lonely planet

Best Road Trips

GREAT BRITAIN

AF621802

CATHERINE LE NEVEZ, KERRY WALKER,
NEIL WILSON, ISABEL ALBISTON, OLIVER BERRY,
JOE BINDLOSS, FIONN DAVENPORT, BELINDA DIXON,
ANTHONY HAM, DAMIAN HARPER, ANNA KAMINSKI,
ANDY SYMINGTON, TASMIN WABY, LUKE WATERSON

CONTENTS

0 200 km
0 100 miles
SCOTLAND
p247
LAKE DISTRICT & NORTHERN ENGLAND
p177
CENTRAL ENGLAND
p145
WALES
p213
SOUTHWEST ENGLAND
p107
SOUTHERN & EASTERN ENGLAND
p71
NORTHERN IRELAND
IRELAND
ENGLAND
FRANCE
ATLANTIC OCEAN
North Sea
Irish Sea
St George's Channel
Bristol Channel
English Channel
Strait of Dover
The Minch
Sea of the Hebrides
South Ronaldsay
Lewis
Harris
North Uist
South Uist
Barra
Skye
Mull
Jura
Islay
Arran
St Kilda
Isle of Man
Isles of Scilly
Land's End
Loch Ness
Loch Lomond
Ben Nevis
Durness
Thurso
John O'Groats
Wick
Stornoway
Tarbert
Ullapool
Helmsdale
Dornoch
Lochmaddy
Uig
Gairloch
Elgin
Fraserburgh
Inverness
Nairn
Kyle of Lochalsh
Portree
Lochboisdale
Fort Augustus
Aviemore
Newtonmore
Aberdeen
Stonehaven
Mallaig
Fort William
Glencoe
Montrose
Oban
Perth
Dundee
St Andrews
Inveraray
Stirling
EDINBURGH
Dumbarton
Glasgow
Berwick-upon-Tweed
Kilmarnock
Peebles
Kelso
Melrose
Campbeltown
Ayr
Derry
Dumfries
Stranraer
Newcastle-upon-Tyne
Carlisle
Durham
Donegal
Omagh
BELFAST
Middlesbrough
Whitehaven
Keswick
Sligo
Armagh
Ambleside
Darlington
Scarborough
Douglas
Dundalk
Harrogate
York
Blackpool
Hull
Leeds
Manchester
Galway
DUBLIN
Liverpool
Sheffield
Llandudno
Lincoln
Stoke-on-Trent
Skegness
Caernarfon
Betws-y-Coed
Nottingham
Tarbert
Limerick
Shrewsbury
Leicester
Kilkenny
Norwich
Birmingham
Wexford
Aberystwyth
Cambridge
Waterford
Llanwrtyd Wells
Stratford-upon-Avon
Northampton
Ipswich
Cork
Gloucester
Cheltenham
Luton
Colchester
Pembroke
Abergavenny
Oxford
Southend-on-Sea
Swansea
CARDIFF
Windsor
LONDON
Bristol
Bath
Canterbury
Reading
Ilfracombe
Maidstone
Dover
Barnstaple
Salisbury
Calais
Southampton
Brighton
Exeter
Portsmouth
Worthing
Eastbourne
Bournemouth
Torquay
Plymouth
Penzance
Dieppe

WELCOME TO GREAT BRITAIN

Great Britain brims with rich seams of history, art and culture. There's no better way to explore its varied landscapes – from Scotland's dramatic mountains and lochs, and England's quaint villages and hedgerow-edged farmland to the haunting beauty of the Welsh and West Country coastlines – than by car. On your way you'll encounter wild open moors, elegant university towns and world-famous cities.

Our 37 drives take you through it all via Britain's most scenic roads. Discover enough palaces, stone circles, gourmet hot spots, castles, wildlife, stately gardens, historic ships and literary locations to fill a book. From top attractions to those well-hidden, these trips enable you to experience the best of modern-day Britain while being the master of your own transport and itinerary.

If you only have time for one drive, make it one featured in Our Picks (p8), such as our 'Epic Trip: North Coast 500'. And next time, come back and explore some more.

Road near Kyle of Durness, North Coast 500 (p22)
EDDIECLOUD/SHUTTERSTOCK

MY PERFECT ROAD TRIP

CATHERINE LE NEVEZ

NORTHUMBRIA, p206

Surf breaks, seafood, cosy bookshops and real-ale pubs are some of my favourites. Northumbria has them all and more: clifftop walks, crumbling castles, ornate gardens, a mirage-like tidal causeway to Holy Island (Lindisfarne), and wildlife including seals and puffins. Driving north from Newcastle-upon-Tyne (and extraordinary Roman legacy Hadrian's Wall), I love detouring to the wild expanses and dark skies of Northumberland National Park before rejoining the coast road to Berwick-upon-Tweed.

KERRY WALKER

SOUTHWEST COAST, p216

The Southwest Coast drive is Wales in microcosm, skipping from the tide-sculpted sands of the Gower Peninsula to timber-beamed pubs once frequented by poet Dylan Thomas. En route to St Davids, you can walk on dune-fringed sands and across wave-pounded clifftops, dig into freshly caught crab at seaside shacks, and tune into the country's fascinating past at Iron Age hillforts, neolithic burial chambers and medieval cathedrals swirling in the legends of early Celtic saints.

ALEXEY FEDORENKO/SHUTTERSTOCK

Windermere (p180), England

BEST SCENIC DRIVES

01 **North Coast 500** These 500 miles of Scotland's Highlands will make you want to drive 500 more.

02 **Classic Lakes** A painting come to life, with blazing falling leaves, wildflowers and snowy peaks.

03 **Southwest Coast** Sandy beaches, sheltered coves and sheer cliffs link Swansea and St Davids.

04 **North Devon & Exmoor** Wild moorland where ponies roam and quaint villages and quays.

05 **Coastal Cornwall** Turquoise bays, golden sands and picture-perfect fishing villages dot the Cornish coast.

BEST URBAN DRIVES

01 **Best of Britain** Hit a trio of capitals and more dynamic cities on this showcase of Britain's finest.

02 **Urban & Art Odyssey** Street art in Bristol, stunning galleries in Birmingham and sculptures in Yorkshire.

03 **Industrial Heritage** Trace industrial history via former mines, potteries and Ironbridge Gorge's museums.

04 **Seaside Jaunt** Highlights span Folkestone's creative quarter, and Brighton's Royal Pavilion and bold nightlife.

05 **Winchester, Glastonbury & Bath** A feast of Roman ingenuity, stately homes, pre-history and more.

NEIL WILSON

NORTH COAST 500, p22

It's not a race. It's not a challenge. It's not just a line to be followed on the map. The North Coast 500 is an adventure, an inspiration, a revelation. I've lost count of the number of times I've driven the section between Lochinver and Torridon but it hits me in the gut every time – the ever-changing light on otherworldly landscapes, the deeply moving history, the tight-knit but welcoming communities. Pure enchantment.

MACIEJ OLSZEWSKI/SHUTTERSTOCK

Lighthouse, Chanonry Point (p25), Scotland

BEST FAMILY DRIVES

01 **Royalty & the Thames Valley** Discover the behind-the-scenes magic of *Harry Potter*.

02 **Jurassic Coast** Dinosaur-obsessed kids can fossil-hunt along aquamarine bays, beaches and striking cliff stacks.

03 **Northwest Wales** Seaside stops include a Punch and Judy show, birdwatching, boat trips and castles.

04 **North York Moors & Coast** Stream-train rides and railway museums for whole-family fun.

05 **Great Glen** Scottish adventure featuring 'outdoors capital' Fort William and Loch Ness monster hunts.

INSPIRATIONAL LANDSCAPES

Britain's landscapes abound in drama-filled views: ocean-dashed coasts, glinting lochs and imposing mountains. A quieter, contemplative beauty is also found in smaller details: a red kite hovering over a lichen-covered stone wall, wildflowers blooming in an ancient forest and sea creatures spotted from the shore. On these gloriously scenic drives through Britain, you'll see why this natural wonderland continues to provide a wellspring of inspiration for poets, playwrights and storytellers.

01 CLASSIC LAKES

Visit the Lake District's fells, lakes and waterfalls, William Wordsworth's homes and Beatrix Potter's farmhouse. p. 180

02 THE COTSWOLDS & LITERARY ENGLAND

See the Georgian grandeur of Bath, honey-hued Cotswolds villages and Tudor-era Stratford-upon-Avon. p. 148

03 NORTH YORK MOORS & COAST

The haunting, rugged beauty of England's north, with wild moors, mountains and rich history. p. 194

04 SOUTHWEST COAST

Journey along Wales' coastline from Dylan Thomas' hometown of Swansea to Britain's smallest city, St Davids. p. 216

05 THE BORDERS

The Scottish Borders inspired Sir Walter Scott through to Dan Brown's *The Da Vinci Code*. p. 250

Left: St Catherine's Island, Tenby (p220), Wales; Right: Blencathra, the Lake District (p182), England

LEFT TO RIGHT: COUNTRYWIDE IMAGES/ALAMY, DANIEL_KAY/SHUTTERSTOCK

HERITAGE RAILWAYS

Britain has more than 170 heritage railways, including steam trains, cliff railways, tramways and rail museums with scheduled trips. Check dates and book tickets ahead.

SHAKESPEARE COUNTRY

Pre-book tickets for an outstanding night of theatre by the Royal Shakespeare Company in Stratford-upon-Avon.

HISTORY RETOLD

Check heritage websites for historical re-enactments. Catch famous battles replayed or a slice of medieval life with jousting and falconry.

WINTER CLOSURE

Some stately homes are closed over winter and others carry out extensive garden-maintenance works. Check individual websites for details.

CASTLES & STATELY HOMES

Britain's wealth of castles and stately homes is one of its greatest treasures. See the grandeur of Castle Howard, the World Heritage–listed fortresses of Beaumaris, Conwy, Caernarfon and Harlech in Wales, and the largest occupied castle in the world (and one of the royal residences of King Charles III) at Windsor. Plus, there are intricate manicured gardens, baroque furnishings and Regency-era flourishes to admire on these driving tours.

01 SEASIDE JAUNT

Take in Channel views from 12th-century Dover Castle, where the Dunkirk evacuation was planned from secret WWII tunnels. p.74

02 ROYALTY & THE THAMES VALLEY

Begin at the surprisingly exquisite Windsor Castle and finish in the grand gardens of baroque Blenheim Palace. p.88

03 MIDLANDS BATTLEFIELDS, CASTLES & STATELY HOMES

Indulge your inner royalty enthusiast or medieval knight on this trip to famous castles and palatial manors. p.170

04 NORTH YORK MOORS & COAST

Tour the setting for *Brideshead Revisited*, Castle Howard, then the fabulously atmospheric remains of Whitby Abbey. p.194

05 NORTHWEST WALES

Admire gloriously intact examples of medieval military architecture on the North Wales coast. p.242

LEFT TO RIGHT: TOMAS MAREK/SHUTTERSTOCK, MISTERVLAD/SHUTTERSTOCK

Left: Conwy Castle (p243); Above: Windsor Castle (p88)

FOOD & DRINK

There's been nothing short of a revolution in British food over the last few decades. Celebrity chefs, Michelin-starred restaurants, organic farm shops and Antipodean-style cafes abound. You'll be able to find something delicious to eat – and drink – no matter where you travel. Indulge in local specialities from haggis in Scotland (yes, you can get a vegetarian or gluten-free version) to seafood on the coast and British cheeses across the land.

01 THE BEST OF BRITAIN

Savour afternoon teas to some of the world's best restaurants on this mighty road trip. p.36

02 KENT: GARDEN OF ENGLAND

Stop for oysters, fine dining and traditional ales in England's rural southeast. p.80

03 SOUTH DEVON

Discover top-class wines and cheeses, quality seafood and Devon's farm-fresh-produce stores and restaurants. p.130

04 COASTAL CORNWALL

From Cornish pasties to St Ives ice cream via fish and chips in Padstow. p.134

05 WHISKY TRAILS

Where spectacular Scottish scenery, distillery tasting tours and historic crafts come together. p.290

Left: Whitstable oysters (p82);
Right: Glenfiddich Distillery (p295)

LEFT TO RIGHT: LEONIE VICTORIA/SHUTTERSTOCK, TRAVELLING TOURIST/SHUTTERSTOCK

WHISKY BUSINESS

Scotland has more than 150 active distilleries. Learn the difference between single malt and single grain on a visit.

WHITSTABLE OYSTERS

Oysters have been harvested in Whitstable since Roman times. Locals say Julius Caesar came to Britain to dine on them.

Winchester Cathedral (p110)

PABLO L MENDOZA/SHUTTERSTOCK

OUR PICKS

ART, ARCHAEOLOGY & ARCHITECTURE

From the mysterious stone circles of Stonehenge to contemporary galleries dotted across the land, Britain's human environment tells a story of culture and innovation. You'll visit baths built by the Romans; churches, castles and cathedrals that pay homage to power and prosperity; plus stone villages and thatched-roof cottages where Britons have led their lives for centuries.

01 URBAN & ART ODYSSEY

A roll call of modern Britain's contemporary art, from the street to its museums and galleries. p.62

SUSTAINABLE ARCHITECTURE

Net-zero carbon for Britain's built environment is an urgent goal. Retrofitting historic buildings for a sustainable future is the challenge.

IS THAT A BANKSY?

Hailing from Bristol, the internationally renowned street artist and activist, Banksy, continues to surprise Britons with fresh work.

02 SEASIDE JAUNT

Brighton might be famously artsy, but the whole south coast is now awash with creatives. p.74

03 AROUND THE CAM

Beautifully preserved half-timbered houses, historic lanes and Cambridge University's centuries-old colleges. p.94

04 WINCHESTER, GLASTONBURY & BATH

An inspiring mix of prehistoric monuments, soaring cathedrals, historic streetscapes and Arthurian mythology. p.110

05 LYRICAL SOUTHEAST WALES

Journey along a valley flanked by ruined abbeys and castles, then explore Britain's most bookish town, Hay-on-Wye. p.232

OUTDOOR ADVENTURES

BRITAIN'S BEACHES

Black-and-white-chequered flags indicate areas for surfboards, paddleboards, kayaks and other non-powered craft; no swimming. Red-and-yellow flags mean lifeguards are on duty.

What's the best way to slow down, meet the locals and get off the beaten track as you travel around Britain? Hop out of the car and head outdoors. From the wild Highlands in the north to the salt-crusted coastal cliffs of the south, Britain offers an extraordinary diversity of terrain that's waiting to be explored. Allow time on these drives to walk, cycle or go for a wild swim.

01 EPIC TRIP: NORTH COAST 500

Ascend Ben Loyal, the 'Queen of Scottish Mountains', along the Highlands' unforgettable northwest coast. p.22

02 PEAK DISTRICT

Hike up to scenic viewpoints of lush green hills and ancient stone villages. p.160

03 CLASSIC LAKES

The Lake District invites you to explore its unforgettable rural beauty on foot. p.180

04 ERYRI (SNOWDONIA) NATIONAL PARK

One of Britain's iconic wild places, with mountains, forests and waterfalls to explore. p.226

05 ROYAL HIGHLANDS & CAIRNGORMS

Walk, cycle, canoe or raft sensational Cairngorms National Park, then stroll Balmoral Castle's gardens. p.276

Eryri (Snowdonia) National Park (p226)

PAJOR PAWEL/SHUTTERSTOCK

WHEN TO GO

Any time is a good time for a road trip in Great Britain, but early summer brings longer days, warmer weather and brighter colours.

I LIVE HERE

I LOVE DRIVING HERE

Tasmin Waby, writer

Tasmin Waby moved back to London from her home in Australia a decade ago. She loves to road trip and has explored most of Britain in her trusty green Volvo estate.

I love to hit the road in spring. Fresh green leaves and pink-and-white cherry blossoms transform naked trees. Grass verges awaken with daffodils and crocuses. Fields are dotted with snow-white lambs, calves and foals. Ducklings and cygnets flit about the rivers. You can explore village shops and local museums that can be busy in summer.

I break up a long drive with a brisk country walk, ideally followed by a pub roast.

Summer is the best – and busiest – time to visit Britain: the weather is at its finest. Many Brits will be on holiday, though, putting pressure on roads, car parks and accommodation, particularly in seaside towns, national parks and anywhere famous.

In the shoulder seasons (May, June, late September and early October) you can still catch the sunshine, but evenings will be cooler.

March to May you'll see the landscape starting to pop with springtime colour. The chance of a sudden downpour means packing wellies (gumboots) and rainwear in your boot (trunk) is a must.

October and November are best for autumn colours. Driving conditions can be hazardous, and accidents create huge delays.

December to February cloaks Britain in wintry darkness. Snow, ice, fog, hail and torrential rain aren't uncommon. But this is the

Stargazing, North York Moors (p194), an International Dark Sky Reserve

AMSLEEPING/SHUTTERSTOCK

WEATHER WATCH: LONDON

JANUARY	FEBRUARY	MARCH	APRIL	MAY	JUNE
Avg daytime max: **7.6°C**	Avg daytime max: **8°C**	Avg daytime max: **10.6°C**	Avg daytime max: **13.5°C**	Avg daytime max: **16.8°C**	Avg daytime max: **19.6°C**
Days of rainfall: **12.7** (London)	Days of rainfall: **10.7** (London)	Days of rainfall: **9.9** (London)	Days of rainfall: **9.7** (London)	Days of rainfall: **9.2** (London)	Days of rainfall: **9.3** (London)

JESSICAGIRVAN/SHUTTERSTOCK

Notting Hill Carnival (p41)

best time to visit if spontaneous days (no bookings needed!), cosy cottages, open fires and quiet snowy mountains are your thing.

ACCOMMODATION

Some rural accommodation, seaside attractions and many stately homes close over winter, usually from the end of October.

GRITTY GRITTY BANG BANG

Scotland is geared up for winter snow and ice. Its road gritters are given punny names each year – Gritty Gritty Bang Bang, Sled Zeppelin. Their movements are shown on Transport Scotland's 'trunk-road gritter tracker' *(traffic.gov.scot)*.

LOOK AT THE STARS

Light pollution is an issue in densely populated Britain. The best places to see the stars on a (rare) cloudless night are national parks. Stargazing events are held throughout the year at Britain's seven International Dark Sky Reserves.

FAMOUS FESTIVALS

Glastonbury Festival is a summer favourite held on a farm in Somerset. Drawing top international and local performers. June

Edinburgh Festival is excellent for books, art, theatre, music, comedy and marching bands. August

National Eisteddfod of Wales celebrates Welsh culture, music and poetry. August

Guy Fawkes Festival (Bonfire Night) commemorates a failed attempt to blow up parliament on 5 November 1605, with firework displays and epic bonfires all over Britain. November

Jorvik Viking Festival is when York celebrates its rich Norse history with longship races. February

Henley Royal Regatta is a six-day boating extravaganza on the Thames. June/July

Notting Hill Carnival is London's multicultural celebration of Afro-Caribbean culture with music and partying. August

Stonehaven Fireball Festival marks Hogmanay (Scottish for New Year's Eve) with an ancient tradition of fireball swinging. December

JULY
Avg daytime max: **21.8°C**
Days of rainfall: **9.5** (London)

AUGUST
Avg daytime max: **21.6°C**
Days of rainfall: **10** (London)

SEPTEMBER
Avg daytime max: **19°C**
Days of rainfall: **9.9** (London)

OCTOBER
Avg daytime max: **14.7°C**
Days of rainfall: **12** (London)

NOVEMBER
Avg daytime max: **10.7°C**
Days of rainfall: **13.1** (London)

DECEMBER
Avg daytime max: **8°C**
Days of rainfall: **12.9** (London)

GET PREPARED FOR GREAT BRITAIN

Useful things to load in your bag, your ears and your brain

WATCH

- **Wild Isles** *(David Attenborough, BBC; 2023)* Nature documentary looking at Britain's landscapes and wildlife.
- **Art That Made Us** (*BBC; 2022*) A journey through Britain's history via 80 pieces of art.
- **Britain's Most Historic Towns** *(Channel 4; 2018)* Prof Alice Roberts uncovers local stories emblematic of different historical eras.
- **Great British Menu** *(BBC; 2006–)* Top British chefs compete by region in this prestigious cooking competition.
- **A History of Britain by Simon Schama** (*BBC; 2000*) Journeys through 5000 years of life in the British Isles.

CLOTHING

Sunglasses You'll need these when you're heading west into the setting sun.

Comfortable, smart-looking clothes Choose clothes that are both comfy enough that you could sleep in them in a pinch and presentable enough that you could drop into a stately home or village teashop without raising eyebrows.

Swimwear Whether driving the coast, where the sea will beckon you in for a splash, or inland to tempting rivers, lakes and public lidos, you'll need your swimsuit, a beach towel and, in winter, a dry robe. Cold-water swimming is hot here right now.

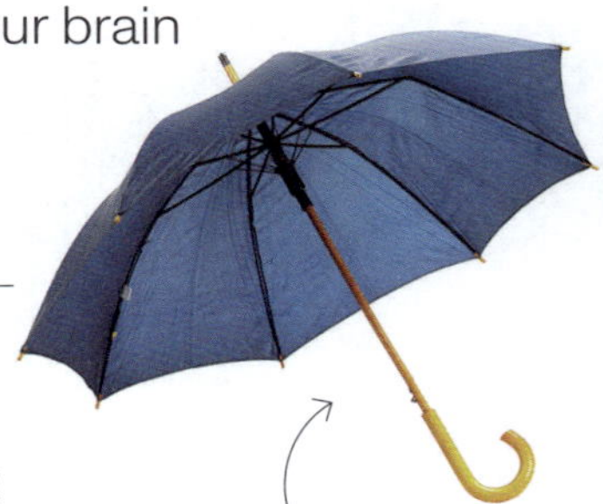

Umbrella You'll need one close to hand in autumn or winter, and probably spring and summer too.

Raincoat You never know when a light shower – or torrential rainstorm – will come between you and that museum just across the road.

Wellington boots Have a pair at the ready for forest walks and muddy car parks.

Walking shoes For country walks in the summer months, when puddles and mud are less of a problem.

FROM LEFT TO RIGHT: LTUMMY/SHUTTERSTOCK, NYS/SHUTTERSTOCK, OKCAMERA/SHUTTERSTOCK, JAKUB KRECHOWICZ/SHUTTERSTOCK, WOZZIE/SHUTTERSTOCK

M53 Motorway

WORDS

Motorways Denoted with an M in the name – M1, M11, M25 – are multilane highways and usually the quickest way to a destination, but they have very little interaction with the surrounding countryside.
Services These are signposted along motorways. Expect a petrol station and a large concourse with major food chains, plus toilets. Outdoor seating is usually limited.
A-roads The busiest and most direct main roads, away from motorways, sometimes with dual lanes. A-roads (eg A30) often go through towns, but they might circumnavigate larger cities. Petrol stations, shops, public conveniences and playgrounds feature in larger towns, but expect to pay for parking. Small villages might have one shop but nowhere to fill up your tank.
B-roads They're often winding, and lack places to pass slow-moving vehicles. Definitely the scenic routes.
Tolls Signposted, as is the last chance to exit before you must pay the toll. Occasionally, you'll need to pay online or by phone – the Dartford Crossing charge is one example.

LISTEN

Radio Times
(Kelly-Anne Taylor) Celebrity guests talk about what's on screen and their own careers.

The Rest Is Politics
(Alastair Campbell and Rory Stewart) Podcast by Westminster insiders on local and global issues of the day.

BBC 6 Music Playlist
(BBC Radio 6) Tune in for good music curated by musical artists and DJs, or catch up online at BBC Sounds.

The Outdoors Fix
(Liv Bolton) Podcast guests recount wild swimming, hiking, climbing, rewilding and more.

READ

On This Holy Island
(Oliver Smith; 2024) Ancient to contemporary pilgrimages, from neolithic tombs to football stadiums.

The Hidden Ways
(Alistair Moffat; 2018) This book traverses the lost paths of Scotland.

Notes from a Small Island
(Bill Bryson; 1995) This American perspective on Britain is funny and educative.

Empireland: How Imperialism Has Shaped Modern Britain
(Sathnam Sanghera; 2021) An award-winning portrait of contemporary society.

ROAD TRIPS

Broadway Tower (p152), the Costwolds, England
ROBERT HARDING VIDEO/SHUTTERSTOCK

CONTENTS

01

EPIC TRIP: NORTH COAST 500

The North Coast 500 was launched in 2015 as a signposted, 516-mile road trip around the northwest Highlands of Scotland, linking harbour villages, imposing castles, whisky distilleries, golden beaches and majestic mountains, and passing through some of the finest coastal and mountain scenery in the country.

It's been driven in sports cars, vintage vehicles, coaches and campervans, ridden on road bikes, mountain bikes and motorbikes; it has even been run on foot (the record time is 5 days, 23 hours, 4 minutes and 17 seconds). But however you choose to experience the North Coast 500, it's an epic journey that will live long in your memory.

BY NEIL WILSON

HIGHLIGHTS

1

Golspie, p27
This appealing seaside town provides the ideal introduction to the history of northern Scotland: Dunrobin Castle was the seat of the Duke of Sutherland, and his controversial monument glowers from a nearby hilltop.

2

Durness, p29
Gorgeous beaches and spectacular coastal scenery mark the midpoint of the North Coast 500, where the clifftop village of Durness sits atop the dramatic limestone cavern of Smoo Cave.

3

Glen Torridon, p33
Some of Scotland's most magnificent mountain scenery lines the single-track road that winds enticingly through Glen Torridon to the village of Shieldaig with its splendid campsite and seafood restaurant.

Dunrobin Castle, Golspie (p27)
JOSE MIGUEL SANCHEZ/SHUTTERSTOCK

EPIC TRIP

DURATION: 5-10 DAYS

DISTANCE: 516 MILES / 830KM

BEST TIME TO GO: AVOID THE CROWDS BY TRAVELLING IN APRIL, MAY, SEPTEMBER OR OCTOBER.

01 Inverness

Inverness, the capital of the Highlands, is the start and finish point of the North Coast 500. It lies around 160 miles north of Edinburgh and a three-hour drive from my home in Perthshire in my 1982 VW campervan. I arrive in time for lunch – the **Mustard Seed** *(mustardseedrestaurant.co.uk)* does great value two-course lunches – leaving the afternoon free for a visit to the newly opened interactive exhibitions on Highland history and culture at **Inverness Castle** *(invernesscastle.scot)* and a riverside stroll to Ness Islands before I spend the night in the motorhome parking at Torvean car park.

I have chosen late April to make this trip – the roads are quiet, the days are lengthening and the weather is improving, but winter snow still lingers on the Highland peaks, adding to the majesty ofthe mountain scenery.

LINK YOUR TRIP

33 Upper West Coast
Continue south from Lochcarron to do the first part of this trip in reverse.

35 Great Glen
Do this trip before you start, or in reverse after you're done

36 Whisky Trails
Head west from Inverness to link up with this whisky route.

★ BEST FOR:

HISTORY

Learn about the Highland Clearances at Strathnaver Museum (p28).

JAN JIRAT/SHUTTERSTOCK

Inverness Castle

THE DRIVE: Head north from Inverness across the Kessock Bridge and turn right on the B9161 to Munlochy, before following the A832 to Fortrose.

02 Fortrose

And we're off! Driving across the Kessock Bridge from Inverness feels like a grand opening to the NC500, soaring over the Beauly Firth to the Black Isle. OK, it's not really an island, but this lozenge of land, bypassed by the main A9 road to the north, is well worth the detour. At Fortrose I take the opportunity to drive out to the car park at the tip of **Chanonry Point** in the hope of spotting the Moray Firth's famous bottlenose dolphins, who follow the schools of salmon as they pass through the narrows here on their way to spawn in the River Ness. But April is a bit early in the year – June to August offer the best chance of seeing them.

THE DRIVE: Head north from Inverness across the Kessock.

03 Cromarty

I studied geology at Edinburgh University, where I learned about the pioneering works of Hugh Miller, a 19th-century stonemason, newspaper editor and amateur palaeontologist from the Black Isle village of Cromarty. The life and achievements of this local lad made good are celebrated and put on display in the village's **Courthouse Museum** *(cromartymuseum.org.uk)* and the neighbouring **Hugh Miller Birthplace Cottage** *(nts.org.uk)*.

THE DRIVE: Follow the B9163 along the north coast of the Black Isle to rejoin the A9, and cross the Cromarty Bridge to Evanton.

04 Evanton

From April to October a small car ferry (two cars max) shuttles back and forth between Cromarty and Nigg, cutting 32 miles off the journey north. But I head back along the north side of the Black Isle – the road follows the shoreline of **Udale Bay nature reserve** where in autumn you can see huge flocks of migrating wigeon (a species of duck with distinctive chestnut-coloured head and creamy yellow crest) – and cross the Cromarty Bridge.

Having parked in the middle of the village opposite the Co-op, I walk to the end of Chapel St, where a signposted woodland walk of about 25 minutes brings me to the **Black Rock Gorge**. Invisible until you're on the footbridge that crosses over it, the gorge is an impressive natural feature – 1.5km long, 35m deep and rarely more than 3m wide with vertical walls draped in moss and ferns – gouged out by torrential meltwater floods as the glaciers retreated at the end of the last Ice Age.

POUL BRIX/SHUTTERSTOCK

Duke of Sutherland Monument, Ben Bhraggie

DON'T MISS THE MANNIE

From its perch on top of Ben Bhraggie, a colossal **monument** to the 1st Duke of Sutherland dominates the skyline above Golspie, just as the man himself once dominated the surrounding country. Completed in 1837 and known locally as the Mannie, the 9m-tall statue stands atop a 24m-tall plinth, visible for many miles in all directions.

George Granville Leveson-Gower (1758–1833), the 2nd Marquess of Stafford, became Britain's wealthiest landowner when he married Elizabeth, Countess of Sutherland in 1785; he was created 1st Duke of Sutherland in 1833, just six months before he died. Later known as 'the great improver', he opened up Sutherland by building roads, bridges and harbours, but became notorious for his part in some of the cruellest episodes of the Highland Clearances, overseeing the eviction of thousands of tenant farmers to make way for more profitable sheep farms.

Although the monument's inscription reads 'of loved, revered and cherished memory, erected by his tenantry and friends', the statue remains controversial to this day. Some locals see it as a symbol of aristocratic power, oppression and greed; decades before the toppling of statues during the Black Lives Matter protests of 2020 there were attempts to blow it up or demolish it, and it is occasionally vandalised or sprayed with graffiti.

The full story of the Sutherland Clearances, and how the evicted families emigrated across the Atlantic to found the Canadian city of Winnipeg, is told in James Hunter's book *Set Adrift upon the World*.

THE DRIVE: Continue on the A9 for 21 miles from Evanton to the Dornoch Firth Bridge.

05 Dornoch Firth

The A9 lounges lazily through rural Easter Ross past the pleasant town of Tain, with the malty whiff of fermenting barley wafting from the **Glenmorangie Distillery** *(glenmorangie.com)*, before curving elegantly across the Dornoch Firth Bridge. There are a few choices of route to be made on the east coast, and this is the first.

You could ignore the bridge and continue west towards Lairg, pausing to tick off another whisky distillery at **Balblair** *(balblair.com)* before heading to the **Falls of Shin** *(forestryandland.gov.scot)* – one of the best places in Scotland to watch salmon leaping upstream (best in late summer and autumn). From the pretty village of Lairg you can return to the coast via the A839, adding 27 miles to the journey. But today I go with the bridge.

THE DRIVE: Cross the Dornoch Firth Bridge and continue for 3 miles, then turn right on the A949 to Dornoch.

06 Dornoch

A short detour east from the A9 leads to Dornoch, an old market town famous for its two championship links golf courses. When it comes to golf, I'm with the anonymous wit who described it as 'a good walk spoiled'. But Dornoch has other attractions, and I grab some lunch in the **Milk & Honey café** before whiling away a pleasant hour browsing the shelves at the next-door bookshop and visiting the medieval **cathedral** across the street.

I'm looking for the tomb of the 1st Duke and Duchess of Sutherland, who paid for the cathedral's restoration in the 1830s; they are buried beneath the chancel, but it turns out their last resting place is unmarked. Despite being the richest couple in Britain during their lifetimes, their controversial association with the Highland Clearances meant that the people of Dornoch preferred not to remember them.

THE DRIVE: Return to the A9 via the B9168 and continue north for 8 miles to Golspie.

07 Golspie

When exploring the Highlands by campervan I always travel with my mountain bike loaded on the rear rack. Golspie is a pretty little village with a family-friendly beach and a couple of good coffee shops. Campervans are not allowed in the central car park, so I head up Fountain Road to the **Highland Wildcat Trails** *(highlandwildcat.com)* car park and unload the bike for a bit of exercise. I opt for the easier blue trail which leads to Queen's Drive and on to a 4WD track which continues to the summit of Ben Bhraggie.

The hill is topped by a huge **monument** to the Duke of Sutherland, and enjoys a magnificent view; on a clear day you can see the Cairngorm Mountains across the Moray Firth to the south. (If you don't have a mountain bike, you can hike to the top and back in around four hours.)

The double black diamond trail (experts only) here sports the biggest single-track descent in the country, dropping around 390m over 7km from the top of Ben Bhraggie almost to sea level. But I wimp out and go down the way I came up.

Dunrobin Castle *(dunrobincastle.co.uk)*, just outside Golspie, is well worth a stop (open April to October). Although it dates back to 1275, most of what you see today was built in French style between 1845 and 1850. One of the homes of the earls and dukes of Sutherland, it offers an intriguing insight into the aristocratic lifestyle. A classic fairy-tale castle adorned with towers and turrets, it has only 22 of its 189 rooms on display, with hunting trophies much to the fore. The exhibits also include innumerable gifts from farm tenants (probably grateful that they weren't victims of the Clearances).

THE DRIVE: Continue north on the A9 for 17 miles to Helmsdale.

08 Helmsdale

After a night at the motorhome parking spot in Brora (there are several of these informal overnight stops along the route, with more popping up each year), a few miles north of Golspie, I set off towards Helmsdale. A historical curiosity that most visitors drive straight past can be seen in a layby beside the A9 halfway between Brora and Helmsdale. I once stopped here to stretch my legs and found the **Wolf Stone** – a grey granite memorial that marks the spot 'near which... the last wolf in Sutherland was killed... in or about the year 1700'.

Helmsdale is an attractive former fishing port with a good museum and famous fish-and-chip shop – **La Mirage** *(lamirage.co.uk)* – but it's too early for lunch. Helmsdale is another decision point: if you're pushed for time you can take the cross-country route from here via the A897 to Melvich on the north coast, shortening your journey by 50 miles.

THE DRIVE: It's another 18 miles on the A9 from Helmsdale to Latheron; here the A9 heads north to Thurso, but keep straight on the A99 towards Wick for another 10 miles to reach Whaligoe.

09 Whaligoe

Beyond Helmsdale the road climbs up onto the bleak moors 200m above sea level to avoid the coastal cliffs at the Ord of Caithness. This is where the driving begins to get more interesting, with a series of tight bends leading to the steep hairpins of the Berriedale Braes (note the snow gates after the Helmsdale roundabout – the road can be closed during severe winter conditions). It's not as interesting as it used to be though – before road improvements in 2020 the hairpin here was so tight that trucks could not pass each other.

At the tiny hamlet of Whaligoe I stop for a spot of exercise on the **Whaligoe Steps**. This spectacular staircase was cut into the cliff face in 1792 to provide access to a tiny natural harbour ringed by vertical cliffs and echoing with the cackle of nesting fulmars.

THE DRIVE: At the traffic lights in Wick, keep straight on across the bridge over the Wick River on the A99 towards John O'Groats.

10 Duncansby Head

I'm not a huge fan of Wick, so I drive straight through on my way to John O'Groats, where the **Taste Coffee Shop** *(facebook.com/TasteJohnOGroats)* is a reliable lunch stop. However, this end point of the 874-mile trek from Land's End in Cornwall is a less-than-inspiring spot, so I head 2 miles east to Duncansby

Head, where an easy 20-minute stroll along the grassy clifftops leads to the pyramidal sandstone pinnancles of the **Stacks of Duncansby**, the scenic highlight of this leg of the NC500.

THE DRIVE: From John O'Groats follow the A836 west through Thurso and along the north coast for 50 miles to Bettyhill.

11 Bettyhill

The cuteness of Bettyhill belies the sombre history that accounts for the emptiness of the surrounding area. I never fail to be moved by the memories of the Highland Clearances recorded in the village's **Strathnaver Museum** (*strathnavermuseum.org.uk*) and at the various sites along the **Strathnaver Trail** between Bettyhill and Altnaharra. But it's been a long day in the driving seat and I gladly retire to a pitch in the village campsite.

THE DRIVE: Follow the A836 west for 13 miles to Tongue.

12 Tongue

Up till now the east and north coast scenery has been relatively low key, but from here on the landscape gets more and more dramatic. The village of Tongue overlooks the turquoise, sand-choked waters of the Kyle of Tongue where a causeway carries the main road across. I drive down the minor road on the east side of the Kyle for a mile and a half to a parking area where a farm track forks left towards Ribigill.

If you do one hill walk on the North Coast 500, make it **Ben Loyal** (764m). I get the mountain bike off the van and follow a 4WD track south for a couple of miles before continuing on foot. Boggy paths and rough ground lead to the summit of this 'Queen of Scottish Mountains' and an all-encompassing view along the whole north coast. The trek takes around six hours, so that's me done for the day and I head to Durness for the night.

THE DRIVE: Continue on the A838 for 30 miles to Durness; the last section around Loch

Smoo Cave

JONATHAN MILLS/SHUTTERSTOCK

Eriboll is single-track with passing places.

13 Durness

Durness has to be one of my favourite stopovers on the North Coast 500. The clifftop pitches at the **Sango Sands campsite** *(sangosands.com)* enjoy one of the best views in Scotland, looking out over a crag-girt bay of golden sand and turquoise waters frilled with white breakers; in clear conditions you might be able to see the hills of Hoy in the Orkney Islands, 55 miles to the northeast. (The site can be very busy, especially from May to August, so book as far ahead as possible).

I spend a rest day here at the halfway point of the NC500, taking the opportunity to visit **Smoo Cave** *(smoocavetours.com)* and Ceannabeinne beach – not for the excitement of the **zip line** *(durnesszipline.com)* but for the contemplative **Ceannabeinne Township Trail**, a short walk through the sad remains a Clearance village to a superb viewpoint overlooking the beach.

THE DRIVE: Follow the A838 and A894 south for 26 miles to Scourie.

14 Scourie

I always sense a change in the atmosphere as I leave Durness, turning south and striking out across a sea of bog and heather, with rounded hills bulking on the horizon. The underlying geology changes from the limestone that lends Durness its green pastures and sandy coves, to the distinctive 'cnoc-and-lochan' (small hill and small lake) landscape of the Lewisian gneiss.

The shining, silvery-grey screes of Foinaven fill the view to my left, while the bleak bogland on my right finally gives way to more expansive coastal vistas as the road skims the west coast sea lochs at Rhiconich and Laxford Bridge. There's no time today for a detour to Oldshoremore and the iconic hike to gorgeous **Sandwood Bay**, so I forge on to the picturesque village of Scourie for a brisk walk on the beach. I would normally

ARTERRA PICTURE LIBRARY/ALAMY

Ceannabeinne Township Trail

THE NC500 & ME

So many of my lifelong interests and obsessions converge in the northwest Highlands, and the North Coast 500 is a wonderful way to link them all together. I started fly fishing for wild brown trout aged 13, began hill walking at 14, got into rock climbing at 16, was fascinated by geology and went to university at 18 to study for the first of two degrees in the subject. And it was one of my dad's books – *The Companion Guide to the West Highlands of Scotland* by WH Murray – picked up on a rainy weekend when I was still at school, that fired my interest in Highland history.

All these activities are showcased to perfection along the North Coast 500, be it wandering the ridges of mini-mountains like Stac Polly, Ben Stack and Ben Loyal, untangling the complex geology of the Moine Thrust at Knockan Crag or following in the footsteps of poet and angler Norman MacCaig to cast a fly at Assynt's 'Loch of the Green Corrie'. Highland history is written in the stones of abandoned Clearance townships and the crumbling ramparts of ruined castles and recorded in countless museums, monuments and memorials strung out along the route.

I must have been around most of the NC500 at least a dozen times now, but still I haven't seen all there is to see – a lifetime isn't long enough to take in all its varied wonders.

stop for lunch at the **Crofters Kitchen** *(crofterskitchen.com)*, an award-winning food truck parked beside the beach, but it's not open yet, so I crack on.

THE DRIVE: Continue south on the A894 for 10 miles to Kylesku.

15 Kylesku

The narrow entrance to Loch Glencoul was the last ferry crossing on the west coast to be replaced by a bridge. The **Kylesku Bridge**, an elegantly curved span designed by Ove Arup (best known for the Sydney Opera House), opened in 1984. After crossing the bridge I turn left to park near the old ferry slip and nip into the cosy dining room of the **Kylesku Hotel** *(highlandcoasthotels.com/kylesku-hotel)* for a warming lunch of mussels and chips; this early in the season the log fire is still burning.

THE DRIVE: Turn right 2 miles south of Kylesku on the B869 to Lochinver via Drumbeg (25 miles). If you're pushed for time, you can fast forward to Ullapool on the A837 and A835 (33 miles).

16 Lochinver

The B869 Drumbeg loop is another typical west coast roller-coaster ride, weaving up, down and around trout lochs, waterfalls, pretty beaches and its namesake village, before reaching **Strone viewpoint** just short of Lochinver, where I stop to photograph the stunning vista of the Assynt hills – Suilven's sugarloaf framed between the lopsided pyramids of Canisp and Cùl Mòr.

After filling up with petrol at **Lochinver** (p274) I have a choice to make. I could follow the main

THE LEGACY OF THE HIGHLAND CLEARANCES

As you travel the North Coast 500, reflect on the fact that the empty landscapes you see in the north and west weren't always so empty. All along the route you will find monuments, museums and relics of one of the most notorious episodes in Scottish history: the Highland Clearances.

In the wake of the Jacobite rebellions, which ended in defeat for Bonnie Prince Charlie and his army of Highland clansmen at Culloden in 1746, the British government outlawed the wearing of Highland dress and playing the bagpipes. The Highlands were put under military control and there was a concerted effort to wipe out traditional Gaelic language and culture, which were looked down on as barbaric.

The ties of kinship and duty that once marked the relationship between Highland laird and clansman gradually transformed into the merely economic relationship of landlord and tenant. Lands that had been confiscated after Culloden were returned to their owners in the 1780s, but by then the chiefs had tasted the aristocratic high life and were tempted by the easy profits to be made from sheep farming. The people who lived on the land were seen as a burden, with no economic utility.

So began the Highland Clearances, when thousands of people were driven from their homes between 1750 and 1860. By no means all who left their townships in the late 18th and 19th centuries were forcibly evicted; in the Hebridean islands, for example, a combination of poverty, overcrowding and lack of suitable land led many to choose emigration. But some of the forced clearances, especially in Sutherland, were so brutal that newspaper reporting of the events caused a national scandal.

Under the pretext of agricultural 'improvement', the peasant farmers, no longer of any use as soldiers and uneconomical as tenants, were evicted from their homes and farms to make way for flocks of hardy Cheviot sheep – in the Highlands the year 1792 (when Cheviots were first introduced) was known for decades afterwards as Bliadhna nan Caorach (the Year of the Sheep).

After the evictions a few cottars stayed behind to work the sheep farms, but most were relocated to desperate crofts on poor coastal land or fled to the cities of central Scotland and northern England in search of work. Many thousands emigrated – some willingly, some under duress – to the developing colonies of North America, Australia and New Zealand. All over the Highlands today, only a ruckle of stones amid the bracken marks where there was once a thriving township.

Though the Clearances took place two centuries ago, they remain an emotive subject in the Highlands today.

Kylesku Bridge

HELEN HOTSON/SHUTTERSTOCK

CAOLAS CUMHANN

NC500 route east to Skiag Bridge then south to Ullapool, taking in lonely Loch Assynt and the romantic ruins of **Ardvreck Castle**, a hike to the **Bone Caves of Inchnadamph**, and the geological delights of **Knockan Crag**. Or detour south on the Wee Mad Road into the heart of Coigach and some of the most splendid scenery Scotland has to offer.

I decide on the latter and set off along the **Wee Mad Road**, 12 miles of corkscrew single-track with dramatic views of the Coigach hills, turning left at Badnagyle to pass beneath the sandstone pinnacles of Stac Polly before returning to the main road for the final 10 miles to Ullapool.

THE DRIVE: The official route follows the A837 east to Inchnadamph and on to Ledmore Junction, where you turn right onto the A835 to Ullapool. For the Wee Mad Road, find the minor road to Inverkirkaig at the south end of Lochinver and continue to Badnagyle (a single white house) where you turn left to return to the main road.

17 Ullapool

The town of Ullapool (population 1500) is the metropolis of the northwest, a planned town laid out in 1788 as a herring fishing port. Today it's a popular overnight on the NC500, with dozens of B&Bs, a couple of hotels, a campsite and a dozen places to eat. I roll into my pitch at **Broomfield Holiday Park** *(broomfieldhp.com)* and walk to the nearby **Ceilidh Place** *(theceilidhplace.com)* for a seafood dinner and a browse of the next-door bookshop (it stays open late).

THE DRIVE: Continue south on the A835 for 12 miles to Braemore, where you turn right to follow the A832 for 44 miles to Gairloch. Note that the 56 miles from Ullapool to Gairloch is the longest stretch on the NC500 without a petrol station – fill up in Ullapool if you're running low.

18 Gairloch

Immediately after the junction at Braemore I pull off into the Corrieshalloch visitor centre car park to stretch my legs with a short walk to the **Falls of Measach**, which plummet 45m into a narrow, sheer-sided gorge draped in moss and ferns, and spanned by a 19th-century suspension footbridge. From here the road skirts the flanks of mighty An Teallach, one of the region's most impressive mountains – there's a great view back from a layby above Gruinard Bay – and continues through enchanting coastal scenery.

En route I pass up the chance to stop and explore WWII history at the **Arctic Convoy Museum** *(arcticconvoymuseum.org)* in favour of wandering the pinewoods at **Inverewe Garden** *(nts.org.uk)* in

Knockan Crag

DAVID W BIRD/SHUTTERSTOCK

the hope of spotting red squirrels, which are particularly active in April. Then it's onward to Gairloch; I have booked a table for lunch at the **Badachro Inn** *(badachroinn.com)*, where tables have a view over a cute little harbour – the scallops with black pudding and pea puree are sensational.

THE DRIVE: The A832 heads southeast for 18 miles to Kinlochewe, where a right turn on the A896 leads through Glen Torridon to Shieldaig.

19 Shieldaig

The road from Gairloch along the shores of Loch Maree is another feast of fantastic scenery, with a grand panorama across the loch's pine-fringed islands to the soaring heights of Slioch. At Kinlochewe I hang a right onto the mostly single-track A896 beneath the quartzite screes of **Beinn Eighe**, the first of Torridon's famous peaks. After 3 miles I pull into a small parking area on the right (look out for a small green sign saying 'Public Path to Glen Carron') and walk along the estate track opposite for 10 minutes to **Loch Clair**; the view across the loch to Liathach, the second of Torridon's mighty mountains, is one of the finest in the country.

The road continues through **Glen Torridon** with the scenery level cranked up to 11. I can't resist the temptation to visit the **Celtic Jumble** *(ukclimbing.com/logbook/crags/torridon_celtic_jumble-2860)* at the foot of the glen for an hour or two of bouldering before heading to the **Shieldaig campsite** *(shieldaigcampingandcabins.co.uk)* for the final overnight of my journey.

THE DRIVE: From Shieldaig the main NC500 route circumnavigates the Applecross peninsula via a minor road before returning east across the Bealach na Bà. To avoid this difficult road, you can stay on the A896 through Lochcarron and continue on the A890, A832, A835 and A862 to return to Inverness (78 miles; or 106 miles via Applecross).

20 Applecross

My last day dawns cold and grey as I pack the van and set off. A mile south of Shieldaig a signpost on the right teases with the legend 'Lochcarron (Scenic Route)'. No contest: I turn right and follow yet another bucking bronco of a single-track road for 25 miles around the coast to Applecross village. A pub lunch at the famous **Applecross Inn** *(applecrossinn.co.uk)* is a must.

The road from here over the Bealach na Bà (the Pass of the Cattle) is the highpoint of the North Coast 500, scenically and literally – the road climbs to 626m above sea level, the third-highest public road in Scotland – and you really want good visibility, both to see where you're going and to enjoy the spectacular views.

THE DRIVE: The road from Applecross village to the A896 Lochcarron road is 11 miles of narrow, twisting single-track with passing places, and a handful of hairpin bends with big drops on one side. Not a place for nervous drivers, and road signs warn you that it's not suitable for caravans, and is 'normally impassable in wintry conditions'.

21 Bealach na Bà

I've been over the Bealach na Bà many times, groaning uphill in second gear in my campervan or growling through the hairpins as a passenger in a friend's Maserati Quattroporte. The worst time was September 2020 when the relaxation of the coronavirus lockdown saw the Highlands fill with cabin-feverish visitors hungry for travel, and the pass was gridlocked from top to bottom with cars and motorhomes.

But today I have the road to myself, and as I begin the climb out

NC500 DOS & DON'TS

Passing places
Do use passing places to allow faster traffic behind you to overtake; check your rear view mirror regularly.

Motorhomes
Don't take caravans or motorhomes on unsuitably narrow and twisting roads, such as the Wee Mad Road and the Bealach na Bà.

Explore further
Do explore away from the main NC500 route. There are lots of detours and side roads that lead to less-visited highlights.

Clean up
Don't be a dirty camper. Empty motorhome waste tanks only at designated sites and dispose of litter in official bins (or take it home with you).

of the village the clouds begin to thin. Soon the green fields around the village drop away and I enter a wasteland of boulder-studded bog, the road a black ribbon of tarmac unfurling towards a craggy bluff where a couple of sharp bends dodge around the cliffs to the summit plateau, the last few hundred metres white with a fresh dusting of April snow.

I pull into the summit car park and walk west to a prominent cairn, where I'm rewarded with an unforgettable panorama over almost the full length of the Isle of Skye, from the jagged snowcapped cluster of the Cuillin Hills to the long, level ridge of the Trotternish Peninsula. But it's not over yet. A half mile beyond the car park the ground drops away in a breathtaking swoop down the steep eastern side of the pass – there's space to park and gawp 60m before the first hairpin, where a view of the distant sea is framed between sheer cliffs of Torridonian sandstone.

I shift into low gear and take the hairpins slowly, pulling into passing places to allow faster locals to pass, picking up speed as the angle eases and the road straightens on the final approach to the **Bealach Cafe** *(thebealach.co.uk)*, which I can never pass without calling in for coffee and a scone. After that, the prospect of the two-hour drive back to my starting point in Inverness feels like a bit of an anticlimax. But hang on... a right turn past Lochcarron village would lead to Kyle of Lochalsh and the Isle of Skye. Hmmm... I flick the indicator and turn right.

THE DRIVE: The official return route continues past Lochcarron on the A890 to Achnasheen, then heads east on the A832 and A835 to Muir of Ord and Beauly, and finally along the A862 to Inverness (66 miles).

PLAN AHEAD

⍟ Overtourism

Overtourism is the biggest issue facing the North Coast 500. The huge increase in visitor numbers to the northern Highlands has led to a number of problems, from a rise in irresponsible wild camping to traffic congestion to a spike in accidents, as well as rubbish and waste discarded by the roadside. Consider making the trip in shoulder season or even in winter; enough hotels, eateries and campsites stay open all year round to make this a realistic option.

⍟ Accommodation

The biggest limiting factor on the NC500 in peak season (May to August) is accommodation. At this time of year it is strongly recommended to book your accommodation, whether B&B, hotel or campsite – the latter can be fully booked for weeks ahead and those without reservations may well find themselves without a place for the night. Car-free cyclists and hikers, however, will usually get by without prebooking.

Applecross Inn (p33)

SCOTIMAGE/ALAMY

The Applecross Inn

02

EPIC TRIP

THE BEST OF BRITAIN

DURATION: 21 DAYS

DISTANCE: 1121 MILES / 1804KM

GREAT FOR: HISTORY, OUTDOORS

BEST TIME TO GO: MYRIAD FESTIVALS TAKE PLACE BETWEEN MAY AND SEPTEMBER.

London's blockbuster attractions and stirring history bookend this epic expedition around three countries. In between, you'll explore ancient ruins and historic architecture, follow trails that lead from King Arthur to Shakespeare, and discover masterpiece-filled museums, all connected by quaint villages and glorious rolling green open countryside. Rest from life on the road with the best of British drinking, dining and nightlife.

LINK YOUR TRIP

16 The Cotswolds & Literary England
From Bath, you can set out for a spin through the picturesque Cotswolds.

22 North York Moors & Coast
York is the starting point for a glorious drive through wild moorland and charming coastal villages.

01 London

Prepare for your trip with at least a couple of days in Britain's most exhilarating city. Traversed by the serpentine River Thames, London is awash with instantly recognisable landmarks and open spaces, from **Trafalgar Square** to the **London Eye** *(londoneye.com)*. Other unmissable sights include the **Houses of Parliament** *(parliament.uk)*, topped by clock tower **Big Ben** *(parliament.uk/visiting/visiting-and-tours/big-ben-tour)*; **Westminster Abbey** *(westminster-abbey.org)*; **St James's Park** *(royalparks.org.uk/parks/st-jamess-park)* and **Palace** *(royal.uk/royal-residences-st-jamess-palace)*; **Buckingham Palace** (rct.uk/visit/buckingham-palace); **Hyde Park** *(royalparks.org.uk/parks/hyde-park)*; **Kensington Gardens** *(royalparks.org.uk/parks/kensington-gardens)* and **Palace** *(hrp.org.uk/kensington-palace)*; and **Tower Bridge** *(towerbridge.org.uk)*. World-leading museums and art

★ BEST FOR

HISTORY

Britain's oldest chalk figure, the extraordinary Uffington White Horse.

VALERIE2000/SHUTTERSTOCK

Uffington White Horse

galleries include the **Tate Modern** *(tate.org.uk)* and the **British Museum** *(britishmuseum.org)*. These are often free.

London's drinking, dining and nightlife options are limitless (Soho and Shoreditch make great starting points), as are its entertainment venues, not least grand theatre stages such as **Shakespeare's Globe** *(shakespearesglobe.com)*.

THE DRIVE: Take the M40 northwest through High Wycombe and the Chilterns National Landscape to Oxford (59 miles in total).

02 Oxford

The elegant honey-toned buildings of the university's colleges, scattered throughout the city, wrap around tranquil courtyards and along narrow cobbled lanes. The oldest colleges date back to the 13th century and little has changed inside since, although there's a busy, lively world beyond the college walls. **Christ Church** *(chch.ox.ac.uk)* is the largest of all of Oxford's colleges, with the grandest quad. From there, you can access 12th-century **Christ Church Cathedral** *(chch.ox.ac.uk/cathedral)*, originally the abbey church and then the college chapel, before it was declared a cathedral by Henry VIII.

Other highlights include Oxford's **Bodleian Old Library** *(bodleian.ox.ac.uk/libraries/old-library)*, one of the oldest public libraries in the world; and Britain's oldest public museum, the 1683-established **Ashmolean Museum** *(ashmolean.org)*, second in repute only to London's British Museum.

THE DRIVE: Head southwest on the A420 to Pusey and continue southwest on the B4508. You'll reach the car park for the White Horse 2.3 miles southwest of Uffington off the B4507, a 24-mile journey altogether.

03 Uffington White Horse

Just below Oxfordshire's highest point, the highly stylised **Uffington White Horse** *(nationaltrust.org.uk)* image is the oldest chalk figure in Britain, dating from the Bronze Age. It was created around 3000 years ago by cutting trenches out

WHY I LOVE THIS TRIP

CATHERINE LE NEVEZ, WRITER

This grand tour is the ultimate British highlights reel. Between three dynamic capitals, London, Cardiff and Edinburgh, star sights like Stonehenge's standing stones, Bath's Roman and Georgian architecture, Oxford and Cambridge's universities, and the Tudor buildings and willow-lined riverbanks in Shakespeare's Stratford-upon-Avon share the stage with chocolate-box villages, castles, cathedrals and the nation's other religion, football. It shows off everything that makes Britain great.

of the hill and filling them with blocks of chalk; local inhabitants have maintained the figure for centuries. Perhaps it was planned for the gods: it's best seen from the above. It's a half-mile walk east through fields from the hillside car park.

THE DRIVE: It's a 49-mile trip to Winchester: return to the B4507 and drive southeast to Ashbury and take the B4000 southeast to join the southbound A34.

04 Winchester

Set in a river valley, this ancient cathedral city was the capital of Saxon kings and a power base of bishops. It also evokes two of England's mightiest myth-makers: famous son Alfred the Great (commemorated by a statue) and King Arthur – a 700-year-old copy of the round table resides in Winchester's cavernous **Great Hall** *(historicwinchester.co.uk)*, the only part of 11th-century Winchester Castle that Oliver Cromwell spared from destruction during the English Civil War.

Winchester's architecture is exquisite, from the handsome Elizabethan and Regency buildings in the narrow streets to the wondrous **Winchester Cathedral** *(winchester-cathedral.org.uk)* at its core. One of southern England's most awe-inspiring buildings, the 11th-century cathedral has a fine Gothic facade and one of the longest medieval naves in Europe (164m). Other highlights include intricately carved medieval choir stalls, Jane Austen's grave (near the entrance, in the northern aisle) and one of the UK's finest illuminated manuscripts, the dazzling, four-volume Winchester Bible dating from the 12th century.

Salisbury Cathedral
ROBERT HARDING VIDEO/SHUTTERSTOCK

THE DRIVE: From Winchester, hop on the B3049 then the A30 for the 26-mile drive west to Salisbury.

05 Salisbury

Salisbury has been an important provincial city for more than a thousand years, and its streets form an architectural timeline ranging from medieval walls and half-timbered Tudor town houses to Georgian mansions and Victorian villas. Its centrepiece is the majestic 13th-century **Salisbury Cathedral** *(salisburycathedral.org.uk)*. This Early English Gothic–style structure has an elaborate exterior decorated with pointed arches and flying buttresses, and is topped by Britain's tallest spire at 123m, which was added in the mid-14th century. Beyond the cathedral's highly decorative West Front, a small passageway leads into the 70m-long nave. In the north aisle look out for a fascinating medieval clock dating from 1386, probably the oldest working timepiece in the world.

Don't miss the cathedral's original, 13th-century copy of the Magna Carta in the chapter house or a 90-minute tower tour, where you climb 332 vertigo-inducing steps to the base of the spire for jaw-dropping views across the city and the surrounding countryside.

THE DRIVE: It's just 9.6 miles northwest from Salisbury via the A360 to epic Stonehenge.

> ☑ TOP TIP
>
> ### LONDON'S CONGESTION CHARGE
>
> Central London levies a congestion charge from 7am to 6pm weekdays and noon to 6pm weekends. Entering the 'C'-marked zone costs £18 (paid on the day or in advance) or £21 (up to three days afterwards). If your car is not a new, cleaner, greener model, the Ultra Low Emission Zone (ULEZ) charge (£12.50) needs to be paid throughout London 24/7. For full details on both charges and how to pay, see the TFL website *(tfl.gov.uk)*.

06 Stonehenge

Mighty **Stonehenge** *(english-heritage.org.uk)* is one of Britain's most enduring archaeological mysteries: despite countless theories about the site's purpose, ranging from a sacrificial centre to a celestial timepiece, no one knows for sure what drove prehistoric Britons to expend so much time and effort on its construction. The first phase of building started around 3000 BCE, when the outer circular bank and ditch were erected. A thousand years later, an inner circle of granite stones, known as bluestones, was added. Visits start from the ultramodern visitor centre.

A pathway frames the ring of massive stones. Although you can't walk in the circle, unless on a recommended Stonehenge Explorer Tour or special out-of-hours **Stone Circle Access Visit** *(english-heritage.org.uk)*, you can get close-up views. Admission is through timed tickets – secure a place well in advance if you want to visit.

THE DRIVE: Drive east to Durrington and take the A345 north, climbing over the grassy Pewsey Downs National Nature Reserve (home to another chalk figure, the Alton Barnes White Horse dating from 1812), to reach Avebury (24 miles in total).

07 Avebury

With a diameter of 348m, **Avebury** *(nationaltrust.org.uk)* is the largest stone circle in the world. It is also one of the oldest, dating from 2500 to 2200 BCE. Though it lacks the dramatic trilithons of its sister site, Stonehenge, the massive stone circle is just as rewarding to visit. Today, more than 30 stones are in place (pillars show where missing stones would have been) and a large section of the village is actually inside the stones – footpaths wind around them, allowing you to really soak up the extraordinary atmosphere. National Trust–run guided walks of the site regularly take place.

THE DRIVE: It's a 27-mile drive along the A4 past patchwork fields, country pubs and a smattering of villages to the Georgian streetscapes of Bath.

08 Bath

World Heritage–listed Bath was founded on top of natural hot springs and has been a tourist draw for some 2000 years. Its 18th-century heyday saw the construction of magnificent Georgian architecture. The best way to explore the city's **Roman Baths complex** and beautiful neoclassical buildings is on foot.

Bath is known to many as a location in Jane Austen's novels, including *Persuasion* and *Northanger Abbey*. Austen lived in Bath for five years, from 1801 to 1806, and remained a regular visitor and a keen student of the city's social scene. At the **Jane Austen Centre** *(janeausten.co.uk)*, guides in Regency costumes regale you with Austenesque tales as you tour memorabilia. September's 10-day **Jane Austen Festival** *(janeausten.co.uk)* takes place citywide.

THE DRIVE: It's 56.5 miles from Bath to Welsh capital Cardiff. Take the A46 north and join the westbound M4 over the Severn Estuary on the six-lane Second Severn Crossing bridge.

09 Cardiff

Set between an ancient fort and an ultramodern waterfront, Cardiff has been the capital of Wales since only 1955, but has embraced the role with vigour and is now one of Britain's leading urban centres, as you can see on a stroll through its compact streets.

Cardiff Castle *(cardiffcastle.com)* was originally a Roman fort and has a medieval keep at its heart, but it's the later additions that transformed it into an opulent Victorian residence that really capture the imagination.

Devoted mainly to art and natural history, the **National Museum Cardiff** *(museum.wales/cardiff)*

Roman Baths, Bath

SHEILA SAY/SHUTTERSTOCK

fills a grand neoclassical building. It's both a part of the Welsh National Museum and one of the best of its kind in Britain. If you time it right, you can catch a fired-up rugby test at Cardiff's **Principality Stadium** *(principalitystadium.wales)*; otherwise, take a stadium or 'rugby legends' tour.

THE DRIVE: Take the A48 northeast for 32 miles, bypassing Newport, to riverside Chepstow.

10 Chepstow

Nestled in an S-bend in the River Wye, Chepstow (Welsh: Cas-gwent) was first developed as a base for the Norman conquest of southeast Wales, later prospering as a port for the timber and wine trades. As river-borne commerce gave way to the railways, Chepstow's importance diminished to reflect its name, which means 'market place' in Old English.

One of Britain's oldest castles, imposing **Chepstow Castle** *(cadw.gov.wales)*, perches atop a limestone cliff overhanging the river, guarding the main river crossing from England into South Wales. Building commenced in 1067, less than a year after William the Conqueror invaded England, and it was extended over the centuries. Today there are plenty of towers, battlements and wall walks to explore. A cave in the cliff below the castle is one of many places where legend says King Arthur and his knights are napping until the day they're needed to save Britain.

THE DRIVE: Farmland makes up most of this 68-mile drive. Head northeast on the A48 along the River Severn to Gloucester then continue northeast on the A46 to Stratford-upon-Avon.

BRITAIN'S BEST FESTIVALS

Britain holds magnificent festivals throughout the year.

In London, see stunning blooms at the **Royal Horticultural Society's Chelsea Flower Show** *(rhs.org.uk/chelsea)* in May; military bands and bear-skinned grenadiers during the martial pageant **Trooping the Colour** *(householddivision.org.uk/trooping-the-colour)* marking the official birthday of the British Sovereign in June; or steel drums, dancers and outrageous costumes at the famous multicultural Caribbean-style street festival **Notting Hill Carnival** *(nhcarnival.org)* in August.

Also in August, Wales' **National Eisteddfod** *(eisteddfod.wales)* is descended from ancient Bardic tournaments. It's conducted in Welsh, but welcomes all entrants and visitors. It moves to a different location each year, attracting some 150,000 visitors.

Edinburgh's most famous happenings are the **International Festival** *(eif.co.uk)* and **Fringe** *(edfringe.com)* in August, but the city also has events throughout the year. Check the full list at *edinburghfestivalcity.com*.

11 Stratford-upon-Avon

Experiences linked to the life of Stratford's fêted son William Shakespeare range from the touristy (medieval recreations and Bard-themed tearooms) to the humbling – Shakespeare's modest grave in **Holy Trinity Church** *(stratford-upon-avon.org)* – and the sublime: a play by the **Royal Shakespeare Company** *(rsc.org.uk)*. One of the best ways to get a feel for the town's Tudor streets and willow-lined riverbanks is on foot.

Combined tickets are available from the Shakespeare Birthplace Trust *(shakespeare.org.uk)* for **Shakespeare's Birthplace** and **Shakespeare's New Place Gardens**, plus **Anne Hathaway's Cottage** (the childhood home of his wife) and **Shakespeare's Schoolroom** *(shakespearesschoolroom.org)*.

Don't miss a pint with the locals at Stratford's oldest and most atmospheric pub, the **Old Thatch Tavern** *(oldthatchtavernstratford.co.uk)*, built in 1470.

THE DRIVE: The fastest route from Stratford-upon-Avon to Manchester is to head northwest on Birmingham Rd and pick up the northbound M42, which becomes the M6. You'll see the hilly Peak District National Park to your east. It's a 116-mile journey; this stretch incurs road tolls that vary according to the time of day.

12 Manchester

A rich blend of history and culture is on show in this northern powerhouse's array of museums, galleries and innovative multigenre art centres, which include **HOME** *(homemcr.org)*.

The **Manchester Art Gallery** *(manchesterartgallery.org)* has a superb collection of British art and a hefty number of European masters. The older wing has an impressive selection that includes 37 Turner watercolours, as well as the country's best assemblage of Pre-Raphaelite art, while the newer gallery is home to 20th-century

British art starring Lucien Freud, Francis Bacon, Stanley Spencer, Henry Moore and David Hockney. A wonderful collection of British watercolours are also displayed at Manchester's **Whitworth Art Gallery** *(whitworth.manchester.ac.uk)*, which has an exceptional collection of historic textiles.

Manchester is famed for its rival football teams Manchester United *(manutd.com)* and Manchester City *(mancity.com)*, while its **National Football Museum** *(nationalfootballmuseum.com)* charts British football's evolution from its earliest days to the multibillion-pound phenomenon it is today.

The city is also world renowned for its live music, with gigs in many genres most nights.

THE DRIVE: This trip's longest drive, at 216 miles, takes you northwest via the M61 and M6, passing between the Yorkshire Dales National Park to your east and the Lake District National Park to your west. Once you cross into Scotland, the road becomes the A74 and climbs into the Southern Uplands, then becomes the A702 as it leads into Edinburgh.

13 Edinburgh

The Scottish capital is entwined with its landscape, with buildings and monuments perched atop crags and overshadowed by cliffs. From the Old Town's picturesque jumble of medieval tenements along the Royal Mile, its turreted skyline strung between the black, bull-nosed Castle Rock and the russet palisade of Salisbury Crags, to the New Town's neat neoclassical grid, the city offers a constantly changing perspective.

Along with a walk through the Old Town, unmissable experiences here include visiting **Edinburgh Castle** *(edinburghcastle.scot)*, which has played a pivotal role in Scottish history, both as a royal residence – King Malcolm Canmore (r 1058–93) and Queen Margaret first made their home here in the 11th century – and as a military stronghold; and climbing to the famous hilltop Arthur's Seat for city panoramas.

Edinburgh has hundreds of pubs. Sample a dram of Scots whisky at icons like the **Malt Shovel** *(belhaven.co.uk)*, with dozens of single malts behind the bar.

THE DRIVE: Drive southeast on the A68, passing through the Scottish Borders, and enter Northumberland National Park at the English border. Join the southbound A1 at Darlington, then take the eastbound A59 to York (191 miles altogether).

14 York

A magnificent ring of 13th-century walls encloses York's medieval spider's web of streets. At the heart of it all lies the immense, awe-inspiring sight of **York Minster** *(yorkminster.org)*. Constructed mainly between 1220 and 1480, it encompasses all the major stages of Gothic architecture. The transepts (1220–55) were built in Early English style; the octagonal chapter house (1260–90) and nave (1291–1340) in the Decorated style; and the west towers, west front and central (or lantern) tower (1470–72) in Perpendicular style.

Don't miss a walk on York's **City Walls** *(york.gov.uk/citywalls)*, which follow the line of the original Roman walls and give a whole new perspective on the city. Cover just the highlights or allow up to two hours for the full circuit of 4.5 miles.

THE DRIVE: From York, it's 163 miles to Cambridge. Take the A64 southwest to join onto the A1 heading southeast.

15 Cambridge

Surrounded by meadows, Cambridge is a university town extraordinaire, with a tightly packed core of ancient colleges and picturesque riverside 'Backs' (college gardens), which you can stroll around.

The colossal neoclassical pile containing the **Fitzwilliam Museum** *(fitzmuseum.cam.ac.uk)*, locally called 'the Fitz', was built to house the treasures that the seventh Viscount Fitzwilliam bequeathed to his old university. Standout exhibits include Roman and Egyptian grave goods, artworks by many of the great masters and quirkier collections such as banknotes, literary autographs, watches and armour.

For the full Cambridge experience, rent a river boat from operators such as **Scudamore's Punting** *(scudamores.com)*.

THE DRIVE: Hop on the M11 for the 60-mile zip south to London.

SCOTLAND'S CRAFT GIN

Scotland is world famous for its whisky, but **Scottish craft gin** *(thescottishginsociety.com)* is also hugely popular. Over 70% of gin produced in the UK comes from Scotland – there are more than 90 gin distilleries in the country. Bars all over Edinburgh are offering cocktails based on brands such as Pickering's, 56 North, Edinburgh Gin and Holyrood Distillery.

Fitzwilliam Museum
ARIJEET BANNERJEE/SHUTTERSTOCK

03

EPIC TRIP

BRITAIN'S WILD SIDE

DURATION: 21 DAYS

DISTANCE: 1435 MILES / 2310KM

GREAT FOR: WILDLIFE, OUTDOORS

BEST TIME TO GO: JUNE TO SEPTEMBER OFFERS THE BEST CONDITIONS FOR OUTDOOR ACTIVITIES.

Leave the city lights behind on this adventure into Britain's wild natural heartland. On this intrepid trip you'll get up close to soaring mountain peaks, desolate moorland, sea-sprayed beaches, scalloped bays, lush hills, green dales, high, barren fells and glassy lakes, some of which teem with wildlife. Along the way, get out and explore the breathtaking countryside on foot, bicycle, horseback and kayak.

LINK YOUR TRIP

16 The Cotswolds & Literary England
The New Forest is 48 miles southeast of Bath, from where you can travel through more picturesque British countryside in the Cotswolds.

33 Upper West Coast
The Isle of Skye's main town, Portree, is the departure point for a voyage through jaw-dropping Scottish highland and island scenery.

01 New Forest

With typical, accidental, English irony the **New Forest** *(thenewforest.co.uk)* is anything but new – it was first proclaimed a royal hunting preserve in 1079. It's also not much of a forest, being mostly heathland ('forest' is from the Old French for 'hunting ground'). For an overview of the New Forest, which was designated a national park in 2005, stop by the **New Forest Heritage Centre** *(newforestheritage.org.uk)* in Lyndhurst. Wild ponies mooch around pretty scrubland, deer flicker in the distance and rare birds flit among the foliage. Genteel villages dot the landscape, connected by a web of walking and cycling trails. The heritage centre stocks maps and guides, or check *newforestnpa.gov.uk*.

New Forest is also a popular spot for horse riding; **Burley Villa** *(burleyvilla.co.uk)* organises rides using traditional English and also Western saddle styles and offers lessons.

RADDSS/SHUTTERSTOCK

★ BEST FOR

WILDLIFE

Spot wild red deer, especially in autumn, at Exmoor National Park.

Lyme Regis

THE DRIVE: Take the A31 then the A35 southwest to Weymouth and Chesil Beach. Follow the Jurassic Coast northwest along the B3157 to Lyme Regis (86 miles in total).

02 Lyme Regis

Fossils regularly emerge from the unstable cliffs surrounding Lyme Regis, exposed by the landslides of a retreating shoreline, making this a key stop along the UNESCO-listed Jurassic Coast. For an overview, **Dinosaurland** *(dinosaurland.co.uk)* overflows with fossilised remains; look out for belemnites, a plesiosaurus and an impressive locally found ichthyosaur. Kids love the lifelike dinosaur models, rock-hard tyrannosaur eggs and 73kg dinosaur dung.

Three miles east of Lyme, the **Charmouth Heritage Coast Centre** *(charmouth.org)* runs regular fossil-hunting trips. In Lyme itself, **Lyme Regis Museum** *(lymeregismuseum.co.uk)* also organises fossil walks. Book walks ahead.

THE DRIVE: Drive west on the A3052 through the dazzling East Devon National Landscape to Exeter and take the B3212 up into Postbridge, a small village in the middle of Dartmoor National Park (62 miles all told).

MILITARY RANGE

Live ammunition is used on Dartmoor's training ranges. Check the Firing Information Service *(mod.uk/access)* or tourist offices. Red flags fly at the edges of in-use ranges by day; red flares burn at night.

03 Dartmoor National Park

Covering 368 sq miles, this vast **national park** *(visitdartmoor.co.uk)* feels like it's tumbled straight out of a Tolkien tome, with its honey-coloured heaths, moss-covered boulders, meandering streams and eerie granite tors (hills). It's one of Britain's most wildly beautiful corners.

On sunny days Dartmoor is idyllic: ponies wander and sheep graze beside the road, as seen in Steven Spielberg's WWI epic *War Horse*. But Dartmoor is also the setting for Sir Arthur Conan

Doyle's *The Hound of the Baskervilles*, and in sleeting rain and swirling mists the moor morphs into a bleak wilderness where tales of a phantom hound can seem very real. Be aware too that the military uses live ammunition in its training ranges.

Dartmoor is a haven for outdoor activities, including hiking, cycling, riding, climbing and white-water kayaking; the Dartmoor National Park Authority *(dartmoor.gov.uk)* has detailed information. And there are plenty of rustic pubs to cosy up in when the fog rolls in.

THE DRIVE: Head west through Tavistock to pass through the Tamar Valley National Landscape, on the A390. At Dobwalls, pick up the A38 and drive west along the forested River Fowey to join the southwest-bound A30. Take the Victoria turn-off and travel northwest past Newquay Cornwall Airport to Carnewas at Bedruthan (67 miles altogether).

04 Carnewas at Bedruthan

On Cornwall's surf-pounded coast loom the stately rock stacks of **Bedruthan** *(nationaltrust.org.uk)*. These mighty granite pillars have been carved out by thousands of years of wind and waves, and the area is now owned by the National Trust. While rockfalls have prevented access to the beach (check the National Trust website for updates), it's a superb spot for wildlife-spotting, picnicking and surveying the views. Towards the north end is a rocky shelf known as **Diggory's Island**, which separates the main beach from another little-known cove.

THE DRIVE: Drive east to join the northeast-bound A39, which runs parallel to the Cornish coast, to the town of Lynmouth in Exmoor National Park (94 miles in total).

05 Exmoor National Park

Right in the middle of **Exmoor National Park** *(visit-exmoor.co.uk)* is the higher moor, an empty, expansive, otherworldly landscape of tawny grasses and huge skies.

Exmoor supports one of England's largest wild red deer populations, which is best experienced in autumn when the annual rutting season sees stags bellowing, charging at each other and clashing antlers in an attempt to impress prospective mates.

At the **Exmoor Pony Centre** *(moorlandmousietrust.org.uk)*, visitors have the chance to meet – and ride – Britain's oldest native pony breed.

The Exmoor Dark Sky Reserve was Europe's first. Astronomy advice, telescope rental and activities are available at the **Exmoor National Park Authority** *(exmoor-nationalpark.gov.uk)*.

Hiking is fantastic here. Cycling is also popular; **Exmoor Adventures** *(exmooradventures.co.uk)* runs a mountain-biking skills course and also rents out bikes.

THE DRIVE: From Lynmouth to Libanus in the Brecon Beacons National Park it's 143 miles. Take the A39 east along the coast to join the M5 at

HIKING EXMOOR

The open moors and a profusion of marked bridleways make Exmoor an excellent area for hiking. The best-known routes are the Somerset & North Devon Coast Path, which is part of the **South West Coast Path** *(southwestcoastpath.org.uk)*, and the Exmoor section of the **Two Moors Way** *(twomoorsway.org)*, which starts in Lynmouth and travels 102 miles south over Dartmoor to Ivybridge. From there, a 15-mile extension leads to the south Devon coast at Wembury.

Another superb route is the **Coleridge Way** *(visit-exmoor.co.uk/coleridge-way)*, which winds for 51 miles from Lynmouth to Nether Stowey, crossing Exmoor, the Brendon Hills and the Quantocks. Part of the 180-mile **Tarka Trail** *(tarkatrail.org.uk)* cuts through the park. The coastal section sweeps from Lynton to Bideford, before making its way down into north Devon.

Check to see if walks overseen by the **Exmoor National Park Authority** *(exmoor-nationalpark.gov.uk)* are running. Past events include deer safaris, nightjar birdwatching walks and dark-sky strolls.

ENPA tourist offices also sell a great range of day-walk leaflets.

Exmoor National Park

ADAM BURTON/ALAMY

Bridgwater. Take the Second Severn Crossing bridge and head west towards Cardiff to join the northwest-bound A470.

06 Bannau Brycheiniog (Brecon Beacons) National Park

Brecon Beacons National Park ripples for 45 miles from the English border to near Llandeilo in the west. High mountain plateaux of grass and heather, their northern rims scalloped with glacier-scoured hollows, rise above wooded, waterfall-splashed valleys and green, rural landscapes.

Within the park there are four distinct regions: the wild, lonely Black Mountain (Mynydd Du) in the west, with its high moors and glacial lakes; Great Forest (Fforest Fawr), whose rushing streams and spectacular waterfalls form the headwaters of the Rivers Tawe and Neath; the Brecon Beacons (Bannau Brycheiniog) proper, a group of very distinctive, flat-topped hills that includes Pen-y-Fan (886m), the park's highest peak; and the rolling heathland ridges of the Black Mountains (Y Mynyd-doedd Duon) – not to be confused with the Black Mountain (singular) in the west. The park's main **visitor centre** *(beacons-npa.gov.uk)* has details of walks, hiking and biking trails, outdoor activities, wildlife and geology (call first to check it's open).

The Brecon Beacons is just one of a handful of places in the world to be awarded Dark-Sky Reserve status. With almost zero light pollution, this is one of the UK's finest places for stargazing. Meteor showers, nebulae, strings of constellations and the Milky Way twinkle brightly in the night sky when the weather is clear. Among the 10 best spots are **Carreg Cennen** *(cadw.gov.wales)*, Sugar Loaf (Mynydd Pen-y-Fâl) and **Llanthony Priory** *(cadw.gov.wales)*.

Visitor centres throughout the park can give you information about stargazing events or check out *bannaubrycheiniog.org/thingstodo/stargazing*.

THE DRIVE: Drive north along the A470 to reach the southern boundary of Eryri (Snowdonia) National Park at Mallwyd (79 miles altogether).

Pen-y-Pass, Eryri (Snowdonia) National Park

NICOLA PULHAM/SHUTTERSTOCK

07 Eryri (Snowdonia) National Park

Wales' best-known and most-visited slice of nature, Eryri (Snowdonia) National Park became the country's first national park in 1951. Every year more than 600,000 people walk, climb or take the rack-and-pinion railway *(snowdonrailway.co.uk)* to the 1085m summit of Snowdon. The park's 823 sq miles embrace stunning coastline, forests, valleys, rivers, bird-filled estuaries and Wales' biggest natural lake.

The **Eryri National Park Information Centres** *(eryri.gov.wales)* are an invaluable source of information about walking trails, mountain conditions and more.

THE DRIVE: Continue north on the A470 and take the A5 northwest to Bangor. Cross Robert Stephenson's Britannia Bridge, built in 1850, over the Menai Strait and take the A545 northwest to Beaumaris (a 72-mile trip).

08 Isle of Anglesey

The 276-sq-mile Isle of Anglesey (Ynys Môn) offers miles of inspiring coastline, hidden beaches and the country's greatest concentration of ancient sites.

Almost all of the Anglesey coast has been designated a National Landscape (formerly known as as an Area of Outstanding Natural Beauty). Beyond the handsome Georgian town of **Beaumaris** (Biwmares), there are hidden gems scattered all over the island. It's very much a living centre of Welsh culture, too, as you can see for yourself at **Oriel Môn** *(orielmon.org)*. A great, introductory day walk from Beaumaris takes in the ancient monastic site of **Penmon Priory** *(cadw.gov.wales)*, **Penmon Point** with stunning views across to

GAIL JOHNSON/SHUTTERSTOCK

Penmon Point, with Pufflin Island in the background

Puffin Island, and long, sandy beach **Llanddona**.

THE DRIVE: Return to the mainland and take the A55 northeast, crossing the border into England where the road becomes the M56. Continue northeast towards Manchester before turning off on the southeast-bound M6. At Sandbach turn east on the A534 and follow the signs to Leek, then take the A53 northeast before turning east towards Longnor then Bakewell (138 miles all told).

09 Peak District National Park

Founded in 1951, the Peak District was England's first national park and is Europe's busiest. But even at peak times, there are 555 sq miles of open countryside in which to soak up the scenery. Caving and climbing, cycling and, above all, walking (including numerous short walks) are the most popular activities.

The **Peak District National Park Authority** *(peakdistrict.gov.uk)* has reams of information about the park and also operates several cycle-hire centres. The charming town of Bakewell also has a helpful **vistor centre** *(visitpeakdistrict.com)*.

THE DRIVE: From Bakewel take the A623 northwest towards Manchester and pick up the northbound M66, then at Burnley take the northeast-bound M65 to Skipton. Enter the Yorkshire Dales National Park on the B6265 to Grassington and head northwest to Aysgarth. Then take the A684 along the River Ure to Hawes (a total of 113 miles).

10 Yorkshire Dales National Park

Protected as a national park since the 1950s, the glacial valleys of the **Yorkshire Dales** *(yorkshiredales.org.uk)*, named from the old Norse word *dalr*, meaning 'valleys', are characterised by a distinctive landscape of high heather moorland, stepped skylines and flat-topped hills above valleys patchworked with drystone dykes and little barns.

Hawes is home to the **Wensleydale Creamery** *(wensleydale.co.uk)*, producing famous Wensleydale cheese. In the limestone country of the southern Dales you'll encounter extraordinary examples of karst scenery (created by rainwater dissolving the underlying limestone bedrock).

THE DRIVE: Head southwest on the B6255 to Ingleton. Take the A65 northwest to Sizergh then the A590 southwest to the Lake District's southern reaches at Newby Bridge. Drive north along Lake Windermere before veering northwest to Hawkshead (53 miles all told).

11 Lake District National Park

The Lake District (or Lakeland, as it's commonly known round these parts) is by far the UK's most popular national park. Ever since the Romantic poets arrived in the 19th century, its postcard panorama of craggy hilltops, mountain tarns and glittering lakes has stirred visitors' imaginations. It's awash with outdoor opportunities, from lake cruises to mountain walks.

Many people visit for the region's literary connections: among the many writers who found inspiration here are William Wordsworth, Samuel Taylor Coleridge, Arthur Ransome and Beatrix Potter, a lifelong lover of the Lakes, whose delightful former farmhouse, **Hill Top** *(nationaltrust.org.uk/visit/lake-district/hill-top)*, inspired many of her tales, including *Peter Rabbit*.

THE DRIVE: Drive northwest on the A591 to join the A595 to Carlisle. Then take the A689 and A69 northeast to Walltown along Hadrian's Wall (68 miles in total).

12 Hadrian's Wall

Hadrian's Wall is one of Britain's most revealing and dramatic Roman ruins; its 2000-year-old procession of abandoned forts, garrisons, towers and milecastles marches across the wild and lonely landscape of northern England. The wall was about defence and control, but this edge-of-empire barrier also symbolised the boundary of civilised order – to the north lay the unruly land of the marauding Celts, while to the south was the Roman world of orderly taxpaying, underfloor heating and bathrooms.

There's an excellent visitor centre at **Walltown** *(northumberlandnationalpark.org.uk)*. The finest sections of the wall run along the southern edge of remote **Northumberland National Park** *(northumberlandnationalpark.org.uk)*, one of Britain's finest wilderness areas.

THE DRIVE: Follow the B6318 northeast along Hadrian's Wall. Turn north on the B6320 to Bellingham. Continue northwest alongside the North Tyne river and Kielder Water lake to the village of Kielder (a 43-mile journey).

13 Kielder Water & Forest Park

Adjacent to Northumberland National Park, the **Kielder Water & Forest Park** *(visitkielder.com)* is home to the vast artificial lake Kielder Water, holding 200 billion litres. Surrounding its 27-mile-long shoreline is England's largest plantation forest, with 150 million spruce and pine trees. Kielder Water is a watersports playground (and midge magnet; bring insect repellent), and also has walking and cycling as well as great birdwatching.

The lack of population here helped see the area awarded Dark Sky Reserve status by the International Dark Skies Association with controls to prevent light pollution. For the best views of the Northumberland International Dark Sky Park, attend a stargazing session at state-of-the-art **Kielder Observatory** *(kielderobservatory.org)*. Book ahead and dress warmly as it's seriously chilly here at night.

THE DRIVE: It's a 139-mile drive from Kielder to Balloch on the southern shore of Loch Lomond. Head north into Scotland and join the A68 towards Edinburgh. Take the M8 to

♥ WHY I LOVE THIS TRIP

ANTHONY HAM, WRITER

This classic journey through wild Britain will leave you wondering how such diversity can possibly be within reach on one relatively short trip. Forests and cliffs, mountains and moors – Great Britain is one beautiful place, and this stirring exploration of lakes and national parks showcases the best that Britain's natural world has to offer.

ROBERT HARDING VIDEO/SHUTTERSTOCK

Winshield Crags, Hadrian's Wall

Glasgow and then the A82 northwest to Balloch.

14 Loch Lomond

Loch Lomond is mainland Britain's largest lake and, after Loch Ness, the most famous of Scotland's lochs. It's part of **Loch Lomond & the Trossachs National Park** *(lochlomond-trossachs.org)*, which extends over a sizeable area from Balloch north to Tyndrum and Killin, and from Callander west to the forests of Cowal.

From Balloch, **Sweeney's Cruises** *(sweeneyscruiseco.com)* offers, among other trips, a popular one-hour return cruise to the island of Inchmurrin (operating year-round). The quay is directly opposite Balloch train station. With departures from Tarbet and Luss on the loch's western shore, **Cruise Loch Lomond** *(cruiselochlomond.co.uk)* runs circular cruises from 80 to 90 minutes, has a waterbus service and hop-on, hop-off options for hikes.

THE DRIVE: Follow the A82 along Loch Lomond's western shoreline and pick up the northeast-bound A85 at Crianlarich, then the A827. Then take the northwest-bound A9 to Aviemore (a total of 141 miles).

15 Cairngorms National Park

The vast **Cairngorms National Park** *(cairngorms.co.uk)* stretches from Aviemore in the north – which has a handy **visitor information centre** *(visitaviemore.com)* – to the Angus Glens in the south, and from Dalwhinnie in the west to Ballater and Royal Deeside in the east.

The park encompasses the highest landmass in Britain – a broad mountain plateau, riven only by the deep valleys of the Lairig Ghru and Loch Avon, with an average altitude of over 1000m and including five of the six highest summits in the UK. This wild mountain landscape of granite and heather has a subarctic climate and supports rare alpine tundra vegetation and high-altitude bird species, such as snow bunting, ptarmigan and dotterel. Lower down, scenic glens are softened by beautiful open forests of native Scots pine, home to rare animals and birds such as pine martens, Scottish wildcats, red squirrels, ospreys, capercaillies and crossbills.

THE DRIVE: Take the A9 northwest to Inverness, then the southwest-bound A82 along Loch Ness. At Invermoriston join the westbound A887, which becomes the A87, and continue to Kyle of Lochalsh, where you'll cross the Skye Bridge to the Isle of Skye. Continue along the A87 to reach Portree (145 miles all up).

16 Isle of Skye

The Isle of Skye (an t-Eilean Sgiatheanach in Gaelic) takes its name from the old Norse *skya*, meaning 'cloud island', a Viking reference to the Cuillin Hills, which are often enshrouded in mist. It's a 50-mile-long patchwork of velvet moors, jagged mountains, sparkling lochs and towering sea cliffs.

Lively Portree (Port Righ) is the main base.

Skye offers some of the finest walking in Scotland, including short, low-level routes (check *isleofskye.com/skye-guide/skye-walks*). The sheltered coves and sea lochs around the coast of Skye provide magnificent sea-kayaking. **Sea Kayak Plockton** *(seakayakplockton.co.uk)* runs expeditions and courses for beginners and experienced paddlers to otherwise inaccessible places.

Skye's stunning scenery is the main attraction, but there are castles, crofting museums, and cosy pubs and restaurants, along with art galleries and craft studios.

DETOUR

Outer Hebrides

Start: 16 Isle of Skye

If you're not ready to return to the mainland after visiting the Isle of Skye, consider a trip to the Outer Hebrides (aka the Western Isles; Na h-Eileanan an Iar in Gaelic) – a 130-mile-long string of islands west of Skye. More than a third of Scotland's registered crofts are here, and no less than 60% of the population are Gaelic speakers. With limited time, head straight for the west coast of Lewis with its prehistoric sites, preserved black houses, beautiful beaches, and arts and crafts studios – **Stornoway's Visit Outer Hebrides Information Hub** *(visitouterhebrides.co.uk)* can provide a list. **Ferries** *(calmac.co.uk)* run from Uig on Skye.

WALKING SAFETY TIPS

The British countryside may appear gentle, and often is, but conditions can deteriorate quickly. Year-round on the hills or open moors, you should carry warm waterproof clothing, a map and compass, and high-energy food (eg chocolate) and drinks. If you're really going off the beaten track, leave your route details with someone.

Cairngorms National Park (p51)

PETE STUART/SHUTTERSTOCK

04

★ BEST FOR

SURPRISES

The world's biggest stone circle: Avebury (not Stonehenge).

EPIC TRIP

THE HISTORIC SOUTH

DURATION: 9–11 DAYS

DISTANCE: 450 MILES / 720KM

GREAT FOR: HISTORY, OUTDOORS

BEST TIME TO GO: SPRING AND AUTUMN. PLUS SUMMER IF YOU DON'T MIND MORE CROWDS.

Leeds Castle

Tour some of the world's most beautiful castles and memorable archaeological sites. Take in three of England's most impressive cathedrals, Georgian cityscapes, Churchill's palace and Oxford's spires. Discover guerrilla art and this country's fine tradition of seaside kitsch. Motor to a car museum, explore unspoiled villages and encounter 14th-century fellow travellers' tales. And in doing so, take a road trip through the best of Britain's past.

LINK YOUR TRIP

07 Kent: Garden of England
Encounter seashores, seafood and modern art along with Kent's fertile landscapes. Start at Margate, 17 miles northeast of Canterbury.

16 The Cotswolds & Literary England
The New Forest is 48 miles southeast of Bath, from where you can travel through more picturesque British countryside in the Cotswolds.

01 London

Vibrant London is so packed with historic sights, it can be difficult to know where to start. Try the cathedral that is the capital's touchstone: **St Paul's** *(stpauls.co.uk)*. Designed by Sir Christopher Wren in 1675 after the Great Fire, its vast dome is famed for avoiding Luftwaffe raids during the Blitz. Head inside and up 257 steps to the walkway called the Whispering Gallery, then 528 steps in total to the Golden Gallery at the top for unforgettable London views. Next walk north to explore the capital's rich history at the historic Smithfield market buildings now housing the **London Museum** *(londonmuseum.org.uk)*. Then head east to elegant **Tower Bridge** *(towerbridge.org.uk)* to learn in its exhibition just how they raise the arms – and the road – to let ships through.

THE DRIVE: London's streets and suburbs meet bursts of the Kent countryside; you're heading for the A20 towards Sidcup, then the M20 towards Dover. Shortly after Maidstone, leave

ROLF E. STAERK/SHUTTERSTOCK

the motorway behind, picking up A20 signs for Lenham and then Leeds Castle, some 40 miles from the capital.

02 Leeds Castle

Immense and moat-ringed, for many **Leeds Castle** *(leeds-castle.com)* is one of the world's most romantic. The formidable, intricate structure balancing on two islands is known as something of a 'ladies castle'. This stems from the fact that in its more than 1000 years of history, it has been home to a who's who of queens, most famously Henry VIII's first wife, Catherine of Aragon.

THE DRIVE: Next up is a 25-mile cruise, high up over the vast chalk ridge of the North Downs. Behind you stretch the villages and fields of the Weald of Kent. But you're headed northeast, largely along the A252/A28 – the Canterbury Rd which echoes the old pilgrim footpath to the cathedral city.

03 Canterbury

Canterbury is at the top of the charts for English cathedral cities – and no wonder. Here, you'll find medieval alleyways framing exquisite architecture, with **Canterbury Cathedral** *(canterbury-cathedral.org)* the centrepiece. This towering Gothic masterpiece features fine stonework, a cavernous crypt and the site of English history's most famous murder: Archbishop Thomas Becket was killed here in 1170 after 'hints' from King Henry II, and has been drawing pilgrims for more than 800 years since.

Knowledgeable guides double up as energetic oarsmen at **Canterbury Historic River Tours** *(canterburyrivertours.co.uk)* for fascinating, multi-award-winning River Stour minicruises. For a taste of even older Canterbury, head to the mosaics of the **Roman Museum** *(canterburymuseums.co.uk)*.

THE DRIVE: Now for a 35-mile drive. Head back up and over those creamy North Downs on the A28 towards Ashford. Then plunge down to roll, along the A2070, through the verdant valley of the Weald of Kent, then take the A259. Soon you're edging the flatlands of Romney Marsh and arriving at Rye.

04 Rye

Welcome to one of England's prettiest seaside towns. Here cobbled lanes, wonky Tudor buildings and tales of smugglers abound. The best place to start stretching your legs is Mermaid Street. It bristles with 15th-century timber-framed houses with quirky names such as 'The House with Two Front Doors' and 'The House Opposite'. The **Rye Heritage Centre** *(ryeheritage.co.uk)* offers themed walking tours.

THE DRIVE: The next 50-mile leg sees you taking a string of A roads west. They lead past the woods and farms of the High Weald National Landscape and up another chalk ridge, this time the amphitheatre of hills known as the South Downs. Eventually, it's time to descend to Brighton on the shore.

DETOUR

Beachy Head

Start: 04 Rye

An 8-mile detour off your route leads to a truly remarkable view. Around 25 miles west of Rye, peel off the A27 onto the A22 to Eastbourne. Head to the seafront to take the signposted route that climbs to Beachy Head. Pick from several parking spots and follow the footpaths to the cliffs themselves. These 162m-tall sheer chalk faces are the highest point of cliffs that slice across the rugged coastline at the southern end of the South Downs. Far below sits a squat lighthouse with red and white stripes. Appealing walks include the 1.5-mile hike west to the beach at Birling Gap.

05 Brighton

Famously hedonistic, exuberant and home to the UK's biggest gay scene, Brighton rocks the south. The bright and breezy seafront boasts the grand, century-old **Brighton Pier** *(brightonpier.co.uk)*, complete with fairground rides, amusement arcades and candy-floss stalls.

Stroll inland to the magnificent **Royal Pavilion** *(brightonmuseums.org.uk/visit/royal-pavilion-garden)*, the glittering palace of Prince George (later King George IV). It's one of the most opulent buildings in England, and Europe's finest example of early-19th-century

Portsmouth Historic Dockyard

GALLWIS/SHUTTERSTOCK

chinoiserie. Take in the Salvador Dalí sofa modelled on Mae West's lips at the **Brighton Museum & Art Gallery** *(brightonmuseums.org.uk)*, then gear up for a lively night out of some shopping amid the tightly-packed boutiques of The Lanes.

THE DRIVE: Next is a 50-mile blast due west, largely along A roads, to the historic port of Portsmouth. As the 170m-high Spinnaker Tower gets closer on the horizon, pick up signs for the Historic Dockyard Car Park.

06 Portsmouth

For a world-class collection of maritime heritage, head to **Portsmouth Historic Dockyard** *(historicdockyard.co.uk)*. The blockbuster draw is Henry VIII's favourite flagship, the *Mary Rose*. A £35-million, boat-shaped museum has now been built around the ship, giving uninterrupted views of the preserved timbers of the massive hull. Equally impressive is *HMS Victory*. Other nautical sights include the Victorian *HMS Warrior* and a wealth of imaginative museums. Round it all off by strolling around the defences in the historic district Portsmouth Point (aka Spice Island).

THE DRIVE: Time to head inland; a 30-mile motorway cruise (the M27 then the M3) takes you to Winchester.

AGSAZ/SHUTTERSTOCK

Canterbury Cathedral (p55)

THE CANTERBURY TALES

The Canterbury Tales is the best-known work of English literature's father figure: Geoffrey Chaucer (1342–1400). Chaucer was the first English writer to introduce characters – rather than 'types' – into fiction. They feature strongly in *The Canterbury Tales*, an unfinished series of 24 vivid stories told by a party of pilgrims travelling between London and Canterbury. The text remains a pillar of the literary canon. But more than that, it's a collection of rollicking good yarns about adultery, debauchery, crime and edgy romance, and is filled with Chaucer's witty observations about human nature.

07 Winchester

Calm, collegiate Winchester is a mellow must-see. One of southern England's most awe-inspiring buildings, 11th-century **Winchester Cathedral** *(winchester-cathedral.org.uk)* adorns its core. It boasts a fine Gothic facade, one of the longest medieval naves in Europe (164m) and intricately carved medieval choir stalls, sporting everything from mythical beasts to a mischievous green man. Jane Austen's grave is near the entrance, in the northern aisle.

The fantastical crumbling remains of **Wolvesey Castle** (Old Bishop's Palace; *english-heritage.org.uk*) sit nearby, as does one of England's most prestigious private schools: **Winchester College** *(winchestercollege.org)*, which you can visit as part of a tour.

THE DRIVE: Leave Winchester's ancient streets to take the motorways towards Southampton (initially the M3). After 14 miles turn off onto the A35 towards Lyndhurst. From here it's a 9-mile drive to Beaulieu through the New Forest's increasingly wooded roads. It's 27 miles in all.

08 Beaulieu

The vintage car museum and stately home at **Beaulieu** *(beaulieu.co.uk)* is centred on a 13th-century Cistercian monastery that passed to the ancestors of the current proprietors, the Montague family, after Henry VIII's 1536 monastic land-grab. Today its motor museum includes F1 cars and jet-powered land-speed record-breakers, as well as wheels driven by James Bond and Mr Bean. The palace began life as a 14th-century Gothic abbey gatehouse, and received a 19th-century makeover from Baron Montagu.

THE DRIVE: The satnav wants to start this 28-mile leg by routing you on to the A326. Resist! Opt for the A and B roads that wind through the villages of Lyndhurst, Cadnam, Brook and North Charford, revealing the New Forest's blend of woods and open heath. Eventually, join the A338 to Salisbury. Soon an immense cathedral spire rises from the town.

09 Salisbury

Salisbury's skyline is dominated by the tallest spire in England, which soars from its central, majestic 13th-century **cathedral** (p111).

The surrounding Cathedral Close has a hushed, other-worldly feel. Nearby, the hugely important finds at **Salisbury Museum** *(salisburymuseum.org.uk)* include Iron Age gold coins, a Bronze Age gold necklace and the Stonehenge Archer, the bones of a man found in the ditch surrounding the stone circle.

THE DRIVE: Next: a 10-mile drive taking you back 5000 years. The A345 heads north. Soon after joining the A303, detail a passenger to watch the right windows – the world's most famous stone circle will soon pop into view. The entry to the site is just beyond.

10 Stonehenge

Welcome to the best-known of Britain's archaeological sites: **Stonehenge**, a compelling ring of monolithic stones that dates, in parts, back to 3000 BCE.

Head into the visitor centre to see 300 finds from the site and experience an impressive 360-degree projection of the stone circle through the ages and seasons.

Next hop on a shuttle (or you can walk; it's 1.5 miles) to the monument. There, as you stroll around it, play 'spot-the-stone': look out for the bluestone horseshoe (an inner

Avebury Stone Circle

DENIS CHAPMAN/SHUTTERSTOCK

semicircle), the trilithon horseshoe (sets of two vertical stones topped by a horizontal one) and the Slaughter Stone and Heel Stone (set apart, on the northeast side). Then try to work out what on earth it all means. Note that entrance is by timed ticket; secure yours well in advance.

THE DRIVE: Now for a 24-mile, A-road meander through rural England. After dodging through Devizes, it's not long before signs point left to Avebury's main car park.

11 Avebury

A two-minute stroll from the car park leads to a ring of stones that's so big an entire village sits inside. Fringed by a massive bank and, and with a diameter of 348m, Avebury (p40) is the largest stone circle in the world. Dating from 2500 to 2200 BCE, more than 30 stones are still in place and you can wander at will between them and clusters of other stones. Houses, the **Henge Shop** *(hengeshop.com)* and a pub, the **Red Lion** *(oldenglishinns.co.uk)*, also nestle inside the circle.

THE DRIVE: Drive due west, as the A4 winds for 30 miles past fields and through villages to the city of Bath.

DETOUR

Lacock

Start: 11 Avebury

Around 16 miles into your Avebury-to-Bath cruise, consider a detour south. Because a drive of just an extra 4 miles leads to a real rarity: a medieval village that's been preserved in time. In Lacock, the sweet streets framed by stone cottages, higgledy-piggledy rooftops and mullioned windows are a delight to stroll around. Unsurprisingly, it's a popular movie location – it's popped up in the *Harry Potter* films, *The Other Boleyn Girl* and a BBC adaptation of *Pride and Prejudice*. The 13th-century former Augustinian nunnery of **Lacock Abbey** *(nationaltrust.org.uk)* is a must-see: its deeply atmospheric rooms and stunning Gothic entrance hall are lined with bizarre terracotta figures – spot the scapegoat with a lump of sugar on its nose. The **Fox Talbot Museum** *(nationaltrust.org.uk)* features an intriguing display on early photography, while the garden includes an orchard, a botanic garden and a historic rose garden.

12 Bath

Sophisticated, stately and ever-so-slightly snooty, Bath is graced with some of the finest Georgian architecture anywhere in Britain. Wandering around the streets here is a real joy. The **Bath Assembly Rooms** *(nationaltrust.org.uk)*, where socialites once gathered, gives an insight into the Georgian world; after renovations, it's expected to reopen in 2027.

To discover the city's culinary heritage head for **Sally Lunn's** *(sallylunns.co.uk)*, which bakes the famous **Bath Bunn** (a brioche-meets-bread treat). For a free glass of the spring water that made the city rich, stop by the **Pump Room** *(romanbaths.co.uk)*. Then soak yourself at **Thermae Bath Spa** *(thermaebathspa.com)*, with its steam rooms, waterfall showers and a choice of swimming pools (including a gorgeous rooftop one).

THE DRIVE: It's a 13-mile blast from Bath to Bristol along the A36/A4.

13 Bristol

In Bristol, a fascinating seafaring heritage meets an edgy and contemporary vibe. The mighty ***SS Great Britain*** *(ssgreatbritain.org)* sits on the city's waterfront. Designed in 1843 by engineering genius Isambard Kingdom Brunel, its interior has been impeccably refurbished, including the galley, the surgeon's quarters and a working model of the original steam engine. The whole vessel is contained in an air-tight dry dock, dubbed a 'glass sea'.

At the **Bristol Museum & Art Gallery** *(bristolmuseums.org.uk)* take in the *Paint-Pot Angel* by

STONEHENGE'S RITUAL LANDSCAPE

As you drive along the roads around Stonehenge, it's worth registering that the site forms part of a huge complex of ancient monuments. North of Stonehenge and running roughly east–west is the Cursus, an elongated embanked oval; the smaller Lesser Cursus is nearby. Two clusters of burial mounds, the Old Barrow and the New Kings Barrow, sit beside the ceremonial pathway, The Avenue. This route cuts northeast of Stonehenge's Heel Stone and originally linked the site with the River Avon, 2 miles away. Theories abound as to what these sites were used for, ranging from ancient sporting arenas to processional avenues for the dead.

world-famous street artist Banksy. In the suburb of Clifton explore Georgian architecture, especially in Cornwallis and Royal York Cres.

The **Clifton Observatory** *(cliftonobservatory.com)*, meanwhile, features a rare camera obscura which offers incredible views of the deep fissure that is the Avon Gorge.

THE DRIVE: Travelling partly on the M4 and partly on A roads, the next 80-mile leg sees you skirting Oxford (for now) and arriving at the tree-lined avenue that leads to one of Britain's finest stately homes.

14 Blenheim Palace

A monumental baroque fantasy designed by Sir John Vanbrugh and Nicholas Hawksmoor, **Blenheim Palace** *(blenheimpalace.com)*, was built between 1705 and 1722. The house is filled with statues, tapestries, ostentatious furniture, priceless china and giant oil paintings. Highlights include the Great Hall, a soaring space topped by a 20m-high ceiling adorned with images of the first duke. Britain's legendary WWII prime minister Sir Winston Churchill was born here in 1874 – the Churchill Exhibition is dedicated to his life, work, paintings and writings.

The house is encircled by vast, lavish gardens and parklands, parts of which were landscaped by the great Lancelot 'Capability' Brown. A mini-train whisks you to the Walled Garden, which features a yew **maze**, an adventure playground, a lavender garden and a butterfly house.

THE DRIVE: From Blenheim's grandeur, it's a 10-mile trip down the A44/A34/A4144 to Oxford's dreaming spires.

15 Oxford

One of the world's most famous university towns, the centre of Oxford is rich in history and studded with august buildings. The city has 39 colleges – Christ Church (p90) is among the largest, with 680 students, and has the grandest quad. Christ Church was founded in 1524 by Cardinal Thomas Wolsey. It's also famous as a location for the *Harry Potter* films.

At the Ashmolean (p37), Britain's oldest public museum has had a modern makeover; interactive displays and glass walls revealing multilevel galleries help showcase treasures that include Egyptian mummies, Indian textiles and Islamic art. Beautiful **Magdalen College** *(magd.ox.ac.uk)* is worth a visit for its medieval chapel, 15th-century cloisters and 40-hectare grounds. Nearby, head to **Magdalen Bridge Boathouse** *(oxfordpunting.co.uk)* for a ride on a chauffeured punt.

PHOTO OPPORTUNITY

PICTURE IN A PUNT

Lounging in a punt with a backdrop of Oxford's divine buildings.

Clifton Observatory

LEIGHTON COLLINS/SHUTTERSTOCK

❤ WHY I LOVE THIS TRIP

CATHERINE LE NEVEZ, WRITER

Britain's immense and influential past is around every bend on this southern trip. Along with outstanding museums, it brings you to sites where defining events have shaped the nation (and the world) through the centuries: mystifying stone circles, awe-inspiring cathedrals, steadfast castles, royal palaces, naval dockyards, engineering marvels and literary locations. History filters into the present before your eyes.

05

EPIC TRIP

URBAN & ART ODYSSEY

DURATION: 13–15 DAYS

DISTANCE: 671 MILES / 1080KM

GREAT FOR: ART, CRAFTS, HISTORY

BEST TIME TO GO: AUTUMN AVOIDS THE WORST OF THE WEATHER ON THE NORTHERN LEGS.

This exploration of England's urban and artistic soul makes for an exhilarating, creative drive. The visual art ranges from prehistoric chalk figures to old masters to sprayed-on street designs. Discover classical composers and design classics; exquisite bridges and hand-crafted motorcars. Experience film locations, stunning sculptures and pop culture ranging from the Beatles to football. And it all takes place against a beautiful backdrop.

LINK YOUR TRIP

22 North York Moors & Coast
A tour of Yorkshire's gorgeous moors and shores. Starts just 15 miles south of this trip's Castle Howard at York.

25 Southwest Coast
A cracking cruise along a spectacular stretch of surf-dashed coast. Starts 40 miles west of Cardiff.

01 Bristol

The creative, edgy city of Bristol is the perfect place to see works by the anonymous street artist Banksy. The central *Well Hung Lover* (Frogmore St) depicts an angry husband, a two-timing wife and a naked man dangling from a window. The startling Paint-Pot Angel (think pink paint meets funerary monument) resides in the foyer of the **Bristol Museum & Art Gallery** *(bristolmuseums.org.uk)*. Banksy's *Mild Mild West* (80 Stokes Croft) features a Molotov cocktail-wielding teddy bear facing three riot police, while his stencil of the Grim Reaper rowing a boat is now on the 1st floor of the city's **M Shed museum** *(bristolmuseums.org.uk)*. The city's **tourism website** *(visitbristol.co.uk)* has downloadable maps and trails.

THE DRIVE: It's a 45-mile drive along the M4 to Cardiff, a route enlivened by the journey across the six-lane, cable-stayed Second Severn Crossing bridge.

★ BEST FOR

CAR FANS

The classic lines on show at Great Malvern's Morgan Motor Company.

IVAN MAGUIRE/SHUTTERSTOCK

Cardiff Castle

In Cardiff, follow signs for City Centre car parks; Greyfriars and Westgate St are ideal.

02 Cardiff

The capital of Wales has a vibrant, confident air. The **National Museum Cardiff** (p40) is one of Britain's best museums. Highlights include a trio of Monet's *Water Lilies*, alongside his scenes of London, Rouen and Venice; Sisley's *The Cliff at Penarth* (the artist was married in Cardiff); Renoir's shimmering *La Parisienne*; a cast of Rodin's *The Kiss*; and Van Gogh's anguished *Rain: Auvers*. At nearby **Cardiff Castle** (p40) the artistic decor includes zodiac symbols in the winter smoking room, mahogany and mirrors in the bedrooms, and marble and acres of gold leaf in the Arab room.

Cardiff is a great city to explore on foot – stroll 1 mile south to Cardiff Bay to take in the grand modern architecture of the **Wales Millennium Centre** *(wmc.org.uk)*.

THE DRIVE: Head back over the Second Severn Crossing bridge for the 70-mile jaunt up the M4/M5 to Cheltenham.

03 Cheltenham

Gracious, 18th-century spa town Cheltenham offers some fine Regency buildings, including the **Pittville Pump Room** *(pittvillepumproom.org.uk)*. Built in 1830, it was modelled on an ancient Athenian temple and has a pillared exterior and a park with lake, lawns and blue-green gates.

Famed as one of the most beautiful streets in England, the Promenade is a broad, tree-lined boulevard flanked by imposing period buildings that are now filled with fancy shops. It leads to Montpellier, with a village-like feel and a lively assortment of bars, restaurants, hotels, independent shops and boutiques.

THE DRIVE: Make for the M5 to glide north for 14 miles before peeling off onto the A38 for the climb to hillside Great Malvern, a further 11 miles away (25 miles in total).

DETOUR

Uffington White Horse

Start: 03 Cheltenham

A 40-mile detour southeast from Cheltenham leads to the oldest chalk figure in Britain. The **Uffington White Horse** (p37) was created in the Bronze Age, some 3000 years ago, on the crest of Oxfordshire's highest point. A highly stylised horse image, it was crafted by cutting trenches out of the hill and filling them with blocks of chalk; local inhabitants have maintained the figure for centuries. From Cheltenham, head south on A roads towards Swindon, then join the A420 towards Oxford; the horse is signposted from that road. It's a 0.5-mile walk east through fields from the National Trust car park to the chalk figure itself.

04 Great Malvern

The gateway to the towering, 9-mile-long ridge of the Malvern Hills, Great Malvern is a picturesque spa town. The **Great Malvern Priory** *(greatmalvern priory.org.uk)* showcases designs ranging from Norman pillars via 15th-century tiles to surreal modernist stained glass.

The town's other great attraction is the **Morgan Motor Company** *(morgan-motor.com)*, where Britain's famous sports cars are made. The firm has been handcrafting the vehicles since 1909, and you can still see mechanics at work on two-hour guided tours of the unassuming shed-like buildings comprising the factory (pre-booking essential). Then view a fleet of vintage classics next to the museum.

THE DRIVE: Time to leave the wooded ridge of the Malvern Hills behind on a 30-mile leg east; it's an A-road meander alongside green fields to Stratford-upon-Avon.

05 Stratford-upon-Avon

For many, a trip to Tudor Stratford, birthplace of the man who wrote some of the most quoted sentences in the English language, is a literary pilgrimage and an opportunity to retrace his steps. **Shakespeare's Birthplace** *(shakespeare.org.uk)* has restored Tudor rooms and live presentations from famous Shakespearean characters.

The playwright died in a house on the site of **Shakespeare's New Place** *(shakespeare.org.uk)* in 1616; an attractive Elizabethan knot garden occupies part of the grounds. Next, visit **Holy Trinity Church** (p153), Shakespeare's final resting place. Look out for handsome 16th- and 17th-century tombs, some fabulous carved choir stalls and the grave of the Bard, with its ominous epitaph: 'cvrst be he yt moves my bones'.

THE DRIVE: Make for the M40 to start your 40-mile drive north. This is true motorway territory; you'll navigate the M42 and the M6 before arriving in Birmingham. Head for the central Bull Ring Car Park.

06 Birmingham

Birmingham delivers a big-city vibe and culture by the truckload. Britain's second-biggest city is (rightly) hugely proud of its glittering £189 million **Library of Birmingham** *(birmingham.gov.uk/libraryofbirmingham)*. Designed by Francine Houben, it features a subterranean amphitheatre, spiralling interior, viewing decks and glass elevator to the 7th-floor 'secret garden' with panoramic city views.

Nearby, Victoria Sq features civic architecture of another era in the **Council House**, built in 1870s. To the west Centenary Sq is home to the art deco **Hall of Memory War Memorial**. From there it's a short stroll to the **Birmingham Museum & Art Gallery** *(birmingham museums.org.uk)* and its fine collection of Victorian art and major Pre-Raphaelite works by Rossetti and Edward Burne-Jones.

THE DRIVE: Time for more motorways (M6/M42), initially, on this 45-mile leg. After about 18 miles, though, it's onto the A38 for a more rural route to Derby.

07 Derby

One of the crucibles of the Industrial Revolution, these days Derby is home to cultural developments and a rejuvenated riverfront. The central **Quad** *(derbyquad.co.uk)*, a striking modernist cube on Market Pl, contains a futuristic art gallery and an art-house cinema. A short walk away, at the **Derby Museum & Art Gallery** *(derbymuseums.org)*, local history and industry displays include fine ceramics produced by Royal Crown Derby – the Royal Crown Derby Factory, still produces some of the finest china in England.

THE DRIVE: Next, a 60-mile drive, at first on the A38, then the A61, but largely via that great route north: the M1. Around 57 miles in, pick up signs for the Yorkshire Sculpture Park.

Great Malvern Priory
IAN KENNEDY/SHUTTERSTOCK

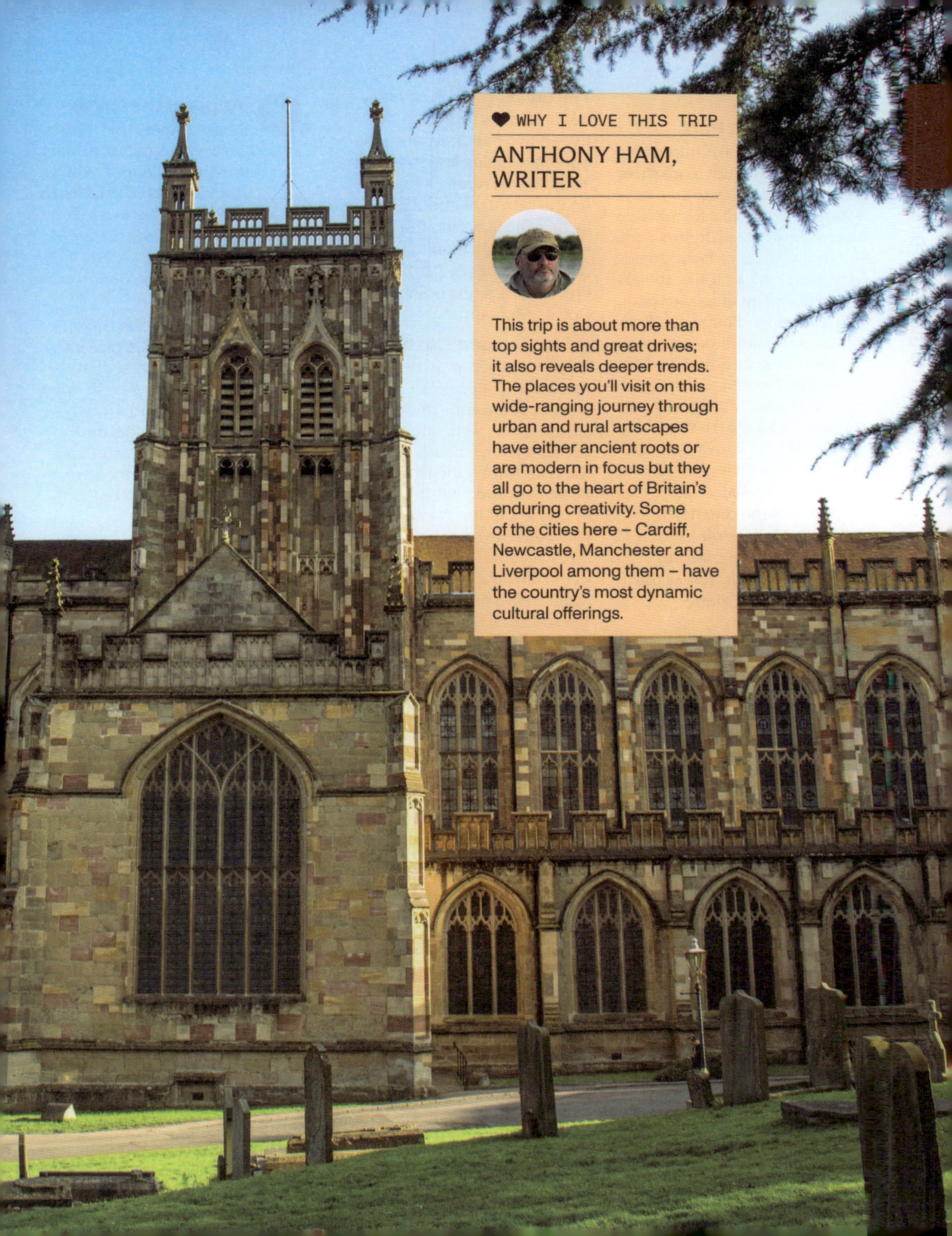

WHY I LOVE THIS TRIP

ANTHONY HAM, WRITER

This trip is about more than top sights and great drives; it also reveals deeper trends. The places you'll visit on this wide-ranging journey through urban and rural artscapes have either ancient roots or are modern in focus but they all go to the heart of Britain's enduring creativity. Some of the cities here – Cardiff, Newcastle, Manchester and Liverpool among them – have the country's most dynamic cultural offerings.

08 Yorkshire Sculpture Park

One of England's most impressive collections of sculpture, **Yorkshire Sculpture Park** *(ysp.co.uk)* is scattered across the formidable 18th-century estate of Bretton Park, 200-odd hectares of lawns, fields and trees. Think of it like the art world's equivalent of a safari park.

The Yorkshire Sculpture Park showcases the work of dozens of sculptors both national and international. But the main attractions of this outdoor gallery are the sculptures of local artists Barbara Hepworth (1903–75), who was born in nearby Wakefield, and Henry Moore (1898–1986).

THE DRIVE: Head due north again, but this time on a much shorter leg: 18 miles, largely up the M1. At Leeds, follow the signs for the City Centre.

09 Leeds

One of the UK's fastest-growing cities, Leeds is a vision of 21st-century urban chic. **Leeds Art Gallery** *(museumsandgalleries.leeds.gov.uk)* is packed with heavyweights – Turner, Constable, Stanley Spencer and Wyndham Lewis. Plus pieces by recent arrivals such as Antony Gormley, sculptor of the Angel of the North. Nearby, the **Henry Moore Institute** *(henry-moore.org/hmi)* showcases the work of 20th-century sculptors.

For a different culture fix, the **Victoria Quarter** *(victorialeeds.co.uk)* delivers striking architecture in the form of mosaic paving, and stained-glass-roofed Victorian arcades. There are also cutting-edge fashion boutiques, including Louis Vuitton, Vivienne Westwood and Swarovski, plus the flagship Harvey Nichols store.

THE DRIVE: Your art odyssey continues north, slicing between two national parks: the Yorkshire Dales and the North York Moors. Again, it's largely up the M1/A1. At about 58 miles in, turn off, first onto the A66 towards Brough, then to the town of Barnard Castle (13 miles). From there, signs point to the Bowes Museum.

10 Barnard Castle

Tucked in at the edge of the town of Barnard Castle, the **Bowes Museum** *(thebowesmuseum.org.uk)* is a monumental French-style château. Funded by the 19th-century industrialist John Bowes and opened in 1892, this brainchild of his Parisian actress wife, Josephine, was built by French architect Jules Pellechet. The aim was to display a collection the Bowes had travelled the world to assemble. The star attraction is the marvellous 18th-century mechanical swan, which performs every day at 2pm. If you miss it, a film shows it in action.

THE DRIVE: Here is a chance to bypass the motorway for a bit on this 52-mile journey. Take the A688 through Bishop Auckland and Spennymoor for 23 miles. Then rejoin the A1 (M), towards Newcastle; the university city of Durham, with its magnificent cathedral and castle, is just to your west. Take the A167 towards Gateshead South, and watch out the windows for the towering Angel of the North. There's a free car park by the base.

PHOTO OPPORTUNITY

Standing, arms outstretched, beside the 20m-high Angel of the North.

11 Angel of the North

Nicknamed the Gateshead Flasher, the extraordinary 200-tonne, rust-coloured, winged human-form **Angel of the North** *(gateshead.gov.uk)* has loomed over the A1 (M) since 1998. Sir Antony Gormley's iconic work is 20m high, with a wingspan wider than a Boeing 767.

THE DRIVE: Hop on the A167/B1318 for the 6-mile cruise into Newcastle City Centre. Just after 3 miles in, stand by to drive along one of England's most famous river crossings: the mighty Tyne Bridge. Head for a City Centre car park; those at Dean St, Akenside Hill or Painters Heugh are ideal.

12 Newcastle-upon-Tyne

Historic, sophisticated and bursting with nightlife, Newcastle is one of England's most appealing cities. Stroll to the Quayside to contemplate its most striking pieces of engineering. The imposing Tyne Bridge (1925–28) resembles the Sydney Harbour Bridge – no wonder, both were built by the same firm, Dorman Long of Middlesbrough. The quaint Swing Bridge (1876), just to the west, pivots in the middle to let ships through.

Next, walk 500m to the east over the gorgeous Millennium Bridge (2002). This opens like an eyelid to enable vessels to pass and leads to the **BALTIC – Centre for Contemporary Art** *(www.baltic.art)*. Once a huge mustard-coloured grain store, this art gallery rivals London's Tate Modern. Rotating shows feature the work of some of the art world's biggest showstoppers. You'll also find artists in residence, a performance space,

DAVIDGRAHAM86/SHUTTERSTOCK

Angel of the North

a cinema, a cafe and a 4th-floor outdoor platform and a 5th-floor viewing box, both with fabulous panoramas of the Tyne.

THE DRIVE: After hundreds of miles driving north, it's time to head 84 miles south. Drive back over the Tyne Bridge, making for the A19 towards York. At Thirsk (local vet and author James Herriot's fictional Darrowby), take the A170 towards Helmsley. Peel off right onto the B1257 and follow the brown signs to Castle Howard, a route of rolling fields and woods.

13 Castle Howard

Grand, theatrical **Castle Howard** *(castlehoward.co.uk)* is one of the world's most beautiful buildings, instantly recognisable from its starring role in both the 1980s TV series *Brideshead Revisited* and in the 2008 film of the same name.

The great baroque house, which was commissioned in 1699, features a magnificent central cupola and plentiful treasures – the breathtaking Great Hall with its soaring Corinthian pilasters, Pre-Raphaelite stained glass in the chapel, and corridors lined with classical antiquities. A wander around the peacock-haunted grounds reveals views of the Howardian Hills and architect Sir John Vanbrugh's playful Temple of the Four Winds.

THE DRIVE: Another near-90-mile stretch, this time heading southwest largely along the A64 towards Leeds and then the M62 to Manchester, eventually leaving the motorways to follow City Centre signs.

DETOUR

Haworth

Start: 13 Castle Howard

As you arrive at Leeds, en route from Castle Howard to Manchester, consider a 20-mile detour west, past Bradford to Haworth. This village set beside the moors of the South Pennines has an impeccable artistic pedigree. It was home to the Brontë sisters – Charlotte, Emily and Anne, responsible for *Jane Eyre*, *Wuthering Heights* and *The Tenant of Wildfell Hall* respectively. The house where they lived from 1820 to 1861 is now the **Brontë Parsonage Museum** *(bronte.org.uk)*. Rooms are decorated as they were in the Brontë era, including Charlotte's bedroom, filled with her clothes and her writing paraphernalia.

14 Manchester

Packed with history and culture, Manchester is the uncrowned capital of the north. Here, football is acknowledged as passion and art form in equal measure.

The National Football Museum explores the evolution of the beautiful game, while engaging, hands-on displays include Football Plus, a series of interactive stations allowing you to test your skills in simulated conditions. A 500m walk south leads to the Manchester Art Gallery (p41), where a superb collection of British and European art includes 37 Turner watercolours and the country's best assemblage of Pre-Raphaelite art. The 20th-century galleries include works by Lucien Freud, Francis Bacon, Stanley Spencer, Henry Moore and David Hockney.

Next, hop on to one of the city's swish trams to MediaCityUK, making for the **Lowry** *(thelowry.com)* to study 300 beautifully humanistic depictions of urban landscapes by LS Lowry (1887–1976). Lowry, a local artist, has become famous for painting matchstick figures amid the north's various mill-dotted towns and cityscapes.

THE DRIVE: A final, 35-mile, motorway cruise: after the A57 (M), join the M62 to roll towards Liverpool, eventually picking up the brown tourist signs for the car parks at the Albert Dock.

DETOUR

Wedgwood Visitor Centre
Start: 14 Manchester

A 50-mile detour south from Manchester, largely via the M56/M6, leads to the **Wedgwood Visitor Centre** *(worldofwedgwood.com)*, 5 miles south of Stoke-on-Trent. The modern production plant for Josiah Wedgwood's porcelain empire, it also offers an insight into this whole area's defining industrial and artistic characteristic: ceramics – the region is still known as the Potteries to this day. Look out for extensive displays of historic pieces, including plenty of Wedgwood's delicate, neoclassical blue-and-white jasperware. The fascinating industrial process is revealed, and there's an interesting film on Josiah's life and work, including his involvement in canal-building and opposition to slavery.

15 Liverpool

A thriving city famous for music, football and wit, Liverpool also has, at **Albert Dock**, the country's largest collection of protected buildings.

This World Heritage Site includes the **Tate Liverpool** *(tate.org.uk/visit/tate-liverpool)*, with its substantial checklist of 20th-century artists, plus exhibitions from the mother ship on London's Bankside. Just paces away, the **International Slavery Museum** *(liverpoolmuseums.org.uk/ism)* is a clear, uncompromising and profoundly affecting depiction of slavery's unimaginable horrors.

The nearby **Beatles Story** *(beatlesstory.com)* features plenty of genuine Fab Four memorabilia, plus a full-size replica of the Cavern Club (which was actually tiny) and a recreation of the Abbey Rd studio in London where the lads recorded their first singles.

A short walk north at **Pier Head** discover the trio of Edwardian buildings beloved by locals: the domed **Port of Liverpool Building** (1907), the Italian palazzo-style **Cunard Building** and the 1911 **Royal Liver Building**, crowned by Liverpool's symbol, a 5.5m copper *Liver Bird*.

Albert Dock
SONGQUAN DENG/SHUTTERSTOCK

0
50 km
0
25 miles
North Sea
Wells-next-the-Sea
Cley-next-the-Sea
Blakeney
Cromer
10
North Walsham
Fakenham
Sandringham
King's Lynn
Wroxham
Broads National Park
Norwich
Great Yarmouth
Swaffham
Oakham
Leicester
Peterborough
Nene
March
Thetford Forest
Loddon
Beccles
Thetford
Scole
Southwold
Ely
Kettering
Huntingdon
Rugby
Wellingborough
Bury St Edmunds
Minsmere
Leiston
Aldeburgh
Northampton
St Neots
Newmarket
Cambridge
Grantchester
Stowmarket
Long Melford
Lavenham
Woodbridge
Ipswich
Saffron Walden
Sudbury
9
Flatford
Felixstowe
Harwich
Banbury
Bletchley
Buckingham
Baldock
Bishop's Stortford
Baintree
Blackwater
Colchester
Luton
Stevenage
Clacton-on-Sea
Woodstock
Aylesbury
Witham
Thames (Isis)
Oxford
St Albans
Harlow
Chelmsford
Cheshunt
Amersham
Watford
Potters Bar
Abingdon
Brentwood
Leigh-on-Sea
8
Southend-on-Sea
Henley-on-Thames
LONDON
Dagenham
Canvey Island
Reading
Windsor
Dartford
Herne Bay
Reculver
Margate
Richmond
Rochester
Chatham
Whitstable
Broadstairs
Newbury
7
Seasalter
Ramsgate
Maidstone
Faversham
Canterbury
Farnborough
Basingstoke
Sevenoaks
Deal
Guildford
Farnham
Reigate
Tonbridge
Ashford
Dover
Royal Tunbridge Wells
Crawley
Haslemere
Folkestone
Horsham
Winchester
Haywards Heath
6
Rye
Eastleigh
Petworth
Lewes
Bexhill
Hastings
Chichester
Havant
Arundel
Hove
Brighton
Fareham
Portsmouth
Worthing
Eastbourne
Strait of Dover
Seaford
West Cowes
Bognor Regis
Beachy Head
Ryde
Isle of Wight
English Channel
A149
A140
A17
A47
A10
A11
A12
A1
A45
A140
M1
M11
A12
A41
A1
A12
M40
M25
M11
M25
M4
M3
M25
A2
A3
A23
A27
A259

PREMIER PHOTO/SHUTTERSTOCK

Punting on the River Cam (p97)

SOUTHERN & EASTERN ENGLAND

EXPLORE

SOUTHERN & EASTERN ENGLAND

Britain's warmest, driest and most populated region is ripe for classic road trips year-round. Driving distances are manageable, and you can easily escape the crowded motorways radiating from London to find beautiful bucolic vistas as soon as you leave the city.

The variety is astonishing, too – northeast of London are the quiet villages and gentle nature reserves of East Anglia's Constable Country. To the east lie the historic seaside towns of Kent, enjoying a revival. Surrey, Sussex and Hampshire abound in wealthy hamlets and scenic roads. To the west are the foodie and farming centres of Berkshire, Oxford and Buckinghamshire.

Cambridge

The enchanting university town of Cambridge is an excellent base for the 'Suffolk-Norfolk Shore' (p100), 'Around the Cam' (p94) and, at a stretch, 'Royalty & the Thames Valley' (p88) trips. It's easily accessed by regular trains from London in under an hour, has plenty of car-hire and accommodation options, and is well served for eating out and local shopping. Cyclists will want to hire a bike and tour the city, too.

Norwich

Historically one of England's greatest urban centres, gentrified by the medieval wool trade, Norwich is an elegant cathedral city and the perfect base for the 'Suffolk-Norfolk Shore' (p100) and 'Around the Cam' (p94) drives. A two-hour train journey (or drive) from London, it has good accommodation options, plus access to the relatively wild Norfolk coast.

Oxford

England's oldest university town is a delightful and fully stocked base from which to plan drives through the Thames Valley and even into central England. If you're booking accommodation here, be sure to enquire about parking. Oxford is conveniently sited near the northern end of the 'Royalty & the Thames Valley' (p88) route and can be accessed from London in 1½ hours by coach, train or car.

WHEN TO GO

Any time of year is feasible for driving in southern and eastern England's generally mild climate. Ice and snow are always possible in winter, but you'll also enjoy smaller crowds (note that some sights close for the season). Crocuses, snowdrops, daffodils and other spring flowers begin to emerge in March, and the busy summer school holidays are in August.

Margate

Once neglected as a faded Victorian resort town, Margate has become the unofficial cultural capital of the northern Kentish coast. Its new-found popularity means you'll have freshly renovated B&Bs, a mix of restaurants, plus shops and galleries to explore. Two hours from London by car, it's a good base for coastal routes, particularly if you plan to allow time for a few swims at the tidal baths.

Canterbury

If you'd prefer an ancient, inland base to tackle the 'Seaside Jaunt' (p74) or 'Kent: Garden of England' (p80) routes, then Canterbury is an excellent choice. Centred on a World Heritage–listed cathedral, its medieval maze of alleys hides charming provedores and places to rest your head. Collect your car before you arrive, as hire options here are limited.

London

The nation's capital is a prime hub for access to southern and eastern England. While driving in London itself might be overwhelming for the newcomer, traffic is slow and drivers are pretty considerate. London is one of the world's foremost tourist destinations, and of course there are plenty of car-rental outfits in every corner of the city. Basing yourself here, before you hire a vehicle to explore beyond it, is the way to go.

TRANSPORT

London is the natural gateway to southern and eastern England, as it is for most of Britain. Served by five international airports, including Heathrow, one of the world's busiest, the city is the centre of a railway network that reaches all the hub towns in this region. Car-hire options at the airports and in the city are abundant.

WHERE TO STAY

If you're on a budget, look at university rooms for inexpensive and basic student rooms in Oxford and Cambridge university colleges outside term time.

Hipcamp is super for finding summer campsites, cabins, bell tents and more.

The Reading Rooms, Margate, is a seaside B&B occupying an entire floor of a Grade II–listed 1770 townhouse within easy walking distance of Margate's Old Town.

The Varsity Hotel & Spa, Cambridge, is a modern boutique hotel with a roof terrace overlooking some of the university's most famous colleges. The Pig at Bridge Place, Canterbury, comes highly recommended as a foodie-focused country inn outside the city.

RESOURCES

Kent
Tourist-info hub for the 'Garden of England'. *visitkent.co.uk*

East of England
Has East Anglia and Cambridgeshire covered. *visiteastofengland.com*

Oxford
A complete guide to the university town and surrounds. *experienceoxfordshire.org*

Cycling
Advice on cycling routes for a change of pace. *walkwheelcycletrust.org.uk*

Folkestone
All the reasons to visit Folkestone. *folke.life*

WHAT'S ON

Oxford Literary Festival
Famous authors descend on Oxford in March.

Cambridge Folk Festival
Folk and Americana in Cambridge in late July.

Latitude
Music, dance and frivolity at Henham Park estate, Southwold, in July/early August.

Where It All Began
Boutique camping festival for the theatrical and creative music lover, in July.

Brighton & Hove Pride
Parties and a parade mark the UK's biggest LGBTQ+ event every August.

06

SOUTHERN & EASTERN ENGLAND

SEASIDE JAUNT

★ BEST FOR

SHOPPING

Brighton's Lanes and North Laine areas have some of the UK's best shopping.

Dover Castle

DURATION: 8 DAYS

DISTANCE: 123 MILES / 198KM

GREAT FOR: HISTORY, VIEWS, BEACHES

BEST TIME TO GO: APRIL TO OCTOBER, WHEN THE FICKLE BRITISH WEATHER IS AT ITS WARMEST AND DRIEST.

This scenic meander along the coast of Kent and Sussex constitutes a quintessentially British seaside escapade. It takes you across undulating chalk cliffs, over rolling downs and around marshes, Victorian resorts and medieval castles, calling at some of the most famous names on the south's coastal map. London's riviera, Brighton, is stuffed with history and heritage.

LINK YOUR TRIP

07 Kent: Garden of England
This north Kent route starts in Margate, just 22 miles north of Dover.

11 Winchester, Glastonbury & Bath
Chichester is 42 miles from historic Winchester.

01 Dover

The maritime city of Dover on the south coast, though bombed to pieces in WWII, possesses a principal chunk of Kent heritage – a huge **castle** *(english-heritage.org.uk)* that has guarded England's closest point to France since medieval times.

The 12th-century Great Tower, with walls up to 7m thick, is a medieval warren filled with interactive exhibits and light-and-sound shows that return visitors to the times of Henry II. The remains of a Roman lighthouse are also within the castle grounds.

The biggest draw, however, is the network of secret **wartime tunnels**. The claustrophobic chalk-hewn passageways were first excavated during the Napoleonic Wars and then expanded to house a command post and hospital in WWII. The highly enjoyable 50-minute guided tour (every 20 minutes, included in the ticket price) tells the story of one of Britain's most

MARCUS_PHOTO_UK/SHUTTERSTOCK

famous wartime operations, code-named Dynamo, which was directed from here in 1940 and oversaw the evacuation of thousands from the beaches at Dunkirk.

THE DRIVE: Follow London-bound foreign lorries out of Dover on the A20, which climbs steeply onto the chalk cliffs. After a couple of miles, find the turn-off for Capel-le-Ferne, home to a Battle of Britain Memorial. The suburbs of Folkestone, your next stop, lie just beyond (9 miles in total).

02 Folkestone

This formerly grand resort was once a favourite stomping ground of royal bon viveur King Edward VII and today is a rejuvenating piece of England's seaside past.

Stroll through the seafront **Lower Leas Coastal Park** with its subtropical flora, then stop for fish and chips at the old fish market before ambling up through the **Creative Quarter**, Folkestone's old town, now home to artists' studios and craft shops.

THE DRIVE: Satnavs may send you to the M20 but instead follow the coastal A259 to Hythe. This is the terminus of the idyllic Romney Hythe & Dymchurch narrow-gauge railway, worth a day off the road itself. At New Romney the road swings inland and crosses Romney Marsh, a sweep of wetland flats dotted with grazing sheep and wind turbines. Total distance 25 miles.

03 Rye

Possibly southern England's quaintest town, Rye is a little nugget of the past, a medieval settlement that looks like it's been sealed in amber. Cobbled lanes, mysterious passageways and crooked half-timbered Tudor buildings echo to tales of resident smugglers, ghosts and writers.

Aimless wandering and browsing are the way to go here, but the most picturesque scene is **Mermaid Street**; American writer Henry James lived in **Lamb House** *(nationaltrust.org.uk)*, while views over town extend from the tower of the **Church of St Mary the Virgin**.

THE DRIVE: Just 12 miles separate Rye from your next stop west, Hastings. The A259 passes through chocolate-box-pretty Winchelsea – watch out for the steep hairpin turn below the village. There's another steep climb through the suburbs of Hastings before a quick descent back to sea level and Hastings' seafront.

04 Hastings

Forever associated with the Norman invasion of 1066, Hastings thrived as one of the Cinque Ports and, in its Victorian heyday, was among the country's most fashionable resorts. After a period of steady postwar decline, the town has enjoyed a mini-renaissance. The beach and restored pier are the biggest draws, but Hastings also has several worthwhile museums and bucketloads of independent shops.

Away from the old town, the most intriguing neighbourhood is the **Stade** (Rock-A-Nore Rd), home to distinctive black clapboard structures known as net shops (built to store fishing gear back in the 17th century, but some now house fishmongers).

THE DRIVE: Follow the A259 along the coast as far as Bexhill, where architecture aficionados will want to see the De La Warr Pavilion in Bexhill-on-Sea. Stick to the A259 (as opposed to the A27) at Pevensey, site of a castle first built by the Romans – this will eventually bring you past Eastbourne's Sovereign Harbour and along Britain's most impressive seafront. Total distance 17 miles.

DETOUR

Battle

Start: 04 Hastings

If there's one date that sears itself into every English schoolchild's mind, it was 1066, the year of the most famous battle in the country's history: the Battle of Hastings, which saw invading French duke William

Eastbourne Pier

SERGII FIGURNYI/SHUTTERSTOCK

of Normandy, aka William the Conqueror, score a decisive victory over local King Harold. This major bend in the road in English history actually took place 6 miles north of Hastings in what is now the town of Battle.

Battle Abbey *(english-heritage.org.uk)* was built on the battlefield, a penance ordered by the pope for the loss of life incurred here. Only the foundations of the original church remain; the altar's position is supposedly the spot where King Harold famously took an arrow in his eye. Other impressive monastic buildings survive and make for atmospheric explorations.

The battlefield's lush rolling hillsides do little to evoke the ferocity of the event, but high-tech interactive presentations and a film at the visitor centre, as well as blow-by-blow audio tours, do their utmost to bring the battle to life. You can survey the battlefield from the rooftop viewing platform, a good place to start a visit.

The biggest crowds turn up mid-October to witness the annual re-enactment taking place on the original battlefield.

05 Eastbourne

'Britain's sunniest town' welcomes visitors with a grand seafront, whitewashed late-Victorian hotels and palm trees lining the Channel, with the scene given focus by one of the country's finest Victorian **piers** *(eastbournepier.com)*. Associated primarily with sedate retirement, Eastbourne has had a shot in the arm in recent years with Polish and student communities arriving to lower the average age considerably.

The traditional seaside duo of beach and pier are the main draws, but the **Towner Art Gallery** *(townereastbourne.org.uk)* energises the town's artistic character. The town is the start or end point for a hike along the 100-mile South Downs Way, which passes through the South Downs National Park.

THE DRIVE: To reach Beachy Head (3.5 miles away), drive west along Eastbourne's seafront until the road turns inland and begins to climb. A brown tourist sign points the way to the famous cliff along a narrow road. There's ample parking around the area.

DETOUR

South Downs National Park

Start: 05 Eastbourne

The UK's newest national park is more than 600 sq miles of rolling chalk downs stretching west from Eastbourne to Winchester, a distance of about 100 miles. The long-distance South Downs Way famously unfurls along its entire length – the ridge hike takes at least 10 days, consisting largely of breathtaking views. Many of the route's most interesting and prettiest locations can be found just west of Eastbourne and can be reached on a there-and-back day walk or by using local buses.

06 Beachy Head

At 162m tall, the cliffs of Beachy Head are the highest point of the chalky rock faces that slice across the coastline at the southern end of the South Downs. This is a spot of thrilling, windswept beauty, the brilliant white chalk rising high into the blue Sussex sky. At the foot of the cliffs stands a much-photographed, candy-striped lighthouse.

If you follow the clifftop path, you'll head down to the tiny seaside hamlet of Birling Gap, where the secluded beach is a sun-trap popular with locals and walkers taking a breather. You'll also find a handy National Trust–run cafe here.

On a darker note, Beachy Head is also known as one of Europe's most frequented suicide spots, with its own dedicated chaplaincy team whose job it is to talk people off the edge.

WHY I LOVE THIS TRIP

CATHERINE LE NEVEZ, WRITER

Along England's south-easternmost edge, you'll see sublime natural landscapes of white chalk cliffs and green rolling hills that could be lifted from a watercolour painting. These contrast with creative towns and cities filled with independent shops, galleries, classic pubs and vibrant nightlife venues. There's also history to be found in spades: from Roman relics to hefty medieval defensives and revived Victorian resorts. Linking them all is the horizon-stretching sea, which is never far from view.

THE DRIVE: Your next stop, the Seven Sisters, are best viewed from Cuckmere Haven, 6 miles west of Beachy Head. From the clifftop, head to Birling Gap then join the A259 at East Dean. Leave your car at the Cuckmere Inn in Exceat and walk 1 mile south to the sea, following the River Cuckmere.

07 Seven Sisters

The undulating chalk cliffs of the **Seven Sisters** create one of the southeast's classic views. The best vantage point is at Cuckmere Haven, the only undeveloped spot on England's south coast where a river meets the sea with no town to keep it company. The pleasant walk from the car park at Exceat down to the shingle beach follows the crazily meandering River Cuckmere.

THE DRIVE: Some 17 miles divide Cuckmere Haven from Brighton, your next stop. The A259 passes straight through Seaford and Newhaven, the latter home to a regular cross-Channel ferry service to Dieppe. Nearer to Brighton, Rottingdean was home to writer Rudyard Kipling from 1897 to 1902. The A259 then becomes the Brighton seafront just beyond.

08 Brighton

Brighton warrants a couple of days' exploration. With its bohemian, cosmopolitan and hedonistic vibe, Brighton is where England's seaside experience goes from cold to cool. Outside London it revels in the south's best shopping and nightlife, and is the de facto gay capital of the UK.

Away from the beach, top billing goes to the **Royal Pavilion** *(brightonmuseums.org.uk/visit/royal-pavilion-garden)*, the eye-popping palace party pad of Prince George, later Prince Regent and then King George IV. It's one of the most opulent buildings in England, packed with weird and

Seven Sisters cliffs

PHOTO OPPORTUNITY

The Seven Sisters chalk cliffs from Cuckmere Haven or Hope Gap.

MIN JING/SHUTTERSTOCK

wonderful interiors and outrageous chinoiserie.

The **i360 Tower** *(brightoni360.co.uk)* rises from the point where the now-defunct West Pier used to make landfall. Take the huge glass doughnut 138m above the city for gobsmacking vistas of the coast.

THE DRIVE: There are two routes you can take to reach Arundel, 23 miles to the west. The A259 and the A27 run parallel to each other – the latter is a much quicker option; the former is a more interesting drive through Worthing, a vibrant seaside town on the ascendant (with cheaper parking than Brighton, too), and Littlehampton.

09 Arundel

Arguably the prettiest town in West Sussex, Arundel is clustered around a vast fairy-tale **castle** *(arundelcastle.org)*, home to the Dukes of Norfolk for centuries. An imposing bastion rising above the picturesque streets below, the castle was first built in the 11th century. Ransacked during the English Civil War, much – but not all – of the castle is the result of reconstruction between 1718 and 1900.

When you are done with the sights, Arundel's hilly streets overflow with antique emporiums, teashops, eateries and excellent art galleries.

THE DRIVE: A mere 11 miles separate Arundel from your final stop, the cathedral city of Chichester, the capital of West Sussex. The only feasible route is to take the fast A27 the whole way.

GARETH L EVANS/SHUTTERSTOCK

Chichester Cathedral

10 Chichester

Founded by the Romans, this lively Georgian market town is still almost encircled by its Roman and medieval town walls. Away from the sights, Chichester has four pedestrianised shopping streets that meet at the Chichester Cross, the town's epicentre.

Chichester Cathedral *(chichestercathedral.org.uk)* was begun in 1075 and largely rebuilt in the 13th century. The free-standing church tower went up in the 15th century; the spire dates from the 19th century, when its predecessor famously toppled over. Inside, three storeys of beautiful arches sweep upwards and Romanesque carvings are dotted around. Interesting features to track down include a smudgy stained-glass window added by artist Marc Chagall in 1978 and a glassed-over section of Roman mosaic flooring.

The **Novium** *(thenovium.org.uk)* is Chichester's purpose-built museum, a home for the eclectic collections of the erstwhile District Museum, built around a set of Roman thermae (baths) discovered in the 1970s

07

SOUTHERN & EASTERN ENGLAND

KENT: GARDEN OF ENGLAND

★ BEST FOR

FOODIES

The Sportsman Pub and Fordwich Arms are Michelin-starred and superb.

DURATION: 4 DAYS

DISTANCE: 49 MILES / 79KM

GREAT FOR: FOOD & DRINK

BEST TIME TO GO: APRIL TO OCTOBER SEES THE MILDEST TEMPERATURES, LEAST RAINFALL AND MOST SUN.

Reculver Towers

From Margate's seafront to the oyster houses of gentrified Whitstable, from the shipping heritage of Chatham to Britain's oldest brewery in Faversham, the theme along Kent's north coast is local tradition. Kent is the 'Garden of England' and produces the tastiest of ingredients – most notably, the country's finest hops – but on this trip you'll also discover what a vital role the sea has played in the county's traditional life.

LINK YOUR TRIP

06 Seaside Jaunt
It's just 22 miles from Margate to Dover, the start of an epic route along the south coast.

11 Winchester, Glastonbury & Bath
It looks a long way on the map, but it's only two hours (103 miles) from Chatham to Winchester.

01 Margate

This grand old seaside town, with fine-sand beaches, artistic associations and the famous **Dreamland** *(dreamland.co.uk)* vintage amusement park, endured a long period of decline but has bounced back splendidly in recent years. There's no greater symbol of this rejuvenation than the eye-catching **Turner Contemporary** *(turnercontemporary.org)* art gallery, bolted together on the site of the seafront guesthouse where artistic genius and pioneer JMW Turner used to stay. Top-notch contemporary installations by high-calibre artists, such as Tracey Emin (who grew up in Margate) are on the gallery menu.

Add a bevy of superb restaurants and boho cafes to the carefully curated junk emporia and period architecture of the rejuvenated old town and Margate has even emerged with a fashionable nickname: Shoreditch-on-Sea,

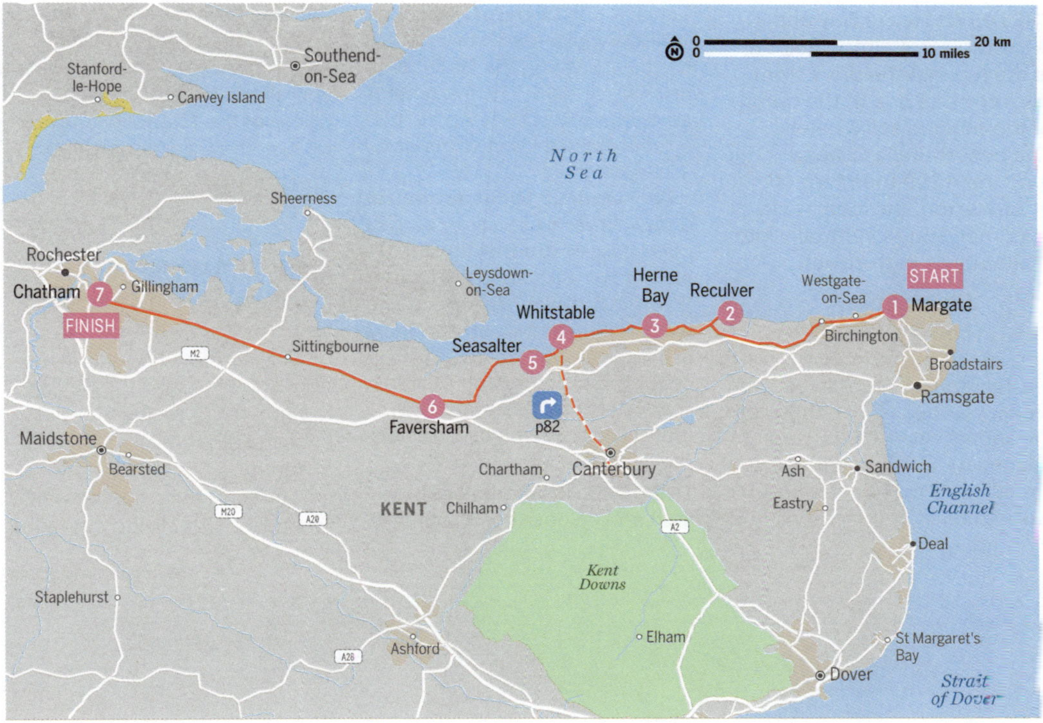

FOTOGENIX/SHUTTERSTOCK

in honour of the hipster neighbourhood in London.

THE DRIVE: From the Margate seafront head west along Canterbury Rd until you come to the roundabout junction with the A299. Turn right and follow this until you see the turn-off for Reculver. The journey is 12 miles.

02 Reculver

When the Romans first arrived in Britain, they built two fortresses at either end of the strategic Wantsum Channel, a stretch of water that divided the Isle of Thanet from the mainland. The channel silted up in the 16th century, but the **ruins** of the fortresses remain – Richborough near Sandwich, and Reculver on the north Kent coast.

The Roman remnants here are not as impressive as the **ruins** of the 12th-century church, the twin towers of which can be seen for miles along the coast. This was part of an Anglo-Saxon monastery but today the site, with the sea creeping ever closer, is deserted.

THE DRIVE: Just 4.5 miles divide Reculver and Herne Bay, your next stop. Don't take the A299; instead follow the back roads along the coast through residential areas and with the occasional sea view.

> **PHOTO OPPORTUNITY**
>
> The Reculver Towers rising high above the sea are one of the Kent coast's most memorable images.

03 Herne Bay

The seaside town of **Herne Bay** may be light on sights but it does have a long shingle beach that extends for miles either side of town. The shingle shelves ever so gradually into the North Sea, making this ideal territory for water sports and hot-weather water fun. **Reculver Country Park**, a wild stretch of rocky shore backed by cliffs, and operated by the Kent Wildlife Trust, lines the coast west of the town.

THE DRIVE: Herne Bay and Whitstable are almost joined at the hip, but the drive from the centre of one to the centre of the other is still 5 miles. The best route is to head onto the A299 then turn off at Tankerton, the local main road morphing eventually into Whitstable's high street.

04 Whitstable

Oysters, weatherboard houses, a shingle beach, an old-fashioned high street and an easy-going vibe – these are the things that attract so many Londoners to Whitstable, just a few miles north of Canterbury. It's most famous for its oysters, best sampled at **Wheelers Oyster Bar** *(wheelersoysterbar.co.uk)*, which has been serving the fabled molluscs since 1856. The town holds an annual oyster festival *(whitstablerocksoysterfestival.com)* in September.

The modest **local museum** *(whitstablemuseum.org)* has glass cases examining Whitstable's oyster industry, the Crab & Winkle Railway that once ran from Canterbury, and the local fishing fleet. There's also a corner dedicated to actor Peter Cushing, star of several Hammer horror films and the town's most famous resident, who died in 1994.

THE DRIVE: It's 4 miles to the next stop, Seasalter. From the centre of Whitstable, follow Joy Lane until it becomes Faversham Rd – this will take you all the way to the village home of the Michelin-starred tavern, the Sportsman Pub.

DETOUR

Canterbury

Start: 04 Whitstable

It's an easy 8-mile drive south from Whitstable (follow the B2205 south to the roundabout and then take the A290) to Canterbury, a chart-topping English cathedral city and one of southern England's biggest attractions. Many consider the World Heritage–listed cathedral

Whitstable harbour

CHRISTINE BIRD/SHUTTERSTOCK

that dominates its centre to be one of Europe's finest, and the town's narrow medieval alleyways, riverside gardens and ancient city walls are a joy to explore. But Canterbury isn't just a showpiece for the past – it's a bustling, busy place with an energetic student population and a wide choice of contemporary bars, restaurants, live venues and independent shops.

Canterbury Cathedral *(canterbury-cathedral.org)* is a rich repository of over 1400 years of Christian history, and the Church of England's mother ship is a truly extraordinary place. This Gothic cathedral, the highlight of the city's World Heritage Sites, is southeast England's top tourist attraction as well as a very active place of worship. It's also the site of one of English history's most famous murders: Archbishop Thomas Becket violently met his maker here in 1170. Allow at least two hours to do the cathedral justice.

Of the city's other landmarks, the **Roman Museum** *(canterburymuseums.co.uk)* is a subterranean archaeological site that affords fascinating glimpses into everyday life in Canterbury almost two millennia ago. Stroll a reconstructed Roman marketplace and rooms, including a kitchen, and examine Roman mosaic floors. Almost everything you see here was only discovered after WWII bombs delivered impromptu excavation. A highlight is the almost entirely intact Roman soldier's helmet, which dates from Caesar's invasion and was unearthed near the village of Bridge in 2012. It's the most complete example ever found in the UK.

For a different perspective of the city's history, take a River Stour cruise with **Canterbury Historic River Tours** *(canterburyrivertours.co.uk)*. Knowledgeable guides double as energetic oarsmen on these fascinating, multi-award-winning trips, which depart from King's Bridge.

Amid the half-timbered streetscapes, on cobbled Burgate, wine bar **Corkk** *(corkk.co.uk)* has bottles and by-the-glass wines, particularly local-speciality sparkling wines, from vineyards in the surrounding area, including **Gorsley Vineyard**, **Domaine Evremond** and **Heppington Vineyard** (all of which can be visited).

HISTORIC HOTEL

The rather wonky 13th-century beamed inn **House of Agnes** *(houseofagnes.co.uk)* in Canterbury was mentioned in Charles Dickens' novel *David Copperfield*.

It has nine themed rooms bearing names such as 'Marrakesh' (Moorish), 'Venice' (carnival masks) and 'Canterbury' (antiques, four-poster, heavy fabrics), plus eight 'stable' rooms in the garden annexe.

Adding to its historical prowess, back in 2005 an on-site archaeological dig led to the discovery of a late 14th-century navigational instrument known as an astrolabe (used to calculate the position of celestial bodies). This became known as the 'Canterbury Quadrant' and is now on display at the British Museum. It is one of only eight in the world to have survived from the Middle Ages.

05 Seasalter

The anonymous village of Seasalter would barely deserve a mention without the **Sportsman Pub** *(thesportsmanseasalter.co.uk)*, one of east Kent's eateries decorated with a Michelin star (held since 2008). Local ingredients from the sea, marsh and woods are crafted by Whitstable-born chef Stephen Harris into taste-packed Kentish creations that have food critics drooling. Oysters dominate the starter line-up, fish the mains menu. All the butter, salt and cured meats here are made by the chef himself. It's a real treat and proof that Michelin-standard food can be served in an informal bar setting and at an affordable price.

THE DRIVE: From the culinary delights of Seasalter take the 5-mile drive west to Faversham for one of Kent's drinking highlights. From the Sportsman Pub take Seasalter Rd south until just after Goodnestone, then turn right onto

THE CITY ARMS INN
Aztec
Silver Designs
SHEPHERD NEAME
SHAKESPEARE
HAPPY SAMURAI
Pho
MATCH
ALL ABOUT THE SOCIAL
CANTERBURY ROMAN MUSEUM

Whitstable Rd – this will take you into Faversham.

06 Faversham

The little-visited but pleasant old market town of Faversham is packed with architecture from medieval times right up to the present day. Light on top-tier sights, it does have one big draw: the **Shepherd Neame Brewery** *(shepherdneame.co.uk)*, Britain's oldest, established in 1698, and the pride of Kent for its traditional ales brewed from the county's unrivalled hops. There are brewery tours but you'll have to book ahead as they're very popular. You can also stop in at the visitor centre and brewery shop. Otherwise Shepherd Neame ale is available across the county, the most famous brand being the aptly named Spitfire.

THE DRIVE: Faversham to Chatham is the longest uninterrupted stretch on this route, at 19 miles. Shun the M2 for the 'old' A2, the original Roman road that runs almost arrow-straight from Canterbury to the River Medway.

07 Chatham

On the Medway riverfront, the **Chatham Historic Dockyard** *(thedockyard.co.uk)* occupies a third of what was once the Royal Navy's main dock facility. It is possibly the most complete 18th-century dock in the world and has been transformed into a maritime museum examining the Age of Sail. Exhibits include well-restored ships, exhibitions on a variety of shipbuilding themes and a working steam railway (check dates of operation), as well as a range of tours, talks and events throughout the year.

ANDREW FLETCHER/SHUTTERSTOCK

The Guildhall, Faversham

♥ DON'T MISS

FAVERSHAM GUILDHALL

While visiting Faversham, take a stroll to Market Place and you'll spot the green-coloured Guildhall. This is a Grade II* listed building featuring a ground-floor timber arcade (built for market trading) that dates back to its 1574 construction, plus octagonal supporting columns. The first floor houses a council chamber.

Butchery Lane and the Roman Museum, Canterbury (p83)

BAX WALKER/ALAMY

STAY AWHILE

MARGATE

BY CATHERINE LE NEVEZ

Margate's incredible regeneration makes it top of my list to stay in the southeast. With gold-sand beaches, candyfloss sunsets and miles of sea and sky inspiring artists including JMW Turner and Tracey Emin, this once-grand Isle of Thanet resort has had a wild ride since steamboats and railways brought crowds. When cheap flights diverted holiday makers, Margate tipped into decline, until its 21st-century revival, rocket-boosted by the glass-fronted gallery **Turner Contemporary** and reimagined **Dreamland** with its century-old coaster, roller disco and concerts.

I love soaking up the seaside kitsch and creative energy in Margate Old Town, Harbour Arm and Cliftonville, where artists and makers have salvaged derelict buildings now home to art spaces, live music venues, vintage shops, indie fashion, great coffee and an absolutely fizzing food scene. In a cherry-coloured ex-cinema that became a bingo then snooker hall, among later incarnations, the **Old Kent Market** *(oldkentmarket.com)* is a brilliant starting point. It's now home to an artisanal bakery, coffee house with cupcakes and homemade fudge, double-decker bus cafe, pub, and vinyl and retro treasures.

Main Sands gets busy; neighbouring Westbrook and St Mildred's are quieter, and Thanet has 16 sandy beaches and rockpool-strewn bays. Cycle the **Viking Coastal Trail** *(explorekent.org/activities/viking-coastal-trail)*, a 32-mile loop along the coast past Victorian-charm-filled Broadstairs, where Charles Dickens spent summers (stop off at old-fashioned ice-cream parlour **Morelli's**; morellisgelato.com) and stylish **Ramsgate**, where boats moor in Britain's only Royal Harbour, passing fishing cottages, beach huts, cliffs, chalk stacks and surfers, then inland via rural villages back to Margate.

LINK YOUR TRIP

From Margate, discover history, art, hops and grapes in 07 **Kent: Garden of England**, or take a 06 **Seaside Jaunt** from Dover, 22 miles south.

WIRESTOCK CREATORS/SHUTTERSTOCK

MONICA WELLS/ALAMY

Left: Old Kent Market; Right: No 42 Margate

PLACES TO STAY

Margate has loads of cool, arty hotels; Broadstairs and Ramsgate also make great bases. Book way ahead in summer.

No 42 Margate
Designer pad with polaroid cameras, turntables and vinyl, and a guest pantry, plus an open-flame restaurant and summertime rooftop bar overlooking Main Sands.
guesthousehotels.co.uk

Fort Road Hotel
Boutique hotel in an 1820 boarding house with local art and original postcards, vintage-furnished rooms, a summer roof terrace and basement cocktail bar.
fortroadhotel.com

George & Heart Hotel
Renovations exposed original brick, timber and stone fireplaces in this 1700-built coaching inn; above the pub/restaurant are one-of-a-kind designer rooms and a 'Zen den' treatment room.
georgeandheart.com

08

SOUTHERN & EASTERN ENGLAND

★ BEST FOR

FAMILIES

Disappear into Harry Potter's magical world on the Warner Bros Studio Tour.

ROYALTY & THE THAMES VALLEY

DURATION: 5–6 DAYS

DISTANCE: 105 MILES / 169KM

GREAT FOR: HISTORY, FAMILIES

BEST TIME TO GO: ANY TIME; CHOOSE APRIL TO JULY FOR WARMER WEATHER AND FLOWER-FILLED GARDENS.

Windsor Castle

Venture into a rewarding world of timeworn castles, literary legends, glorious gardens, Harry Potter frenzy and architectural wizardry. This richly varied trip whisks you off to some of south England's most magical destinations. You'll find royal fanfare and the world's oldest continually occupied fortress in Windsor. Then there's architectural wonders and historical curiosities in Oxford, plus Woodstock's prosperous charm.

LINK YOUR TRIP

16 The Cotswolds & Literary England
Head 20 miles west from Oxford to Burford to get lost in this in-depth tour of the dreamy gold-tinged Cotswolds.

07 Kent: Garden of England
From Windsor, skirt 70 miles around London's southern edge to join this culture-fuelled jaunt at Chatham.

01 Windsor

Flaunting royal pomp at every turn, from the ceremonious changing of the guards to the magnificent outdoors treasure that is **Windsor Great Park** *(rct.uk/visit/windsor-castle)*, Windsor has a rather surreal atmosphere. Crowning the Thames-side town is **Windsor Castle** *(royalcollection.org.uk)*, a majestic vision of battlements and towers.

The castle is one of the king's principal residences; if he's at home, the Royal Standard flies from the Round Tower. William the Conqueror first established a royal dwelling here in 1080. Since then, successive monarchs have rebuilt, remodelled and refurbished the complex to create the massive, sumptuous palace that stands here today. In 1992, the castle was devastated by fire;

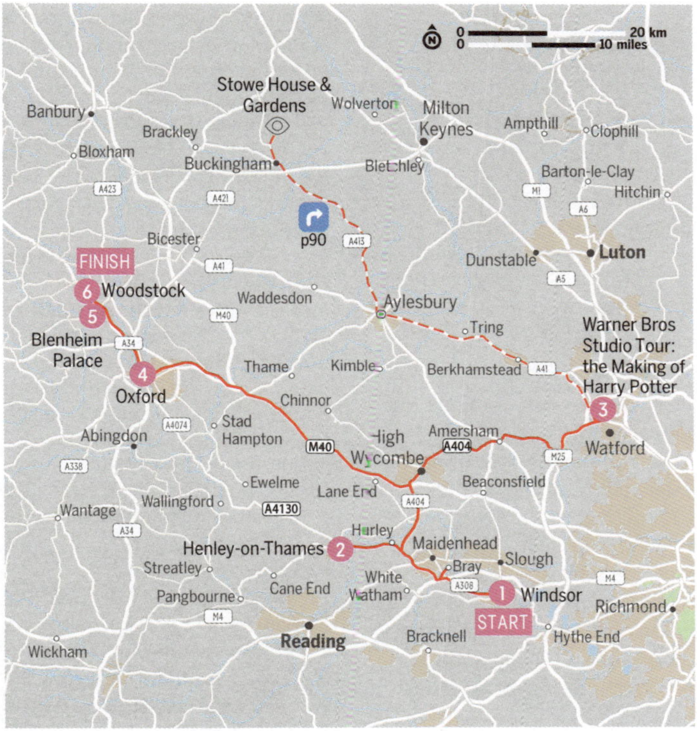

ALEXEY FEDORENKO/SHUTTERSTOCK

restoration took five years. Book tickets online to avoid queues.

Castle tickets include a multimedia guide. Among the highlights are the gilded, chandeliered Grand Reception room, the State Apartments decked with art by Holbein, Van Dyck and Rubens, and the intricate details of Queen Mary's Dolls' House. Within the grounds, in Gothic **St George's Chapel**, 11 monarchs' tombs include that of Queen Elizabeth II.

The triumphant changing of the guard usually takes place at 11am Tuesdays, Thursdays and Saturdays; check the schedule at *householddivision.org.uk*.

THE DRIVE: This section of the drive involves some big roads, but they'll speed by! Head west out of Windsor along Arthur Rd (which becomes Maidenhead Rd), taking the A308 5 miles northwest to bypass the M4 motorway. Follow signs onto the A404(M), head 3.5 miles northwest and exit onto the A4130. It's 6 miles northwest to Henley-on-Thames.

02 Henley-on-Thames

Standing elegantly beside the Thames, Henley is an attractive commuter town of red-brick and half-timbered houses, characterful pubs, lovely riverside saunters and a long-established rowing tradition.

If you're lucky enough to be visiting in July, book ahead for the world-famous **Henley Royal Regatta** *(hrr.co.uk)*, a high-calibre rowing tournament that doubles as a major social fixture for England's elite.

THE DRIVE: Whizz 10.5 miles northeast from Henley to High Wycombe (A4130 and A404). It's mostly major roads into London from here, but for a prettier, more rural drive, continue 15 miles northeast along the A404, passing Amersham, through the Chilterns National Landscape. Join the M25; 5 miles northeast is Warner Bros Studio Tour (signposted)

03 Warner Bros Studio Tour: the Making of Harry Potter

Whether you're a fair-weather fan or a full-on Potterhead, this magical **studio tour** *(wbstudiotour.co.uk)* is worth its out-of-the-way Watford location and admittedly hefty-sounding admission price. You'll need to pre-book your visit for an allocated time slot; arrive 20 minutes beforehand and allow around 3½ hours inside. The tour starts with a short film before you're ushered through giant doors into the film studios – the first of many 'wow' moments.

You're then free to explore the rest of the complex, including a large hangar featuring all the most familiar interior sets (Dumbledore's office, the Gryffindor common room, Hagrid's Hut), another starring Platform 9¾ and the Hogwarts Express, and an outdoor section displaying Privet Drive, the purple triple-decker Knight Bus, Sirius Black's motorbike and a shop selling butterbeer (sickly sweet). Other highlights include a stroll down Diagon Alley, but the most enchanting treat is saved for last – a shimmering, gasp-inducing 1:24 scale model of Hogwarts.

THE DRIVE: Exit the major M25 5 miles southwest of Watford and backtrack along the scenic A404, past Amersham, to High Wycombe. Zip 17 miles northwest on the M40, take the A40 5 miles west and follow Oxford signs. Driving and parking in central Oxford is near impossible; use one of five Park & Ride car parks around the city edge (£2 to £4 per day, plus bus fare).

DETOUR

Stowe House & Gardens

Start: 03 Warner Bros Studio Tour: The Making of Harry Potter

From the Harry Potter studios, it's a rewarding 41-mile diversion northwest to Stowe, home to some of England's most spectacularly beautiful gardens. Take the A41 23 miles northwest to Aylesbury, then the A413 16 miles northwest to Buckingham. From here, brown signs lead along fabulous 1.5-mile-long tree-lined Stowe Ave to Stowe.

Covering 160 hectares, **Stowe's glorious gardens** *(nationaltrust.org.uk)* were shaped in the 18th century by Britain's greatest landscape gardeners. Among them was master landscape architect Lancelot 'Capability' Brown, who kick-started his career at Stowe.

The gardens are best known for their many temples and follies, commissioned by the super-wealthy Richard Temple (1st Viscount Cobham), whose family motto was *Templa Quam Dilecta* (How Delightful are Your Temples). Paths meander past lakes, bridges, temples, fountains and cascades, and through Capability Brown's Grecian Valley.

Lording over the gardens, neoclassical Stowe House is now an exclusive private school. Although rooms are left bare (the house's contents were sold off to rescue the original owners from financial disaster), the sheer scale and ornamentation of the building is impressive.

From Stowe, head 32 miles southwest via the A421, A43, M40 and A34 to Oxford to rejoin the main route. This detour totals 72 miles; you'll need at least half a day to explore Stowe properly.

☑ TOP TIP

DON'T MISS CHRIST CHURCH CATHEDRAL

Christ Church's grand quad is world famous, but this 12th-century, vaulted cathedral is as glorious as it is serene.

04 Oxford

One of the world's most famous university cities, Oxford is a beautiful, privileged place, and deserves at least two days on your itinerary. Loved by literary greats JRR Tolkien, CS Lewis and Oscar Wilde, it's steeped in history and studded with august honey-toned buildings, yet maintains a young, lively student feel.

The university's 39 colleges are scattered throughout the city, the oldest dating back to the 13th century. Seek out your own corner of studious calm, but don't miss extraordinary, wealthy **Magdalen College** *(magd.ox.ac.uk)*, peaceful and exclusive **All Souls College** *(asc.ox.ac.uk)*, and magnificent, popular **Christ Church** *(chch.ox.ac.uk)*, with the grandest of quads. Christ Church is Oxford's largest college, famous as a location for the Harry Potter films (check out the Great Hall and staircase) and for its wonderful vaulted **cathedral** *(chch.ox.ac.uk/cathedral)*.

Explore the fantastic **Ashmolean Museum** *(ashmolean.org)* and stroll down exquisite Catte St, flanked by golden colleges, the steeped 1914 **Bridge of Sighs** (Hertford Bridge; New College Lane), the relatively unadorned (but historically important) **University Church of St Mary the Virgin** *(universitychurch.ox.ac.uk)*, and the striking, circular, columned **Radcliffe Camera** *(bodleian.ox.ac.uk)*. Also here is Oxford's **Bodleian Old Library** *(bodleian.ox.ac.uk/bodley)*, one of the oldest public libraries in the world and quite possibly the most impressive you'll ever see; admission is by guided tour.

Outstanding buildings aside, punting is a quintessential and unmissable Oxford experience: **Magdalen Bridge Boathouse** *(oxfordpunting.co.uk)* is the most

Warner Bros Studio Tour: the Making of Harry Potter (p89)
GAUTIER STEPHANE/ALAMY

PHOTO OPPORTUNITY

Spectacular sets at Warner Bros Studio Tour: The Making of Harry Potter.

central location to take to the water. Oxford's many literary-linked pubs, such as the **Turf Tavern** *(greeneking.co.uk/pubs/oxfordshire/turf-tavern),* offer the perfect post-punt retreat.

THE DRIVE: It's a quick 8-mile trip northwest on the A44 to Blenheim Palace, which has a sprawling free car park.

05 Blenheim Palace

Absolutely worth travelling for, **Blenheim Palace** *(blenheimpalace.com),* one of Britain's greatest stately homes, is a monumental baroque fantasy. The site was designed by Sir John Vanbrugh and Nicholas Hawksmoor, and built between 1705 and 1722. The land and funds to build the house were granted to John Churchill, Duke of Marlborough, by a grateful Queen Anne, after his victory over the French at the 1704 Battle of Blenheim. Sir Winston Churchill was born here in 1874. Now a UNESCO World Heritage Site, Blenheim (blennum) is home to the 12th duke.

Leave enough time and energy to walk the lavish gardens and parklands, parts of which were landscaped by the great Lancelot 'Capability' Brown.

THE DRIVE: Leaving Blenheim Palace, you'll emerge on the A4095. Turn left, skirting the splendid palace grounds. From the roundabout, signs lead 1 mile northwest into Woodstock.

06 Woodstock

Though the main reason to swing by Woodstock is, of course, to visit nearby Blenheim Palace, the town itself is blessed with a delightful, affluent centre dotted with old pubs, antique stores, fine stone houses and several luxuriously stylish hotels. It's well worth exploring, and makes the perfect final overnight stop to your trip.

If you're craving a stroll, **Wychwood Way** is a historic, 37-mile loop route from Woodstock through ancient royal forest, divided into manageable sections for those who fancy tackling a smaller part.

Blenheim Palace
INGA KEBLERYTE/SHUTTERSTOCK

09

SOUTHERN & EASTERN ENGLAND

AROUND THE CAM

★ BEST FOR

CULTURE

One of the world's most important centres of learning: historic Cambridge.

Willy Lott's House

DURATION: 6–7 DAYS

DISTANCE: 130 MILES / 210KM

GREAT FOR: HISTORY, OUTDOORS

BEST TIME TO GO: MID-JUNE TO SEPTEMBER BRINGS FINE WEATHER AND LONGER OPENING HOURS.

Settle in for a grand tour through the heart of old England; a journey not just into history, but into landscapes that define what it means to be English. Stops include a spectacular cathedral, wonky villages of timbered houses, scenery immortalised by famous painters and some of England's grandest stately homes. Then there's Cambridge, a bewitching university city where history and tradition emanate from the bicycle-crowded streets.

LINK YOUR TRIP

10 Suffolk-Norfolk Shore
A glorious voyage along a sublime stretch of sandy, marsh-backed seafront. Starts 45 miles east of Bury St Edmunds at Aldeburgh.

04 The Historic South
An exploration of the pick of southern England's heritage sights. Starts in London, 60 miles south of Saffron Walden.

01 Lavenham

One of England's most immaculately preserved medieval towns, the former wool-trade centre of Lavenham is dominated by beautiful timbered houses that tip and lean at crazy angles.

If it's open, browse the museum inside whitewashed **Lavenham Guildhall** *(nationaltrust.org.uk)*, a superb example of close-studded, timber-framed, early-16th-century architecture, and caramel-coloured, 14th-century **Little Hall** *(littlehall.org.uk)*, where rooms have been restored to their period splendour. Even if the museums are closed, the whole town is a living museum of medieval architecture – drop into the 15th-century church of **St Peter & St Paul** *(lavenham.church)*, with its churchyard of skull and cherub gravestones.

THE DRIVE: Your first leg is a 5-mile countryside cruise southwest, initially along the B1071, then Bridge St Rd, towards Long Melford. Turn left onto the A134 then turn right onto the A1092;

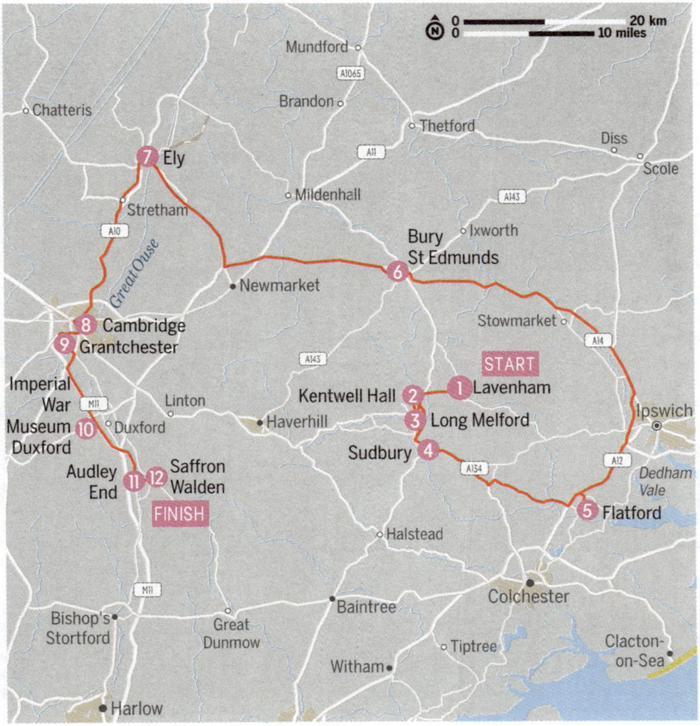

KEV GREGORY/SHUTTERSTOCK

seconds later you'll reach the long, tree-lined driveway to Kentwell Hall.

02 Kentwell Hall

Gorgeous, turreted, Tudor-era **Kentwell Hall** *(kentwell.co.uk)* may date from the 1500s but it's still used as a private home, lending it a wonderfully lived-in feel. The mansion is framed by a rectangular moat and lush gardens, and during Tudor re-enactment events, the whole estate bristles with bodices, codpieces and hose.

When events are hosted at Kentwell, the regular house and garden visits are unavailable, so check the website first to make sure it's open to the public.

THE DRIVE: Continue south once you exit Kentwell Hall to waft alongside Long Melford's famous village green, passing a medieval hospital and the village church, with its fine 15th-century stained glass.

03 Long Melford

The charming village of Long Melford has a second ace up its sleeve: the romantic Elizabethan mansion of **Melford Hall** *(nationaltrust.org.uk)*, which from the outside has changed little since it entertained Queen Elizabeth I in 1578.

> **PHOTO OPPORTUNITY**
>
> The Flatford Mill view that has hardly changed since Constable's time.

Inside, there's a panelled banqueting hall, masses of Regency and Victorian finery, and a display on writer Beatrix Potter, who was a cousin of the owners. Call for current hours and prices.

THE DRIVE: Continue south through the village to get back onto the A134/131 for the 6-mile stretch to Gainsborough's House in the town of Sudbury.

04 Sudbury

Today a quiet little market town, Sudbury was the 18th-century birthplace of painter Thomas Gainsborough. His family home, **Gainsborough's House** *(gainsborough.org)*, now houses a museum and gallery with one of the world's most comprehensive collections of his work. Look out for *Portrait of Harriet, Viscountess Tracy*, with its delicate portrayal of drapery.

THE DRIVE: The road onwards winds through bucolic, hedgerow-framed fields for 18 miles, following the A131/134, then the B1068. There's a brief zoom on the A12 to reach the B1070 through East Bergholt; turn off to the right for Flatford.

05 Flatford

If the languid landscape looks familiar, thank local boy John Constable – his romantic visions of springtime fields and babbling brooks were inspired by this serene corner of the country.

Centred on the historic mill that features in *The Hay Wain*, the tiny hamlet of **Flatford** *(nationaltrust.org.uk)* is now a National Trust-run window onto Constable's time. Check if you can enter tiny **Bridge Cottage**, with its restored interior, then stroll past **Flatford Mill**, where the view across the mill pond to **Willy Lott's House** has hardly changed since 1821.

♥ DON'T MISS

ELY CATHEDRAL

Marvel at the cathedral's ship's mast-like spire and 14th-century Octagon.

THE DRIVE: Retrace your route back to the A12, then zip along A roads (the A14 and A134) to curve round into Bury St Edmunds; 35 miles in all.

06 Bury St Edmunds

History-rich Bury is a delight to explore. In the picturesque **Abbey Gardens** *(westsuffolk.gov.uk)*, the mighty walls of a once-vast abbey have crumbled and eroded into fantastical shapes. Next door, partly 16th-century **St Edmundsbury Cathedral** *(stedscathedral.org)* was once just a small part of the enormous abbey; look inside to see if tours of the 45m-high tower have resumed.

You'll detect brewing smells from the **Greene King Brewery** (prebook tours of its 1938 Victorian brewhouse at greeneking.co.uk) as you loop round to reach the fascinating but macabre **Moyse's Hall** *(moyseshall.org)* museum.

THE DRIVE: Pick up the A14 towards Newmarket, turning off 15 miles later to head northwest onto the A142. From here it's a 12-mile drive through the flat Fenland landscape, with Ely Cathedral's towering spire beckoning you onwards.

07 Ely

Sleepy Ely's city status is conferred by **Ely Cathedral** *(elycathedral.org)*, dubbed the 'Ship of the Fens' because its spire rises like a mast above the flat Fens. Inside, gaze up to see the 14th-century Octagon that transfers the weight of the tower on to vast columns, then enter the Lady Chapel, preserved in the ravaged state in which it was left at the end of the English Civil War.

A few minutes' walk away, timbered **Oliver Cromwell's House** *(olivercromwellshouse.co.uk)* is where the man who initiated that war (and executed a king) lived in the mid-1600s. It's now an engaging museum.

Ely Cathedral

ANGELINA DIMITROVA/SHUTTERSTOCK

PETER MOULTON/SHUTTERSTOCK

Oliver Cromwell's House

FAMOUS CAMBRIDGE STUDENTS

The honour roll of famous Cambridge students and academics is an international who's who of high achievers. This is the town where Newton refined his theory of gravity, where Whittle invented the jet engine, where Stephen Hawking penned *A Brief History of Time* and where Crick and Watson discovered DNA. Alongside Britain's favourite comedians – everyone from Rowan Atkinson to the Monty Python team found an audience thanks to the university's Footlights sketch comedy troupe – you'll find 126 Nobel Prize winners, 14 British prime ministers, 18 archbishops of Canterbury and numerous scientists, poets and authors. Statesman Oliver Cromwell attended Sidney Sussex College, Cambridge (where his head is now buried) for about a year before leaving due to his father's death.

THE DRIVE: This one's simple: 16 miles south along the A10, through the low-lying Fens to Cambridge. Make for the car park under the Grand Arcade in the centre.

08 Cambridge

Awash with exquisite medieval and Regency architecture and oozing tradition, Cambridge is a perfect city to explore on foot. There are more than 30 colleges here; perhaps the greatest and grandest is **King's College** *(kings.cam.ac.uk)* with its extravagant **chapel**. Climb the tower of **Great St Mary's Church** *(greatstmarys.org)* for eagle's-eye views over the college rooftops, and take a **punt trip** along the River Cam.

Don't miss the fabulous **Fitzwilliam Museum** *(fitzmuseum.cam.ac.uk)*, with its Roman and Egyptian grave goods, pottery and old-master paintings, and intriguing **Kettle's Yard** *(kettlesyard.cam.ac.uk)* with its eccentric artworks assembled by a former curator from the Tate in London.

THE DRIVE: Take a 4-mile drive south through Cambridge's streets – you're making for the A603, aka the Fen Causeway. Soon, take the left to Grantchester, via Grantchester Rd, and roll into the Orchard Tea Garden car park.

09 Grantchester

With its thatched cottages, flower-filled gardens, breezy meadows and cafes with classic cream teas, Grantchester is the picture-postcard image of England and the setting for a popular TV detective show. The quintessentially **English Orchard Tea Garden** *(theorchardteagarden.co.uk)*, beside the church, has deckchairs spread beneath the apple trees and reassuringly calorific cakes and light lunches. It was a favourite haunt of the Bloomsbury Group, who came to camp, picnic, swim and push back social boundaries.

THE DRIVE: Leaving Grantchester, snake south via the A1134 onto the speedy M11, southbound. Leave it at junction 10, heading for Duxford, then pick up signs for the Imperial War Museum. It's a 7-mile trip in all.

10 Imperial War Museum Duxford

Plane-spotters will be in aviation heaven at Europe's biggest **aircraft museum** *(iwm.org.uk)*, with around 200 vintage aircraft - including many veterans of WWI and WWII – spread across a series of enormous hangars. You'll see everything from dive bombers to biplanes, Spitfires, Hurricanes and Concordes, which was moved here after ending service in 2003 and can be explored on tours (included in admission).

THE DRIVE: Another short drive, this time just under 10 miles on minor roads: first the A505, then the A1301, before the B1383 leads lazily to the exquisite Audley End.

11 Audley End

Palatial in scale, the fabulous early Jacobean **Audley End House** *(english-heritage.org.uk)* was clearly designed to place its creator, the 1st Earl of Suffolk, at the top table of the English gentry. The house eventually did become a royal palace when it was purchased by Charles II in 1668. The rooms inside are lavishly decorated with heirloom furniture, oil paintings, priceless silverware, woodcarvings and taxidermy. Also swing by the lavish gardens, designed by Capability Brown, which include a walled kitchen garden full of traditional varieties.

THE DRIVE: Blink and you'd miss the final leg of this trip – a fraction under 2 miles. Head east from Audley End via Spring Hill and Audley End Rd into the picturesque streets of Saffron Walden.

12 Saffron Walden

The dainty 12th-century market town of Saffron Walden is a delightful knot of half-timbered houses, narrow lanes, crooked roofs and ancient churches. It gets its name from the purple saffron crocus (the source of the world's most expensive spice), which was cultivated in the surrounding fields between the 15th and 18th centuries. Swot up on local history in the **Saffron Walden Museum** *(saffronwalden museum.org)* then swan over to the restored **Victorian Bridge End Garden** *(bridgeendgarden.org)*, an elegant sprawl of water features, gazebos and manicured hedges.

Audley End House
CHRISDORNEY/SHUTTERSTOCK

10

SOUTHERN & EASTERN ENGLAND

★ BEST FOR

ROYALTY

His Majesty the King's country estate: Sandringham.

SUFFOLK-NORFOLK SHORE

DURATION: 8 DAYS

DISTANCE: 138 MILES / 222KM

GREAT FOR: FOOD & DRINK

BEST TIME TO GO: SPRING THROUGH TO SUMMER FOR FINER WEATHER; AUTUMN FOR QUIETER BEACHES.

Aldeburgh

See another facet of the English seaside as you motor from Suffolk's piers to north Norfolk's dune-backed shore. The distances aren't great but the pit stops are: scenic drives lead to creeks full of bobbing boats; salt marshes teem with fluttering and wading birds; and hidden beaches lurk behind grass-topped dunes. If you've only experienced the English seaside full of gambling arcades and fairground rides, prepare to be surprised.

LINK YOUR TRIP

09 Around the Cam
A history-rich meander through Fenland countryside to the historic university city of Cambridge. Join it 45 miles west of Aldeburgh at Bury St Edmunds.

04 The Historic South
A cross-country dive into Britain's fascinating past, taking in blockbuster heritage sights. Starts in London, 100 miles southwest of Aldeburgh.

01 Aldeburgh

The coastal town of Aldeburgh (orld-bruh) floats in a charming time warp. Along the pebbly shore, wooden sheds sell ocean-fresh seafood hauled in by the boats perched on the beach, while sightseers stroll along the prom with nary a slot machine in sight. Look out for the town museum in **Moot Hall** *(aldeburghmuseum.org.uk)*, a medieval merchant's house on the seafront, made from ancient oak beams and herringbone brick. Take a wander north along the pebbles towards Thorpeness to view artist Maggi Hambling's 2003 sculpture *Scallop*, celebrating composer Benjamin Britten's links to the town.

THE DRIVE: This first short hop is an 8.3-mile trip north into the marshes. Take the rural B1122, then the B1125 to Westleton, then Mill Rd and Sheepwash Lane to the Royal Society for the Protection of Birds (RSPB) Minsmere car park.

DAVID CALVERT/SHUTTERSTOCK

DETOUR

Sutton Hoo

Start: 01 Aldeburgh

From Aldeburgh, take the A1094, B1069 and A1152 for 15 miles southwest to the remarkable archaeological site of **Sutton Hoo** *(nationaltrust.org.uk)*. In 1939 a tumulus was excavated to reveal the decayed hull of an enormous Anglo-Saxon ship containing the lavish grave goods and earthly remains of the Anglo-Saxon king Raedwald, who ruled over East Anglia until 625 CE. The massive effort that went into Raedwald's burial and the intricate artisanship of the treasure he was buried with gives some idea of his high status. You can see a full-scale reconstruction of the grave ship, due to be launched on the River Deben in 2027, and reproductions of Raedwald's remarkable jewelled sword, helmet and shield (the originals are in London's British Museum). Head to Tranmer House to see archive footage of the original excavation.

02 Minsmere

The nature reserve at **RSPB Minsmere** *(rspb.org.uk)* near Dunwich is home to one of England's rarest birds, the bittern, along with dozens of other resident and migratory bird species, best spotted in the autumn, when the marshes and pools come alive with birdlife.

Trails run through the reeds that line the foreshore to hides that offer prime spotting opportunities. The reserve borders the National Trust-administered **Dunwich Heath** *(nationaltrust.org.uk)*, another fine spot for birdwatching by the coast.

THE DRIVE: From Minsmere return to Westleton and continue to the A12 to cross the River Blyth, then go right onto the A1095 and through rolling farmland to Southwold, a trip of 12 miles. Park near the pier.

03 Southwold

Southwold has been a favourite retreat for well-heeled Londoners since the Regency period, thanks to its lovely sandy beach pebble-walled cottages, clifftop promenade and rows of beachfront bathing huts.

First built in 1899, the 190m-long **pier** *(southwoldpier.co.uk)* is worth a visit for the Under the Pier Show, a kooky collection of handmade amusement machines combining daft fun with political satire. The malty aromas that waft around the centre of town come from the Victorian-era **Adnams** *(adnams.co.uk)* brewery, which produces some of East Anglia's most popular ales. Book for hour-long tours of the high-tech kit and tasting of the house brews. Weekdays see the brewing in action. There are also distillery tours and workshops.

THE DRIVE: Pick up the B1127 then join the A146 for a 30-mile cruise to Norwich. Norfolk's roads are famously straight but they dip into gullies and rise over bridges like a roller coaster, hence the typically East Anglian 'Hidden Dip!' and 'Humpback Bridge' warning signs.

04 Norwich

Norwich (norr-ich) is one of East Anglia's most historic cities, and its winding, part-pedestrianised streets are crammed with ancient flint churches and venerable timbered buildings that speak volumes about the wealth that the wool trade brought to Norfolk in the medieval period. The magnificent **Norwich Cathedral** *(cathedral.org.uk)* has England's second-highest spire, a fan-vaulted ceiling and fantastical ceiling bosses in its vast cloisters. Take a wander through the ancient Tomb-land district to gorgeous Elm Hill.

Head over to the **Sainsbury Centre for Visual Arts** *(sainsburycentre.ac.uk)* at the university for African and Asian treasures, and artworks by Bacon, Giacometti, Henry Moore and others.

About 15 miles north of Norwich, **Blickling Hall** *(nationaltrust.org.uk)*, ancestral seat of the Boleyn family (of Anne Boleyn fame), is a worthwhile detour.

THE DRIVE: Next is an easy 8-mile drive northeast to Wroxham along the A1151, where you'll glide past fields painted (in summer) in colours by terracotta-coloured earth and vivid yellow oilseed rape (used to make vegetable oil).

05 Wroxham

Signs in the shape of sailboats signal your arrival at Wroxham, gateway to the Norfolk Broads. Head for the twin hump-backed bridges dividing Wroxham from twin-town Hoveton, where **Broads Tours** *(broadstours.co.uk)* can book you on a 1½ to two-hour boat trip around the waterways, or let you loose on a rented boat for self-guided day explorations. One charming boat-trip stop is **Toad Hole Cottage** *(howhilltrust.org.uk)* at How Hill, a restored eel-catchers' cottage on the edge of marshes traversed by nature trails and dotted with 'skeleton mills' that were once used to drain sections of the swamps.

Norwich Cathedral

JONO PHOTOGRAPHY/SHUTTERSTOCK

THE DRIVE: It's hedgerows, fields and leafy lanes for most of the next 20 miles (via the A1151 and A149), passing through a string of pretty villages and small market towns. After a burst of woodland, you'll hit the main road into Cromer.

06 Cromer

The once-fashionable Victorian resort of Cromer still flourishes as a busy fishing port, famous for the sweet-tasting brown crabs that are hauled in daily during the March to October crabbing season. The long, cliff-edged seafront is lined with fishing boats and the tractors that pull them onto the pebbles, and the beach sees some impressive swell for surfers. The town is a friendly mix of seaside chintz and Victorian elegance, complete with a vintage **pier** *(cromerpier.co.uk)*.

Just east is the **Henry Blogg Museum** *(rnli.org)*, devoted to lifeboats, where you can take a hands-on lesson in Morse code and semaphore flag signals; check for details of its reopening following renovations. You can rent a surfboard from **Glide Surf School** *(glidesurfschool.co.uk)* on the seafront and brave the breakers. In the streets leading back from the shore, seek out **Davies Fish Shop** *(facebook.com/daviesfishshop)* at 7 Garden St, where the Cromer crab is caught by the owner's day boat and boiled, cracked and dressed on site.

THE DRIVE: Time for an 11-mile drive through the villages of brick-edged flint houses that define the Norfolk coast. The A149 peels west along Cromer's seafront, affording frequent sea views. At Salthouse the scenery changes – the road dips down to a wide sweep of flat, reed-filled marshland, edged to the north by a distant ridge of dunes, hiding the beach beyond.

07 Cley-next-the-Sea

The sleepy flint-stone village of Cley (which is pronounced 'cly') huddles near the shore, but the breakers lie far beyond a sea of reeds. Just east of Cley, **Cley Marshes** *(norfolkwildlifetrust.org.uk)* are one of England's premier birdwatching sites, with a network of walking trails and bird hides that offer excellent chances of spotting marsh harriers, bitterns and bearded reedlings, alongside 300 other species. Wander down sign-posted lanes to reach the postcard-pretty **windmill** (now a lovely B&B; *cleywindmill.co.uk*), sitting serenely beside reed beds.

THE DRIVE: It's just a 1.5-mile jaunt past hedges and houses to Blakeney. Once in the village, follow signs to Blakeney Quay.

08 Blakeney

The pretty village of Blakeney was once a busy fishing and trading port before its harbour silted up. These days, visitors come to sit down beside the creek and watch the boats bobbing between the mudflats, before taking a trip to the nearby **Blakeney National Nature Reserve** *(nationaltrust.org.uk)*, a curving sandspit lined with marshes, that provide a home for myriad seabirds and a huge colony of common and grey seals.

Seals can be spotted year-round at Blakeney Point; take a trip to see them with **Bishop's Boats** *(bishopsboats.co.uk)* from the quayside at Blakeney.

THE DRIVE: Head west on the A149, which weaves through villages of flint-fronted houses, passing through a gentle landscape of salt marshes and meadows. Some 8 miles later, in Wells-next-the-Sea, head down the mile-long straight road that borders the sea defences to the car park near the beach.

09 Wells Beach

Stroll north from the car park and follow the boardwalk past the lifeboat station on the point to one of Norfolk's finest beaches: a sweeping curve of dune-backed sand, lined with pastel-coloured beach huts on stilts. The shore stretches for miles to the west, offering long, uplifting and often windy walks. Closer to the boardwalk, the shallow water is perfect for paddling.

THE DRIVE: Head back down Beach Rd to the centre of Wells, and park up near the quay – parking fees apply.

10 Wells-next-the-Sea

In charming Wells-next-the-Sea, rows of attractive Georgian houses and flint cottages snake down to a busy, boat-lined fishing quay bordered by creeks and marshes. Take a peek at what the boats are hauling in, then wander inland to explore the pretty back lanes around a tiny park, the Buttlands.

Head to Stiffkey Rd to board the charming 10.25in narrowgauge **Wells & Walsingham Railway** *(wwlr.co.uk)*, the world's smallest public railway. This tiny loco puffs for a picturesque 5 miles (30 minutes) to the village of **Little Walsingham**, an ancient Catholic pilgrimage site centred on the ruins of the Reformation-ravaged **Walsingham Priory**.

THE DRIVE: The A149 plots your route onwards, tracing the marsh-fringed coast for 2 miles through a flat, open landscape. You'll know you've reached Holkham by the neat houses built to accommodate workers at the stately Holkham Hall, which is a 400m drive south on Park Rd.

11 Holkham Hall

Constructed by Earl Thomas Coke in the 18th century, **Holkham Hall** *(holkham.co.uk)* was the ancestral seat of the Earls of Leicester and the current earl still lives in the palatial Palladian mansion.

The perfectly symmetrical, Italianate house was essentially constructed as a display case for the earl's astonishing collection of classical sculpture and painting, assembled during a grand tour of Europe from 1712 to 1718. Guided visits explore the guest rooms, with their original tapestry and wall coverings, and the hidden passageways used by servants.

THE DRIVE: Head back up the drive from Holkham Hall and park over the road in the car park on Lady Anne's Dr, then stroll north on the earth-and-boardwalk trail to the beach (a mile in all).

> PHOTO OPPORTUNITY
>
> Grassy dunes and an endless sweep of sand at Holkham National Nature Reserve.

12 Holkham National Nature Reserve

The track from the car park runs through pine forests and over salt marshes to a distant line of dunes hiding the marvellous beach at **Holkham National Nature Reserve** *(holkham.co.uk)*. This 4000-hectare (10,000-acre) nature reserve throngs with birdlife (easily spotted from hides dotted behind the shore) and the endless sweep of fine golden sand is one of England's most beautiful coastal vistas.

THE DRIVE: Running west, the A149 follows a winding, undulating route, passing a picturesque windmill at Burnham Overy, before crossing the marshes at the mouth of the River Burn. Stick to the A149, which turns back towards the coast and weaves through Burnham Deepdale and Titchwell village to reach Titchwell Marsh nature reserve – a 10-mile leg in all.

13 Titchwell Marsh

At **RSPB Titchwell Marsh** *(rspb.org.uk)* nature reserve, sandbars, marshes and lagoons attract vast numbers of birds, including pied avocets, marsh harriers, Eurasian bitterns and bearded reedlings in summer. In winter the marshes throng with wading birds and countless ducks and geese. There are pubs and a pretty beach nearby in Brancaster Staithe.

THE DRIVE: Take the A149 onwards through the flatlands, past the broad sweep of golf-course-framed sea at Hunstanton, before peeling off onto the B1440 for the gentle cruise

GILLIAN PULLINGER/ALAMY

RSPB Titchwell Marsh

to Sandringham, 15 miles from Titchwell Marsh.

14 Sandringham

The king's lavish **country estate** *(sandringham-estate.co.uk)* is set in 25 hectares of beautifully landscaped gardens, and the sumptuous reception rooms – still regularly used by the royals – contain a wealth of objets d'art and glinting gifts from European royal families.

Sandringham was built in 1870 by the then Prince and Princess of Wales (who later became King Edward VII and Queen Alexandra) and the features and furnishings remain much as they were in Edwardian times.

Sandringham House, gardens, church and stables cafe, open March to October; the parkland (including the playground, courtyard restaurant, terrace cafe and shop) is open year-round.

THE DRIVE: From Sandringham it's a 10-mile hop along well-signposted A and B roads to King's Lynn.

15 King's Lynn

Historically one of England's most important ports, King's Lynn was long known as 'the Warehouse on the Wash' after the nearby bay at the mouth of the River Great Ouse. In its heyday, it was said you could cross from one side of the river to the other by simply stepping from boat to boat.

The 15th-century town hall houses a museum of local history, **Stories of Lynn** *(storiesoflynn.co.uk)*, which covers everything from mercantile history to crime and punishment. Follow a genteel row of townhouses along Queen St to Purfleet Quay, where a statue of Charles II crowns **Custom House**, built in 1683. Continue along King St, past the 15th-century **St George's Guildhall** *(stgeorgesguildhall.com)*, where Shakespeare reputedly performed, and a succession of courtyards crowded with medieval merchants' warehouses. Beyond is charming **True's Yard** *(truesyard.co.uk)*, where two restored fisher's cottages explore the lives and traditions of King's Lynn's fisherfolk.

Dolgellau
Shrewsbury
Newport
Leicester
Wolverhampton
Birmingham
Coventry
Llanidloes
Aberystwyth
Royal
Leamington Spa
Llandrindod
Wells
Leominster
Worcester
Stratford-
upon-Avon
Cardigan
WALES
Hereford
Banbury
Fishguard
St George's
Channel
Talgarth
Brecon
Carmarthen
Abergavenny
Gloucester
Cheltenham
Sherborne
Haverfordwest
Monmouth
Stroud
Oxford
Merthyr Tydfil
Chepstow
Severn
ENGLAND
Pembroke
Pontypridd
Swansea
Newport
Swindon
Cardiff
Bristol
Bath
Newbury
Bristol Channel
Bridgwater
Bay
Mendip
Hills
Salisbury Plain
Lundy
Island
Lynmouth
Minehead
Amesbury
Andover
Ilfracombe
Dunster
Glastonbury
Wells
Croyde
12
Bridgwater
11
ATLANTIC
OCEAN
Barnstaple
Winchester
Clovelly
Dulverton
Taunton
Salisbury
Shaftesbury
Southampton
Tiverton
Yeovil
Sherborne
Bude
Cullompton
Wareham
Cowes
Okehampton
Bridport
Bournemouth
Tintagel
Exeter
Dorchester
Bovey
Tracey
Lyme
Regis
Poole
Bodmin
Moor
13
Padstow
Exmouth
Lyme
Bay
Weymouth
ISLE OF
WIGHT
Wadebridge
St Just-in-
Penwith
Newquay
Bodmin
Liskeard
Torquay
Perranporth
Fowey
Brixham
St Agnes
14
Plymouth
St Ives
St Austell
Dartmouth
Truro
Bigbury-on-Sea
Bantham
Penzance
Falmouth
Kingsbridge
English
Channel
Sennen
15
Porthcurno
Cherbourg
GUERNSEY
St Peter
Port
FRANCE
JERSEY
St Helier
0
0
100 km
50 miles

IAN WOOLCOCK/SHUTTERSTOCK

River Frome, Wareham (p125)

SOUTHWEST ENGLAND

EXPLORE

SOUTHWEST ENGLAND

The gently stirring southwest is for many the ideal England. Driving here can feel like an exercise in blissful escapism. Industrial centres and highways are close but easy to avoid, creating the sense of travelling to a bygone era.

Cornwall justifies its fame for its idyllic fishing villages and dramatic coastline. Dartmoor and Exmoor are vestiges of a wild England, with rugged landscapes to rival those of Scotland and Wales. Devon and Dorset offer some of Britain's loveliest seaside drives.

But the southwest isn't all about rural relaxation. Urban adventures await in the historic port of Bristol, one of the country's most happening cities.

Winchester

Winchester is closest to London when you're heading to southern and western England. A mere 75 to 90 minutes away by train or car, this venerable cathedral city was capital to Alfred the Great's Anglo-Saxon Kingdom of Wessex. The natural launch pad for the 'Winchester, Glastonbury & Bath' (p110w) route, Winchester is blessed with delightful Elizabethan and Regency buildings, some now housing boutique hotels and B&Bs. There are plenty of places to shop and a useful scattering of car-hire outfits.

Bath

Founded by the Romans as the spa resort Aquae Sulis, Bath is famous today for its gorgeous Georgian architecture. As a tourist hub, it has abundant restaurants, bars, B&Bs and hotels, although these fluctuate both in price and availability so book well ahead in peak season. It's a convenient base for the 'Winchester, Glastonbury & Bath' (p110) and 'Jurassic Coast' (p124) drives.

Bristol

While Bristol is the biggest centre in the southwest and a fantastic cultural and historical destination in its own right. It also has an international airport that serves UK and European destinations, frequent rail links to London (1½ hours) and the broadest range of accommodation, car hire and food outlets in the southwest. If you're planning on staying a while and tackling more than one drive, it

WHEN TO GO

These are by no means Britain's coldest regions, but high, wild areas (such as Dartmoor) can experience ice and snow in winter, while the Cornish seas can become extremely rough, limiting chances to get out and explore. Cornwall is definitely best avoided during the summer school-holiday period, if possible, when tiny roads become choked with traffic.

may appeal as the natural point of entry to the region.

Exeter

Handy for the 'North Devon & Exmoor' (p118) and 'South Devon' (p130) itineraries, Exeter is a university town of some historical interest, and has plenty of accommodation, car-hire and catering options. Its one downside is its inaccessibility from London (it's an expensive 2½-hour train journey from Paddington).

Plymouth

Linked by direct trains to London (3½ hours), Britain's 'Ocean City' Plymouth is undergoing a process of urban regeneration. It's handy for both the 'South Devon' (p130) and 'Coastal Cornwall' (p134) driving routes, and provides options for car hire, food and accommodation. Don't miss its art-deco saltwater lido.

Penzance & Newquay

Two of the larger centres in Cornwall, these seaside resort towns are both potential bases for the 'Coastal Cornwall' (p134) drive. Each has a scattering of car-hire places, while Penzance has good eating and sleeping options. Only Penzance has direct rail links with London (5¼ hours). Book ahead in summer for accommodation and bring your beach gear.

TRANSPORT

Coming from London, the train to Bristol is perhaps the smartest way to access this region: it's frequent and takes only 1½ hours. Bristol International Airport is a limited option, only connecting to a handful of destinations. Given how reliant you'll be on your car, consider hiring one in London and setting the GPS for the southwest.

WHERE TO STAY

South Penquite Farm, Bodmin Moor, is just off the 'Coastal Cornwall' route. This bucolic organic farm offers yurts, camping and bunks year-round.

Sitting in the photogenic fishing village of the same name, the six-suite Georgian Padstow Townhouse is in the old centre.

Wykeham Arms, Winchester, was once a coaching inn and is now a family-friendly pub. The Wykeham Arms has been taking care of travellers since 1755 and Lord Nelson reportedly stayed here en route to Portsmouth.

For a taste of history, Chapter House, Salisbury, is more than 800 years old, and has 17 timber-beamed suites with such modern luxuries as Egyptian cotton sheets and goose-down duvets.

RESOURCES

Cornwall
Official tourism site and the go-to resource for beaches, walks, historic sights, restaurants and more. *Visitcornwall.com*

Devon
Online port of call for events, activities and classic sights in Devon. *visitdevon.co.uk*

Wiltshire
Comprehensive guide to Wiltshire's ancient monuments, towns and events. *visitwiltshire.co.uk*

Muddy Stilettos
Local's guide to pub gardens, restaurants and weekend escapes. *muddystilettos.co.uk*

WHAT'S ON

May Day (1 May)
'Obby Oss Day' in Padstow, where red and blue 'osses' (pantomime horses) parade through town.

Golowan Festival
Animates Penzance with Cornish music, art and culture in June.

Boomtown
Britain's alternative subcultures flock to a site near Winchester in August.

Sidmouth Folk Festival
International folk performances, dancing and ceilidhs in August.

11

SOUTHWEST ENGLAND

WINCHESTER, GLASTONBURY & BATH

★ BEST FOR

CITYSCAPES

The ancient architecture in UNESCO World Heritage city Bath.

DURATION: 12–14 DAYS

DISTANCE: 165 MILES / 265KM

GREAT FOR: FOOD & DRINK, HISTORY

BEST TIME TO GO: MARCH TO JUNE TO ENJOY BETTER WEATHER AND FEWER CROWDS.

Salisbury Cathedral

This is a trip for encountering England's most extraordinary constructions. You'll circle the 5000-year-old stones at Stonehenge, prowl the still-stunning Roman baths in Bath and wonder at the soaring cathedrals of Salisbury and Wells. Add a safari park, stalactite-filled caverns and a saucy chalk figure, and it's your chance to tour the essence of old England and experience the best archaeological and architectural sights.

LINK YOUR TRIP

04 The Historic South
Even more history awaits on this tour of southern England's big-name heritage sights, which links to the final stop: Bath.

05 Urban & Art Odyssey
Just 14 miles northwest of Bath, Bristol is the launch pad for an exciting exploration of some of Britain's best cities for culture.

01 Winchester

The past still echoes strongly around the flint-flecked walls of this ancient cathedral city, which was the power base of bishops and a capital to Saxon kings. Start with an exploration of 11th-century **Winchester Cathedral** *(winchester-cathedral.org.uk)*. One of southern England's most awe-inspiring buildings, it combines a fine Gothic facade, one of the longest medieval naves in Europe (164m) and a fascinating jumble of features from all eras. Highlights include the intricately carved medieval choir stalls, which sport everything from mythical beasts to a mischievous green man. Check the website to see if you can book a crypt tour or tower tour up onto the roof for panoramic views and whether one of the UK's finest illuminated manuscripts, the

DAVID DENNIS/SHUTTERSTOCK

dazzling **Winchester Bible**, will be on display. Next, stroll just 10 minutes west to Winchester's 11th-century **Great Hall** *(historicwinchester.co.uk)*. It holds the Round Table, a copy of the mythical piece of furniture that King Arthur and his knights reputedly sat around. Although it's actually thought to have been made some 700 years after King Arthur died, it's impressive nonetheless.

THE DRIVE: Pick up the 'Salisbury A30' signs for a 31-mile, often-dual-carriageway cruise. Eventually, Salisbury Cathedral's soaring spire glides into view. Head for one of the central car parks signposted from the ring road.

02 Salisbury

The mid 13th-century cathedral that points your way into the city was constructed in the early English Gothic style. **Salisbury Cathedral** *(salisburycathedral.org.uk)* has the tallest spire in Britain (at 123m) and an elaborate exterior with pointed arches, flying buttresses and a highly decorative West Front. The 70m-long nave houses a 1386 medieval clock, which is probably the oldest working timepiece in the world. The cathedral's prized **Magna Carta** is one of only four surviving original copies of the historic agreement made in 1215 between King John and his barons. It's located in a display box designed to prevent fading and increase security. Like all sights on this trip, you may need to pre-book your visit to Salisbury Cathedral; check the website beforehand.

THE DRIVE: From Salisbury, it's a 3-mile drive west to gorgeous Wilton House.

03 Wilton House

Stately **Wilton House** *(wiltonhouse.co.uk)* provides an insight into the rarefied world of the British aristocracy. One of England's finest stately homes, it is where the Earls of Pembroke have lived since 1542. Highlights are the Single and Double Cube Rooms, designed by the pioneering 17th-century architect Inigo Jones. Look out for magnificent period furniture, frescoed ceilings and elaborate plasterwork; they frame paintings by van Dyck, Rembrandt and Joshua Reynolds. That will be why *The Madness of King George*, *Sense and Sensibility* and *Pride and Prejudice* were shot here.

THE DRIVE: Peel back east on the A36 towards Salisbury, before darting north on the A345 to Old Sarum. Total distance is 4.5 miles.

04 Old Sarum

The huge ramparts of **Old Sarum** *(english-heritage.org.uk)* sit on a grass-covered mound. It began life as a hill fort during the Iron Age, before its later occupation by the Romans, but by the mid-11th century it was an important town, and the first cathedral was built in 1092. Today it's a place to wander grassy defences, see the cathedral's original stone foundations and take a look across the Wiltshire countryside to the spire of the Salisbury Cathedral.

THE DRIVE: Hop back onto the A345, joining the tour buses for the 10-mile blast (via the A303) to Stonehenge. You'll see the stone circle, suddenly, thrillingly, on the right; carry on to the signposted visitor centre beyond.

05 Stonehenge

One of England's most recognisable sights, ancient **Stonehenge** *(english-heritage.org.uk)* has had an ultra-modern makeover, including an impressive visitor centre, the closure of an intrusive road and a powerful sense of historical context. A pathway frames the ring of massive stones and, although you can only walk in the circle itself on tours and out-of-hours experiences, you can get close-up views of a striking sight – the remaining sets of stones, some forming huge doorways, others towering towards the sky.

> **PHOTO OPPORTUNITY**
>
> Standing beside the massive 5000-year-old monument at Stonehenge.

The **visitor centre** charts the site's 5000-year past; it also sees you standing in the middle of a 360-degree projection of the stone circle through the ages and seasons – complete with midsummer sunrise and swirling starscape. The visitor centre is 1.5 miles from the stones. Buses make the 10-minute trip – you can also walk via a 2.6-mile circular trail through the ancient landscape.

THE DRIVE: Next comes an 18-mile drive as the A303/A36 slices through the high chalk plateau of Salisbury Plain. After Warminster, follow the signs for Longleat.

06 Longleat

Half ancestral mansion, half safari park, **Longleat** *(longleat.co.uk)* was transformed into Britain's first safari park in 1966, turning Lancelot 'Capability' Brown's landscaped grounds into an amazing drive-through zoo, populated by a menagerie

Longleat

TJOGR/SHUTTERSTOCK

of animals more at home in the African wilderness than the fields of Wiltshire. There's a throng of attractions, too: the historic house, narrow-gauge railway, mazes and playgrounds including an adventure castle.

THE DRIVE: Time for a meander off the main roads as the B3092 winds gently past ploughed fields and through woodland and scattered villages to Stourhead, 8.5 miles away.

07 Stourhead

Overflowing with vistas, temples and follies, **Stourhead** *(nationaltrust.org.uk)* is landscape gardening at its finest. The magnificent 18th-century gardens spread across the valley, with a picturesque 2-mile garden circuit taking you past ornate follies, around a centrepiece lake and to the Georgian Temple of Apollo. A 3.5-mile walking detour leads from near the Pantheon to a 50m-high folly called King Alfred's Tower.

THE DRIVE: Keep heading south, as more B roads snake for 11 miles beside pastoral meadows and hogbacked hills. Then climb the ridge to Shaftesbury.

08 Shaftesbury

The appealing market town of Shaftesbury circles around the ruins of **Shaftesbury Abbey** *(shaftesburyabbey.org.uk)*. Once England's largest and richest nunnery, it was founded in 888 by King Alfred the Great; Alfred's daughter, Aethelgifu, was its first abbess. Most of the buildings were dismantled by Henry VIII, but you can still spot the foundations amid swathes of grass and wildflowers, and discover the medieval-inspired collection of herbs and fruit trees.

LAURENCE BERGER/SHUTTERSTOCK

Stonehenge

STONEHENGE TICKETS

Stonehenge operates by pre-booked, timed tickets, even for English Heritage and National Trust members entitled to free admission. To be sure you can visit when you want, book your ticket well in advance.

A few paces away sits Gold Hill, an often-photographed, painfully steep, quaint cobbled slope, lined by chocolate-box cottages.

THE DRIVE: Join the A30 as it swoops down out of town and undulates besides fields for 17 miles to Sherborne. As you approach, follow signs for the town's short-stay parking.

DETOUR

Blandford Forum

Start: 08 Shaftesbury

A 13-mile drive south of Shaftesbury, largely along the B3081/2 leads to the architectural oddity that is Blandford Forum. In 1731 the whole town was consumed in a fire and the subsequent rebuild (by leading architects, the Bastard brothers) resulted in a rarity: a town centre that dates from just one period.

A short stroll pretty much anywhere here rewards the eye – a good route sees you starting at central Market Place, beside the cupola-crowned Parish Church of St Peter and St Paul; the imposing town hall sits nearby. To the west, Salisbury St heads up past bow windows and mathematical tiling. The Plocks darts off to the right to reveal more grand buildings, before The Tabernacle and Church Walk lead you back, 30 minutes later, to the start.

09 Sherborne

Sherborne gleams with mellow, orangey-yellow stone, which has been used to build a cluster of 15th-century buildings and the impressive **Sherborne Abbey** *(sherborneabbey.com)* at their core. At the height of its influence, this magnificent building was the central cathedral of 26 succeeding Saxon bishops. Established early in the 8th century, it became a Benedictine abbey in 998 and functioned as a cathedral until 1075. The church has mesmerising fan vaulting that's the oldest in the country, a central tower supported by Saxon-Norman piers and an 1180 Norman porch.

One mile east, on the outskirts of town, sits impressive **Sherborne Castle** *(sherbornecastle.com)*. Sir Walter Raleigh began building this fine stately home in 1594, but only got as far as the central block before being imprisoned by James I. James promptly sold the castle to Sir John Digby, who added the splendid wings you see today. In 1753 the grounds received a mega-makeover at the hands of landscape-gardener extraordinaire Capability Brown, who added a massive lake and the 12-hectare waterside gardens.

THE DRIVE: Time to head north for 20 miles, along an A- and B-road blend that winds past a patchwork of fields. As you

Cheddar Gorge

MARCHAUGH/SHUTTERSTOCK

near Glastonbury, look out for the iconic hump of Glastonbury Tor rising out of the pan-flat landscape.

DETOUR

Cerne Giant
Start: 09 Sherborne

An 11-mile detour south from Sherborne (along the B3145 and A352) leads to a truly eye-opening sight. The **Cerne Giant** *(nationaltrust.org.uk)* is a 60m-high, 51m-wide depiction of a man, etched into a chalk hillside. Nude, full frontal and notoriously well endowed, he's revealed in a state of excitement that wouldn't be allowed in most magazines. Once you've got over his assets, ponder his age; in 2021, National Trust archaeologists dated his likely construction to the late Saxon period.

10 Glastonbury

Thanks to converging ley lines and ranks of legends, Glastonbury is England's premier counterculture town. It centres around the scattered ruins of **Glastonbury Abbey** *(glastonburyabbey.com)*, which was once one of England's great seats of ecclesiastical power. Today's striking ruins include some of the nave walls, the remains of St Mary's Chapel, and crossing arches.

A 20-minute stroll southeast leads to the reputedly holy waters of the **Chalice Well** *(chalicewell.org.uk)* and then **Glastonbury Tor** *(nationaltrust.org.uk)*, a vast mound that's the focal point of Arthurian legends and is home to a ruined medieval chapel. The half-hour hike to the top reveals wrap-around views.

GLASTONBURY TRAFFIC

To many, Glastonbury is synonymous with the **Glastonbury Festival** *(glastonburyfestivals.co.uk)*, a majestic extravaganza of music and culture that attracts over 150,000 people in mid-June. If you're not festival-bound, avoid the area then as traffic jams can be horrendous.

THE DRIVE: From Glastonbury it's a relatively routine 6-mile zip up the A39 to Wells.

11 Wells

England's smallest city contains one of the country's grandest medieval buildings: **Wells Cathedral** *(wellscathedral.org.uk)*, a gargantuan Gothic confection built between 1175 and 1490. Highlights include a West Front decorated with more than 300 carved figures, and some fine scissor arches.

In surrounding Cathedral Close, hunt out the 14th-century cobbled Vicar's Close, then make for the nearby **Bishop's Palace** *(bishopspalace.org.uk)*, a moat-ringed, 13th-century manor house with state rooms, a ruined great hall and delightful gardens, complete with natural springs.

THE DRIVE: Peeling out of town on the A371, it's a mere 3 miles to Wookey Hole.

12 Wookey Hole

Yes, the **Wookey Hole** *(wookey.co.uk)* limestone caverns are incredibly touristy (the local legend of a witch inhabiting them is played for all it's worth), but the caves themselves are rightly famous for striking stalagmites and stalactites, one of which is the infamous witch herself, purportedly turned to stone by a local priest.

THE DRIVE: Continue northwest for 8 miles through a string of villages on the A371, which skirts the Mendip Hills on the right (you'll be up there later). Once in Cheddar, continue through the village, following signs to Cheddar Gorge.

13 Cheddar Gorge

Pick any one of the parking spots in **Cheddar Gorge** *(cheddargorge.co.uk)*, and then get out and explore. Carved out by glacial meltwater during the last Ice Age, these limestone cliffs form England's deepest natural canyon, in places towering 138m above the twisting B3135. Of the gorge's caves, Cox's Cave and Gough's Cave are the easiest to reach, and are decorated with impressive stalactites and stalagmites.

The 274-step staircase known as Jacob's Ladder leads to a spectacular viewpoint over the gorge and a 3-mile clifftop trail. Day tickets cover Jacob's Ladder and entry to the caves.

THE DRIVE: The short drive up the gorge itself is along a twisting, sometimes single-track road that cuts through towering rock formations. At the top, the B3135 becomes a rolling, field-framed route across the roof of the Mendip plateau. Next, a series of A roads cut down from the hills and on to Bath, 23 miles from Cheddar Gorge.

14 Bath

Home to some of Britain's grandest Georgian architecture, Bath is also one of the nation's most beautiful cities. On the southern fringes sits 18th-century **Prior Park** *(nationaltrust.org.uk)*. Partly designed by landscape architect Capability Brown, the grounds of this exquisite 18th-century estate feature cascading lakes and a graceful Palladian bridge, one of only four such structures in the world (look out for the period graffiti, some of which dates back to the 1800s). Of the estate's lovely pathways, the pick is the Bath Skyline, a 6-mile circular trail offering truly inspirational views.

Get back in the car for the 1-mile cruise to Bath itself. Here, a walk around the streets is richly rewarded. The **Museum of Bath Architecture** *(museumofbath architecture.org.uk)* was closed for repairs at the time of writing; check the website for updates and details of ongoing events.

Bath is also famously a location featured in Jane Austen's novels, including *Persuasion* and *Northanger Abbey*. The writer was a city resident for five years and remained a regular visitor and keen student of the city's social scene. In the **Jane Austen Centre** *(janeausten.co.uk)*, guides in Regency costumes regale you with Austenesque tales as you tour memorabilia relating to her life in Bath.

BATH'S HISTORY

Legend has it King Bladud, a Trojan refugee and father of King Lear, founded Bath some 2800 years ago when Lear was cured of leprosy by a dip in the muddy waters, after noticing his pigs contracted no skin diseases after being dipped. The Romans established the town of Aquae Sulis in 44 CE and built the extensive Roman Baths complex and a temple to the goddess Sulis-Minerva.

Long after the Romans decamped, the Anglo-Saxons arrived, and a monastery was founded on the site of the present Bath Abbey. Throughout the Middle Ages, Bath was an ecclesiastical centre and a wool-trading town, but it wasn't until the early 18th century that Ralph Allen and the celebrated dandy Richard 'Beau' Nash made Bath the centre of fashionable society. Allen developed the quarries at Coombe Down, constructed Prior Park and employed the two John Woods (father and son) to create Bath's signature buildings.

In WWII Bath was hit by the Luftwaffe during the so-called Baedeker raids, which targeted historic cities in an effort to sap British morale. Several houses on the Royal Crescent and the Circus were badly damaged, and the city's Assembly Rooms were gutted by fire, though all have since been restored.

In 1987 Bath became the only city in Britain to be declared a UNESCO World Heritage Site in its entirety.

Prior Park

FRANCESCO BONINO/ALAMY

WHY I LOVE THIS TRIP

BELINDA DIXON, WRITER

For me, this trip is a classic because it delivers truly memorable moments. Encountering mighty Stonehenge is an experience you never forget; the beauty of the cathedrals also lingers in the mind. The drives are special too, taking in high plateaux, ancient villages, stylish cities and chalk plains. It's a trip into the heart of England's heritage, which reveals how that history still echoes today.

12

SOUTHWEST ENGLAND

★ BEST FOR

SURFING

The broad sandy beach at picture-postcard pretty Croyde.

NORTH DEVON & EXMOOR

DURATION: 3–4 DAYS

DISTANCE: 121 MILES / 195KM

GREAT FOR: FAMILIES, OUTDOORS

BEST TIME TO GO: SPRING BRINGS WILDFLOWERS; SUMMER, WARMER SEAS; AUTUMN, BATTLING STAGS.

Dunster Castle

It's the kind of road trip that cars were made for. From quaint villages you'll climb to open moorland topped by an overarching sky. Here, single-track roads wind between free-roaming ponies; you might even spot wild deer. Motor down to picturesque quays, burn your brakes on white-knuckle descents, then bump along toll roads. Coal-black cliffs fill your windscreen en route to surfing beaches and swimming coves. It's an unforgettable drive.

LINK YOUR TRIP

15 Coastal Cornwall
From Clovelly, head 17 miles southwest to Bude to link up with a charismatic, spray-dashed drive around the end of England.

11 Winchester, Glastonbury & Bath
A history-rich tour of the west's best big-name cultural sights. Pick it up 40 miles east of Dunster at Glastonbury.

01 Dunster

The pretty town of **Dunster** is a tempting tangle of cobbled streets and bubbling brooks. It's presided over by rose-stone, 13th-century **Dunster Castle** *(nationaltrust.org.uk)*; check whether you need to pre-book a visit. The colourful terraced gardens have views across Exmoor's shores and lead to an 18th-century watermill, which still has most of its original working mechanisms. A short walk leads to picturesque **St George's Church**; a 16th-century dovecote sits just behind it.

THE DRIVE: Motoring 15 miles south along the A396, a steep wooded ridge rises to the west. But on this stretch you're not driving on the higher moor; that comes later. Instead, it's a rolling route through tree-framed valleys.

02 Dulverton

Dulverton is the definition of an Exmoor market town.

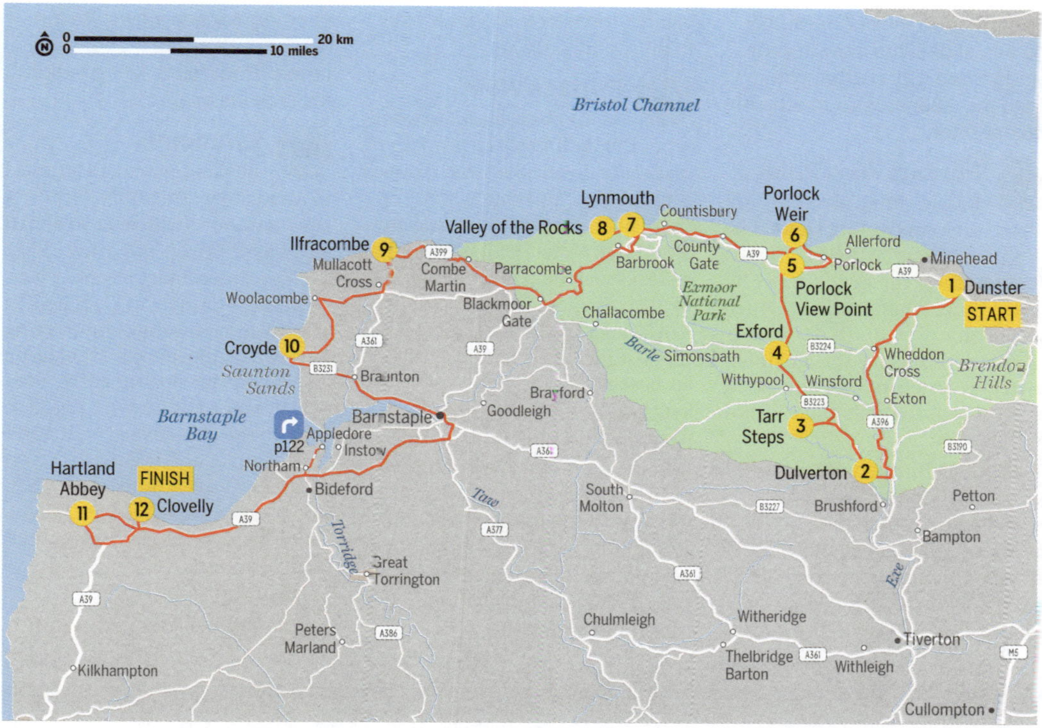

BILLY STOCK/SHUTTERSTOCK

Sitting at the base of the Barle Valley, it's home to a collection of independent shops selling fishing tackle, antiques and crafts. Pick up visitor information in Exmoor House at the **Dulverton National Park Centre** *(exmoor-nationalpark.gov.uk)*.

South of town, **Carnarvon Stores** *(carnarvonstores.co.uk)* stocks local picnic fare.

THE DRIVE: From the centre of town, take the B3223 north towards Exford (also signposted Tarr Steps). Soon woods clear and, after rattling across a couple of cattle grids, you're onto the open, undulating moor. Five miles out of Dulverton, follow signs to Tarr Steps, a mile away down steep, winding lanes. Park at the car park, continuing 450m on foot.

03 Tarr Steps

Exmoor's most famous landmark, **Tarr Steps** is an ancient stone clapper bridge shaded by gnarled old trees. Its huge slabs are propped up on stone columns embedded in the River Barle. Local folklore (which declares it was used by the Devil for sunbathing) aside, it first pops into the historical record in the 1600s, and had to be rebuilt after 21st-century floods.

A few paces away, **Tarr Farm** *(tarrfarm.co.uk)* is a charming inn that dishes up snacks and meals that feature local fish and game.

THE DRIVE: Back up the hill, peel left, following signs for Exford. It's a 7-mile roof-of-the-moor meander, with swathes of honey-brown bracken unfolding on either side. Cross the bridge by the Exmoor White Horse Inn, parking beside the village green.

04 Exford

There's not much to Exford but what there is defines quaint. This tiny village clusters around a pleasant muddle of cottages and slate-roofed houses.

Time then to stroll beside the rushing River Exe and sip a drink on the terrace of the waterfront pub.

THE DRIVE: Next, a 6-mile leg. Head up the hill with the village green to your left, signposted Porlock. It's another steep climb (you'll feel your ears pop) that's rewarded with a prolonged burst of open moor. Eventually, the sea slides into view in your windscreen. Soon after, you meet the A39; cross it to stop in the car park.

05 Porlock View Point

Rarely, surely, has a car park offered such captivating views. The sweep of beach far below frames **Porlock Bay**; the headland at its eastern (right-hand) edge is Hurlstone Point.

The shoreline on the horizon, dotted with cliffs and toy-sized structures, is actually the coast of South Wales.

THE DRIVE: Turn left at the carpark entrance for a second-gear descent down the infamous, 25% gradient Porlock Hill; expect hairpin bends, escape lanes and 'try your brakes' signs. Once in Porlock village, turn left to Porlock Weir. In all, a 4-mile drive.

06 Porlock Weir

At the charismatic breakwater of **Porlock Weir** *(porlockweir.co)*, an arching pebble beach frames a pint-sized harbour – watching small boats navigate their way in is absorbing. A short walkway stretches beside the water and over the lock to a tiny terrace of cottages clinging to a slender spit of sea-framed land. A pub, cafes, and gift and art shops sit nearby.

THE DRIVE: Take the lane between the Ship Inn and the Locanda On The Weir hotel. It cuts sharply right, signposted Worthy. At the toll gate pay £3. A bouncing road climbs through woods; sea glimpses emerge below. The A39 rolls along a moorland plateau to spectacular sea views. As the road plunges, signs speak volumes: 'Rockfalls', '12% gradient'. It's 12 miles in all.

07 Lynmouth

Bustling Lynmouth is tucked in amid steep, tree-lined slopes. A busy harbour leads west to a **cliff railway** *(cliffrailwaylynton.co.uk)*.

This extraordinary piece of water-powered engineering opened in 1890 water-powered engineering sees two connected cars shuttle up and down the sloping cliffs. They deliver you to hill-town Lynton to head to the churchyard of St Mary the Virgin (Church Hill) for views of precipitous Countisbury Hill (the one you've just driven down).

Hop back on the cliff railway and back to your car.

THE DRIVE: Now, there's a 2-mile drive. From Lynmouth

Porlock Weir

IAN WOOLCOCK/SHUTTERSTOCK

seafront take the right fork up the hill for another set of 25% gradient switchbacks. Ignore the turn for Simonsbath and pick up the Valley of the Rocks signs. Soon you're heading into a deep, broad dip, framed by towering rocks.

08 Valley of the Rocks

Welcome to a perfect pit stop for a dramatic stroll. The awesome geology in the shoreside **Valley of the Rocks** includes formations dubbed the Devil's Cheesewring and Ragged Jack. Look out, too, for feral goats wandering the tracks.

THE DRIVE: Head back into Lynton, picking up signs to Ilfracombe, initially along a climbing A39 (signposted Barnstaple). At Blackmoor Gate, turn right onto the A399, heading down Combe Martin's long High St, to emerge at Ilfracombe. It's 20 miles in all.

09 Ilfracombe

In Ilfracombe, steep headlands plummet down to pint-sized beaches and paths cling to sheer cliffs. At the harbour mouth, Damien Hirst's towering, 20m-high 2012 statue, ***Verity*** (The Pier), depicts a naked pregnant woman holding aloft a sword. On the seaward side her skin is peeled back, revealing muscles and foetus. Stop here for a striking photo opportunity.

On the other side of the harbour, beside the Royal National Lifeboat Institution (RNLI) lifeboat house, hunt out the **S&P** *(sandpfish.co.uk)* cafe. Opt for some cockles or go all out for a bumper seafood platter.

THE DRIVE: Take the A361 south. At Mullacott Cross, ignore the satnav and take the B3343 down into Woolacombe. At the shore, turn left to follow the coast along a web of unclassified lanes, then

TOM MEAKER/SHUTTERSTOCK

Valley of the Rocks

DON'T MISS

The strange rock shapes of the Valley of the Rocks — watch out for feral goats.

pick up signs for Croyde. It's a 10-mile leg in all.

10 Croyde

The cheerful, chilled village of Croyde is Devon's surf central. Thatched roofs peep out over racks of wetsuits and cool types in board shorts sip beer beside 17th-century inns. **Ralph's** *(facebook.com/ralphssurfshop)* hires out surf equipment. Lessons are provided by **Surf South West** *(surfsouthwest.com)* and **Surfing Croyde Bay** *(surfingcroydebay.co.uk)*. The sandy beach is 10 minutes' walk from the village centre.

THE DRIVE: Time to cover some miles – 33 to be exact. The B3231 winds west, revealing the 3-mile sweep of Saunton Sands. After Barnstaple, the A39 (aka the 'Atlantic Hwy') glides southwest. After Higher Clovelly the B3248 branches off to Hartland village; your next stop is 1.5 miles further on.

11 Hartland Abbey

History seems to flow from the walls of enchanting **Hartland Abbey** *(hartlandabbey.com)*. Built in the 12th century, it was a monastery until Henry VIII grabbed it in the Dissolution and gave it to the sergeant of his wine cellar. His descendants, the Stucley family still live in the abbey today. It's encircled by a fernery, walled garden, camellia garden and woodland walks.

THE DRIVE: A 6.5-mile leg, largely retracing your route to Higher Clovelly. From there pick up signs to Clovelly village.

12 Clovelly

Picture-postcard-pretty **Clovelly** *(clovelly.co.uk)* is privately owned, so park up beside the hilltop visitor centre and pay your admission.

Then walk down cobbled streets so steep cars can't cope – supplies are brought in by sledge; spot these big bread baskets on runners leaning outside homes. Look out for the former home of Charles Kingsley, author of the children's classic *The Water Babies*, the atmospheric fisher's cottage and the twin chapels.

DETOUR

Northam Burrows
Start: 12 Clovelly

A detour of just 3 miles off the A39 between Barnstaple and Clovelly leads to a vast, wildlife-rich expanse. The 253-hectare **Northam Burrows** *(torridge.gov.uk/northamburrows)* reserve encompasses grassy plains, dunes, salt marshes, a sandy shore, and grazing sheep and horses. It's home to wheat-ear, linnet, stonechat, curlew and little egret. A pebble ridge sits between the burrows and 2-mile-long Westward Ho! beach, forming a natural sea defence.

INTERESTING PLACES TO STAY AND EAT

This region of England is awash with picturesque and historic places to stay or have a meal.

With its deer antlers, hunting prints and big wood-burning stove, multi-award-winning **Woods** *(woodsdulverton.co.uk)* in Dulverton is Exmoor to its core. No surprise then to find menus with full-bodied ingredients: expect confit leg of guinea fowl, slow-roast lamb shoulder, and asparagus-and-wild-garlic risotto. The clutch of tables outside and in the flower-framed courtyard garden are first-come, first-served.

The **Ancient Mariner** *(bathhotellynmouth.co.uk)* brings a burst of shipwreck chic to Lynmouth, thanks to a copper bar top, curved ship's decking, covered outdoor seating and memorabilia including a full-scale torpedo. Drink it all in while tucking into a stacked-high Mariner Burger, complete with Exmoor ale and black-treacle-braised brisket, onion jam and blue-cheese mousse.

In the 1600s, **Millstream Cottage** *(facebook.com/millstreamcottagedunster)* was Dunster's workhouse. Now it's a sweet-as-pie guesthouse with country-cottage-style rooms featuring beams, pine doors and stone fireplaces. Breakfast treats include porridge, toast with Exmoor jams, and smoked haddock and poached eggs.

Clovelly

ROLF E. STAERK/SHUTTERSTOCK

CAPTURE EVERY MOMENT

This picturesque drive has plenty of breathtaking views and impressive buildings, so you'll want to keep pulling over to take photos. Make sure your camera or phone has plenty of battery power – you can always keep it charged up in the car – so you can capture every moment.

13

★ BEST FOR

DISCOVERIES

Fossil hunting in Lyme Regis.

SOUTHWEST ENGLAND

JURASSIC COAST

DURATION: 7 DAYS

DISTANCE: 90 MILES / 145KM

GREAT FOR: FAMILIES, HISTORY

BEST TIME TO GO: SPRING AND AUTUMN ARE COOLER AND LESS CROWDED TIMES TO VISIT.

Guildhall, Poole

On this road trip to remember, the route ribbons along a World Heritage–listed shore. Expect gorgeous bays, iconic castles and a windscreen full of views. One of the southwest's best drives, this route rolls up chalk ridges, through thatched villages and along sea-fringed roads. It takes in vast beaches, unforgettable swimming spots, a soaring rock arch and fossils galore. History is everywhere, from fairy-tale castles to an art-packed quarry.

LINK YOUR TRIP

11 Winchester, Glastonbury & Bath
Stonehenge, soaring cathedrals and the sumptuous city of Bath. Pick it up at Sherborne, 27 miles north of Weymouth.

14 South Devon
Some 50 miles southwest of this trip's end, Torquay leads to a charming tour of historic ports, an eco-town, a vineyard and Agatha Christie's home.

01 Poole

The attractive historic buildings in the old port of Poole include the Tudor **King Charles pub** on Thames St, the cream **Old Harbour Office** (1820s) next door and the impressive red-brick **Custom House** (1813) opposite. A few metres away, **Poole Museum** *(poolemuseum.org.uk)* is a beautifully restored 15th-century warehouse housing a 2300-year-old, 10m-long, 14-tonne Iron Age logboat dredged up from Poole Harbour. From Poole Quay, boats shuttle to the wooded nature reserve of **Brownsea Island** *(nationaltrust.org.uk)* which is just offshore.

THE DRIVE: Pick up signs for the A350 to Dorchester/Blandford, then peel off onto the A351 to Wareham for a 10-mile drive.

DOUBLELEE/SHUTTERSTOCK

02 Wareham

The Saxons built sturdy Wareham in the 10th century, and their legacy lingers in surviving remnants of the market town's defensive walls – explore them on the 45-minute Walls Walk, or make a beeline for one section: the 11th-century **St Martin's on the Walls church** at the top of North St. It features a 12th-century fresco and a marble effigy of TE Lawrence (aka *Lawrence of Arabia*), who lived locally.

THE DRIVE: Continue south on the A351, a tree-lined but unremarkable drive. Unremarkable, that is, until 4 miles on, when the startling, shattered hilltop ruins of mighty Corfe Castle leap into view.

03 Corfe Castle

From the National Trust car park, walk two minutes to **Corfe Castle** *(nationaltrust.org.uk)* itself. Once home to Sir John Bankes, Charles I's right-hand man, the castle was besieged by Cromwellian forces in the English Civil War. In 1646 the plucky Lady Bankes directed a six-week defence, and the castle fell only after being betrayed from within. The Roundheads then gunpowdered Corfe Castle apart; turrets and soaring walls still sheer off at precarious angles – the splayed-out gatehouse looks like it's just been blown up.

THE DRIVE: Put Corfe Castle in your rear-view mirror, heading back towards Wareham then onto the B3070 to East Lulworth (some 10 miles). Rattle over the cattle grid and into Lulworth Castle's grounds.

04 Lulworth Castle

Creamy, dreamy **Lulworth Castle** *(lulworth.com)* looks more like a French château than a traditional English castle; it was built in 1608 as a hunting lodge, and has survived extravagant owners, extensive remodelling and a fire in 1929. Tour the reconstructed kitchen and cellars; if the tower has reopened, take in sweeping coastal views.

THE DRIVE: Turn right for a 3-mile dawdle along rural roads, past a military tank camp and through West Lulworth, to the main visitor centre car park at Lulworth Cove.

05 Lulworth Cove

At the village of **Lulworth Cove**, a pleasing jumble of thatched cottages and fishing gear leads down to the eponymous bay – a perfect, narrow-mouthed crescent of white cliffs. After admiring the views, pop into the **visitor centre** *(lulworth.com)* to learn how rock types and erosion have shaped this remarkable shore. Then walk two minutes southeast to see geology in action at Lulworth Crumple, where layers of rock form dramatically zigzagging folds.

THE DRIVE: From the visitor centre, exit the roundabout onto the B3070. Shortly after, turn left onto Church Road. Driving uphill, turn left again at the brown signs to Durdle Door – it's a steep 1-mile climb beside hummocky hills. Head into the campsite; your Lulworth Cove parking ticket is valid at either of the two car parks furthest from the shore.

06 Durdle Door

The walk from the car park that brings the **Durdle Door** *(lulworth.com)*, near Lulworth Cove, into view is well worth the effort. This immense, sea-fringed, 150-million-year-old Portland stone arch was created by a combination of massive earth movements and erosion. Today it's framed by shimmering bays; bring a swimsuit and head down the hundreds of steps for an unforgettable dip.

The beaches and car park here can get busy; in summer, visit early in the day.

THE DRIVE: Next comes an 8-mile drive. Head up the B3070/3071 to Wool. After Wool train station turn right, across the tracks, to pick up signs featuring the cute, long-tailed residents of your next stop: Monkey World.

07 Monkey World

As attractions go, **Monkey World** *(monkeyworld.org)* overflows with the 'aah' factor. The sanctuary's 26 hectares are home to bounding, noisy colonies of chimpanzees, orang-utans, gibbons, marmosets and some ridiculously cute ring-tailed lemurs. Most have been rescued from primate smuggling rings, circuses, laboratories, working on beaches or being mistreated as pets.

THE DRIVE: Head back through Wool, then join the A352/353 for the 15-mile cruise through rolling hills southwest to Weymouth. There, pass the reed-filled lagoons of the bird reserve and ranks of B&Bs to park up on the seafront or beside the waterfront Pavilion theatre.

08 Weymouth

The appealingly kitsch-rich seaside resort of **Weymouth** centres on its historic harbour and 3-mile beach, where you can rent a deckchair and soak in the nostalgic charm along its fine sandy shore. A grid of sweet streets leads to an old harbour packed with boats. The cannon-studded defences of 19th-century **Nothe Fort** *(nothefort.org.uk)* sit nearby.

Then head out to **Sandworld** *(sandworld.co.uk)* to see lifelike sand sculptures of fairy-tale castles, sly dragons and scenes from blockbuster films.

THE DRIVE: Join the A354 south to Portland. The long straight road onto the isle is an exhilarating stretch, sweeping between a vast harbour and a high-ridged pebble beach. The twisting climb through Chiswell on the Fortuneswell road reveals Portland's unique character: remote, rugged, sometimes bleak, but beautiful. At the hill's crest follow the signs to Tout Quarry Park (7 miles in all).

FIRING RANGES

The picturesque Purbeck Hills are also tank live-firing ranges: road signs warn: 'Sudden Gunfire'. Our route avoids restricted areas, but the ranges are sometimes accessible; see *gov.uk/government/publications/lulworth-access-times*. A southerly Corfe Castle to East Lulworth route (offering sea glimpses and tank remnants) is often open holidays and weekends; call 01929404714 to check.

Durdle Door

MARK GODDEN/SHUTTERSTOCK

PHOTO OPPORTUNITY

The massive 150-million-year-old Durdle Door stone arch.

09 Tout Quarry

Portland's white limestone has been quarried for centuries and features in some of the world's finest buildings, such as the British Museum and St Paul's Cathedral in London. The disused workings at **Tout Quarry Sculpture Park & Nature Reserve** *(learningstone.org)*, near Fortuneswell, now house more than 60 sculptures carved into the rock in situ. It results in a fascinating combination of raw materials, the detritus of the quarrying process and the beauty of chiselled works. Stroll to the cliffs at the quarry's edge for 180-degree views down to the awe-inspiring sweep of Chesil Beach.

THE DRIVE: Retrace your route down off the plateau (passengers can delight in drinking in the remarkable views) and back along the thin road to the mainland. Near the end, head left into the Chesil Beach car park; in total, it's a mere 3 miles away.

10 Chesil Beach

One of Britain's most breathtaking beaches, Chesil is 18 miles long, 15m high and moving inland at the rate of 5m a century.

The stones on this mind-boggling, 100-million-tonne pebble ridge range from pea-sized in the west to hand-sized here in the east. The **Wild Chesil Centre** *(dorsetwildlifetrust.org.uk)* details its ecosystem and geology.

From the car park, it is an energy-sapping hike up sliding pebbles to the constant surge and rattle of waves on stones and dazzling views of the sea, with the thin pebble line and the expanse of the Fleet Lagoon behind.

THE DRIVE: Time to drive the road you saw from Portland: a 9-mile sweep along the B3157, rolling beside undulating fields and hills. In the midst of the thatched-cottage-rich village of Abbotsbury, turn sharp left for the Swannery.

11 Abbotsbury Swannery

Every May some 600 free-flying mute swans choose to nest at **Abbotsbury Swannery** *(abbotsburyswannery.co.uk)*, which shelters in the Fleet Lagoon. Wandering the network of trails winding between the swans' nests is an awe-inspiring experience that's punctuated by

Abbotsbury Swannery

GARTLAND/SHUTTERSTOCK

occasional territorial displays (including stand-up flapping), ensuring that even the liveliest children are stilled.

THE DRIVE: Continue through Abbotsbury for another glorious, second-gear climb, pausing at the lay-bys for cracking views back onto Chesil Beach. Next, a ridgetop roller-coaster of a road, framed by green fields and an improbably wide bay. Some 20 miles later you descend into Lyme Regis.

12 Lyme Regis

Beach-framed and quaint, Lyme Regis is one of Dorset's most delightful towns. It's also fantastically fossiliferous – rock-hard relics of the past pop out repeatedly from the surrounding cliffs, exposed by the landslides of a retreating shore.

Delve into that rich heritage at **Lyme Regis Museum** *(lymeregismuseum.co.uk)*. On the site of the former home and fossil shop of Mary Anning, the museum also relates how local teenager Anning found the first full ichthyosaur skeleton near Lyme Regis in 1811–12, propelling the town onto the world stage, and pioneering the science of modern-day palaeontology.

To find your own fossils, go on a guided walk run by the museum or the nearby **Charmouth Heritage Coast Centre** *(charmouth.org)*. During the season, the centre shows a catch and release tank to demonstrate the assorted marine life of Lyme Bay rockpools. Entry to the centre is free, with donations welcomed.

DORSET DRONE PHOTOGRAPHY / SHUTTERSTOCK

Chesil Beach

SUPER PLACES TO STAY AND EAT

For quirky stays and to eat like a local, these are our top tips:

To sample seafood while drinking in Chesil Beach's fine views, **Crab House Cafe** *(crabhousecafe.co.uk)* is where locals head on hot summer days, to sit beside Fleet Lagoon in beach-shack-chic, tucking into fresh-as-it-gets seafood. Fish is enlivened by chilli, curry, lemon and herbs, crab comes spicy Chinese-style or whole for you to crack, and the oysters are served with either pesto and parmesan or bacon and cream.

Bishops Cottage *(bishopscottage.com)* of Lulworth has an idyllic setting, pared-down designs, top-notch linen and pamper-yourself toiletries, combining to make this a memorable place to stay, especially if you opt for a room with Lulworth Cove views. Or just lounge beside the pool, which also overlooks that circle of bay.

In Lyme Regis, the **Alexandra** *(hotelalexandra.co.uk)* was built in 1735 for the Dowager Countess Poulett and became a hotel in 1901. Glorious views of Lyme Bay extend from its best bedrooms but back-facing ones are charming, too. In the orangery, its Ammonite Restaurant showcases West Country produce, and tiered afternoon teas with Dorset clotted cream are a treat.

14

★ BEST FOR

FAMILIES

Bodyboarding at Bantham Beach.

SOUTHWEST ENGLAND

SOUTH DEVON

DURATION: 4 DAYS

DISTANCE: 89 MILES / 143KM

GREAT FOR: HISTORY, NATURE, BEACHES

BEST TIME TO GO: EARLY SUMMER (JUNE OR JULY) BEFORE THE BEACHES GET TOO BUSY.

Babbacombe Cliff Railway

Green, gentle and gorgeous, the coastline of south Devon is made for a road trip. From old seaside villages and thatched cottages to quaint harbours and riverside towns, south Devon serves up the essence of rural, coastal England. It's a wonderful landscape to drive through – a patchwork of open fields, old farms, pebble beaches, art-deco swimming spots and sudden flashes of bright blue sea. Pack a picnic, take your time and revel in the drive.

LINK YOUR TRIP

13 Jurassic Coast
More awesome coastal adventures await further to the east – it's 53 miles from Torquay to Lyme Regis.

15 Coastal Cornwall
From Plymouth, it's just a quick jaunt across the Tamar Bridge into Cornwall: head 45 miles north to reach Bude.

01 Torquay

Sometimes dubbed the heart of the English Riviera, this classic seaside resort is the perfect place to begin a south Devon tour. With its palm trees and russet-red cliffs, there's a dash of elegance to Torquay's seafront, though windbreakers and buckets and spades define most of the town's 20-odd beaches.

The best thing to do is just embrace it: take a trip on Babbacombe's 1926-opened funicular **railway** *(babbacombecliffrailway.co.uk)*, soak up the kitsch miniatures of the **Babbacombe Model Village** *(model-village.co.uk)* and take a sunset stroll along Paignton Pier, candy floss in hand.

THE DRIVE: The easiest route is just to follow the main coast road around the bay to Paignton and Brixham (partly the A379); it's a pleasant 9-mile drive, though you'll inevitably run into traffic jams in summertime.

PETER TITMUSS/SHUTTERSTOCK

02 Brixham

This horseshoe-shaped harbour is as salty and shipshape as it gets. The **Fish Market** *(brixhamfishmarket.co.uk)* sells more than £77 million of fish a year, making it England's biggest by value of fish sold.

A replica of Francis Drake's globe-trotting ship, the **Golden Hind** *(goldenhind.co.uk)*, is moored along the historic harbour, while gorgeous art-deco, open-air **Shoalstone Pool** *(shoalstonepool.com)* is built into natural rock to the east of the breakwater.

THE DRIVE: Follow signs out of Brixham pointing you towards Dartmouth. Veer left off Slappers Hill onto Broad Road following the brown tourist signs for Coleton Fishacre (initially, it'll also be signed Lower Ferry). It's 4.5 miles in all.

03 Coleton Fishacre

Echoes of the Jazz Age still ring through the beguiling art-deco estate of **Coleton Fishacre** *(nationaltrust.org.uk)*.

The croquet terrace leads to deeply shelved subtropical gardens and suddenly revealed vistas of the sea. Pop inside the house as its interior is sublime – you'll see original Lalique tulip uplighters, comic bathroom tiles and a stunning saloon.

THE DRIVE: Backtrack along the road to take the first sign to Kingswear on the B3205 (2 miles). This will take you down to the Dartmouth–Kingswear Lower Ferry (£7.50), the latest iteration of a service that's been running since the 14th century.

04 Dartmouth

South Devon isn't short on photogenic seaports, but Dartmouth still dazzles. Its boat-filled estuary and quaint 17th- and 18th-century architecture are framed by green hills and the bright-blue waters of the River Dart. It's a place to explore at leisure – don't miss the half-timbered houses of South Embankment, Fairfax Pl and Duke St, and the crooked buildings of the **Butterwalk**.

Book ahead for a **river cruise** *(greenwayferry.co.uk)* to **Greenway** *(nationaltrust.org.uk)* where

SOUTH DEVON SOUTHWEST ENGLAND

writer Agatha Christie dreamt up some of her best-loved tales of murder.

THE DRIVE: The next stage of the drive, along the coastal A379 past shingly beaches and green fields, offers glorious views. It's easy to navigate as far as the Slapton Ley nature reserve (10 miles away) and Torcross, but it's very easy to get lost along the minor roads leading south to Hallsands, Beesands and Start Point. Bring a decent road map. It's 15 miles altogether.

DETOUR

Totnes

Start: 04 Dartmouth

The counterculture town of Totnes has a fine **castle** *(english-heritage.org.uk)* and is awash with Tudor architecture and interesting shops, but there are two other irresistible reasons to visit: a meal at the nearby **Riverford Field Kitchen** *(fieldkitchen.riverford.co.uk)*, a farm that hosts lavish feasts of locally grown produce; and the 324-hectare **Dartington Estate** *(dartington.org)* on the outskirts of town, which has a deer park, walking trails and riverbanks from which you can kayak and swim. Totnes is 15 miles' drive northwest from Dartmouth.

05 Start Bay

Surging down the coast towards Start Point, the first essential stop is **Slapton Sands** (a pebble ridge, despite the name). Rehearsals here for the D-Day landings in 1944 went disastrously wrong when an attack by German E-boats resulted in more than 800 Allied deaths. A Sherman tank stands as a memorial at the southern end of the peaceful **Slapton Ley** nature reserve.

Further south, the village of **Beesands** and the ruined village of

Slapton Sands, with Slapton Ley (background)

PHOTO OPPORTUNITY

A Sherman tank selfie at Slapton Ley.

GLEN BERLIN/SHUTTERSTOCK

Hallsands make good stops, but the best views lie in wait at the end of the bay's road at **Start Point** *(startpointdevon.co.uk)*, where a photogenic lighthouse bookends a slender ridge.

THE DRIVE: Backtrack along the backroads to the A379, then turn left towards Kingsbridge (11 miles from Start Point). From here it's pleasant driving through fields and farmland onto the A381 to Salcombe (a further 7 miles).

06 Kingsbridge & Salcombe

Though they're on the same river estuary, the neighbouring towns of Kingsbridge and Salcombe feel very different.

Kingsbridge has the vibe of a sleepy country town, with weekly markets and lots of independent shops. A few miles further south, Salcombe is an altogether more chi-chi affair: a muddle of winding lanes, old cottages and sandy coves. Salcombe's South Sands beach is the perfect place for a swim. Either hop on the **South Sands Ferry** *(southsandsferry.co.uk)* or walk up Fore St, then continue south for 2 miles, sticking to the waterfront. Or hire a sit-on-top **kayak** *(salcombe watersports.com)* and explore the estuary. Round the day off with dinner at the **Crab Shed** *(crab shed.com)* seafood shack.

THE DRIVE: Follow the A381 back the way you came, but don't turn off to Kingsbridge; stay on the A381 (signposted to Plymouth/Modbury A379) and follow it till you see a roundabout with a left turn to Bantham Beach (8 miles in total).

DARTMOUTH–KINGSWEAR FERRIES

There are two car ferries that shuttle across the River Dart. The **Lower Ferry** *(southhams.gov.uk)* is a floating platform that's pulled and pushed along by a tug boat; it runs from Kingswear, right into Dartmouth's town centre. The **Higher Ferry** *(dkfb.co.uk)* chugs across the river on Dartmouth's northern edge, avoiding the centre of town.

07 Bantham

It has stiff competition, but some say that at low tide the beach at Bantham might just be Devon's best. Backed by dunes, ringed by golden sand and with stunning views across the water to Burgh Island, it's certainly a beauty – and perfect picnic territory. It also happens to have the best surf on the south Devon coast, and thanks to **Bantham Surfing Academy** *(banthamsurfingacademy.co.uk)*, it's a good place to hire kit and learn the basics.

THE DRIVE: Return to the roundabout and turn left onto the A379, signposted to Aveton Gifford. Follow this road through the countryside until you see the left turn onto the B3392 to Bigbury. It's a gorgeous drive down to the sea from here. It's 12 miles in all.

08 Bigbury-on-Sea

At Bigbury-on-Sea elegant townhouses line the hills down to a sandy beach that is expansive at low tide. From here, you can hop across to **Burgh Island** *(burghisland.com)*, a 10-hectare outcrop of rock that's home to a circular footpath and a stunning art-deco hotel. At low tide you can walk across to the island, but it's more fun at high tide, when you have to catch the sea-tractor, with its passenger platform perched 2m above the waves.

THE DRIVE: Return to the A379 and follow signs to Plymouth, which is 19 miles away through the countryside.

09 Plymouth

Some knock Plymouth's post-Blitz rebuild, but the port city has much to tempt visitors.

Displays at the **Box** *(thebox plymouth.com)*, a shimmering, £46-million museum, include a series of 14 massive, suspended ships' figureheads.

In the historic Barbican area wonky buildings and cobbled lanes surround the Mayflower Steps, which mark the departure of the Pilgrim Fathers to North America. Stroll up to the café-dotted grassy headland called the Hoe to look out over a beautiful natural harbour. Don't miss a bracing dip in **Tinside Lido** *(www.tinsidelido.co.uk)*, an open-air salt-water pool set into the shore. Built in 1935 in curving art-deco style, it's a spectacular spot for a swim.

15

SOUTHWEST ENGLAND

COASTAL CORNWALL

DURATION: 10 DAYS

DISTANCE: 211 MILES / 340KM

GREAT FOR: HISTORY, FAMILIES

BEST TIME TO GO: NOVEMBER TO APRIL, BUT TRY TO AVOID SCHOOL HOLIDAYS, CHRISTMAS AND EASTER.

There can be few corners of Britain where scenery packs such a heart-in-the-mouth, jaw-on-the-floor punch as Cornwall. This unforgettable adventure travels right the way round Britain's most westerly county: top-to-bottom, coast-to-coast. Along the way, you'll encounter sparkling beaches, surf bays and seaside ports galore, as well as curiosities such as a clifftop theatre and a trio of space-age biomes. It's wild and wonderful out west.

LINK YOUR TRIP

12 North Devon & Exmoor
Take in under-explored Exmoor and its famous starry skies. From Clovelly, it's an 18-mile hop across the Cornish border to Bude.

14 South Devon
From the stark drama of Cornwall to the gentler countryside of Devon – it's a 38-mile drive from Fowey to Plymouth.

01 Bude

This breezy sea town makes a great place to start your cruise around Cornwall – or Kernow, as it's known in the Cornish language. The town is surrounded by beaches: the family favourite is Summerleaze, right in the centre of town. If you don't feel up to tackling the waves, you can take a dip in the bracing waters of **Bude Sea Pool** *(budeseapool.org)*. This saltwater lido was built into an existing rock bowl back in the 1930s. It means you can swim in the sea but are sheltered from its force.

More beaches can be found north and south of town, ranging from tiny coves to impressive sweeps such as Crackington Haven, where rock shelves and pebbly sand are bordered by black cliffs, and Widemouth Bay, which has hectares of sand at low tide, plenty of facilities, good swimming and lifeguards in the summer. Many visitors never quite travel this far north, so the

UCG/GETTY IMAGES

★ BEST FOR

SWIMMING

Sheltered sea swimming in saltwater lido Bude Sea Pool.

Bude Sea Pool

Bude beaches are often a little quieter than their better-known counterparts along the coast.

THE DRIVE: Head south, initially on the A39 (sometimes called the Atlantic Hwy on road signs). Soon you cut right, onto the B3263, following signs to Boscastle, a pretty village with an even prettier harbour. From there the road tracks the coast all the way to Tintagel, a distance of 20 miles.

02 Tintangel

Cornwall's most legend-strewn location is the crumbling clifftop castle of **Tintagel** *(english-heritage.org.uk)*, rumoured to be where England's most heroic of heroes, King Arthur was born (or at least conceived). In truth, there's more fiction than fact in that – the present castle is largely the work of Richard, Earl of Cornwall, who built a base here during the 1230s. But there's no denying the truly epic setting: a fairy-tale ruined fortress teetering above black cliffs and booming surf. An elegant new footbridge now spans a plunging 60m gully, linking the two sides of the medieval castle and recreating a land bridge that existed 500 years ago. Take a blustery wander among the ruins, then head down at low tide to explore the beach and the murky **Merlin's Cave**.

It's also worth walking over to teeny **St Materiana Church**, which was built between 1080 and 1150 and occupies a dramatic position atop Glebe Cliff. Look out for signs from the castle.

THE DRIVE: The most scenic route to Padstow is to explore the backroads via Polzeath and Rock, but it's easy to get lost, so we route you south to the main A39 to follow it past Wadebridge, then turn off towards Padstow. It's a drive of 21 miles this way; there's a large car park above town.

DETOUR

Bodmin Moor
Start: 02 Tintangel

Sprawling over an area of some 77 sq miles along Cornwall's eastern edge, Bodmin Moor might not be everyone's idea of classic Cornwall, but it has a bleak, magisterial beauty all of its own. Pockmarked with heaths and granite hills, including Cornwall's highest point, **Brown Willy** (420m), it's a desolate place that works on the imagination – for years there have been reported sightings of the Beast of Bodmin, a large, black, cat-like creature, though no one's ever managed to snap a decent picture.

It's a fine place for hiking and cycling, and is strewn with many beauty spots, such as the underground slate chambers of **Carnglaze Caverns** *(carnglaze.com)* and tumbling Golitha Falls (near Redgate). It's also home to the **Jamaica Inn** *(jamaicainn.co.uk)*, made famous by Daphne du Maurier's novel of the same name – though it's been ruthlessly modernised since then.

There are various routes onto the moor. Try heading from Tintagel to just northeast of Camelford, and circling east then southwest across the moor from there.

03 Padstow

Famous for its foodie culture thanks to celebrity chef Rick Stein, Padstow has to rank as one of north Cornwall's prettiest ports. It's beautifully situated on the Camel Estuary, opposite the treacherous sandbank known as the **Doom Bar** (after which a popular local beer is named). It's a lovely place for a wander: explore the backstreets, browse the shops, dangle your toes over the harbour wall, then catch the **ferry** *(padstow-harbour.co.uk)* across the estuary to the chi-chi seaside village of Rock – a favourite of the poet John Betjeman, who holidayed here as a child, and now one of Cornwall's priciest patches of real estate. Nearby, the sands of Daymer Bay are perfect sunbathing territory. While there, hunt out tiny St Enodoc Church. Betjeman adored this chapel so much he asked to be buried here; it doesn't take long to find his headstone – it's a surprisingly ornate affair.

THE DRIVE: Head around the Padstow peninsula, initially following signs towards Trevone. After Trevose Head comes a roller-coaster coast, dipping and swerving past a string of stunning white-sand beaches. Soon a line of dramatic rock towers loom out of the surf: called Carnewas at Bedruthan (or Bedruthan Steps), they make for a great photo op. Then comes party-town Newquay. Total distance is 14 miles.

04 Newquay

Welcome to Cornwall's surf central. Impressive beaches on the eastern outskirts of town include

Newquay

TIM WOOLCOCK PHOTOGRAPHY/SHUTTERSTOCK

Mawgan Porth, while at nearby **Watergate Bay** the **Wavehunters** *(wavehunters.co.uk)* offers surf lessons. Or just hire a wetsuit and surfboard, and have a play in the waves on your own.

Newquay itself is a love-it-or-hate-it affair. Brash and busy, it's notorious for its nightlife, but it is home to several beautiful beaches, most notably the magnet for British surfers: **Fistral**. Although purists scoff that it's way too busy to be worth surfing these days – and they may be right – its consistent swell and close-to-town facilities make it a fine place for beginners and novices.

THE DRIVE: The best road along this stretch of coast is the A3075, which passes detours to the photogenic beaches at Crantock and Holywell Bay. Take the turn-off to Perranporth (perhaps stopping to gaze at its sweeping beach), then follow the B3285 out of town past Perranporth Airfield and into St Agnes (12 miles in total).

05 St Agnes

Pretty St Agnes, once a centre for Cornwall's tin industry, is strewn with reminders of its mighty mining past. At the beautiful beach of **Chapel Porth** *(nationaltrust.org.uk)*, on the west side of St Agnes Head, a trail leads up to the abandoned mine at Wheal Coates, towering above heather-covered cliffs and rust-red rock. Hiking trails radiate all around from here, including a path that leads to the panoramic hilltop called the Beacon. Alternatively, you can just head back down to the car park for a hot cup of tea and ice cream with a dollop of clotted cream at the beach cafe.

THE CAMEL TRAIL

If you fancy swapping four wheels for two, try cycling along the old Padstow–Bodmin railway line. It was closed in the 1950s, but re-emerged decades later as the **Camel Trail** *(cameltrail.co.uk)*. It's now Cornwall's most popular cycle route. The main section starts in Padstow and heads east through Wadebridge (5.75 miles), but the full trail runs on all the way to Poley Bridge on Bodmin Moor (18.3 miles). Bikes can be booked from **Trail Bike Hire** *(cameltrailcyclehire.co.uk)* at the Padstow end, or from **Camel Trail Cycle Hire** *(bridgebikehire.co.uk)* at the Wadebridge end. Most people ride the route from Padstow and back, so it's quieter (and much easier to find parking) if you start from the Wadebridge side.

THE DRIVE: There are some wonderful backroads to explore from here, but they're a maze, so the easiest option is to take the road back to Chiverton Cross and join the main A30, which will zip you all the way past Hayle. From there, follow signs to St Ives. It's 24 miles stop to stop.

06 St Ives

Few spots in Cornwall have such a wow factor as St Ives. Occupying a graceful curving bay, framed by a jumble of slate rooftops, dazzling blue water and white beaches, it's postcard perfect – so it's not hard to see why artists find themselves drawn here. Among them was the abstract sculptor Barbara Hepworth, who made her home here in the 1930s. Her **house and studio** *(tate.org.uk/visit/tate-st-ives)* have remained almost untouched since her death and the adjoining garden contains several of her most notable sculptures, many of which were inspired by the elemental forces she discovered in her adopted Cornish home: rock, sea, sand, wind and sky.

There are galleries and studios scattered along St Ives' warren of backstreets, but the flagship is the **Tate St Ives** *(tate.org.uk/visit/tate-st-ives)*, which displays key works by local artists such as Barbara Hepworth, Terry Frost, Peter Lanyon and Patrick Heron, and has been impressively extended.

After soaking up some art and culture, head for one of the town's beaches to soak up some sun. There's Porthmeor, opposite the Tate, or little Porthgwidden around the headland, with an excellent **beach cafe** *(porthgwiddencafe.co.uk)*, but most people favour **Porthminster**, a curl of white sand not far from the train station home to the sophisticated **Porthminster Beach Café** *(porthminstercafe.co.uk)*.

THE DRIVE: An epic 11-mile stretch of tarmac lies in store. Take the road up Higher Stennack onto the B3306, signposted Zennor. From here the wilds of Penwith's moors open up all around; you'll pass ancient fields, rock formations and abandoned mine stacks, all framed by the sea to your right

DETOUR

Hayle
Start: 06 St Ives

Six-and-a-half miles east of St Ives, across the Hayle Estuary, the dune-backed flats of Gwithian and Godrevy unfurl in a golden curve that joins together at low tide to form Hayle's '3 miles of golden sand'. This is one of Cornwall's most glorious beach panoramas, fringed by hectares of rock pools and grassy dunes (known in Cornish as *towans*) and, at the northern end, the lighthouse that inspired Virginia Woolf's stream-of-consciousness classic *To the Lighthouse*. Pick up a healthy, homemade takeaway snack at the excellent **Godrevy Café** *(@godrevybeachcafe)* and settle down to enjoy the views.

07 Geevor Tin Mine

Penwith is one of Cornwall's wildest corners but was once a mining heartland. Hardly surprising then that it features heavily in the BBC's 2015–19 series *Poldark*, an 18th-century historical drama with a mining subplot. To get a true taste of a miner's life, head for **Geevor Tin Mine** *(geevor.com)*, where you can view the original machinery used to sort the minerals and ores, before taking a guided tour into some of the underground shafts.

Other photogenic ruins dot the area. One mile west of Geevor sits **Levant Mine** *(nationaltrust.org.uk)*, with its working beam engine. Two miles southwest of Geevor, **Botallack** *(nationaltrust.org.uk)* clings to the cliffs. This dramatic complex of crumbling mine workings is one of the most atmospheric sights from Cornwall's industrial past. The main mine stack teeters on the cliff edge above a cauldron of surf. It's famously photogenic and *Poldark* fans will recognise the views. The National Trust website has a 1-mile, looped walking trail taking in Botallack.

THE DRIVE: From the tin sites around Geevor, hop back on the B3306. Travel through the mining village of St Just before joining the A30 and following signs to Sennen. It's a drive of 8 miles in all.

08 Sennen

Many secret beaches await in Cornwall for those intrepid enough to find them, but with its white sands unfurling right from the road, the pretty village of Sennen is rather easier to find. Sennen is also a great launch pad for hiking the coast path around to **Land's End** (a 2.5-mile walk

Jubilee Pool

IAN WOOLCOCK/SHUTTERSTOCK

PHOTO OPPORTUNITY

A seaside selfie with the sleek backdrop of the art-deco Jubilee Pool.

each way). This is where mainland Britain comes to a screeching halt.

Though it's now home to an uninspiring theme park, there's still something thrilling about standing on Britain's westernmost point: you'll see cliffs, seagulls and lighthouses, and on a clear day, perhaps, glimpse the silhouettes of the Isles of Scilly, 28 miles west.

THE DRIVE: You'd have to try really hard to get lost from here: there's only one road from Sennen to Porthcurno, the B3315, for 5 miles. Follow the signs to Porthcurno and the Minack Theatre.

09 Porthcurno

Forget Stratford-upon-Avon or London's West End: if you're looking for Britain's most dramatic place to watch a play, you'll find it above the beach of Porthcurno. Dreamt up by an eccentric theatre lover called Rowena Cade, and inspired by the amphitheatres of ancient Greece, the **Minack** *(minack.com)* was painstakingly carved out from the granite cliffs during the 1930s and '40s. It now hosts a season of plays throughout the summer: on a clear night it's utterly magical, though experienced theatregoers remember to pack a cushion, a picnic and rain gear in case the Cornish weather decides to stage an unscheduled appearance.

Down below you'll find sandy Porthcurno beach, one of the best coves in west Cornwall for swimming and sunbathing.

THE DRIVE: The prettiest route is to follow the B3315 to Penzance, which passes the lovely village of Mousehole and the busy fishing harbour of Newlyn en route. It's around 10 miles this way.

PETER TITMUSS/SHUTTERSTOCK

Geevor Tin Mine

10 Penzance

The salty seafront town of Penzance is pretty much the end of the line for Cornwall (and the last stop for the railway from London Paddington).

Established as a fishing and trading port, Penzance has a blustery, lived-in charm, and has resisted the gentrification that's taken over many of Cornwall's other seaside towns. Reminders of its seafaring heyday can be found along Chapel St, which is lined with grand Georgian mansions and some cracking pubs.

Further down towards the seafront is the town's pride and joy: **Jubilee Pool** *(jubileepool.co.uk)*, a glorious seawater lido that was built in 1935. A bold statement of art-deco styling – sleek, sharp and whitewashed – it's the perfect backdrop for bracing, shoreside alfresco bathing. Sections now have geothermal heating – book well ahead for a much warmer, 28–30°C dip.

THE DRIVE: Head out of Penzance on the A30, cross through a couple of roundabouts and follow signs to Marazion. It's a 4-mile drive.

11 St Michael's Mount

As you approach Penzance, catching your first sight of **St Michael's Mount** *(stmichaelsmount.co.uk)* is an unforgettable experience: it looks like something from the pages of *Harry Potter*. A cluster of spires and battlements looming up from a rocky island in the middle of Mount's Bay, the fairy-tale building dates back to the 1100s, and has variously served as an abbey, a fortress, a prison and a trading port. Later it became the ancestral seat of the St Aubyn family, and is now administered by the National Trust. Highlights include the stately great hall and subtropical gardens, but the crossing is almost the best part: at low tide, you can walk across a cobbled causeway from the nearby town of **Marazion**. From mid-March to October, you may also be able to hop on a boat to visit at high tide.

THE DRIVE: From Marazion the A394 runs past the busy beach at Praa Sands all the way to Helston, gateway town to the Lizard. You can take a direct route from Helston on the A3083 straight to Lizard Point (20 miles), but there are countless detours along the way if you have time.

12 The Lizard

Despite its name, you won't spot too many reptiles on this back-of-beyond peninsula (the word is actually thought to derive from the Cornish *lys ardh*, meaning high court or high fortress). What you will spy is mile after mile of cliffs, beaches, coves and moors – this is another of Cornwall's wildest corners, where summer wildflowers blaze, choughs wheel over the clifftops and countless ships have come to grief on these unforgiving rocks.

The coastline is strewn with quaint little fishing villages, such as Cadgwith and Coverack on the east side of the peninsula. On the west side, gorgeous bays include Church Cove near Gunwalloe, which was used as a ready-made backdrop in *Poldark*.

Some 11 miles south, **Kynance Cove** *(nationaltrust.org.uk)* is truly stunning at low tide – a picturesque concoction of turquoise water, white surf and rocky islands.

The cliffs around the cove are rich in serpentine, a red-green rock popular with Victorian trinket makers. The island opposite the cove is called Asparagus Island, as wild asparagus can be foraged here in spring and summer. Drinks and snacks are available at Kynance's ecofriendly **beach cafe** *(kynancecovecafe.co.uk)*. The cove gets busy in summer; try to arrive before 11am.

Nearby is the sea-smacked headland at Lizard Point, with its striking **lighthouse** *(trinityhouse.co.uk/lighthouses-and-lightvessels/lizard-lighthouse)*.

THE DRIVE: Backtrack to Helston and continue east on the A394 – not the most exciting 25 miles of road, but the fastest way from here to Falmouth.

13 Falmouth

Truro might be the county's capital, but Falmouth surely stakes a claim as Cornwall's coolest town. Thanks to its deepwater harbour, this historic port was once a bustling hub for Britain's maritime trade, welcoming clippers and tall ships from all over the globe. It's now home to Cornwall's only

CORNISH PASTIES

There's nothing more local to tuck into for lunch than a Cornish pasty. Half-moon shaped, stuffed with steak and vegetables and sealed with a decorative crimp on the side, they've been a staple here since the 13th century. They're said to have been created as a portable lunch for tin miners: the crust was designed to allow the miners' filthy fingers to grip the pasty without contaminating their food. When waves of impoverished Cornish miners emigrated in the mid-1800s, they took their pasty techniques with them, particularly to Australia and the USA.

Annually, pasty production employs thousands, and brings millions of pounds into Cornwall's economy. In 2011, the pasty was finally awarded protected status by the European Commission, and the UK's Protected Geographical Indication (PGI) post-Brexit, meaning only those actually made in Cornwall, according to a traditional recipe, can be called 'Cornish pasties'.

Everyone has their favourite pasty shops: two of our top tips are **Ann's Pasties** *(annspasties.co.uk)* in Helston and impressive variations like smoked haddock at **Stein's Deli** *(rickstein.com/padstow-shops/steins-deli)* in Padstow.

MACIEJ OLSZEWSKI/SHUTTERSTOCK

St Michael's Mount

university (based at nearby Penryn), meaning it's awash with trendy bars, hip coffee shops and excellent restaurants. It also has the western outpost of the **National Maritime Museum** *(nmmc.co.uk)*, which presents a fascinating collection of boats and maritime memorabilia in innovative ways.

Out on the town's headland you'll find **Pendennis Castle** *(english-heritage.org.uk)*, an imposing Tudor fortress built by Henry VIII to guard the entrance to Falmouth Harbour in partnership with its sister castle across the bay in St Mawes. It's an atmospheric location, and you can wander round the gun decks and battlements. Don't be too perturbed if you hear a deafening crack at midday – it'll just be the noonday gun going off with a bang.

THE DRIVE: We're taking the most direct route to Eden: the A39 to Truro, then the A390 to St Austell, and another 4 miles further to the Eden Project. It's a pleasant but uneventful drive of 30 miles. Count on an hour, longer if there's traffic.

14 Eden Project

At first glance it looks like something from a sci-fi film set – two gigantic glass biomes, glittering in the sunlight at the bottom of a disused clay pit. But you haven't stumbled onto the set of a Ridley Scott movie – you've just arrived at the **Eden Project** *(edenproject.com)*, a pioneering eco-initiative that aims to recreate habitats from around the globe inside its oversized greenhouses. From tropical jungle to dry desert, soaring palms to spiky cactus, it sometimes feels a bit like wandering through a scene from *Jurassic Park*. Additions, including a canopy walkway and a zip-wire, have added extra thrills and spills.

THE DRIVE: Follow the road back towards St Austell, but after you reach the A390, follow signs to Par and then the A3082 to Fowey. Once you pass Par, it's a lovely drive through quiet countryside. In total it's 7 miles.

15 Fowey

The last stop on your Cornish road trip is the riverside town of Fowey. It's another postcard-perfect scene, a jumble of pastel-coloured town houses, fishers' cottages and winding alleyways, all backed by the River Fowey's banks.

The best way to see it is from the water: book ahead for one of the memorable three-hour guided kayaking trips run by **Encounter Cornwall** *(encountercornwall.com)*. These see you gliding up creeks and backwaters, spotting egrets, kingfishers and seals.

End the day with a pint of ale and a plate of fish and chips at the quayside **King of Prussia** *(thekingfowey.co.uk)*.

STAY AWHILE

PADSTOW

BY CATHERINE LE NEVEZ

Anywhere along the Cornish coast is somewhere I would happily stay for a while, but there's something extra-special about Padstow (Lanwethenek in Cornish). It's an idyllic place to breathe in the briny air as circling seagulls caw overhead and flags on masts flutter in the breeze at the boat-filled harbour. The centuries-old fishing port is ringed by cut-stone, red-brick, whitewashed and ice-cream-coloured buildings set in narrow, winding streets.

For a small town, the food scene here is off the charts. Seafood has always anchored Padstow. It still has a busy fleet hauling in fish, crab and lobsters; estuary shellfish farms raising mussels, cockles, oysters and scallops; and some of the best seafood cookery in the world. Rick Stein is meshed into the town's fabric, opening his flagship **Seafood Restaurant** *(rickstein.com/restaurants/the-seafood-restaurant)* here in 1975 (his other enterprises include a deli, tapas-style seafood bar and fishmonger, and cookery school with evening workshops through to multiday courses.) **Paul Ainsworth at No6** *(paul-ainsworth-no6.co.uk)*, in a Georgian townhouse, has a Michelin star. One of my more affordable favourites treats is a steaming-hot, golden-crusted pasty. The best are from the **Cornish Pasty Co** *(@cornishpastycompany)* on Market Pl.

Surrounded by sandy beaches and sparkling turquoise seas including the Seven Bays (Trevone, Harlyn, Mother Ivey's, Booby's, Constantine, Treyarnon and Porthcothan), Padstow is a fantastic place for swimming, surfing, SUP, coasteering, kayaking and cycling. The 18-mile **Camel Trail** *(cameltrail.co.uk)* links Padstow with Wadebridge and Bodmin, with a branch line to Wenford Bridge. And, of course, there's fishing (both shore and offshore).

LINK YOUR TRIP

Pull up during **15 Coastal Cornwall**, or head north to the wild landscapes and star-filled skies of **12 North Devon & Exmoor**.

Left: Rick Stein's Seafood Restaurant; Right: Padstow Harbour

FROM LEFT: GRAHAM PRENTICE/ALAMY, CAROLYN JENKINS/ALAMY

PLACES TO STAY...

Padstow has plenty of B&Bs, hotels and campsites, but book far ahead for summer and for Padstow's biggest party, **Obby Oss Day** (May Day; 1 May).

Padstow Harbour Hotel
Set on the headland, this restored 1904 Victorian beauty overlooking the harbour, port and estuary has modern, marine-inspired rooms. *harbourhotels.co.uk*

Coswarth House
A five-minute stroll from the harbour, this 1825 B&B sports original features such as flagstone floors blended with vintage decor including 1930s theatre lamps and boudoir chairs, and modern fittings. *coswarthhouse.com*

Seafood Restaurant
Above Rick Stein's flagship are 16 rooms designed by Jill Stein, with breakfast served in the restaurant. *rickstein.com*

0
0
50 km
25 miles
Bradford
Leeds
Selby
Hull
Humber
Halifax
Goole
M62
Huddersfield
Scunthorpe
DONCASTER
M180
Grimsby
Wigan
Bolton
Barnsley
Holmfirth
Doncaster
Manchester
ROTHERHAM
St Helens
A628
Peak District
National Park
Sheffield
Maltby
Gainsborough
Liverpool
Warrington
Stockport
Edale
Castleton
A15
Bebington
M56
Worksop
LINCOLNSHIRE
Eyam
M1
Ellesmere Port
Macclesfield
Tideswell
Lincoln
CHESHIRE
Buxton
Chesterfield
A1(M)
M6
Clwydian
Range
Chester
Bakewell
Matlock
Newark-
on-Trent
Sandbach
Matlock Bath
A515
Leek
Wrexham
Stoke-
on-Trent
A523
Tissington
A41
Ashbourne
NOTTINGHAMSHIRE
Boston
Nottingham
Whitchurch
18
Longton
Derby
Grantham
Oswestry
STAFFORDSHIRE
DERBYSHIRE
A38
A15
Melton
Mowbray
Loughborough
Spalding
Newport
A518
Stafford
Burton-
upon-Trent
A46
Shrewsbury
A1
Welshpool
Telford
Lichfield
Stamford
M6
Rutland
Water
LEICESTERSHIRE
Leicester
Snailbeach
A47
Wolverhampton
Walsall
Hinckley
I6
19
A442
Birmingham
Clun
17
Kidderminster
Coventry
NORTHAMPTONSHIRE
Ludlow
A45
Wellingborough
WORCESTERSHIRE
Brixworth
Huntingdon
Warwick
WARWICKSHIRE
Northampton
Leominster
Bromyard
Worcester
Stratford-
upon-Avon
Bedford
M1
A435
Broadway
Great
Malvern
A438
BEDFORDSHIRE
Evesham
Chipping
Campden
Hereford
Banbury
Milton
Keynes
A6
Talgarth
M5
Moreton-
in-Marsh
Brecon
Beacons
National
Park
Winchcombe
M40
BUCKINGHAMSHIRE
Ross-
on-Wye
Stow-on-the-Wold
GLOUCESTERSHIRE
A5
Luton
The Slaughters
Gloucester
Cheltenham
OXFORDSHIRE
Aylesbury
Northleach
Burford
A40
Abergavenny
Monmouth
Forest
of Dean
Painswick
St Albans
16
Bibury
Oxford
HERTFORDSHIRE
Stroud
Severn
Cirencester
Watford
Tetbury
High
Wycombe
Chepstow
A46
Swindon
Newport
WEST
BERKSHIRE
M4
LONDON
CARDIFF
M4
Bristol
Chippenham
Reading
Clevedon
A4
Marlborough
Newbury
Croydon
Bath
Devizes
Bristol
Channel
Weston-
super-Mare
M3
Basingstoke
Guildford
Burnham-
on-Sea
Wells
Warminster
HAMPSHIRE

ALEXEY FEDORENKO/SHUTTERSTOCK

Peveril Castle (p165)

CENTRAL ENGLAND

EXPLORE

CENTRAL ENGLAND

Driving through central England takes you into the country's heart. This is where you'll find those honey-stoned Cotswolds villages of postcards and dreams, ancient market towns founded on strategic sites by the Romans, rolling countryside straddling the Welsh border, and some of England's lesser-known wild places.

Historic and photogenic sights abound: the 'dreaming spires' of Oxford, one of the world's oldest universities; ecclesiastical masterpieces such as Gloucester Cathedral; and inspirational uplands in the Peak District National Park. World Heritage Sites such as Derbyshire's Derwent Valley Mills and Shropshire's Ironbridge Gorge underscore central England's industrial significance.

Birmingham

'Brum' is the unofficial capital of the Midlands, with everything you need to plan and equip your driving forays into England's heartland. The second-largest city in the UK, it has an international airport serving some 150 domestic and international destinations, linked to the city centre by fast, regular trains. As befits a major city, it offers the full range of accommodation options, car hire aplenty (including multiple offices at the airport), supermarkets, and rail and coach lines radiating in every direction. It's around 1½ hours by train from London.

Sheffield

A natural base for the 'Peak District' (p160) route, this former steel town in south Yorkshire offers plenty of accommodation and a lively eating and drinking scene, courtesy of its student population. You'll find car hire, direct rail links from Birmingham, Manchester and London, and ample opportunities to stock up on supplies.

Manchester

The northern terminus of the 'Industrial Heritage' (p154) itinerary, and convenient for the 'Peak District' (p160) route, Manchester is the cultural capital of the north. Britain's third-largest urban conurbation it's served by an international airport that links with nearly 200 destinations and can be reached from the city centre by train in around 20 minutes. This vibrant student town has a full spectrum of places to stay and eating options, plus excellent shopping and lots of car-rental places. Regular trains and

WHEN TO GO

The shoulder seasons (April/May and September/October) offer the best mix of (hopefully) fine weather and minimal crowds. Summer, especially the August school holidays, can deliver delightful weather, but you'll fight for space and accommodation in hot spots such as the Cotswolds. Winters are cold, but you're generally only likely to be impeded by snow and ice in the Peak District.

coaches run from London in around 2¼ hours.

Nottingham

Sitting at one end of the 'Industrial Heritage' (p154) route, historic Nottingham can be reached by train from London in under three hours. A student town with nightlife to match, it offers everything from hostels to boutique hotels and, of course, shops and car rental.

Coventry

Not high on most tourist itineraries, Coventry in Warwickshire is nonetheless an excellent and good-value base for both the 'Industrial Heritage' (p154) and 'The Cotswolds & Literary England' (p148) itineraries. Just an hour from London by train, it offers reasonable accommodation and all the essentials you'll need for touring.

Cheltenham

The best-situated base for the The Cotswolds & Literary England (p148) route (excepting perhaps Bath) is Regency Cheltenham. Retaining the air of a fashionable Georgian resort, it's flush with appealing accommodation and restaurants, and big enough to rely on for car rental and supplies. The train from London takes around two hours.

TRANSPORT

Birmingham and Manchester airports have domestic and international services; East Midlands airport also serves international destinations. Major cities and towns are also is easily reached by regular trains and coaches from London. While car hire is easily found in the many urban areas of central England, it's perfectly feasible to drive here from London.

WHERE TO STAY

No. 131, Cheltenham, features a luxury collection of 36 beautifully appointed suites, spread across three Georgian townhouses.

At one end of the Peak District (p160) itinerary you'll find the wonderfully atmospheric Old Hall Hotel, Buxton, dating from the 16th century. Mary, Queen of Scots once stayed here (albeit against her will).

On the Industrial Heritage (p154) drive, the Georgian B&B, Library House, Ironbridge, is perfectly located among the local museums and pubs.

Rotunda, Birmingham, is in an iconic city-centre building. It has excellent views and modern interiors.

RESOURCES

The Cotswolds
Comprehensive guide to events, activities, towns and sights in the Cotswolds. *Cotswolds.com*

Visit England
Excellent coverage of central England and the Midlands, including festivals, outdoor activities and maps. Learn about the many historically significant industrial sites in the region. *Visitengland.com*

Masarnen Ramblers
An inspiring couple share all they've learned about hiking in Britain. *Masarnenramblers.com*

WHAT'S ON

Crufts Dog Show
Famous dog show held in Birmingham over four days in March.

Stratford Literary Festival
Shakespeare's home town hosts one of Britain's big literary events in May.

Cotswold Olimpick Games
Chipping Camden revives unique local sports such the 'shin kicking' contest in May/June.

Cheltenham Festivals
Across the year: jazz, science, music, horse racing and a literature festival.

16

CENTRAL ENGLAND

THE COTSWOLDS & LITERARY ENGLAND

DURATION: 7–8 DAYS

DISTANCE: 149 MILES / 240KM

GREAT FOR: HISTORY, FOOD & DRINK

BEST TIME TO GO: APRIL, MAY, JUNE AND SEPTEMBER, FOR BETTER WEATHER, MINUS SUMMER CROWDS

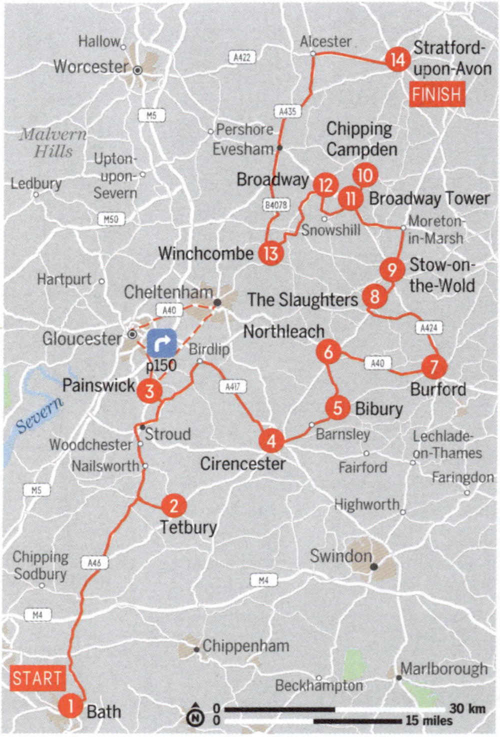

On this bucolic spin into the heart of the Cotswolds, you'll traverse five counties, wander time-warped, gold-washed villages, feast on local produce and pay your respects to William Shakespeare. Glimpse Georgian grandeur in Bath, marvel at Painswick's sleepy beauty, unearth Roman history in Cirencester, stroll Chipping Campden's honey-hued lanes and wrap up in dramatic Tudor style at Stratford-upon-Avon, home of Shakespeare.

LINK YOUR TRIP

07 Royalty & the Thames Valley
From Burford, drive 20 miles west to Oxford to explore fantastical worlds, royal hang-outs and bookish colleges.

18 Midlands Battlefields, Castles & stately homess
Zip 9 miles northeast from Stratford-upon-Avon to Warwick to pick up this history-rich central England trip.

01 Bath

A star among Britain's most beautiful cities, Bath comprises splendid honey-toned Georgian buildings coupled with one of the world's most unspoilt Roman bathhouses. It's a lovely place to explore on foot. Jane Austen set *Persuasion* and *Northanger Abbey* here.

The busy, brilliantly preserved **Roman Baths** *(romanbaths.co.uk)* bubble up at 46°C, surrounded by 18th- and 19th-century buildings. Handsome **Bath Abbey** *(bathabbey.org)* emerged in its current form in the 15th century.

Nowhere is Bath's magnificent Georgian architecture as fine as on semicircular, park-fringed Royal Crescent, where wonderfully restored **No 1 Royal Crescent** *(no1 royalcrescent.org.uk)* provides a peek into the glitzy period lifestyle.

THE DRIVE: Bath's London Rd joins the A46; follow 'Stroud' signs. Drive 24 miles north on the A46 into Gloucestershire. The countryside becomes

★ BEST FOR

HISTORY

Get lost in majestic Sudeley Castle.

CHRISATPPS/SHUTTERSTOCK

Market House, Tetbury

increasingly bucolic and the road narrower as you enter the southern Cotswolds. Turn east onto the A4135; after 4 miles, you'll reach Tetbury. It's 26 miles altogether.

02 Tetbury

Sitting prettily in the Cotswolds' southwestern reaches, Tetbury was once a wealthy wool town. Its easily strolled sandy-gold centre is a delightful tangle of lively streets flanked by medieval cottages, grand townhouses, antique shops and a 17th-century **Market House** (Market Pl).

The Georgian Gothic Church of **St Mary the Virgin & St Mary Magdalen** *(tetburychurch.co.uk)* has a towering spire (a 19th-century replica of its medieval original) and a dramatic interior of 18th-century dark-oak box pews.

In spring and summer, be sure to visit **King Charles' Highgrove** *(highgrovegardens.com)*, a mile southwest of town, for its gorgeous organic gardens.

THE DRIVE: Head 4 miles west from Tetbury on the A4135, then 6 miles north on the A46. Wiggle around Stroud onto the B4070, then it's 3 miles northeast through green-clad Slad Valley – follow 'Painswick' signs 1 mile northwest to Painswick. You'll pass through little Slad, once the beloved home of writer Laurie Lee: stop for a refreshment at the Woolpack Inn. Total distance is 14 miles.

03 Painswick

Hilltop Painswick is the Cotswolds' most perfectly formed village. At its heart stands 1[illegible]th-century **St Mary's Church** *(stmarys painswick.org.uk)*, a resplendent Perpendicular Gothic creation surrounded by 18th-century table-top tombs and 99 clipped yew trees.

Stroll Painswick's slender, twisting streets, passing ancient honey-coloured homes and medieval inns. Just north of town, the exquisite folly-dotted **Painswick Rococo Garden** *(rococogarden.org.uk)* is the only one of its type in England, designed by Benjamin Hyett in the 1740s as a vast 'outdoor room'.

THE DRIVE: Backtrack to the B4070, head 6 miles northeast and, at Birdlip, follow 'Cirencester' signs onto the A417. It's a 10-mile spin southeast past green fields to Cirencester, where the signposted Brewery Car Park has central (short-term) parking. It's a 16-mile trip in all.

DETOUR

Gloucester & Cheltenham

Start: 03 Painswick

Gloucester's spectacular **cathedral** *(gloucestercathedral.org.uk)* is among the first and most exquisite examples of the English Perpendicular Gothic style, with a 14th-century, fan-vaulted Great Cloister so enchanting and beautiful that it features in the first, second and sixth *Harry Potter* films. The cathedral also contains **Edward II's tomb**, a magnificently elaborate work in alabaster created after the king died in suspicious circumstances at nearby Berkeley Castle. From Painswick, head 6 miles northwest on the B4073 to Gloucester; there's plenty of signposted parking.

A 10-mile drive east on the A40 from Gloucester brings you to the handsome Regency town of Cheltenham, a flourishing 18th-century spa resort on the western fringe of the Cotswolds. Fine accommodation and restaurants make Cheltenham an attractive overnight stop.

Cheltenham's **Promenade** is a wide, tree-lined boulevard flanked by imposing period buildings and flower-filled gardens. Also worth a look is Cheltenham's excellent museum, **The Wilson** *(wilsonmuseum.org.uk)*, which depicts local life through the ages and has wonderful displays on William Morris and the Arts and Crafts movement. Modelled on an ancient Athenian temple, the **Pittville Pump Room** *(pittvillepumproom.org.uk)* is the town's outstanding Regency building.

Allow a one-day detour, then from Cheltenham motor 10 miles southwest back to Painswick on the A46.

Alternatively, rejoin the main route at Cirencester, 15 miles southeast (A417), or at Winchcombe, 8 miles northeast (B4632).

Cheltenham Promenade

ROBERT HARDING VIDEO/SHUTTERSTOCK

04 Cirencester

Self-styled capital of the southern Cotswolds, elegant and affluent Cirencester hides a stash of fascinating sights, pretty boutiques, antique shops and striking Victorian architecture around its Market Square.

In Roman times, Cirencester (Corinium) was the second most important settlement in Britain after London. Well-preserved remains can be viewed at the superb **Corinium Museum** *(corinium museum.org)*, where highlights include a beautiful set of floor mosaics plus the towering 2nd-century Jupiter column. Next, head to the remains of a Roman amphitheatre nearby.

Cirencester's cathedral-like **St John the Baptist's Church** *(ciren parish.co.uk)*, commenced in 1100, is one of England's largest parish churches. It features an outstanding Perpendicular Gothic tower with flying buttresses (ca. 1400) and a majestic three-storey south porch dating from the late 15th-century. In the light-filled interior you'll find soaring arches, magnificent fan vaulting, a Tudor nave and the 1535 Boleyn Cup, made for Anne Boleyn.

Cirencester Park, in the town centre, is a great spot for a picnic or to stretch your legs before getting back on the road.

THE DRIVE: Wind 8 miles northeast to Bibury on the tree-lined B4425, traversing mellow, well-heeled Barnsley and peaceful countryside interspersed with sprawling Cotswolds panoramas.

05 Bibury

Once described by William Morris as England's most beautiful village, tiny Bibury embodies the Cotswolds at its most picturesque. With a knot of narrow streets flanked by attractive stone buildings, it's popular.

But the major draw is **Arlington Row**: a perfectly rustic sweep of cottages converted in the 17th century from a 14th-century wool store. Access is by foot only.

THE DRIVE: We'll be sticking to gorgeous, slim, classic-Cotswolds country lanes on this 6-mile stretch. Head south on The St, and then north out of Bibury on the B4425l. After 1.5 miles, turn left, following signs for 4.5 miles to Northleach.

06 Northleach

Little visited, underappreciated and, therefore, well worth a stop on your Cotswolds itinerary, Northleach has been a small market town since 1227. Its centre is made up of late-medieval cottages, imposing merchants' stores and half-timbered Tudor houses.

The grand **Church of St Peter & St Paul** *(northleachbenefice.org)*, a masterpiece of the Cotswold Perpendicular style, is testimony to Northleach's wool-era wealth; its chancel, 30m tower and unusual font date to the 14th century.

A short drive from town, nestled in the Cotswolds coutryside, the **Chedworth Roman Villa** *(national trust.org.uk)* is a well-preserved sight with idyllic rural views.

THE DRIVE: It's a quick 10-mile drive east along the (admittedly unexciting) A40, crossing into Oxfordshire, to Burford. Parking here can be tricky: head for an official car park first, then look for a spot down a side street if they're full.

07 Burford

Tumbling steeply downhill to the River Windrush, Burford is usually one of the Cotswolds' busiest villages, little changed since its high-flying wool-era days. It makes a picturesque overnight stop thanks to its remarkable mix of stone cottages, gold-tinged townhouses, chintzy tearooms, ancient pubs, antique shops and delicatessens.

Commenced in 1175 and added to over the years, Burford's **St John the Baptist's Church** *(burford church.org)* has survived reformers and Roundheads (supporters of parliament against the king in the English Civil War) with its fan-vaulted ceiling, Norman west doorway, 15th-century spire and several grand tombs intact.

If you're craving a stretch after all that driving, there are some good signposted walks.

THE DRIVE: It's time to tackle the wonderfully scenic, undulating northern Cotswolds. Hop on the A424 northwest; after 6 miles, follow 'Little Rissington' signs west. Drive 900m, turn right, then immediately left, continuing 3 miles through Little Rissington and picturesque Bourton-on-the-Water onto the A429. A mile northeast, take the signposted 'The Slaughters' turn-off and 650m west is Lower Slaughter. (An 11-mile journey in total.)

08 The Slaughters

Blissfully charming, the tranquil chocolate-box villages of Upper and Lower Slaughter are the perfect introduction to the golden-stone delights of the northern Cotswolds. Their names are derived from the Old English *slohtre* ('slough' or 'muddy place'). The River Eye meanders peacefully through the villages, flanked by classic honey-washed houses and manors, and Lower Slaughter's picturesque **Old Mill** *(lowerslaughtermill.com)*.

THE DRIVE: Back on the A429, Stow-on-the-Wold is 2.5 miles northeast past rippling fields, along what was once the Roman Fosse Way.

09 Stow-on-the-Wold

Welcome to the Cotswolds' highest town, strategically positioned at 244m on the junction of six roads. Stow has long been an important market town, with thin alleyways (originally for funnelling sheep) feeding into a sprawling market square lined with graceful stone buildings, cute tearooms, a medieval-era church and old-world pubs.

THE DRIVE: Rejoin the A429 and head 4.5 miles north to busy Moreton-in-Marsh, known for its local food shops and Tuesday farmers market. From Moreton, take the A44 6 miles northwest, climbing through tiny Bourton-on-the-Hill. Exit onto the B4081, following signs to Chipping Campden, 2.5 miles north of the A44. It's an 11-mile trip in total.

10 Chipping Campden

Chipping Campden is one of the Cotswolds' most exquisitely beautiful towns and home to many English A-listers. Its elegant High St is flanked by a perfectly picturesque array of stone cottages, fine terraced houses, ancient inns, historic homes and the 14th-century **Grevel House**, with a marvellous Perpendicular Gothic-style gabled window.

The premier attraction is the highly photogenic 17th-century **Market Hall** *(nationaltrust.org.uk/market-hall)*, an open-sided, timber-roofed pillared building that looks like a cross between a barn and a chapel.

Imposing **St James' Church** *(stjameschurchcampden.co.uk)*, built in the late 15th century in Perpendicular Gothic style on wool-trade riches, has an impressive tower and some graceful 17th-century monuments. Just outside, the **Court Barn Museum** *(courtbarn.org.uk)* gives a detailed insight into Chipping Campden's important connection with the Arts and Crafts movement: architect and designer Charles Robert Ashbee moved his Guild of Handicraft here from East London in 1902.

THE DRIVE: Next, a short 4.5-mile hop. Take the B4081 2.5 miles to the A44, then drive 1 mile northwest, crossing into the Cotswolds' Worcestershire pocket. Follow 'Broadway Tower' signs 1 mile southwest to the top of the escarpment.

11 Broadway Tower

A crenulated 18th-century Gothic folly, **Broadway Tower** *(broadwaytower.co.uk)* stands on the windswept crest of the escarpment, offering all-encompassing views from the top. Arts and Crafts Movement pioneer William Morris once summered here. It's also on the Cotswold Way and a 2-mile path links it to St Ead-burgha's Church, a mile south of Broadway.

PHOTO OPPORTUNITY

Broadway Tower perched spectacularly on the crest of the escarpment.

THE DRIVE: Another scenic 4.5-mile stretch. Continue 1 mile south from Broadway Tower and turn right (southwest). Signs soon lead the 1-mile way to pretty little Snowshill, famed for featuring in *Bridget Jones's Diary*. If you're visiting in June or July, you'll pass gorgeously purple fields carpeted with blooming lavender. From Snowshill, it's 2.5 miles north to Broadway.

12 Broadway

Huddling beautifully at the foot of a sloping escarpment, Broadway has one of the lengthiest high streets in England. A quintessentially Cotswolds village, it reels in visitors with its golden cottages, art galleries, boutiques, foodie stops and plush hotels.

Set inside a grand converted coaching inn, the **Broadway Museum & Art Gallery** *(broadwaymuseum.org.uk)* has fascinating displays of local crafts, antiques and history spanning the 17th century to the present day. Collections include Winchcombe pottery, vintage furniture, ornate tapestries, and paintings by Reynolds and Gainsborough.

THE DRIVE: The fastest route from Broadway to Winchcombe is the B4632 southwest; we're turning off 3 miles southwest of Broadway to detour through picture-perfect Stanton (signposted). Next, track 1 mile south on the road that parallels the Cotswold Way to stunning little Stanway, famous for its fabulous Jacobean mansion. Turn west onto the B4077, then southwest onto the B4632; it's 3.5 miles to Winchcombe. It's 7.5 miles in all.

MICHAEL JOHN MANNING/SHUTTERSTOCK

William Shakespeare's birthplace

13 Winchcombe

Once capital of the Anglo-Saxon kingdom of Mercia and a prominent Cotswolds town until the Middle Ages, Winchcombe retains its workaday bustle amid half-timbered houses, gold-stone buildings and ancient inns. It's also popular with walkers.

The main attraction, spectacular **Sudeley Castle** *(sudeleycastle.co.uk)*, has welcomed many a monarch over its thousand-year history, the likes of which include Richard III, Henry VIII and Charles I. It's most famous as the home and final resting place of Catherine Parr (Henry VIII's widow), who lived here with her fourth husband, Thomas Seymour.

You'll find Catherine's tomb in the castle's Perpendicular Gothic St Mary's Church, making this the only private house in England where a queen is buried. Outside lie 10 splendid gardens.

THE DRIVE: Take the B4078 north for 7 miles, then zip along the A46 for 21 miles to Stratford-upon-Avon. Stratford has plenty of central parking, though town car parks charge high fees.

14 Stratford-upon-Avon

A distinctly Tudor town with a huge following, Stratford-upon-Avon is a fascinating place to wander, and a fittingly famous final stop on your itinerary: the birth and burial place of the greatest of English scribes William Shakespeare (1564–1616).

Kick off your Shakespeare story at **Shakespeare's Birthplace** *(shakespeare.org.uk)*, where the playwright spent his childhood. In Stratford's medieval **Holy Trinity Church** *(stratford-upon-avon.org)* you can see the modest, much-visited grave of William Shakespeare, with its menacing epitaph: 'cvrst be he yt moves my bones'.

Book ahead to join the world-renowned **Royal Shakespeare Company** *(rsc.org.uk)* at one of its legendary productions. From here on, you're in the hands of the Bard.

17

CENTRAL ENGLAND

INDUSTRIAL HERITAGE

DURATION: 4 DAYS

DISTANCE: 194 MILES / 312KM

GREAT FOR: HISTORY, FOOD & DRINK

BEST TIME TO GO: MAY TO SEPTEMBER ARE THE MOST PLEASANT MONTHS.

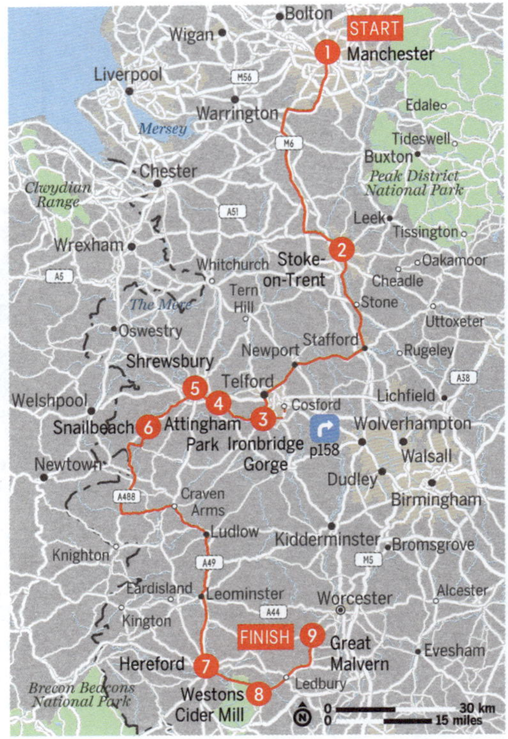

The Industrial Revolution's humble beginnings took place deep in the English countryside: the wooded riverbanks of Ironbridge Gorge are where cast iron was first mass-produced, and today the gorge teems with the factories' legacies, including its namesake bridge. Other industries along this attraction-packed route include pottery, cars, aircraft and cider producers (including one that supplies the Houses of Parliament).

LINK YOUR TRIP

18 Peak District
Head 23 miles east of Stoke-on-Trent via the A52 to pick up the Peak District trip in Ashbourne.

05 Urban & Art Odyssey
The end point of this trip, Great Malvern, intersects with the Urban & Art Odyssey.

01 Manchester

Manchester has a rich blend of history and culture along with a hedonistic swirl of epicurean and entertainment venues.

This northern powerhouse's industrial legacy is explored at the excellent **Science & Industry Museum** *(scienceandindustrymuseum.org.uk)*, set within the enormous grounds of the old 1830-opened Liverpool St station, the oldest rail terminus in the world. The large collection of steam engines, locomotives and original machinery tells the story of the city from the sewers up, and looks to the future.

Housed in a refurbished Edwardian pumping station, the **People's History Museum** *(phm.org.uk)* tells the story of Britain's 200-year march to democracy. Colourful and distinctive protest banners play a prominent role in telling each struggle's story, while posters, badges, tokens and satirical cartoons all become powerful tools in the battle for change.

4KCLIPS/SHUTTERSTOCK

★ BEST FOR

HISTORY

Britain's spirit inspires at the national museum of democracy, the People's History Museum

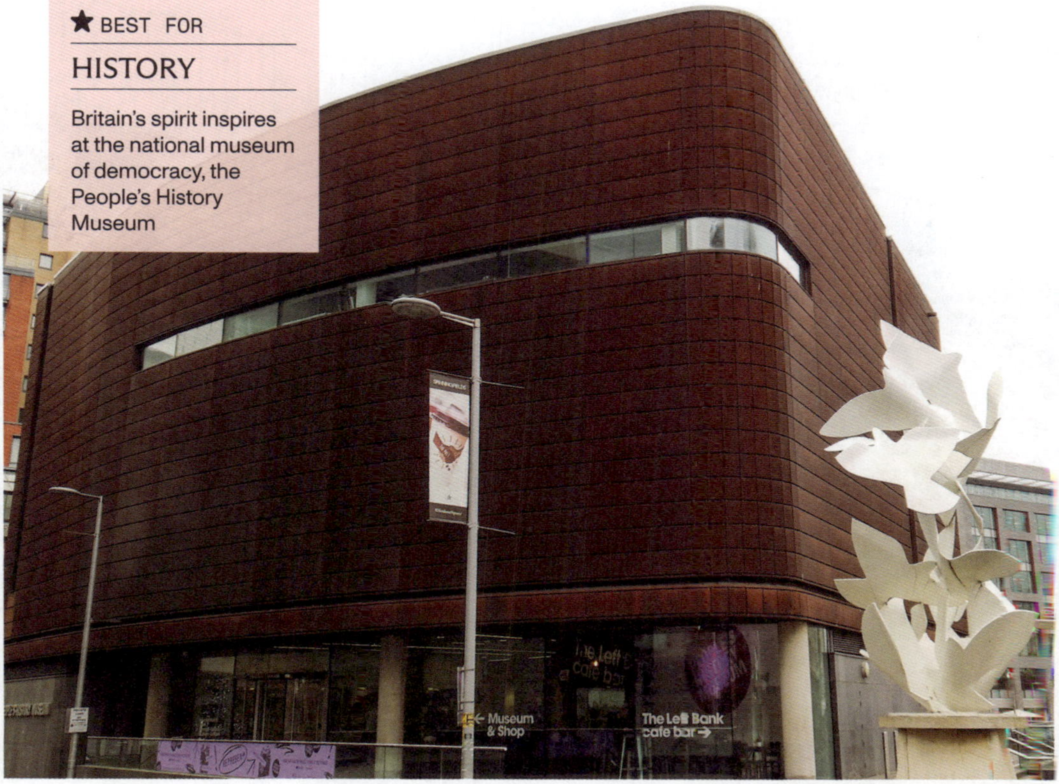

People's History Museum, Manchester

THE DRIVE: It's 45 miles south to Stoke-on-Trent. Take Princess Rd to Manchester Airport, where it becomes the M56, and connect to the southbound M6.

02 Stoke-on-Trent

At the heart of the Potteries – the famous pottery-producing region of Staffordshire – Stoke-on-Trent is famed for its ceramics. Don't expect cute little artisanal producers: this was where pottery shifted to mass production during the Industrial Revolution, and Stoke today is a sprawl of industrial townships tied together by flyovers and bypasses.

For a good overview, visit the **Potteries Museum & Art Gallery** *(stokemuseums.org.uk)*, which houses an extensive ceramics display, from Toby jugs and jasperware to outrageous ornamental pieces. Other highlights include displays on the WWII Spitfire, created by the Stoke-born aviator Reginald Mitchell.

Active potteries that you can visit in the greater area include the **Wedgwood factory** *(worldofwedgwood.com)*. The modern production centre for Josiah Wedgwood's porcelain empire displays historic pieces, including plenty of Wedgwood's delicate, neoclassical blue-and-white jasperware. A film on Josiah's life and work details his involvement in canal-building and opposition to slavery.

THE DRIVE: Drive 36 miles southwest, via the late-20th-century town of Telford (named after civil engineer Thomas Telford), to Ironbridge Gorge.

03 Ironbridge Gorge

It's hard to believe this peaceful, wooded river gorge could really have been the birthplace of the Industrial Revolution. But it was here that Abraham Darby perfected the art of smelting iron ore with coke in 1709, making it

PHOTO OPPORTUNITY

The arched Iron Bridge that first showcased cast-iron technology.

possible to mass-produce cast iron for the first time.

Abraham Darby's son, Abraham Darby II, invented a new forging process for producing single beams of iron, allowing Abraham Darby III to astound the world with the first-ever **iron bridge** *(ironbridge.org.uk)*, constructed in 1779. The bridge remains the focal point of this World Heritage Site, and 10 very different museums tell the story of the Industrial Revolution in the buildings where it took place. All are administered by the National Trust *(national trust.org.uk)*

Start at the Gothic riverside warehouse-housed **Museum of the Gorge** *(www.ironbridge.org.uk)*, which offers an outstanding overview using film, photos and exhibits including a 12m-long 3D model of the town in 1796. Other gorge highlights include the **Museum of Iron**, set in Abraham Darby's original iron foundry.

As ironmaking fell into decline, Ironbridge diversified into manufacturing china pots, using the fine clay mined around Blists Hill. Learn more at the **Coalport China Museum**, dominated by a pair of towering bottle kilns.

Other museums here include the Coalbrookdale **Museum of Iron**, **Jackfield Tile Museum**, and the brilliant **Blists Hill Victorian Town** and **Enginuity museums**.

THE DRIVE: Head west out of Ironbridge on the B4380 along the River Severn; Attingham Park is 11 miles away.

World's first iron bridge
JOE DANIEL PRICE/GETTY IMAGES

ALAN E TAYLOR/ALAMY

Mackie Mayor

FASCINATING PLACES TO EAT AND STAY

The restored former meat market in Manchester is now home to a superb food hall, **Mackie Mayor** *(mackie-mayor.co.uk)*, with a fine selection of nine individual traders. The pizzas from Honest Crust are divine; bowls of Japanese ramen, along with snacks and sake, are in hot demand at New Wave Ramen (aka Taiko Ramen); and Tender Cow serves really tasty steaks. Dining is communal, across two floors.

D'arcys at the Station *(darcysironbridge.co.uk)* in Ironbridge is just over the bridge by the river. The handsome old station building is the backdrop for flavoursome Mediterranean dishes, from Moroccan chicken to Cypriot kebabs and Tuscan bean casserole. Kids aged over 10 are welcome.

Shrewsbury is filled with historic places to eat and sleep. On Wyle Cop, home to 39 of Shrewsbury's almost 800 listed buildings, 16th-century coaching inn the **Lion + Pheasant** *(lionandpheasant.co.uk)* combines historic character with contemporary edge in its boutique rooms and wood-fire-warmed restaurant (don't miss its Sunday lunch).

In a regal Georgian town house where the Bishop of Hereford once resided, the tranquil 16-room **Castle House** *(castlehse.co.uk)* hotel in Hereford has a renowned restaurant using ingredients sourced from its own nearby farm, a sunny garden spilling down to Hereford's former castle moat, and magnificent rooms and suites. Another eight newer rooms (some wheelchair accessible) are a short walk away at 25 Castle St.

DETOUR

Cosford Royal Air Force Museum

Start: 03 Ironbridge Gorge

The famous **Cosford Royal Air Force Museum** *(rafmuseum.org.uk)* is run by the Royal Air Force, whose pilots steered many of the winged wonders here across the skies. Among the more than 70 aircraft on display are the Vulcan bomber (which carried Britain's nuclear deterrent) and the tiny helicopter-like Fa 330 Bachstelze glider that was towed behind German U-boats to warn them of enemy ships. You can also try out a Black Hawk simulator. It's 13 miles east of Ironbridge via the A4169.

04 Attingham Park

Built in imposing neoclassical style in 1785, **Attingham Park** *(nationaltrust.org.uk)* looks like something straight out of a period drama, with its grand columned facade, manicured lawns and stagecoach turning circle in the courtyard. The landscaped grounds swirl around an ornamental lake and are home to some 130 fallow deer. The restored walled garden is a picture.

THE DRIVE: Cross to the southern bank of the River Severn; it's a quick 5-mile drive northwest to Shrewsbury.

05 Shrewsbury

A jumble of winding medieval streets and timbered Tudor houses leaning at precarious angles around its 16th-century **Old Market Hall** *(oldmarkethall.co.uk)*, Shrewsbury was a crucial front in the conflict between English and Welsh in medieval days, and is the birthplace of Charles Darwin (1809–82). He's commemorated by a statue (Castle Gates) outside the town library, formerly the Shrewsbury School, where he was educated.

Hewn from flaking red Shropshire sandstone, **Shrewsbury Castle** *(shropshiremuseums.org.uk/shrewsbury-castle)* contains the **Shropshire Regimental Museum**. There are fine views from Laura's Tower and the battlements.

THE DRIVE: Follow the A488 southwest from Shrewsbury through rolling green countryside, and take the first left after the town of Minsterley to Snailbeach (which, despite its name, is not a beach), on the edge of the Shropshire Hills – a 12-mile journey all told.

06 Snailbeach

You'll see relics, including an abandoned pumping house, explosives magazine, disused railway lines and rusting machinery, such as an ore crusher, at the former lead- and silver-mining village of **Snailbeach** *(shropshiremines.org.uk)*.

Old Market Hall, Shrewsbury

D K GROVE/SHUTTERSTOCK

Self-guided trails let you explore the site, or you can join a guided tour that takes you deep into the mine. Waterproof footwear is a must; hard hats and lamps are provided.

THE DRIVE: Drive southwest through the village of Stiperstones to the town of Bishop's Castle (home to the Three Tuns Brewery, founded in 1642). Continue south on the A488 to the black-and-white village of Clun. From here, it's 18 miles east via the B4368 to market town Ludlow, then 23 miles south via the A49 to Hereford (59 miles in all).

07 Hereford

Surrounded by apple orchards and rolling pastures at the heart of the Marches, straddling the River Wye, Hereford is famed for its prime steaks and its cider – you can learn about the local tipple at the **Museum of Cider & King Offa Distillery** *(cidermuseum.co.uk)*. Displays cover cider-making history and you can sample the delicious modern brews. Look for the fine costrels (minibarrels) used by agricultural workers to carry wages, which were partially paid in cider.

Soaring **Hereford Cathedral** *(herefordcathedral.org)* is home to the extraordinary Mappa Mundi, a single piece of calfskin vellum intricately painted with some fantastical assumptions about the globe's layout in around 1290. The same wing contains the world's largest surviving chained library of rare manuscripts manacled to the shelves.

THE DRIVE: It's 13 miles southeast along the A438 through countryside and farming villages to Westons Cider Mills, just under a mile west of the tiny village of Much Marcle. Most of the journey shadows the River Wye.

TRAVELIB HISTORY/ALAMY

Museum of Cider & King Offa Distillery

♥ DON'T MISS

Sampling a brew at the Museum of Cider, followed by a visit to the on-site shop, which stocks more than 100 craft ciders and perries

08 Westons Cider Mill

Cider producers are scattered across the Herefordshire countryside. One of the most prestigious is **Westons Cider Mill** *(westons-cider.co.uk)* – its house brew is served in the Houses of Parliament. Book ahead for tours (1½ hours), including free cider and perry tastings. There are lovely walks through the surrounding apple orchards.

THE DRIVE: The final stretch of this trip is also the prettiest. Take the A449 northeast, via the postcard-perfect black-and-white Tudor town of Ledbury, up into the wooded hills to Great Malvern (13 miles in total).

09 Great Malvern

Tumbling down the side of a forested ridge about 7 miles southwest of Worcester is the spa town of Great Malvern.

The 11th-century **Great Malvern Priory** *(greatmalvernpriory.org.uk)* is packed with remarkable features, from original Norman pillars to surreal modernist stained glass. The choir is enclosed by a screen of 15th-century tiles and the monks' stalls are decorated with delightfully irreverent 14th-century misericords, depicting everything from three rats hanging a cat to the mythological reptile, the basilisk. Charles Darwin's daughter, Annie, is buried here.

For road-trippers, though, the real treat is the **Morgan Motor Company** *(morgan-motor.com)*, which has been handcrafting elegant sports cars since 1909. You can still see the mechanics at work on two-hour guided tours (book ahead), and view vintage classics adjacent to the museum. If you want to swap your wheels for one of these machines (at least for a while), it's possible to rent one or enjoy a one-hour experience drive.

18

CENTRAL ENGLAND

PEAK DISTRICT

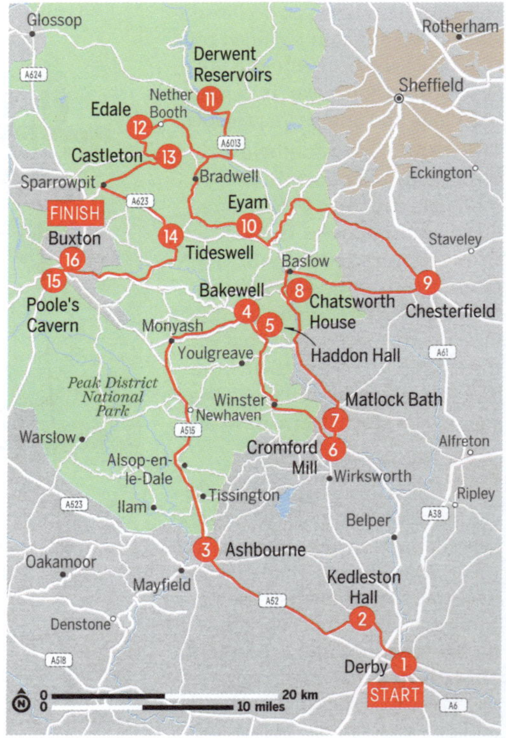

DURATION: 5 DAYS

DISTANCE: 140 MILES / 225KM

GREAT FOR: HISTORY, OUTDOORS

BEST TIME TO GO: EASTER TO SEPTEMBER LETS YOU ENJOY THE BEST WEATHER.

On this adventure-packed trip, you'll wind through the glorious Peak District – founded in 1951 as England's first national park – as it rolls across the Pennines' southernmost hills. The White Peak is made up of the limestone dales, while to the north, the Dark Peak is dominated by exposed moorland and gritstone 'edges'. Ancient stone villages are folded into creases in the landscape and the rocky hillsides are strewn with stately homes.

LINK YOUR TRIP

17 Industrial Heritage
It's a 30-mile drive from Buxton to Manchester to take a spin through British industrial history.

19 Midlands Battlefields, Castles & stately homess
Derby is a 15-mile hop from Nottingham, the starting point to discover historic battlefields and buildings.

01 Derby

Gloriously sited at the southeastern edge of the Derbyshire hills that roll towards the Peak District, Derby is one of the Midlands' most energetic, creative cities. This was one of the crucibles of the Industrial Revolution: almost overnight, a sleepy market town was transformed into a major manufacturing centre, producing everything from silk to bone china, and later locomotives and Rolls-Royce aircraft engines.

With a history dating back to 1750, and supplying every British monarch since 1761, **Royal Crown Derby Factory** *(royalcrownderby.co.uk)* still produces some of the finest bone china in England. Factory visits were closed at the time of writing; check for updates.

The **Derby Museum & Art Gallery** *(derbymuseums.org)* also has ceramics produced by Royal Crown Derby, along with the world's largest collection of works by artist Joseph Wright. Elsewhere, the home

ROBERT HARDING VIDEO/SHUTTERSTOCK

Tissington Trail

of Georgian architect Joseph Pickford has period-furnished rooms and enchanting toy theatres at **Pickford's House**, while Derby's 18th-century Silk Mill, the site of the world's first modern factory, is now the **Museum of Making**.

THE DRIVE: Drive through Derby's outskirts along Kedleston Rd, which gives way to farmland just before the turn-off to Kedleston Hall (5 miles in total).

02 Kedleston Hall

Sitting pretty in vast landscaped grounds, the neoclassical mansion **Kedleston Hall** *(nationaltrust.org.uk)* is a must for fans of stately homes. Entering the house through a grand portico, you'll reach the breathtaking Marble Hall with massive alabaster columns and statues of Greek deities.

The Curzon family has lived here since the 12th century but the current wonder was built by Sir Nathaniel Curzon from 1758. Highlights here include Indian treasures amassed by Viceroy George Curzon and a domed, circular saloon modelled on the Pantheon in Rome, as well as 18th-century-style pleasure gardens.

THE DRIVE: Head west along Buckhazels Lane and join Ashbourne Rd (aka the A52) to drive northwest into Ashbourne (10 miles all up).

03 Ashbourne

Perched at the southern edge of the Peak District National Park, Ashbourne is a pretty patchwork of steeply slanting stone streets lined with cafes, pubs and antique shops.

The main attraction is the chance to walk or cycle along the **Tissington Trail**, part of NCN Route 68, which runs north for 13 miles to Parsley Hay. The track climbs gently along the tunnels, viaducts and cuttings of the disused railway line that once transported local milk to London.

THE DRIVE: It's 17 miles from Ashbourne to Bakewell. Drive north into the rolling countryside (carpeted with daffodils in spring) along Buxton Rd as it winds up through the hills and valleys of the White Peak region.

04 Bakewell

The second largest town in the Peak District (after Buxton), Bakewell is filled with storybook stone buildings. The town is ringed by famous walking trails and stately homes, but it's probably best known for its famous Bakewell pudding, a pastry shell filled with jam and frangipane invented here in 1820.

Up on the hill above Rutland Sq, **All Saints Church** *(bakewellchurch.co.uk)* is packed with ancient features, including a 14th-century font, a pair of Norman arches, heraldic tombs, and a collection of crude stone gravestones and crosses dating from the 12th century.

Nearby, the **Old House Museum** *(oldhousemuseum.org.uk)* explores local history. Check out the Tudor loo and the displays on wattle and daub, a traditional technique for building walls using woven twigs and cow dung.

THE DRIVE: From Bakewell it's just 2 miles southeast along Haddon Rd, following the River Wye, to Haddon Hall.

05 Haddon Hall

With stone turrets, time-worn timbers and walled gardens, **Haddon Hall** *(haddonhall.co.uk)* looks exactly like a medieval manor house should. Founded in the 12th century, it was expanded and remodelled throughout medieval times. The 'modernisation' stopped when the house was abandoned in the 18th century. Spared from the more florid excesses of the Victorian period, Haddon Hall has been used as the location for numerous period blockbusters (such as *Elizabeth*).

THE DRIVE: From Haddon Hall's car park, take your first right (south) onto the B5056 to Grange Mill, then take the A5012 southeast down along a deep gully to Cromford Mill (10.5 miles in all).

06 Cromford Mill

Founded in the 1770s by Richard Arkwright, a leading inventor and entrepreneur during the early Industrial Revolution, **Cromford Mill** *(cromfordmills.org.uk)* was the first modern factory, producing cotton on automated machines powered by a series of waterwheels along the River Derwent. This prototype inspired a succession of mills, ushering in the industrial age.

THE DRIVE: It's a mile-long drive north along the River

Haddon Hall

DARREN MATTHEWS/ALAMY

Derwent to Matlock Bath (not to be confused with the larger, workaday town of Matlock 2 miles to Matlock Bath's north).

07 Matlock Bath

Unashamedly tacky, Matlock Bath looks like a seaside resort that somehow lost its way and ended up at the foot of the Peak District.

Following the River Derwent through a sheer-walled gorge, the main promenade is lined with amusement arcades, tearooms, fish-and-chip shops and pubs. Family-friendly attractions here include **Heights of Abraham** *(heightsofabraham.com)*. A spectacular cable-car ride (accessible with admission ticket only) from the bottom of the gorge brings you to this hilltop leisure park, which has cave and mine tours, and fossil exhibitions.

The enthusiast-run **Peak District Lead Mining Museum** *(peakdistrictleadminingmuseum.co.uk)* provides an educational introduction to Matlock Bath's mining history.

THE DRIVE: Continue north through the valley along the River Derwent and follow the road northeast up into the hills to Chatsworth House, a 9.5-mile journey.

08 Chatsworth House

Known as the 'Palace of the Peak', **Chatsworth House** *(chatsworth.org)* has been occupied by the earls and dukes of Devonshire for centuries. Inside, the lavish apartments and mural-painted staterooms are packed with priceless paintings and period furniture. The house sits in 1.5 sq miles of grounds and ornamental gardens, some landscaped by Lancelot 'Capability' Brown. Kids will love the farmyard adventure playground.

The manor was founded in 1552 by the formidable Bess of Hardwick and her second husband, William Cavendish, who earned grace and favour by helping Henry VIII dissolve the English monasteries. Mary, Queen of Scots was imprisoned at Chatsworth on the orders of Elizabeth I in 1569. Look out for the portraits of the

PA IMAGES/ALAMY

Royal Shrovetide Football Match, Ashbourne (p161)

ROYAL SHROVETIDE FOOTBALL

Some people celebrate Mardi Gras aka Shrove Tuesday (the last day before Lent) by eating pancakes or dressing up in carnival finery. But Ashbourne marks the occasion with a riotous game of football, where the ball is wrestled as much as kicked from one end of town to the other by crowds of revellers.

Following 12th-century rules, villagers are split into two teams – those from north of the river and those from south – and the 'goals' are two millstones, set 3 miles apart. Participants are free to kick, carry or throw the ball, though it's usually squeezed through the crowds like a rugby scrum. Sooner or later, players and the ball end up in the river. Local shops board up their windows and the whole town comes out to watch or play.

Fearless visitors are welcome to participate in the melee but, under a quirk of the rules, only locals are allowed to score goals.

current generation of Devonshires by Lucian Freud.

Also on the estate is an exceptional **farm shop** *(chatsworth.org)* – one of the best in the UK – and an attached cafe, as well as a handful of other delightful eateries and shops.

THE DRIVE: From Chatsworth House it's 15 miles to Chesterfield. Head north along Bakewell Rd to Baslow, then east along the A619 and descend through the forested valley.

09 Chesterfield

Busy Chesterfield is worth a stop to see the astonishing crooked spire rising atop **St Mary & All Saints Church** *(crookedspire.org)*. Dating from 1360, the 68m-high spire is twisted in a right-handed corkscrew and leans several metres southwest. It's the result of the lead casing on the south-facing side having buckled in the sun.

Learn more at the engaging **Chesterfield Museum & Art Gallery** *(chesterfield.gov.uk)*, closed at the time of writing for renovations, which documents Chesterfield's history as a Roman fort through to the present.

THE DRIVE: Take the B6051 northwest through open farmland to Owler Bar. Head west on the B6054 through the Dark Peak region and along the side of the sheer gritstone escarpment Froggatt Edge to Calver, from where Eyam is 2 miles northwest (a 16-mile journey in total).

10 Eyam

Quaint little Eyam (ee-em), a former lead-mining village of sloping streets and old cottages backed by rows of green hills, has a poignant history that's all the more resonant in light of the global COVID-19 pandemic.

In 1665 the town was infected by the dreaded Black Death plague, carried here by fleas on a consignment of cloth from London, and the village rector, William Mompesson, convinced villagers to quarantine themselves. Some 270 of the village's 800 inhabitants succumbed, leaving surrounding villages relatively unscathed. Vivid displays on the Eyam plague are the centrepiece of the engaging **Eyam Museum** *(eyam-museum.org.uk)*, alongside exhibits on the village's history of lead mining and silk weaving. Many victims of the village's 1665 Black Death outbreak were buried at **Eyam Parish Church** (St Lawrence's Church); *(eyamchurch.org)*. Stained-glass panels and moving displays tell the story of the outbreak.

Scenic walking trails surround the village. An interesting short walk leads to **Mompesson's Well**, where supplies were left during the plague by friends from other villages (paid for using coins sterilised in vinegar).

THE DRIVE: Drive west along Main Rd and turn north on the B6049, passing through the villages of Bradwell and Thornhill, to Snake Rd. Cross the two bridges spanning Ladybower Reservoir and head northwest along the western bank to Derwent Reservoirs (16 miles in total).

11 Derwent Reservoirs

The upper reaches of the Derwent Valley were flooded between 1916 and 1935 to create three huge reservoirs – Ladybower, Derwent and Howden – to supply Sheffield, Leicester, Nottingham and Derby with water. These constructed lakes soon proved their worth – the Dambusters squadron carried out practice runs over Derwent Reservoir before unleashing their 'bouncing bombs' on the Ruhr Valley in Germany in WWII.

These days, the reservoirs are popular destinations for walkers, cyclists and mountain bikers – and lots of ducks, so drive slowly!

THE DRIVE: Return to Thornhill and take Hope Rd west to the village of Hope, then turn north on Edale Rd through a wide valley dominated by Dark Peak slopes until you reach Edale (14 miles altogether).

12 Edale

Surrounded by majestic Peak District countryside, this cluster of stone houses is an enchanting

---

♥ WHY I LOVE THIS TRIP

CATHERINE LE NEVEZ, WRITER

What makes this trip so special is its diversity. England's first national park isn't simply an outdoors playground (though there's plenty to do, including incredible walking, so pack your hiking boots!). History lessons here span grand manors to Industrial Revolution–era mills and the site of the Dambusters testing ground. And when you've finished exploring for the day, you can unwind in cosy open-fire-warmed country pubs.

PETER SCHOLEY/ALAMY

Eyam Parish Church

place to pass the time. Walking is the number-one drawcard, with plenty of diverting strolls for less-committed hill walkers.

As well as trips to Hollins Cross and Mam Tor, on the ridge dividing Edale from Castleton, you can walk north onto the Kinder Plateau, dark and brooding in the mist, gloriously high and open when the sun's out. This was the setting for a famous act of civil disobedience by ramblers in 1932 that paved the way for the legal 'right to roam' and the creation of England's national parks.

A fine circular walk starts by following the Pennine Way through fields to Upper Booth, then up a path called Jacobs' Ladder and along the southern edge of Kinder, before dropping down to Edale via the steep rocky valley of Grindsbrook Clough or the ridge of Ringing Roger.

THE DRIVE: Leave Edale to the southwest and climb the steep hill of Mam Tor, before descending precipitous Winnats Pass to Castleton (4.7 miles in total).

13 Castleton

Castleton's village streets are lined with leaning stone houses, with walking trails criss-crossing the surrounding hills. Topping the ridge to the south, a 350m walk from the town centre, sits crag-like **Peveril Castle** *(english-heritage.org.uk)*. Constructed by William Peveril, a favourite of William the Conqueror, the castle was used as a hunting lodge by Henry II, King John and Henry III.

The bedrock below is riddled with fascinating caves. The most convenient, **Peak Cavern** *(peakcavern.co.uk)*, is easily reached by a pretty streamside 250m walk south of the village centre. Dramatic limestone formations are lit with fibreoptic cables.

Just more than half a mile west of Castleton is a claustrophobe's nightmare. **Speedwell Cavern** *(speedwellcavern.co.uk)* is reached via an eerie boat ride through flooded tunnels.

Captivating **Treak Cliff Cavern** *(bluejohnstone.com)*, just under a mile west of Castleton's village centre, has a forest of stalactites and exposed seams of colourful Blue John Stone.

Up the southeastern side of Mam Tor, 2 miles west of Castleton, **Blue John Cavern** *(bluejohn-cavern.co.uk)* is a maze of natural caverns.

THE DRIVE: Retrace your route up spectacular Winnats Pass and head southwest to Sparrowpit. Turn southeast onto the A623 and follow it to Tideswell (a total of 9.5 miles).

14 Tideswell

Dominating the former lead-mining village of **Tideswell**, the massive **parish church** of St John the Baptist – also known as the **Cathedral of the Peak** *(achurchnearyou.com)* – has stood here virtually unchanged since the 14th century. Look out for the wooden panels, inscribed with the Ten Commandments, and the grand 14th-century tomb of local landowner Thurstan de Bower, depicted in full medieval armour.

THE DRIVE: Take the B6049 south to join the forested A6 (you'll see clouds of snowdrops and bluebells in early spring), which shadows the River Wye to Poole's Cavern (9 miles all told).

15 Poole's Cavern

The magnificent natural limestone **Poole's Cavern** *(buxtoncivicassociation.org.uk)* is reached by descending 28 steps; the temperature is a cool 7°C. Tours last 45 minutes. From the cavern's car park, a 20-minute walk leads up through Grin Low Wood to Solomon's Temple, a ruined tower with fine views over the town.

THE DRIVE: The last stretch is also the shortest: from Poole's Cavern (it's just 1 mile northeast along the A515 to Buxton)

16 Buxton

The 'capital' of the Peak District National Park, albeit just outside the park boundary in the rolling hills of the Derbyshire dales, Buxton built its fortunes on its natural warm-water springs, which attracted health tourists in Buxton's turn-of-the-century heyday.

Cathedral of the Peak

MATT SMITH/ALAMY

IRONBELL/SHUTTERSTOCK

Edale (p165)

GET ON YOUR BIKE

The **Peak District National Park Authority** *(peakdistrict.gov.uk)* operates cycle-hire centres at Ashbourne, Derwent Reservoirs and Parsley Hay, renting out road, mountain, tandem, e-bikes and kids' bikes. You can hire from one location and drop it off at another.

Buxton's extravagant baths were built in Regency style in 1854 and are fronted by the **Crescent** *(buxtoncrescentexperience.com)*, a grand, curving facade inspired by the Royal Crescent in Bath. Its pump room, which dispensed the town's spring water for nearly a century, has displays showcasing Buxton's thermal springs heritage spanning their Roman discovery to today. Within the complex is a five-star hotel and lavish spa, including the original Victorian baths with naturally heated 28°C water.

Adjoining Buxton's turreted **Opera House** *(buxtonoperahouse.org.uk)* are the 9-hectare **Pavilion Gardens** *(paviliongardens.co.uk)* with domed pavilions; concerts take place in the bandstand throughout the year. For kids, there are open picnic areas and playgrounds, plus a mini-railway.

Guided walks and character-led tours (eg Robert Rippon Duke's Victorian architecture tour and Miss Florence Cook's Victorian ghost tour) are available through **Discover Buxton Tours** *(discoverbuxton.co.uk)*.

Collections of the **Buxton Museum & Art Gallery** *(derbyshire.gov.uk/leisure/buxton-museum/buxton-museum-and-art-gallery.aspx)* are displayed at the Buxton Library until it finds a new permanent home.

STAY AWHILE

BAKEWELL

BY CATHERINE LE NEVEZ

After a day's hiking in the Peak District, I love returning to stay in Bakewell with its huddle of sandstone and limestone buildings and a five-span, pointed-arch stone bridge (one of England's oldest, dating from around 1300) crossing the willow-lined River Wye, where ducks and geese splash in the cascading weir. It's a gorgeous and relaxing spot amid the surrounding national park.

What I especially love is that the charming town manages to avoid feeling touristy despite its popularity with walkers. It's small enough to be able to park up and wander on foot but big enough for all the essential amenities – traditional shops, delis, bakeries, tea rooms, great restaurants and cosy pubs with crackling open fires and real ales.

On the River Wye, a half-mile meander northwest of the centre, **Thornbridge Brewery** *(thornbridgebrewery.com)* brews vegan, gluten-free and alcohol-free beer varieties through to Cognac barrel-aged stout, runs tours with tastings, and has a fantastic taproom hosting gigs and open-mic nights. It originated at **Thornbridge Hall** *(thornbridgehall.co.uk)*, a fabulously quirky stately home 2 miles northwest, set in 10-acre gardens, with tours of its great hall with William Morris stained-glass windows, a carriage house and a music room.

Whenever possible, I try to catch the Monday stall **market** *(derbyshiredales.gov.uk)*, when 80-plus traders selling fresh produce, flowers, linen, clothing, jewellery and more set up on Market Pl and Granby Rd; even better if I can catch the farmers market (at Bakewell's Agricultural Business Centre, often the last Saturday of the month), the second largest in Britain.

LINK YOUR TRIP

Stop off in the 18 **Peak District** or drive 35 miles east to Nottingham for 19 **Midlands Battlefields, Castles & stately homess**.

UNIVERSAL IMAGES GROUP LTD/ALAMY

KAY ROXBY/ALAMY

Left: Thornbridge Hall, Right: Rutland Arms Hotel

PLACES TO STAY

Accommodation in and around Bakewell and the wider Peak District fills up quickly in the summer months, so lock in bookings well ahead.

Rutland Arms Hotel
Landmark 1804 Georgian coaching inn in the centre of Bakewell; rooms range from small singles to four-poster suites. *rutlandarmsbakewell.co.uk*

Bagshaw Hall & Lodge
A short stroll from the town centre, with period-furnished rooms in the original house from 1649 and contemporary self-catering rooms in the annexe. *bagshawhall.com*

Pilsley Inn
Woodland walks lead from this ivy-clad stone inn 3 miles northeast of Bakewell on the Chatsworth Estate, with estate-grown produce on the restaurant menu. *chatsworthescapes.co.uk*

19

CENTRAL ENGLAND

MIDLANDS BATTLEFIELDS, CASTLES & STATELY HOMES

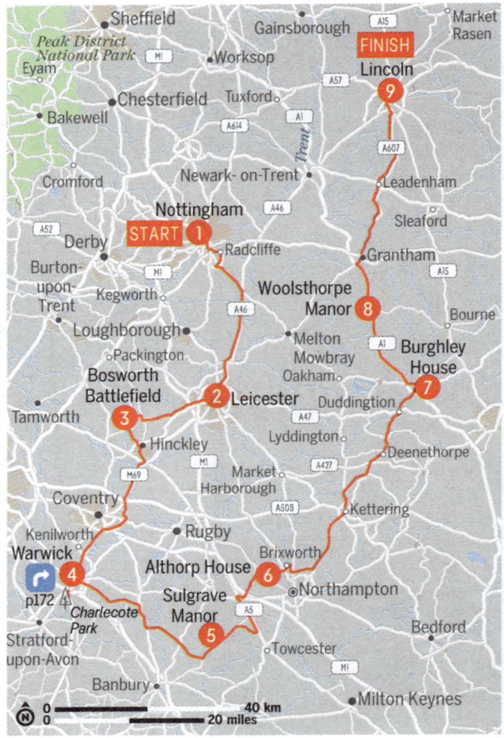

DURATION: 5 DAYS

DISTANCE: 214 MILES / 344KM

GREAT FOR: HISTORY, FAMILIES

BEST TIME TO GO: JUNE TO SEPTEMBER SEES THE BEST WEATHER AND FEWEST CLOSURES.

This grand tour begins and ends with famed castles, and stops at a third mighty fortress en route. In between, you'll see the field where Richard III became the last English king to die in battle, learn the extraordinary story of the recent discovery of his long-lost remains in a city car park, and wander the opulent corridors of stately homes and their magnificently landscaped gardens and deer-roamed grounds.

LINK YOUR TRIP

16 The Cotswolds & Literary England
From Warwick, it's 8 miles southwest to Stratford-upon-Avon for a spin through quintessentially English rolling countryside.

18 Peak District
It's a 15-mile hop west from Nottingham to Derby, from where you can strike out into the glorious Peak District National Park.

01 Nottingham

Nottingham is synonymous with mythologised outlaw Robin Hood. A **bronze statue** (Castle Rd) of the woodsman stands in the former moat of **Nottingham Castle** *(nottinghamcastle.org.uk)*. Founded by William the Conqueror, the original castle was held by a succession of English kings before falling in the English Civil War. Its 17th-century manor-house-like replacement contains a local-history museum and art gallery.

Carved into the cliff beneath the castle, **Ye Olde Trip to Jerusalem** *(greeneking.co.uk)*, founded in 1189, claims to be England's oldest inn.

For more Robin Hood history, take an entertaining, highly informative 2½-hour Robin Hood Town Tour with **Ezekial Bone Tours** *(ezekialbone.com)*. Tours of nearby Sherwood Forest can also be arranged.

The city's bedrock is riddled with caves, which you can delve into on tours of the **City of Caves**

★ BEST FOR

FAMILIES

Relive medieval times at Warwick Castle.

DESTINOS ESPETACULARES/SHUTTERSTOCK

Ye Olde Trip to Jerusalem

(nationaljusticemuseum.org.uk/cityofcaves). Audio guides lead you through a WWII air-raid shelter, a medieval underground tannery, several pub cellars and a mock-up of a Victorian slum dwelling. Book ahead for a time slot.

THE DRIVE: It's an easy 28 miles' drive south to Leicester. The A46, which travels through a dark-green patchwork of dairy and crop fields, makes a scenic alternative to the speedier but busier M1.

02 Leicester

Built directly over the buried ruins of two millennia of history, Leicester (les-ter) suffered at the hands of the Luftwaffe and postwar planners, but a massive influx of textile workers from India and Pakistan since the 1960s has transformed the city into a bustling global melting pot.

The astonishing 2012 discovery and 2013 identification of the remains of King Richard III in a Leicester car park sparked a flurry of developments, including a spiffing visitor centre on the site, **King Richard III: Dynasty, Death & Discovery** *(kriii.com)*, which details the University of Leicester's archaeological dig and identification, and lets you view the site of the grave in which he was found.

The discovery also led to the restoration of **Leicester Cathedral** *(leicestercathedral.org)*, where the king was reburied in 2015; you can visit his grave, which is topped by a contemporary limestone tomb.

THE DRIVE: Travel through open farmland for 14 miles west, via the A47, to Sutton Cheney, where you'll see the turn-off to the site of the Battle of Bosworth.

03 Bosworth Battlefield

Given a few hundred years, every battlefield ends up simply a field, but the site of the Battle of Bosworth – where Richard III met his maker in 1485 – is enlivened by the entertaining **Bosworth Battlefield Heritage Centre** *(bosworthbattlefield.org.uk)*, full of skeletons and musket balls. Although it lasted just a few hours the Battle of Bosworth marked the end of the Plantagenet dynasty and the start of the Tudor era.

This was where the mortally wounded Richard III famously proclaimed: 'A horse, a horse, my kingdom for a horse.' (Actually, he didn't: the quote was invented by that great Tudor propagandist William Shakespeare.) Enthusiasts in period costume re-enact the battle each August.

THE DRIVE: It's 32 miles southwest from Bosworth, via the M69 (skirting the southeastern edge of Coventry) and the A46, to Warwick.

04 Warwick

Regularly name-checked by Shakespeare, Warwick was the ancestral seat of the Earls of Warwick, who played a pivotal role in the Wars of the Roses. Despite a devastating fire in 1694, Warwick remains a treasure-house of medieval architecture with rich veins of history and charming streets, dominated by the many soaring turrets of **Warwick Castle** *(warwick-castle.com)*.

Founded in 1068 by William the Conqueror, the ancestral home of the Earls of Warwick remains impressively intact, and is today filled with flamboyant, family-friendly attractions that bring the castle's rich history to life. Waxworks populate the private apartments; there are also jousting tournaments, regular trebuchet firings, themed evenings and a dungeon. Tickets are cheaper online.

You can even stay here – atmospheric **accommodation options** *(warwick-castle.com)* span tower suites to lodges at its riverside Knight's Village and themed tents in its 'glamping' ground.

THE DRIVE: Take Gallows Hill Rd southeast out of Warwick and continue southeast through farmland of potato and cabbage crops along with golden fields of flowering canola. It's 27 miles in total to Sulgrave Manor.

DETOUR

Charlecote Park

Start: 04 Warwick

From Warwick, you can take a short 6-mile side trip southwest, via Stratford Rd and the southbound A429, to **Charlecote Park** *(nationaltrust.org.uk)*. A youthful Shakespeare allegedly poached deer in the grounds of this lavish pile on the River Avon, and fallow deer still roam the grounds today. It was remodelled over the years, with the interiors restored in Elizabethan Revival style in the 19th century. Highlights include Victorian kitchens, filled with culinary moulds, and an original 1551 Tudor gatehouse.

05 Sulgrave Manor

The impressively preserved Tudor mansion **Sulgrave Manor**

Re-enactment, Warwick Castle

GARY PERKIN/SHUTTERSTOCK

(sulgravemanor.org.uk) was built by Lawrence Washington in 1539. The Washington family lived here for almost 120 years before Colonel John Washington, the great-grandfather of America's first president, George Washington, sailed to Virginia in 1656.

THE DRIVE: From Sulgrave Manor it's a 21-mile drive northeast via Northampton Rd and the A5 to another famous family home, Althorp House.

06 Althorp House

The ancestral home of the Spencer family, **Althorp House** *(althorp.com)* – pronounced 'awl-thorp' – is the final resting place of Diana, Princess of Wales, commemorated by a memorial. The outstanding art collection features works by Rubens, Gainsborough and van Dyck. Hours are seasonal and tickets are limited; pre-book by phone or online.

THE DRIVE: Leaving Althorp House, head northeast, passing through the charming ivy-clad stone villages of Church Brampton and Chapel Brampton. You'll skirt the larger towns of Kettering and Corby, as well as the southern edge of Stamford, before reaching Burghley House (42 miles in all).

07 Burghley House

Set in more than 810 hectares of grounds, landscaped by Capability Brown, resplendent **Burghley House** *(burghley.co.uk)*, pronounced 'bur-lee', was built by Queen Elizabeth I's chief adviser William Cecil, whose descendants still live here. It bristles with cupolas, pavilions, belvederes and chimneys; the lavish staterooms are a particular highlight. In early September the renowned **Burghley Horse Trials** *(burghley-horse.co.uk)* take place here.

The estate is 1.3 miles southeast of **Stamford**, one of England's prettiest towns, with elegant streets lined with honey-coloured limestone buildings and hidden alleyways dotted with alehouses, interesting eating outlets and small independent boutiques. A forest of historic church spires rises overhead and the gently gurgling River Welland meanders through the town centre.

This is a favourite with filmmakers seeking the postcard vision of England, and has appeared in everything from *Pride and Prejudice* to *The Da Vinci Code.*

MARTIN BACHE/ALAMY

Woolsthorpe Manor

> **PHOTO OPPORTUNITY**
>
> The apple tree that inspired Newton's theory of gravity at Woolsthorpe Manor.

THE DRIVE: It's a 17-mile trip from Burghley House via the A1 to Woolsthorpe Manor.

08 Woolsthorpe Manor

Sir Isaac Newton fans may feel the gravitational pull of the great man's birthplace, **Woolsthorpe Manor** *(nationaltrust.org.uk)*. The humble 17th-century house contains reconstructions of Newton's rooms; the apple that inspired his theory of gravity allegedly fell from the tree in the garden. There's a nifty kids' science room and a cafe.

THE DRIVE: The final 33-mile stretch of this trip, via the High Dike road, takes you past cauliflower, corn and wheat fields. At Waddington, look out to your right to see fighter jets landing at its famous RAF air base. As you approach Lincoln, you'll see its cathedral spires and castle crenulations rising up on the ridgeline to the north.

09 Lincoln

Ringed by historic city gates – including the Newport Arch (Bailgate) on Bailgate, a relic from the original Roman settlement – Lincoln's historic centre is a tangle of cobbled medieval streets surrounding a colossal 12th-century **cathedral** *(lincoln cathedral.com)*.

Towering over the city like a medieval skyscraper, it's a breathtaking representation of divine power on Earth. The great tower rising above the crossing is the third highest in England at 83m, but in medieval times, a lead-encased wooden spire added a further 79m, topping even the great pyramids of Giza.

One-hour guided tours (included in admission) take place at least twice daily Mondays to Saturdays; there are also tours of the roof and tower (book in advance).

Nearby **Lincoln Castle** *(lincoln castle.com)* was one of the first castles erected by the victorious William the Conqueror to keep his new kingdom in line, and offers awesome views over the city and miles of surrounding countryside. A major restoration programme has opened up the entire castle walls and given the 1215 Magna Carta (one of only four copies) a swanky, subterranean new home.

It's worth booking ahead for one-hour guided tours, included in castle admission.

The lanes that topple over the edge of Lincoln Cliff are lined with Tudor townhouses, ancient pubs and quirky independent stores. Flanking the River Witham at the base of the hill, the new town is less absorbing, but the revitalised Brayford Waterfront development is a popular spot to watch the boats go by.

CHIC & HISTORIC PLACES TO STAY

In the heart of the gentrified Lace Market in Nottingham, elegant Georgian townhouse, the **Lace Market** *(lacemarkethotel.co.uk)* boutique hotel has 51 sleek rooms with state-of-the-art furnishings and amenities, some with air con. Its adjoining pub, the **Cock & Hoop** *(lacemarkethotel.co.uk)*, serves real ales and traditional pub food all day.

Owned and run by the same family for four generations, the 19th-century **Belmont Hotel** *(belmonthotel.co.uk)* in Leicester has 74 stylish, contemporary, individually designed rooms and a fantastic location overlooking leafy New Walk. Family rooms have a double bed and bunks. **Jaime's Bar & Restaurant** opens all day; afternoon tea is a highlight. Each of the **Castle Hotel**'s *(castlehotel.net)* 18 rooms has been exquisitely refurbished in olive, truffle and oyster tones, as has its family-friendly four-person coach house. It was built on the site of Lincoln's Roman forum in 1852; the red-brick building's incarnations variously included a school and a WWII lookout station. Take advantage of great-value dinner, bed and breakfast deals at its award-winning restaurant **Reform** *(reformrestaurant.co.uk)*.

Lincoln Cathedral

MICHAEL ODDI/SHUTTERSTOCK

EDINBURGH
Grantshouse
A1
Berwick-upon-Tweed
0 50 km
0 25 miles
Duns
A697
Biggar
Peebles
Galashiels
Coldstream
24
Bamburgh
Innerleithen
Melrose
Kelso
A697
Low Newton-by-the-Sea
Megget Reservoir
SCOTLAND
Jedburgh
Craster
Hawick
A68
Alnwick
Warkworth
Amble
A1
North Sea
Moffat
A7
Rochester
A1068
Border Forest Park
Northumberland National Park
Morpeth
Newbiggin-by-the-Sea
A74(M)
Lockerbie
NORTHUMBERLAND
Whitley Bay
Ponteland
Chollerford
Dumfries
23
Tynemouth
Gretna Green
South Shields
Brampton
Hexham
Corbridge
Haltwhistle
Sunderland
Carlisle
Newcastle-upon-Tyne
Seaham
Waverton
Killhope
Durham
M6
Peterlee
Workington
Eamont Bridge
West Auckland
DURHAM
Hartlepool
Cockermouth
Billingham
Keswick
Barnard Castle
Stockton-on-Tees
A5086
Ullswater
Middlesbrough
Glenridding
Buttermere
Brough
Guisborough
Whitby
Robin Hood's Bay
Egremont
Grasmere
CUMBRIA
Bowes
Darlington
Danby
Wasdale
Great Langdale
Ambleside
A19
Goathland
20
Richmond
Buttertubs Pass
Lake District National Park
Coniston
Windermere
22
North York Moors National Park
A171
Hawkshead
Leyburn
Ravenglass
NORTH YORKSHIRE
Lake District National Park
Kendal
Whernside (735m)
Hawes
Thirsk
A170
Scarborough
Great Whrenside (705m)
Helmsley
Millom
Ulverston
Ripon
Malton
Arncliffe
Pateley Bridge
Easingwold
Grassington
Morecambe Bay
Ingleton
A65
A1
Kirkham
Great Driffield
Settle
21
Knaresborough
A64
Irish Sea
Malham
Lancaster
Forest of Bowland
Harrogate
York
Skipton
A6
A59
LANCASHIRE
YORK
Beverley
Keighley
Nelson
Leeds
Blackpool
Selby
Burnley
Bradford
Preston
Humber
Blackburn
Halifax
M62
Goole
SEFTON
M61
Southport
M62
Huddersfield
DONCASTER
Scunthorpe
Bolton
Ormskirk
Bury
Holmfirth
Barnsley
Doncaster
M180
Formby
Wigan
ROTHERHAM
Manchester
St Helens
Maltby
Gainsborough
Sheffield
Liverpool
Peak District National Park
Stockport
Warrington
Mersey
A1
LINCOLNSHIRE

CHRISDORNEY/SHUTTERSTOCK

Whale Bone Arch (p198)

LAKE DISTRICT & NORTHERN ENGLAND

EXPLORE

LAKE DISTRICT & NORTHERN ENGLAND

England's north is its wildest and most romantic region. While millions head annually to the incomparable Lake District, inspired by the Romantic poets and painters who built its legend, fewer explore the delights of the unpeopled national parks, ancient monuments and untamed, castle-studded coastline of Northumbria.

One of the easiest parts of the country to escape the hustle, the north is rich in sites of historical and cultural interest. The Northumberland and Yorkshire Dales National Parks are unsurpassed; York and Durham's museums and medieval streetscapes are perfect for wandering; and Newcastle is the proud, peerless metropolis of the northeast.

Leeds

Yorkshire's unofficial capital is well placed to access the 'Yorkshire Dales' (p188) and 'North York Moors & Coast' (p194) drives and is the best-equipped city in this region. It's served by Leeds Bradford Airport, which has connections to 80+ European destinations (some seasonal). It's directly connected to London by rail (around 2½ hours) and coach (around four hours). There's not much budget accommodation in central Leeds, but you'll find plenty of boutique options, plus places to shop and hire a car.

Newcastle-upon-Tyne

The metropolis of the northeast, Newcastle is the ideal base for the 'Hadrian's Wall' (p200) and 'Northumbria' (p206) itineraries. Accessible by train from London in around three hours, it is on the fast coastal line that continues to Edinburgh (another 1½ hours). A thriving student centre, like Leeds and Durham, it has plenty to recommend it by way of nightlife, eating and accommodation. Rental cars are easily found, and trains and buses run to Carlisle, Alnwick and other centres.

York

York, more of a tourist magnet than Leeds or Newcastle, is perfectly placed for the 'Yorkshire Dales' (p188) and 'North York Moors & Coast' (p194) drives. A historic highlight in its own right, established by the Romans and showing later Viking,

WHEN TO GO

The Lakes are probably England's most traffic-logged beauty spot at peak times, such as the August school holidays. Try to time your visit for the shoulder seasons of April/May and September/October. Avoid school-holiday periods where possible. Midwinter brings snow and ice to higher ground throughout the region, which may put a kink in your driving plans.

Anglo-Saxon and Anglo-Norman influences, it's not a very cheap place to stay, and having a car can be a liability in the medieval centre. It's a well-serviced base with excellent pubs and restaurants.

Carlisle

Historic and not-yet-gentrified, Carlisle is a good base for the 'Hadrian's Wall' (p200) and 'Classic Lakes' (p180) drives. Inexpensive accommodation can be found here, alongside decent shopping and car-rental options. The fastest direct trains to London take around 3½ hours.

Windermere

The most heavily touristed of the Lakes towns is replete with B&Bs and heritage hotels. It's also connected by local bus to more remote parts of the region and can be reached by rail from Carlisle (via Oxenholme) in a little over an hour.

Keswick

The gateway to the northern Lakes, Keswick no longer has a train station; the nearest is 17 miles east in Penrith, linked by bus (40 minutes). A hub for walkers and outdoor enthusiasts, it's blessed with plenty of B&Bs for varying budgets and has an excellent supermarket for supplies. Local buses, fanning out into the region's more remote valleys, pass through.

TRANSPORT

If you're coming from London, the high-speed train to Leeds or Newcastle is your best bet for accessing the north. Both cities have plenty of car-hire options, so you can proceed from there. If you'd rather base yourself in or near the Lakes, you'll need to take a coach or an additional train from Newcastle to Carlisle.

WHERE TO STAY

Dakota, Leeds, is a luxury option in the centre of the city that reflects the northern city's vibrancy and style.

Classy, comfortable and eccentric, Rum Doodle, Windermere, is named after a WE Bowman novel parodying 1950s mountaineering memoirs.

YHA Berwick-upon-Tweed offers cheap, comfortable beds, a bar and lounge, and even an art gallery.

The Inn at Cheltenham Parade, Harrogate, is a boutique hotel in the centre of Harrogate, one of Yorkshire's handsomest towns.

An ideal historic hotel, dating in parts to the 11th century, Grays Court, York, is now all modern sophistication

RESOURCES

- **The Sill**
  An excellent tourist-information centre and exhibition space on the southern verge of Northumberland National Park, near Hadrian's Wall. *Thesill.org.uk*
- **Lake District Guide**
  Comprehensive and well-maintained guide to all there is to do and see in the Lakes. *Visitlakedistrict.com*
- **North East England**
  Packed with info on Newcastle, Northumberland and beyond. *Visitnortheastengland.com*

WHAT'S ON

- **Spring Flower Show**
  This much-loved horticultural festival brings colour and life to Harrogate for four days in late April.
- **Amble Puffin Festival**
  The Northumbrian coastal town of Amble celebrates puffin-hatching season on the bird sanctuary of Coquet Island for two days in late May.
- **Leeds Festival**
  Each August bank holiday draws 50,000 music lovers to Bramham Park, 10 miles outside the city centre.

20

LAKE DISTRICT & NORTHERN ENGLAND

CLASSIC LAKES

★ BEST FOR

FAMILIES

Bike trails, sculptures and zip lines at Grizedale Forest.

Lake Windermere

DURATION: 5 DAYS

DISTANCE: 154 MILES / 248KM

GREAT FOR: HISTORY, FAMILIES, OUTDOORS

BEST TIME TO GO: SUMMER AND EASTER CAN BE HECTIC IN THE LAKES; SPRING AND AUTUMN ARE BEST.

This road trip takes in the scenic wonders of the UK's largest and loveliest national park. William Wordsworth, Samuel Taylor Coleridge and Beatrix Potter are among the literary luminaries who have fallen in love with the Lake District. The national park is studded by England's highest hills (fells), including the highest of all, Scafell Pike. Alongside lakes, forest, hills and valleys, the drive takes in country houses and cosy pubs.

LINK YOUR TRIP

23 Hadrian's Wall
From Windermere, head north to Carlisle to explore Roman England's most ambitious structure.

30 The Borders
The Lake District is an obvious launch pad for travels north of the Scottish border; Glasgow is 130 miles from Ullswater.

01 Bowness-on-Windermere

At 10.5 miles long, Windermere is the largest body of water in England: more a loch than a lake. It's also one of the most popular places in the Lake District, and has been a tourist centre since the late 19th century, especially for lake cruises.

Windermere gets its name from the old Norse, *Vinandr mere* (Vinandr's lake; so 'Lake Windermere' is actually tautologous). Encompassing 5.7 sq miles between Ambleside and Newby Bridge, the lake is a mile wide at its broadest point, with a maximum depth of about 65m. There are 18 islands on Windermere: the largest is Belle Isle, encompassing 16 hectares and an 18th-century Italianate mansion, while the smallest is Maiden Holme, little more than a patch of soil and a solitary tree.

The wonderful **Windermere Jetty Museum** *(lakelandarts.org.uk/windermere-jetty-museum),*

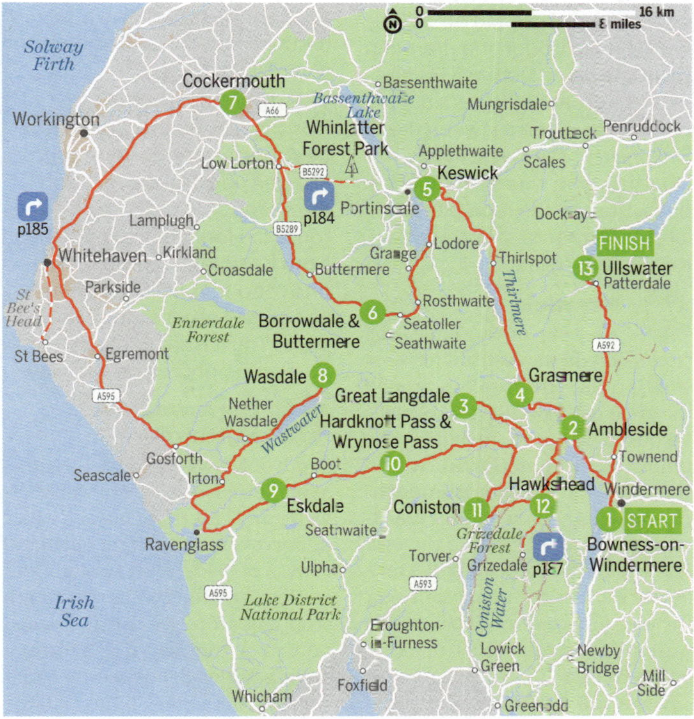

DAVID LYONS/ALAMY

opened after years of development, explores the history of cruising with a glorious collection of vintage boats, punts and steam yachts – including the *Esperance*, which provided the inspiration for Captain Flint's houseboat in Arthur Ransome's *Swallows and Amazons*. Best of all, you can take your own trip aboard the 1902 *Osprey* or the 1930 *Penelope II*. There's simply no more stylish way to see Windermere.

Alternatively, **Windermere Lake Cruises** *(windermere-lakecruises.co.uk)* offers sightseeing trips leaving from Bowness Pier.

THE DRIVE: From Bowness, follow Rayrigg Rd north until it joins the A591, which rolls all the way to Ambleside, for 6 miles.

02 Ambleside

At the northern end of Windermere lies the old mill town of Ambleside. It's a pretty place, well stocked with outdoors shops and some excellent restaurants: don't miss a meal at the fabulous **Lake Road Kitchen** *(lakeroadkitchen.co.uk)*, run by Michelin-starred chef James Cross, who trained at the legendary Noma in Copenhagen.

Afterwards take a half-hour woodland walk to the double-drop waterfall of **Stock Ghyll Force**, a clattering 21m-high waterfall on the edge of town. The trail is signposted behind the old Market Hall at the bottom of Stock Ghyll Lane. If you feel energetic, you can follow the trail beyond the falls up **Wansfell Pike** (482m), a reasonably steep walk of about two hours.

THE DRIVE: Take the A593 west towards Skelwith Bridge, and follow signs to Elterwater and Great Langdale. It's a wonderful 8-mile drive that gets wilder and wilder the deeper you head into the valley. There's a large car park beside the Old Dungeon Ghyll Hotel, but it gets busy in summer; there's usually overflow parking available in a nearby field.

03 Great Langdale

The Lake District has some truly stunning valleys, but Great Langdale definitely ranks near the top. As you pass through the pretty village of Elterwater and its village green, the scenery becomes really wild and empty. Fells stack up like dominoes along the horizon, looming over a patchwork of barns and fields.

If you're up for a hike, then you might consider tackling the multi-peak circuit around the **Langdale Pikes** – a tough, full-day hike into the wild fells above Langdale, which allows you to pick off between three and five summits depending on your route, including the four main 'Pikes' of Pike O' Stickle (709m), Loft Crag (682m), Harrison Stickle (736m) and Pavey Ark (700m). You'll need proper boots, hiking gear and an Ordnance Survey map.

Alternatively, the more sedentary option is to just admire the views over a pint of locally brewed ale from the cosy bar of the **Old Dungeon Ghyll** *(odg.co.uk)*, a classic hikers' haunt.

THE DRIVE: Retrace the road to Ambleside and head north to Grasmere on the A591 for 5 miles; total distance is 10 miles.

04 Grasmere

The lovely little village of Grasmere is inextricably linked with the poet William Wordsworth, who made it his home in the late 18th century and never left unless he really had to. Two of his houses are now open to the public. The most famous is **Dove Cottage** *(wordsworth.org.uk)*, a tiny house where he lived with his sister Dorothy, wife Mary and three children between 1798 and 1808. Guided tours explore the house, and next door the museum has lots of memorabilia and original manuscripts relating to the Romantic poets.

A little way south of Grasmere is the house where Wordsworth spent most of his adult life, **Rydal Mount** *(rydalmount.co.uk)*. It's still owned by the poet's descendants, and is a much grander affair than Dove Cottage: you can have a look around the library, visit the poet's attic study and wander the gardens he designed. Below the house, Dora's Field is filled with daffodils in springtime; it was planted in memory of Wordsworth's daughter, who died of tuberculosis.

If you have a sweet tooth, you'll want to pick up a souvenir at **Sarah Nelson's Gingerbread Shop** *(grasmeregingerbread.co.uk)*, which still makes its gingerbread according to a recipe from 1854.

THE DRIVE: From Grasmere, continue north on the A591. You'll pass through the dramatic pass known as Dunmail Raise, where a great battle is said to have taken place between the Saxons and the Celtic king Dunmail, who was slain near the pass. Stay on the road past the lake of Thirlmere all the way to Keswick (13 miles).

05 Keswick

Another of the Lake District's classic market towns, Keswick is a place that revolves around the great outdoors. Several big fells lie on its doorstep, including the imposing lump of **Skiddaw** and the dramatic ridge of **Blencathra**, but it's the lake of **Derwentwater** that really draws the eye: it was said to be Beatrix Potter's favourite, and she supposedly got the idea for *Squirrel Nutkin* while watching red squirrels frolicking on its shores.

Keswick Launch *(keswick-launch.co.uk)* travels out around the lake February to November: you could combine it with an easy hike up to the top of **Catbells** (451m), a favourite first-time fell for many walkers. The views of the lake and the distant hills are absolutely breathtaking.

Back in town, don't miss a visit to **George Fisher** *(georgefisher.co.uk)*, the most famous outdoors shop in the Lake District: if you need new hiking boots, this is definitely the place to come.

THE DRIVE: The drive into Borrowdale on the B5289 is a beauty, passing several pretty villages as it travels through the valley. You can't get lost en route to Honister Pass (7 miles from Keswick) – there's only one road to take; Buttermere lies on the other side of the pass. You'll want to stop for numerous photos on the way.

06 Borrowdale & Buttermere

South of Keswick, the B5289 tracks along the eastern side of Derwentwater and enters the bucolic valley of Borrowdale, a classic Lakeland canvas of fields, fells, streams and endless drystone walls. It's worth stopping off to see the geological oddity of the **Bowder Stone**, a huge boulder deposited by a glacier, and for a quick hike up to the top of Castle Crag, which has the best views of the valley.

Then it's up and over the perilously steep Honister Pass, where the Lake District's last working **slate mine** *(honister.com)* is still doing a thriving trade. You can take a guided tour down into the mine or brave the heights along the nerve-testing via ferrata,

NATIONAL TRUST MEMBERSHIP

Being a member of the **National Trust** (NT; *nationaltrust.org.uk*), or purchasing a 4-, 8- or 14-day overseas-visitor NT Explorer Pass, comes in very handy in the Lake District. The NT owns several key attractions, including Hill Top and the Beatrix Potter Gallery near Hawkshead, Wordsworth House in Cockermouth, and Fell Foot and Wray Castle near Windermere. Best of all, you get to park for free at most of the NT's car parks – handy in celebrated beauty spots like Buttermere, Borrowdale, Wasdale, Gowbarrow Park and Tarn Hows.

Derwentwater, near Keswick

DANIEL_KAY/SHUTTERSTOCK

to carry 3
41 to carry 4

and pick up slate souvenirs in the shop.

Nearby **Buttermere**, 5.5 miles west of Borrowdale, has a sparkling twinset of lakes, Buttermere and Crummock Water, and is backed by a string of impressive fells. The summit of **Haystacks** (597m) is a popular route: it was the favourite fell of Alfred Wainwright, who penned the definitive seven-volume set of guidebooks on the Lake District's fells between the 1950s and '70s. It's a three- to four-hour return walk from Buttermere.

THE DRIVE: From Buttermere village, bear left on the B5289 signed towards Loweswater and Crummock Water, which continues into the Lorton Valley. At Low Lorton, stay on the B5289, which continues 4 miles to Cockermouth. Total distance is 11 miles.

DETOUR

Whinlatter Forest Park

Start: 06 Buttermere

Encompassing 4.6 sq miles of pine, larch and spruce, **Whinlatter** *(forestryengland.uk/whinlatter)* is England's only true mountain forest, rising sharply to 790m. It's about 5 miles from Keswick.

The forest is a designated red squirrel reserve; you can check out live video feeds from squirrel cams at the visitor centre. It's also home to several exciting mountain-bike trails and a tree-top assault course. You can hire bikes next to the visitor centre.

To get to Whinlatter Forest Park from Buttermere, look out for the right turn onto the B5292 at Low Lorton, which climbs up to Whinlatter Pass.

07 Cockermouth

Grasmere might be Wordsworth central, but completists will want to visit the **poet's childhood home** *(nationaltrust.org.uk/wordsworth-house)* in Cockermouth.

Now owned by the National Trust, it's been redecorated in period style according to details published in Wordsworth's own father's accounts: you can wander round the drawing room, kitchen, pantry and garden, and see the rooms where little Willie and his brother John slept. Costumed

Buttermere Lake

PATRYK KOSMIDER/SHUTTERSTOCK

guides wander around the house for added period authenticity. Outside is the walled kitchen garden mentioned in Wordsworth's autobiographical epic *The Prelude*.

THE DRIVE: Head west on the A66 and detour onto the A595, which tracks the coast all the way to Whitehaven. To reach Wasdale (35 miles all up), turn off at Gosforth, and then follow signs to Nether Wasdale and Wasdale Head. It's quite easy to miss the turning, so keep your eyes peeled; satnavs can be very unreliable here.

DETOUR

St Bees Head

Start: 07 Cockermouth

Cumbria's coastline might not have the white sandy beaches of Wales or the epic grandeur of the Scottish coast, but it has a bleak beauty all of its own – not to mention a renowned seabird reserve at **St Bees Head** *(rspb.org.uk)*, where you can spot species including fulmars, herring gulls, kittiwakes and razorbills – as well as England's only nesting black guillemots at nearby Fleswick Bay. Just try and forget that one of the UK's largest nuclear reactors, Sellafield, is round the corner. The village of St Bees lies 5 miles south of Whitehaven, and the headland is signposted from there.

08 Wasdale

Wild Wasdale is arguably the most dramatic valley in the Lake District National Park. Carving its way for 5 miles from the coast, it was gouged out by a long-extinct glacier during the last Ice Age; if you get an up-close look, you can still see glacial marks on the scree-strewn slopes above Wastwater.

It's a truly dramatic drive that feels rather like heading into the depths of a remote Scottish glen: in terms of mountain scenery, it's probably the most impressive stretch of road this side of the Highlands.

Most people come for the chance to reach the summit of **Scafell Pike**, England's highest point (978m); it's a tough six- to seven-hour slog, but the views from the top are quite literally as good as they get (assuming the weather plays ball, of course).

WHY I LOVE THIS TRIP

CATHERINE LE NEVEZ, WRITER

After you've tackled the Lake District's fells, waterfalls, lakes and meadows its villages and towns are filled with local treats to recharge. Along with Grassmere's 19th-century-recipe gingerbread, specialities include sweet Morecambe Bay shrimps, coiled Cumberland sausage (a staple of Cumbrian breakfasts and traditional dishes like toad-in-the-hole), Cumberland rum nicky (shortcrust pastry filled with spiced, rum-soaked dried fruit), sugary Kendal Mint Cake and sublime Cartmel sticky toffee pudding.

Afterwards, reward yourself with a meal at the **Wasdale Head Inn** *(wasdale.com)*, a gloriously olde-worlde hostelry with lashings of mountain heritage: it was here that the sport of rock climbing was pioneered in the mid-19th century.

THE DRIVE: Retrace your route to Gosforth, take the coast road (A595) south to Ravenglass and follow signs to Eskdale (19 miles). Alternatively, there's a shortcut into Eskdale via Nether Wasdale and Santon Bridge, but it's easy to get lost, especially if you're relying on satnav; a good road map is really handy

09 Eskdale

The valley of Eskdale was once a centre for mineral mining, and a 15in-gauge steam train was built to carry ore down from the hillsides to the coast. Now known as the **Ravenglass & Eskdale Railway** *(ravenglass-railway.co.uk)*, or as the La'al Ratty to locals, its diminutive choo-choos are a beloved Lakeland attraction They chuff for 7 miles along the valley from the station at Ravenglass to the final terminus at Dalegarth, stopping at several stations in between.

Nearby, the **Boot Inn** *(thebooteskdale.co.uk)* makes a pleasant stop for lunch.

THE DRIVE: Since you're driving, the most sensible idea is to park near Dalegarth Station, ride the train to Ravenglass and back, and then set off for Hardknott Pass. There's only one road east. Take it and get ready for a hair-raising, white-knuckle drive. It's 6 (very steep!) miles from Eskdale to Hardknott Pass.

10 Hardknott Pass & Wrynose Pass

At the eastern end of Eskdale lie two of England's steepest road passes, Hardknott and Wrynose. Reaching a 30% gradient in some places, and with precious few passing places on the narrow, single-file road, they're absolutely not for the faint-hearted or for nervous drivers – but the views are amazing, and they're doable if you take things slow (although it's probably best to leave the caravan or motor home in the garage).

Make sure your car has plenty of oil and water, as you'll do much of the road in first gear, and the strain on the engine can be taxing. Take it slow and take breaks – you need to keep your focus on the road ahead.

From Eskdale, the road ascends via a series of very sharp, steep switchbacks to **Hardknott Fort**, a Roman outpost where you can still see the remains of some of the walls. Soon after you reach **Hardknott Pass** at 393m. The vistas here are magnificent: you can see all the way to the coast on a clear day.

Next you'll drop down into Cockley Beck before you continue the climb up to **Wrynose Pass** (393m). Near the summit is a small car park containing the Three Shire Stone, where the counties of Cumberland, Westmorland and Lancashire historically met.

Then it's a slow descent down through hairpins and corners to **Slaters Bridge**, a traditional packhorse bridge, and on into the valley of Little Langdale. Phew! You made it.

THE DRIVE: Once you reach Little Langdale (5.5 miles east of Hardknott Pass), follow the road east until you reach the A593, the main road between Skelwith Bridge and Coniston. Turn right and follow the road for 5 miles.

11 Coniston

South of Ambleside, the old mining village of Coniston is dominated by its hulking fell, the **Old Man of Coniston** (803m), an ever-popular objective for hikers, but it's perhaps best known for the world speed record attempts made here by father and son Malcolm and Donald Campbell between the 1930s and 1960s.

Though they jointly broke many records, in 1967 Donald was tragically killed during an attempt in his jetboat Bluebird; the little **Ruskin Museum** *(ruskinmuseum.com)* has the full story.

Coniston Water is also said to have been the inspiration for Arthur Ransome's classic children's tale, *Swallows and Amazons*. The best way to explore is aboard the **Steam Yacht Gondola** *(nationaltrust.org.uk/steam-yacht-gondola)*, a steam yacht built in 1859 and wonderfully restored. It travels over the lake to the stately home of **Brantwood** *(brantwood.org.uk)*, owned by the Victorian polymath, critic, painter and inveterate collector John Ruskin. The house is packed with furniture and crafts, and the gardens are glorious.

THE DRIVE: Heading north from Coniston, turn right onto the B5285 up Hawkshead Hill. You'll pass Tarn Hows and the Drunken Duck en route to Hawkshead, 4 miles east.

12 Hawkshead

If you're searching for the perfect chocolate-box lakeland village, look no further – you've found it in Hawkshead, an improbably pretty confection of whitewashed cottages, winding lanes and slate roofs. It's car-free, so you can wander at will: don't miss **Tabitha Twitchit's Bookshop** *(nationaltrust.org.uk)*, an enchanting secondhand bookshop in the former office of Beatrix Potter's husband, William Heelis; it also sells trail maps to explore the village.

Nearby, it's worth making a detour to have a stroll around the lake of **Tarn Hows** *(nationaltrust.org.uk/coniston-and-tarn-hows)*

HILL TOP: HOME OF BEATRIX POTTER

Two miles from Hawkshead in the tiny village of Near Sawrey, the idyllic cottage at **Hill Top** *(nationaltrust.org.uk/hill-top)* is the most famous house in the whole of the Lake District. It belonged to Beatrix Potter, and was used as inspiration for many of her tales: the house features directly in *Samuel Whiskers*, *Tom Kitten*, *Pigling Bland* and *Jemima Puddle-Duck*, and you will doubtless recognise the kitchen garden from *Peter Rabbit*.

Following her death in 1943, Beatrix bequeathed Hill Top (along with more than 1600 hectares of land) to the National Trust, with the proviso that the house be left with her belongings and decor untouched.

It's probably the Lake District's most popular attraction, however, so don't expect to have it all to yourself. Prebooking tickets to the property is essential when arriving by car as parking is limited.

DAVID STEELE/SHUTTERSTOCK

Steamer, Ullswater

– a bucolic place, but one that's artificially created (it was made by joining three neighbouring tarns in the 19th century).

After your walk, pop in for lunch at the Lake District's finest dining pub, the wonderfully named **Drunken Duck** *(drunkenduckinn.co.uk)*.

THE DRIVE: Head back to Ambleside and then follow the A591 back towards Windermere. Just before you reach it, take the turn-off onto the A592 to Troutbeck Bridge, which climbs up to the lofty Kirkstone Pass – at 454m this is the highest mountain pass in Cumbria that's open to road traffic. It's steep, but it's a main A road so it's well maintained. Total distance is 19 miles.

DETOUR

Grizedale Forest

Start: 12 Hawkshead

Stretching for more than 2400 hectares across the hilltops between Coniston Water and Esthwaite Water, **Grizedale Forest** *(forestryengland.uk/grizedale)* is a wonderful place for wandering, ziplining or stargazing. It's criss-crossed by cycling trails, and is also home to outdoor sculptures created by artists since 1977. There's an online guide at grizedalesculpture.org. Also here are an observatory and planetarium. As you leave the Hawkshead car park, you'll immediately see a brown sign for Grizedale, heading right onto North Lonsdale Rd. Just follow the brown signs from here – it's 3 miles' drive from the village.

13 Ullswater

From the windlashed heights of Kirkstone Pass, the A592 loops down towards the last stop on this jaunt around the Lake District: stately Ullswater, the second-largest lake (after Windermere) in the national park. It's impressive: its silvery surface is framed by jagged fells and plied by the puttering Ullswater **'Steamers'** *(ullswater-steamers.co.uk)*; you can also hire your own vessels from the **Glenridding Sailing Centre** *(glenriddingsailingcentre.co.uk)*.

As you skirt up the lake's western edge, it's worth stopping for a walk around **Gowbarrow Park** *(nationaltrust.org.uk)*, where there's a tumbling waterfall to admire called **Aira Force** and impressive displays of daffodils in springtime (Wordsworth dreamt up his most famous poem, *I wandered lonely as a cloud*, while walking nearby).

For an epic end to the trip, strap on your hiking boots and tackle the famous ridge climb via Striding Edge to the summit of **Helvellyn**, the Lake District's third-highest mountain at 950m. You'll need a head for heights, but you'll feel a real sense of achievement: you've just conquered perhaps the finest hill walk in all of England.

21

LAKE DISTRICT & NORTHERN ENGLAND

YORKSHIRE DALES

DURATION: 3-4 DAYS

DISTANCE: 129 MILES / 208KM

GREAT FOR: EATING & DRINKING

BEST TIME TO GO: MAY AND JUNE SEE WILDFLOWERS ADD A SPLASH OF COLOUR TO THE SCENERY.

★ BEST FOR

OUTDOORS

Hiking to the top of Malham Cove's spectacular cliff.

Montpellier Quarter, Harrogate

This roller-coaster of a route spins you through the finest scenery in the Yorkshire Dales, from pretty villages and country pubs to limestone crags and windswept moors. The winding road over Buttertubs Pass is regularly voted the most spectacular in England. This trip adds a second thrilling road climb, from Arncliffe to Malham, to link six of the national park's most beautiful dales in a tour de force of scenic splendour.

LINK YOUR TRIP

22 North York Moors & Coast
From Richmond it's a quick 47-mile blast down the M1 to link with our tour of Yorkshire's other national park.

23 Hadrian's Wall
One hour's drive north from Richmond (47 miles) is Newcastle, where you can begin a tour of Britain's most famous Roman legacy.

01 Harrogate

The quintessential Victorian spa town, prim and pretty Harrogate has long been associated with a kind of old-fashioned Englishness – it is fitting that the town's most famous visitor was crime novelist Agatha Christie, who fled here incognito in 1926 to escape her broken marriage. It was also Queen Victoria's favourite spot for a spa break.

Explore the **Montpellier Quarter** *(montpellierharrogate.co.uk)*, an area of pedestrianised streets lined with restored 19th-century buildings that are now home to art galleries, antique shops, fashion boutiques, cafes and restaurants, and learn all about the town's history in the ornate **Royal Pump Room Museum** *(northyorks.gov.uk)*, built in 1842 over the most famous of the town's sulphurous springs.

If you feel like sampling the waters for yourself, take a dip in the town's ornate **Turkish Baths** *(turkishbathsharrogate.co.uk)*, a

JOHN CORRY/SHUTTERSTOCK

Victorian's idea of a Moorish bathhouse. A range of watery delights are on offer here: hot rooms, steam rooms, a plunge pool and so on, plus use of the original wooden changing cubicles and historic Crapper toilets. Opening hours are quite complex (bathing sessions are alternately mixed and single-sex) – check the website for details. There's also a fascinating 45-minute guided tour of the building (8.30am, Wednesday).

THE DRIVE: Head north out of Harrogate on the A61. After 4 miles turn left at Ripley onto the B6165 to the pretty town of Pately Bridge, then continue on the B6265 as it climbs high over Craven Moor before entering the Yorkshire Dales National Park and descending to Grassington (total 24 miles).

02 Grassington

The perfect base for hiking the south Dales, Grassington's handsome Georgian centre teems with walkers and visitors throughout the summer months, soaking up an atmosphere that – despite the odd touch of faux rusticity – is as attractive and traditional as you'll find in these parts.

THE DRIVE: Head north out of Grassington and follow the B6160 along Wharfedale for a few miles. Soon after passing the massive limestone overhang of Kilnsey Crag on your left, take the minor road on the left to Arncliffe, just 8 miles from Grassington. As you enter the village, turn left to find the village green.

03 Arncliffe

The tiny village of Arncliffe sits in the heart of scenic Littondale, its neat stone houses ranged around the village green. On the north side of the green is the **Falcon Inn** (*facebook.com/thefalconarncliffe*), the original for the Woolpack pub in the popular UK TV series *Emmerdale*. It's a lovely rustic inn where beer is still served from a jug on the counter.

THE DRIVE: Exit the far end of the village green, cross the bridge and turn sharp left to follow the steep, twisting, single-track road that climbs up the valley of Cowside Beck (beware of wandering sheep). At a fork near Malham Tarn, bear left and after 700m, at another junction, continue straight across and descend steeply into Malham

04 Malham

Malham is set within the largest area of limestone country in England, stretching west from Grassington to Ingleton – a distinctive landscape pockmarked with potholes, dry valleys, limestone pavements and gorges. Two of the most spectacular features – Malham Cove and Gordale Scar – are within walking distance of Malham's centre.

The huge rock amphitheatre known as **Malham Cove** is ringed with 80m-high vertical cliffs. In the wake of the last Ice Age, this was a waterfall to rival Niagara; today it is a playground for rock climbers. Peregrine falcons nest here in spring, when the Royal Society for the Protection of Birds (RSPB) sets up a birdwatching lookout.

You can hike up the steep steps on the left-hand side of the cove to see the extensive limestone pavement above the cliffs.

For a longer walk, follow the 5-mile circular **Malham Landscape Trail** *(yorkshiredales.org.uk)*, which continues on to spectacular **Gordale Scar**, a deep limestone canyon with scenic cascades, then leads to the remains of an Iron Age settlement and **Janet's Foss waterfall**.

THE DRIVE: Continue south on the minor road from Malham (it can be very busy on summer weekends) to the A65, and turn left to reach Skipton in 11 miles.

05 Skipton

This busy market town on the southern edge of the Dales takes its name from the Anglo-Saxon *sceape ton* ('sheep town') – no prizes for guessing how it made its money.

Skipton's pride and joy is the broad and bustling High Street, one of the most attractive shopping streets in Yorkshire. Mondays, Wednesdays, Fridays and Saturdays are market days, bringing crowds from all over and giving the town something of a festive atmosphere.

No visit to Skipton is complete without a cruise along the Leeds–Liverpool Canal, which runs through the middle of town. **Pennine Cruisers** *(penninecruisers.com)* runs half-hour trips to Skipton Castle and back.

THE DRIVE: Head northwest from Skipton along the A59 onto the busy A65, and continue to Ingleton, 24 miles away. Turn off the main road and follow signs for Village Centre and then Waterfalls Walk.

06 Ingleton

The village of Ingleton, perched precariously above a river gorge, is the caving capital of England. It sits at the foot of one of the country's most extensive areas of limestone, crowned by the dominating peak of Ingleborough and riddled with countless potholes and cave systems.

The town is the starting point for a famous Dales hike, the circular, 4.5-mile **Waterfalls Trail**

MOUNTAIN BIKING IN SWALEDALE

Swaledale – the quietest and least visited of the Dales – stretches west from Richmond, its wild and rugged beauty in sharp contrast to the softer, greener dales to the south. It's hard to imagine that only a century ago this was a major lead-mining area. When the price of ore fell in the 19th century, many people left to find work in England's burgeoning industrial cities, while others emigrated – especially to Wisconsin in the USA – leaving the valley almost empty, with just a few lonely villages scattered along its length.

The many rough tracks that criss-cross the moors and hillsides around the pretty village of Reeth, at the junction of Swaledale and Arkengarthdale, make this part of the Dales a paradise for mountain bikers, with dozens of miles of off-road trails to explore. The **Dales Bike Centre** *(dalesbikecentre.co.uk)*, just half-a-mile east of Reeth, can rent you a bike and provide local trail maps.

Gordale Scar

ALBINONI/SHUTTERSTOCK

(ingletonwaterfallstrail.co.uk), which passes through native oak woodland on its way past a series of spectacular waterfalls on the Rivers Twiss and Doe (allow three to four hours); payment is by card only (no prebooking required).

THE DRIVE: Follow the B6255 northeast from Ingleton. Beyond Chapel-le-Dale you'll see the spectacular 30m-high, 400m-long Ribblehead Viaduct on your left. The road continues over bleak Gayle Moor and down to Hawes (17 miles). Leave the car in the car park beside the national park centre at the eastern end of the village.

07 Hawes

Hawes is the beating heart of Wensleydale, and a thriving and picturesque market town (market day is Tuesday) with several antique, art and craft shops, and the added attraction of its own waterfall in the village centre.

Beside the car park is the **Dales Countryside Museum** *(dalescountrysidemuseum.org.uk)*, a beautifully presented social history of the area that explains the forces shaping the landscape, from geology to lead mining to land enclosure.

At the other end of the town is the **Wensleydale Creamery** *(wensleydale.co.uk)*, devoted to the production of the animated characters Wallace and Gromit's favourite crumbly white cheese. You can drop into the visitor centre, watch cheesemakers in action, and then try-before-you-buy in the shop. There's also a rather good cafe, **Calvert's Restaurant**.

About 1.5 miles north of Hawes is 30m-high **Hardraw Force** *(hardrawforce.com)*, the highest unbroken waterfall in England, but by international standards not that impressive (except after heavy rain).

Access is via a lovely landscaped walk (400m) from the car park behind the Green Dragon Inn. There's an admission fee (coins only) to access the walk, and a cafe selling local ice cream.

Tan Hill Inn

PETE STUART/SHUTTERSTOCK

THE DRIVE: The 13-mile route from Hawes to the Tan Hill Inn is one of the most scenic in the Dales. Turn right and right again out of the car park (signposted Muker) and follow the minor road over **Buttertubs Pass**. Turn left on the B6270 to Keld, then right on the minor road signposted West Stonesdale and Tan Hill.

08 Tan Hill Inn

Sitting in the middle of nowhere at an elevation of 528m, the **Tan Hill Inn** *(tanhillinn.com)* is Britain's highest pub. Despite its isolation it's an unexpectedly comfortable and welcoming hostelry, with an ancient fireplace in the atmospheric, stone-flagged public bar, and an assorted menagerie of dogs, cats and even sheep wandering in and out of the building. An important watering hole on the Pennine Way, the inn offers real ale on tap and decent pub grub.

THE DRIVE: Head east from Tan Hill on a wild and lonely single-track road that cuts across the high Pennine moors then descends through Arkengarthdale to the picturesque village of Reeth. Follow the B6270 along Swaledale through classic Dales scenery patchworked with drystone dykes and little barns, then the A6108 for the final stretch to Richmond (total 23 miles).

09 Richmond

The handsome market town of Richmond is perched on a rocky outcrop overlooking the River Swale and guarded by the ruins of massive **Richmond Castle** *(english-heritage.org.uk)*.

COLIN WARD/SHUTTERSTOCK

Buttertubs Pass

DON'T MISS

The view north from the summit of Buttertubs Pass.

A maze of cobbled streets radiates from the broad, sloping market square (market day is Saturday), lined with elegant Georgian buildings and photogenic stone cottages, with glimpses of the surrounding hills and dales peeking through the gaps. It's a fine spot to end your Yorkshire adventure.

Another key Richmond landmark is the **Georgian Theatre Royal** *(georgiantheatreroyal.co.uk)*. Built in 1788, this is the most complete Georgian playhouse in Britain. It closed in 1848 and was used as an auction house into the early 20th century, reopening as a working theatre again in 1963 after a period of restoration. Illuminating tours (hourly Mondays to Saturdays) include a look at the country's oldest surviving stage scenery, painted between 1818 and 1836.

22

LAKE DISTRICT & NORTHERN ENGLAND

★ BEST FOR

FOODIES

Browsing the market and delicatessens in Helmsley.

NORTH YORK MOORS & COAST

DURATION: 4–5 DAYS

DISTANCE: 87 MILES / 140KM

GREAT FOR: HISTORY, NATURE, FOOD AND DRINK

BEST TIME TO GO: THE MOORS LOOK THEIR BEST IN AUGUST WHEN THE HEATHER IS IN BLOOM.

York Minster

This varied tour takes in ancient architecture, wild moorlands, picture-postcard villages (with steam trains!) and a classic seaside resort. The Blakey Ridge road out of Hutton-le-Hole just keeps climbing, leaving behind the medieval city of York and the aristocratic spendour of Castle Howard. Stop in a Yorkshire food haven and then the bustling fishing harbour of Whitby, with its Gothic abbey and links to Bram Stoker's *Dracula*.

LINK YOUR TRIP

21 Yorkshire Dales
Head west for 22 miles from York to Harrogate to discover the scenic delights of the Yorkshire Dales.

17 Industrial Heritage
A 71-mile drive southwest from York on the A64 and M62 leads to Manchester, starting point for our tour of Britain's industrial heritage.

01 York

Nowhere in northern England says 'medieval' quite like York, a city of extraordinary cultural and historical wealth that has lost little of its pre-industrial lustre. At its heart lies the immense, awe-inspiring **York Minster** *(yorkminster.org)*, the largest medieval cathedral in all of northern Europe, and one of the world's most beautiful Gothic buildings. It was completed in 1472 (Germany's Cologne Cathedral wasn't finished until 1880). Much of its dazzling stained glass is intact. If this is the only cathedral you visit in England, you'll still walk away satisfied.

The **National Railway Museum** *(railwaymuseum.org.uk)* is the biggest in the world, with more than 100 locomotives. It is well presented and crammed with fascinating stuff including a 1960s Japanese bullet train, model railway and much more.

Interactive multimedia exhibits aimed at bringing history

LEON RAFAEL/SHUTTERSTOCK

to life often achieve exactly the opposite, but the much-hyped **Jorvik Viking Centre** *(jorvik vikingcentre.co.uk)* manages to pull it off with aplomb. Thoroughly restored and reimagined, it's a smells-and-all reconstruction of the Viking settlement unearthed here during excavations in the late 1970s, experienced via a 'time-car' monorail that transports you through 10th-century Jorvik (the Viking name for York). You'll need to prebook your tickets online.

And don't miss the chance to walk York's magnificent 2.1-mile circuit of 13th-century **City Walls**.

THE DRIVE: Head northeast out of York on the A64. After 11 miles, at Barton Hill, turn left on the signposted minor road to Castle Howard. After 1.7 miles of twisting and turning, the road becomes arrow-straight as it enters the castle's landscaped grounds and passes through a monumental gate to reach the visitors' car park (16 miles in total).

02 Castle Howard

Stately homes may be two a penny in England, but you'll have to try pretty damn hard to find one as breathtakingly stately as **Castle Howard** *(castle howard.co.uk)*, a work of theatrical grandeur and audacity set in the rolling Howardian Hills.

This is surely one of the world's most beautiful buildings, instantly recognisable from its starring role as Sebastian Flyte's home in both screen versions of Evelyn Waugh's 1945 paean to the English aristocracy, *Brideshead Revisited*. You'll need at least two hours to do the place justice; booking ahead is essential.

THE DRIVE: Continue north from Castle Howard for half a mile, and take a right onto Hepton Hill. Follow the road for 5 miles until you reach Malton (5.5 miles in total).

03 Malton

The sweet market town of Malton was dubbed Yorkshire's food capital by legendary late Italian chef Antonio Carluccio, and with good reason. For a town of its size the food scene is fabulous, with overflowing delis such as **Malton Relish** *(maltonrelish.co.uk)* championing produce from the moors, wolds and dales; pint-sized artisanal food and drink businesses; and food-focused tours.

Although there are no specific sights to speak of, the town does have some lovely Georgian architecture and independent shops – like York, Malton has a crooked Shambles, now crammed with vintage shops, where butchers would have once slaughtered the lambs brought in for the town's sheep markets.

The town also has connections to Charles Dickens, who regularly visited a friend here, which inspired *A Christmas Carol* and who wrote part of *Martin Chuzzlewit* here on one of his trips.

THE DRIVE: Take the narrow B1257 northwest (watch for the sharp bend at Hovingham) for 15 miles to Helmsley.

04 Helmsley

Helmsley is a classic North Yorkshire market town, a handsome huddle of old stone houses, historic coaching inns and a cobbled market square (market day is Friday), all basking under the watchful gaze of a sturdy **Norman castle** *(english-heritage.org.uk)*.

It's also a bit of a foodie town, sporting several good coffee shops, a couple of quality delicatessens on the main square and some renowned restaurants in the surrounding area.

South of Helmsley lies the superb ornamental landscape of the **Duncombe Park estate** *(duncombepark.com)*, laid out in 1718 for Thomas Duncombe (whose son would later build Rievaulx Terrace). Wide grassy walkways and terraces lead through woodland to mock-Classical temples, while longer walking trails are set out in the landscaped parkland, now protected as a nature reserve.

THE DRIVE: Drive east from Helmsley on the A170 and, just past Kirkbymoorside, turn left on the minor road to the picturesque village of Hutton-le-Hole. Continue on the Blakey Ridge road, which climbs high over the moors, peaking at 418m near the remote Lion Inn before swooping steeply down to Danby (total 23 miles).

DETOUR

Rievaulx Abbey

Start: 04 Helmsley

In the secluded valley of the River Rye, amid fields and woods loud with birdsong, stand the magnificent ruins of **Rievaulx Abbey** *(english-heritage.org.uk)*, pronounced 'ree-voh'. The extensive remains give a wonderful sense of the size and complexity of the community that once lived here, and their story is fleshed out in a series of fascinating exhibits in the museum and visitor centre. On the

Vintage steam train, Goathland

PHOTO OPPORTUNITY

A steam train passing through Goathland Station.

MILOSZ MASLANKA/SHUTTERSTOCK

hillside above the abbey is Rievaulx Terrace, built in the 18th century by Thomas Duncombe II as a place to admire views of the abbey (separate admission fee). Rievaulx is 3 miles west of Helmsley and is signposted off the B1257.

05 Danby

Danby is a compact stone-built village set deep amid the moors at the head of Eskdale. It's home to the **Moors National Park Centre** *(northyorkmoors.org.uk)*, the national park's headquarters, which has interesting exhibits on the natural history of the moors as well as a cafe.

There are several short circular walks from the village, but a more challenging objective is **Danby Beacon** (301m), a stiff 2 miles uphill to a stunning 360-degree panorama across the moors. Or you can cheat and just drive your way up.

THE DRIVE: Head east from Danby on steep and twisting minor roads winding along gorgeous Eskdale, passing through the villages of Lealholm and Glaisdale before reaching Egton Bridge, where you turn right and follow signs to Goathland (13 miles).

06 Goathland

This picture-postcard halt on the **North Yorkshire Moors Railway** *(nymr.co.uk)* stars as Hogsmeade train station in the *Harry Potter* films, and the village appears as Aidensfield in the British TV series *Heartbeat*. It's also the starting point for lots of easy and enjoyable walks, often with the chuff-chuff-chuff of passing steam engines in the background.

THE DRIVE: Continue east from Goathland then north on the A169, pausing at the Blue Bank parking area to take in the sweeping view of the North Yorkshire coast, before descending into Whitby (total 9 miles).

07 Whitby

Whitby is both a busy fishing port and a traditional seaside resort that has managed to retain much of its historic character. The narrow streets and alleys of the old town hug the riverside, now lined with restaurants, pubs and cute little shops.

Keeping a watchful eye over the whole scene are the atmospheric ruins of **Whitby Abbey** *(english-heritage.org)*.

James Cook, one of the best-known explorers in British history, lived here – his life is commemorated in the **Captain Cook Memorial Museum** *(cookmuseumwhitby.co.uk)* and the authentic **HMS Endeavour** *(endeavourwhitby.com)* scale replica sailing from the harbour. Bram Stoker found inspiration for his famous horror story *Dracula* while holidaying in Whitby in 1890.

Whitby is famous for its seafood and the town is home to several award-winning fish-and-chip shops, so grab some takeaway and enjoy it while you sit on a harbourside bench.

THE DRIVE: Head 5.5 miles south from Whitby on the A171 and B1447 to Robin Hood's Bay.

08 Robin Hood's Bay

The picturesque fishing village of **Robin Hood's Bay** *(robinhoods-bay.co.uk)* is one of the prettiest spots on the Yorkshire coast.

Leave your car at the parking area in the upper village and walk downhill to **Old Bay**: a maze of narrow lanes and passages is dotted with tearooms, pubs, craft shops and artists' studios.

At low tide you can go onto the beach and look for treasures in the rock pools.

NORTH YORK MOORS WALKS

The wild and windswept North York Moors rise in desolate splendour. Three-quarters of all the world's heather moorland is found in Britain, and this is England's largest expanse. Ridgetop roads climb up from lush green valleys to the bleak open moors, where weather-beaten stone crosses mark the lines of ancient roadways. In summer, heather blooms in billowing drifts of purple haze.

This is classic walking country. The moors are criss-crossed with footpaths old and new; the **North York National Park** *(northyorkmoors.org.uk/things-to-do/walking/our-walks)* has an interactive map with downloadable route guides including accessible 'Miles without Stiles' routes suitable for wheelchairs and pushchairs/buggies.

STAY AWHILE

WHITBY

BY CATHERINE LE NEVEZ

Flowing from the North York Moors to the rugged Yorkshire coast, the River Esk cleaves this historic port in two. It's immediately obvious why Bram Stoker set his gothic masterpiece *Dracula* here – Whitby is one of the most superbly atmospheric places I've encountered, with its pitched red-roofed houses slanting down to the harbour filled with fishing boats and guarded by 19th-century lighthouses.

Wandering here feels more like time travel. On the river's east side, 199 stone steps with views of Whitby's sandy beaches and piers battered by shipwrecks climb past the weathered gravestones of East Cliff's 12th-century **St Mary's Church** to the **Whitby Abbey ruins**, which are silhouetted at sunset and truly ghostly when the mist rolls in.

Whitby's seafaring past echoes in the medieval old town's knot of cobbled streets, alleys and yards that smugglers used to escape. Popping into its quirky shops selling semi-precious Whitby jet jewellery, worn in Victorian mourning periods, and snug pubs such as the preserved-in-time **Black Horse Inn** *(the-black-horse.com)* and Domesday book-recorded **Duke of York** *(heritagepubs.co.uk/duke-of-york-whitby)* is one of my favourite activities.

Across the swing bridge on Whitby's west side, the harbour is lined by boat-cruise operators, classic seaside amusements, and some of England's freshest, crispiest fish and chips at the black-and-white-fronted **Magpie Cafe** *(magpiecafe.co.uk)*.

For me, the most evocative views of Whitby are uphill on West Cliff near 6 Royal Crescent, where Bram Stoker stayed in 1890, at the Bram Stoker Memorial Seat (the bench furthest from Whitby's landmark **Whale Bone Arch**), looking out over his novel's settings.

LINK YOUR TRIP

Stop off on 22 **North York Moors & Coast** or head 75 miles southwest to Harrogate and the 21 **Yorkshire Dales**.

QUENTIN BARGATE/ALAMY

CHRIS276644/SHUTTERSTOCK

Left: Black Horse Inn, Church St
Right: Whitby Abbey ruins

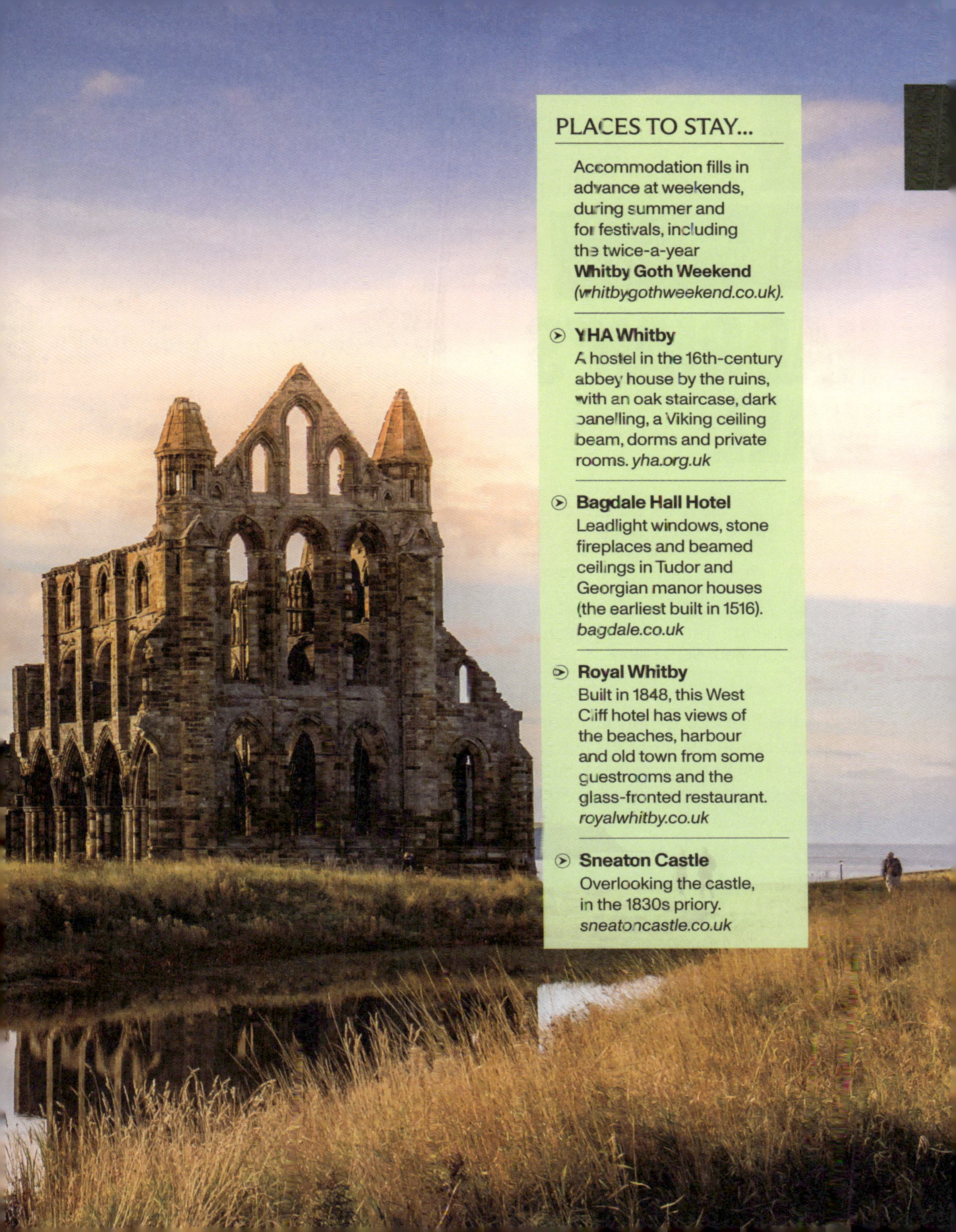

PLACES TO STAY...

Accommodation fills in advance at weekends, during summer and for festivals, including the twice-a-year **Whitby Goth Weekend** *(whitbygothweekend.co.uk)*.

YHA Whitby
A hostel in the 16th-century abbey house by the ruins, with an oak staircase, dark panelling, a Viking ceiling beam, dorms and private rooms. *yha.org.uk*

Bagdale Hall Hotel
Leadlight windows, stone fireplaces and beamed ceilings in Tudor and Georgian manor houses (the earliest built in 1516). *bagdale.co.uk*

Royal Whitby
Built in 1848, this West Cliff hotel has views of the beaches, harbour and old town from some guestrooms and the glass-fronted restaurant. *royalwhitby.co.uk*

Sneaton Castle
Overlooking the castle, in the 1830s priory. *sneatoncastle.co.uk*

23

LAKE DISTRICT & NORTHERN ENGLAND

HADRIAN'S WALL

★ BEST FOR

HISTORY

Intriguing exhibits at Segedunum's museum.

Segedunum

DURATION: 3 DAYS

DISTANCE: 197 MILES / 317KM

GREAT FOR: FOOD & DRINK, OUTDOORS

BEST TIME TO GO: KEY SITES GENERALLY OPEN THROUGHOUT THE WEEK BETWEEN AT LEAST EASTER AND SEPTEMBER.

Follow in the Romans' mighty footsteps as you trace the length of this enormous, enduring wall, built between 122 and 128 CE to separate the Romans and Scottish Picts. Every Roman mile (0.95 miles) had a gateway guarded by a small fort (milecastle), with two observation turrets between them, and many of these remain. Preserved vestiges and intriguing museums punctuate the route, along with easily accessible remnants of the wall.

LINK YOUR TRIP

20 Classic Lakes
It's 35 miles south from Carlisle, via the M6 and A592, to Ullswater, where you can take the picturesque Classic Lakes drive in reverse.

24 Northumbria
Newcastle-upon-Tyne is also the starting point for a spectacular journey along the Northumberland coast to the Scottish border.

01 Newcastle-upon-Tyne

Against a dramatic backdrop of Victorian elegance and industrial grit, this fiercely independent city harbours a spirited mix of heritage and urban sophistication. You can expect excellent art galleries, exceptional restaurants and, of course, interesting bars: Newcastle-upon-Tyne is renowned throughout Britain for its thumping nightlife. The central Bigg Market and Quayside are packed with bars, as are Neville St, Collingwood St (aka Diamond Strip) and Jesmond's Osbourne Rd, for starters.

Newcastle is an ideal place for a debrief on the area's Roman legacies. The **Discovery Museum** *(northeastmuseums.org.uk/discoverymuseum)*, housed in the vast former Co-operative Wholesale Society building, has displays on Pons Aelius (Roman Newcastle) as well as every subsequent era throughout the city's history.

LARRY MCGUIRK/SHUTTERSTOCK

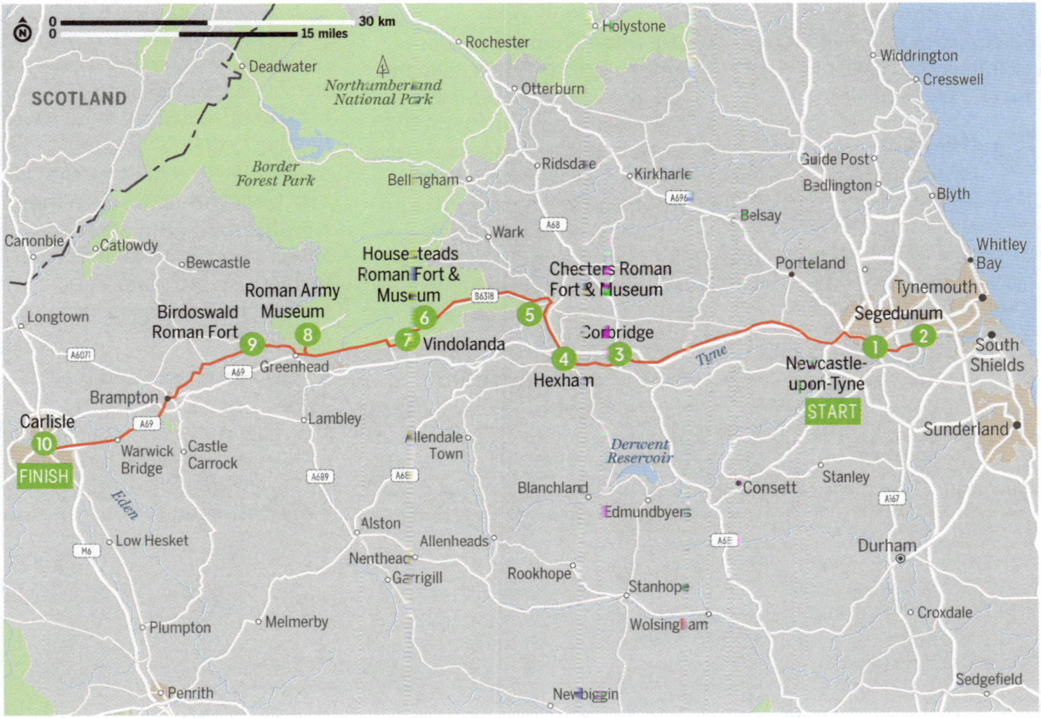

At the **Great North Museum: Hancock** *(northeastmuseums.org.uk/greatnorthmuseum)*, a fantastic interactive model of Hadrian's Wall shows every milecastle and fortress, Roman soldier artefacts and more.

THE DRIVE: Take the A193 and A187 for 5 miles east to reach Segedunum.

02 Segedunum

The last strong post of Hadrian's Wall was the fort of **Segedunum** *(northeastmuseums.org.uk/segedunum)*, at the 'wall's end', now the Newcastle suburb of Wallsend. Beneath the 35m-high tower, which you can climb for terrific views, is an absorbing site that includes a reconstructed Roman bathhouse (with steaming pools and frescoes) and a museum offering a fascinating insight into life during Roman times.

THE DRIVE: Hop on the A167 ring road and head west on the A69. You'll soon enter a patchwork of farmland. After 19 miles, take the B6530 into Corbridge (23 miles in total).

03 Corbridge

Above a green-banked curve in the Tyne, Corbridge's streets are lined with old-fashioned shops and pubs. It's been inhabited since Saxon times when there was a substantial monastery; many of the town's charming buildings feature stones plundered from the nearby Roman garrison town of Corstopitum.

What's left of Corstopitum lies about half a mile west of Market Pl on Dere St, once the main road from York to Scotland. Now preserved as the **Corbridge Roman Town** *(english-heritage.org.uk)*, it's the oldest fortified site in the area, predating the wall itself by some 40 years. Most of what you see here dates from around 200 CE, when the fort had developed into a civilian settlement and was the main base along the wall. You get a real sense of the domestic heart of the town from the visible remains. The museum displays Roman sculpture and carvings, including the amazing 3rd-century **Corbridge Lion**.

THE DRIVE: From Corbridge, set out southwest on the B6321. Cross the River Tyne and follow the road into Hexham (4.3 miles all up).

04 Hexham

Bustling Hexham's cobbled alleyways have more shops and amenities than any other wall town between Carlisle and Newcastle.

Dominating Market Pl, stately **Hexham Abbey** *(hexhamabbey.org.uk)* is a marvellous example of Early English architecture. It cleverly escaped the Dissolution of 1537 by rebranding as Hexham's parish church, a role it still has today. The highlight is the 7th-century Saxon crypt, the only surviving element of St Wilfrid's Church, built with inscribed stones from Corstopitum in 674.

THE DRIVE: From the River Tyne's northern bank, take the A69 west for just under a mile. Turn northwest onto the A6079 and cross the single-lane stone bridge over the North Tyne to the village of Chollerford. Turn left (west) on to the B6318; Chesters Roman Fort & Museum is half a mile ahead on your left (6.8 miles altogether).

05 Chesters Roman Fort & Museum

Now the **Chesters Roman Fort & Museum** *(english-heritage.org.uk)*, this Roman cavalry fort's superbly preserved remains are set among idyllic green woods and meadows. Originally constructed to house up to 500 troops from Asturias in northern Spain, they include part of a bridge (best appreciated from the eastern bank), four gatehouses, a bathhouse and an underfloor heating system. The museum has a large Roman sculpture collection.

THE DRIVE: Head west on the B6318 uphill to Housesteads Roman Fort & Museum (9 miles in total). As you drive, keep a lookout for crumbling remains of the wall.

06 Housesteads Roman Fort & Museum

Hadrian's Wall's most dramatic site – and the best-preserved Roman fort in the country – is the **Housesteads Roman Fort & Museum**

Roman remains, Housesteads Roman Fort & Museum

JENNYT/SHUTTERSTOCK

(english-heritage.org.uk), set high on a ridge and covering 2 hectares. From here you can survey the moors of Northumberland National Park and the snaking wall, with a sense of awe at the landscape and the unmistakable aura of the Roman lookouts.

Up to 800 troops were based at Housesteads at any one time. Its remains include an impressive hospital, granaries with a carefully worked out ventilation system, and barrack blocks. Most memorable are the spectacularly situated communal flushable latrines. Information boards show what the individual buildings would have looked like in their heyday.

There's a scale model of the entire fort in the small museum at the ticket office.

THE DRIVE: It's a short, well-signposted 2-mile hop southwest from Housesteads Roman Fort & Museum to Vindolanda.

07 Vindolanda

The extensive site of **Vindolanda** *(vindolanda.com)* offers a fascinating glimpse into the daily life of a Roman garrison town. The time-capsule museum is just one part of this large, extensively excavated site, which includes impressive parts of the fort and town (excavations continue) and reconstructed turrets and a temple.

Highlights of the Vindolanda museum displays include leather sandals, signature Roman toothbrush-flourish helmet decorations and numerous writing tablets. These include a student's marked work ('sloppy'), and a parent's note with a present of socks and underpants (things haven't changed – in this climate you can never have too many).

THE DRIVE: Rejoin the B6318 at the small hamlet of Once Brewed and turn west. Below you to the south you'll see the village of Haltwhistle – one of the places that claims to be the geographic centre of the British mainland, although the jury is still out. The Roman Army Museum is ahead on your right (7 miles all up).

UMOMOS/SHUTTERSTOCK

Vindolanda

NEED TO KNOW

There are **tourist offices** *(visitnorthumberland.com)* in Hexham, Haltwhistle and Corbridge. The **Walltown Visitor Centre** *(northumberlandnationalpark.org.uk)* is at Greenhead.

Hadrian's Wall Country *(hadrianswallcountry.co.uk)* is the official online portal for the entire area, with information on the Roman Army Museum and Vindolanda, including transport links.

Parking costs £10 per day; tickets are valid at all national-park-operated sites along the wall.

08 Roman Army Museum

On the site of the Carvoran Roman Fort, the revamped **Roman Army Museum** *(vindolanda.com/roman-army-museum)* has three galleries covering the Roman army and the expanding and contracting empire; the wall (with a 3D film illustrating what the wall was like nearly 2000 years ago and today); and colourful background detail to Hadrian's Wall life (such as how the soldiers spent their R&R time in this lonely outpost of the empire).

THE DRIVE: It's 4.7 miles to the Birdoswald Roman Fort. Continue along the B6318 through the hamlets of Greenhead and Gilsland, crossing the River Irthing; Birdoswald is on your left.

09 Birdoswald Roman Fort

The remains of the formerly formidable **Birdoswald Roman Fort** *(english-heritage.org.uk)* are set on an escarpment overlooking the beautiful Irthing Gorge. The longest intact stretch of wall extends from here to Harrow's Scar Milecastle.

THE DRIVE: Head southwest to the small village of Lanercost, where you'll see the raspberry-coloured ruins of the Lanercost Priory, before crossing the River Irthing and entering the town of Brampton. Continue west on the A689 to Carlisle (17 miles in total).

10 Carlisle

Carlisle has history and heritage aplenty. Precariously perched on the frontier between England and Scotland, in the area once ominously dubbed the 'Debatable Lands', it's a city with a notoriously stormy past: sacked by the Vikings, pillaged by the Scots and plundered by the Border Reivers, the city has been on the frontline of England's defences for more than 1000 years.

Reminders of the past are evident in the great crimson **Carlisle Castle** *(english-heritage.org.uk/visit/places/carlisle-castle)* and **Carlisle Cathedral** *(carlislecathedral.org.uk)*, built from the same rosy-red sandstone as most of the city's houses. On English St are two massive **circular towers** that once flanked the city's gateway.

Carlisle's **Tullie** *(tullie.org.uk)* museum covers the city's past, from its Roman foundations onwards. The highlight is the Roman Frontier Gallery, which uses a mix of archaeological exhibits and interactive displays to tell the story of the Roman occupation of Carlisle. The Carlisle Gallery celebrates the city's past and present.

MEMORABLE PLACES TO STAY AND EAT

★ Blackfriars

A 13th-century friary, thought to be the oldest dining room anywhere in the UK, is the setting for **Blackfriars** *(blackfriarsrestaurant.co.uk)* in Newcastle-upon-Tyne. Beautiful stained-glass windows frame the dining room; in summer tables are set up in the cloister garden. It has its own cookery school with day courses such as artisanal bread making or fish and seafood masterclasses, chef's tables, and special events such as building history tours and lunches.

★ Jesmond Dene House

Large bedrooms at the exquisite 41-room **Jesmond Dene House** *(jesmonddenehouse.co.uk)* boutique hotel in Newcastle-upon-Tyne are furnished in a modern interpretation of the Arts and Crafts style and have stunning bathrooms complete with underfloor heating, as well as the latest tech; some have private terraces. The fine-dining restaurant is sublime.

★ Lord Crewe Arms

Book into the **Lord Crewe Arms** *(lordcrewearmsblanchland.co.uk)* to stay in the abbot's house, built in 1165 in the honey-stone North Pennines village of Blanchland, 11 miles south of Corbridge. The entrancing inn has 26 rooms, some in the house while others are in former miners' cottages. Non-guests can also dine on outstanding modern British fare and drink in the vaulted bar, the Crypt, with a monumental medieval fireplace.

Hadrian's Wall at Birdoswald Roman Fort
WHITNEY HUBBELL/SHUTTERSTOCK

PHOTO OPPORTUNITY

The wall's longest intact stretch, from Birdoswald Roman Fort to Harrow's Scar Milecastle.

24

LAKE DISTRICT & NORTHERN ENGLAND

NORTHUMBRIA

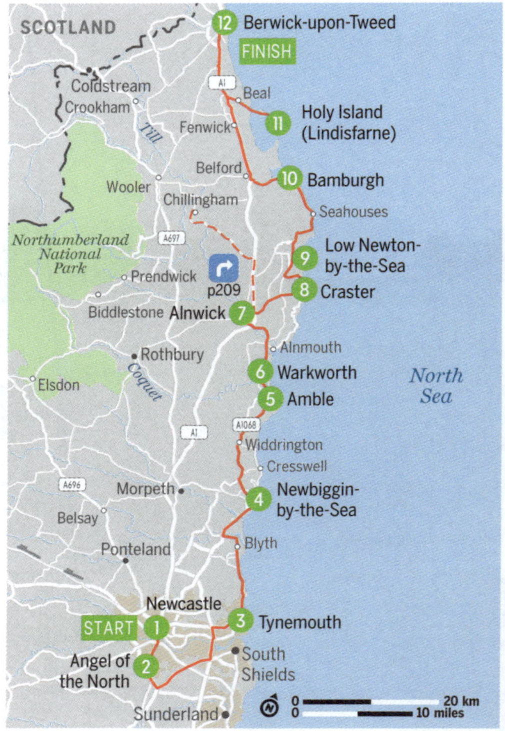

DURATION: 3–4 DAYS

DISTANCE: 113 MILES / 182KM

GREAT FOR: FOOD & DRINK, HISTORY

BEST TIME TO GO: BIRDWATCHING IS BEST FROM MARCH TO JULY.

Newcastle is renowned for its culture and nightlife, but once you hit the open road the pace drops several gears. Wild and remote, this area is sparsely populated: charming, castle-crowned villages are strung along miles of wide, sandy beaches that you might just have all to yourself. Along the way, you'll encounter incredible birdlife and fresh-as-it-gets seafood hauled in at traditional fishing ports and magical islands.

LINK YOUR TRIP

23 Hadrian's Wall
Newcastle is also the jumping-off point for an unforgettable drive through Roman history along Hadrian's Wall.

30 The Borders
From this trip's final stop, Berwick-upon-Tweed, it's 24 miles southwest to Kelso to drive the Scottish Borders trip in reverse.

01 Newcastle

Vibrant Newcastle is famed for its nightlife, but there's plenty to see by day too, including museums showcasing the region's Roman heritage.

Newcastle Castle *(newcastlecastle.co.uk)* – the stronghold that gave the city its name – has been largely swallowed up by the train station, leaving only a few remaining fragments, including the square Norman keep and the Black Gate. Exhibits cover the history of the city, its castle and its residents. The 360-degree city views from the keep's rooftop are superb.

Walking Newcastle's streets, you'd never know the extraordinary **Victoria Tunnel** *(ouseburntrust.org.uk)* runs for 2.5 miles beneath your feet. Built between 1839 and 1842 as a coal-wagon thoroughfare, it was used as an air-raid shelter during WWII. Guided 1¼-hour or more in-depth 2-hour tours take you along an atmospheric level section. Book ahead as numbers are limited, and

★ BEST FOR

HISTORY

Warkworth's castle and boat-accessed hermitage.

JSVIDEOS/SHUTTERSTOCK

Angel of the North

wear good shoes and a washable jacket for the lime-washed walls.

THE DRIVE: Cross the Tyne Bridge (which closely resembles the Sydney Harbour Bridge – both were built by the same company around the same time) and take the A167 south through Gateshead for 6.5 miles to the Angel of the North. There's a free car park by the base.

02 Angel of the North

Nicknamed the Gateshead Flasher, the **Angel of the North** *(gateshead.gov.uk)* – an extraordinary 200-tonne, rust-coloured, winged human frame – has loomed improbably over the A1 (M) motorway since 1998. Sir Antony Gormley's iconic work (which saw him knighted in 2014) stands 20m high, with a wingspan wider than a Boeing 767.

THE DRIVE: Head southeast on the A1 to pick up the northbound A194 and pass under the River Tyne through the Tyne Tunnel (one-way toll £2.60). After you resurface, take the A193 to Tynemouth

03 Tynemouth

The mouth of the Tyne is one of the best surf spots in England, with great all-year breaks off an immense, crescent-shaped Blue Flag beach, which occasionally hosts the National Surfing Championships.

For all your surfing needs, try **Tynemouth Surf Company** *(tynemouthsurf.co.uk)*, which also provides two-hour group lessons (when the surf's up) from April to October. The adjoining chilled **Surf Cafe** *(surfcafetynemouth.co.uk)* morphs into a cool bar and live-music venue at night.

Built by Benedictine monks on a strategic bluff above the Tyne mouth in the 11th-century ruins, **Tynemouth Priory** *(english-heritage.org.uk)* was ransacked during the Dissolution in 1539. The military took over for four centuries, only leaving in 1960, and today the skeletal remains of the priory church sit alongside old military installations, their guns aimed out to sea at an enemy that never came.

Opposite the priory, village-like Front St runs inland from the ocean and is lined with restaurants, cafes and arty shops.

THE DRIVE: Drive north along the coast to the town of Blyth

GABRISIGNO/SHUTTERSTOCK

Puffin colony, Farne Islands

FARNE ISLANDS

The otherwise unmemorable village of Seahouses, located between Low Newton-by-the-Sea and Bamburgh, is the jumping-off point for the more-famous **Farne Islands** *(nationaltrust.org.uk)*.

During breeding season (roughly May to July) you can see feeding chicks of 20 seabird species (including puffin, kittiwake, Arctic tern, eider duck, cormorant and gull), and some 6000 grey seals, on this rocky archipelago 3 miles offshore.

Three boat operators depart from Seahouses' dock, including **Billy Shiel** *(farne-islands.com)*.

Crossings can be rough (impossible in bad weather); wear warm, waterproof clothing and an old hat to guard against the birds!

Inner Farne is the more interesting of the two publicly-accessible islands (with Staple Island); its tiny chapel (1370; restored 1848) commemorates St Cuthbert, who lived here for a spell and died here in 687.

and join the northbound A189 to Newbiggin-by-the-Sea (16.3 miles altogether).

04 Newbiggin-by-the-Sea

Rising above the North Sea 300m offshore from Newbiggin's North Beach, British sculptor Sean Henry's immense 2007 bronze creation *The Couple*, measuring 12m high by 20m wide, depicts a man and woman standing on a pier-like structure looking out to sea. Its installation was part of a major regeneration of the area, which included shifting 500,000 tonnes of sand to the beach here to prevent erosion.

THE DRIVE: Rejoin the A189 and head northwest to pick up the northbound A1068 through patchworked farmland to Amble (a 13-mile trip).

05 Amble

The fishing port of Amble has a boardwalk along the seafront and serves as the departure point for Dave Gray's **Puffin Cruises Amble** *(puffincruisesamble.com)*. Its two boats take birdwatchers on one-hour sailing cruises around Coquet Island (no landing), where you can see some of the 20,000 puffins that nest here each March, as well as other bird species, including eider ducks, kittiwakes and rare roseate terns, and the island's grey seal colony.

In late May Amble celebrates the hatching of puffin chicks on Coquet Island during the **Amble Puffin Festival** *(amblepuffinfest.co.uk)*, with events including local history talks, guided birdwatching walks, exhibitions, water sports, a craft fair, a food festival and live music.

THE DRIVE: It's just 1.7 miles north along the River Coquet to Warkworth.

06 Warkworth

Warkworth's huddle of houses cluster around a loop in the River Coquet, dominated by the craggy ruin of **Warkworth Castle** *(english-heritage.org.uk)*. Looking like the ultimate sandcastle you'd see at the beach, this honey-stone edifice atop a hillock was built around 1200. From the 14th to 17th centuries, it was home to the Percy family (whose descendants still live at Alnwick Castle), and was pivotal in the Wars of the Roses and the English Civil War. It became a national monument in 1915 but the Duke's Rooms remained under the family's control until 1987. Listening-post trails lead you through the castle and grounds, and there are spectacular views from the keep.

Half-a-mile's walk west of Warkworth Castle (no car access), the tiny, magical 14th-century chapel **Warkworth Hermitage** *(english-heritage.org.uk)* is carved into the rock on the northern bank of the River Coquet. It's accessed by a short boat ride (included in admission); ring the brass bell and the ferry operator will row you across. Dappled sunlight illuminates the moss-covered ruin's interior. Look for the stone-carved nativity scene in the window.

THE DRIVE: Continue northwest on the A1068. On your right you'll see the pastel-shaded estuary town of Alnmouth. It's a total of 7.6 miles from Warkworth to Alnwick.

07 Alnwick

Northumberland's historic ducal town, Alnwick (pronounced 'annick') is an elegant tangle of narrow cobbled streets beneath the colossal medieval **Alnwick Castle** *(alnwickcastle.com)*. The imposing ancestral home of the Duke of Northumberland has changed little since the 14th century.

It's a favourite set for film-makers and starred as Hogwarts for the first couple of *Harry Potter* films as well as in British comedy series *Blackadder* and period drama *Downton Abbey*. Broomstick training is one of various activities and guided tours included in the admission price. For the best views of the castle's exterior, take The Peth to the River Aln's northern bank and follow the woodland trail east.

Nearby is spectacular **Alnwick Garden** *(alnwickgarden.com)*. The centrepiece of its series of magnificent green spaces is the breathtaking Grand Cascade – 120 separate jets spurting some 30,000L of water down 21 weirs.

If you're familiar with the renaissance of the WWII 'Keep Calm and Carry On' slogan, it's thanks to the wonderfully atmospheric second-hand bookshop **Barter Books** *(barterbooks.co.uk)* in Alnwick's Victorian former railway station. While converting the station, the owner came across a set of posters – the framed original is above the till – and turned it into a successful industry. Coal fires, velvet ottomans, reading rooms and a cafe make this one of Britain's great bookshops. As you browse the crammed bookshelves, the silence is interrupted only by the tiny toy train that runs along the track above your head.

THE DRIVE: Head northeast through rolling farmland and hidden glens to the little seaside village of Craster (7.3 miles in total), where you'll see fishing boats moored in the harbour and the ruins of Dunstanburgh Castle beyond.

DETOUR

Chillingham Castle

Start: 07 Alnwick

Steeped in history, warfare torture and ghosts, 13th-century **Chillingham Castle** *(chillingham-castle.com)* is said to be one of the country's most haunted places, with spectres from a phantom funeral to Lady Mary Berkeley seeking her errant husband. Owner Sir Humphry Wakefield has passionately restored the castle's extravagant medieval staterooms, stone-flagged banquet halls and grisly torture chambers. It's possible to stay at the medieval fortress in one of eight self-catering apartments where the likes of Henry III and Edward I once snoozed. Double rooms start from £100.

Nearby is **Chillingham Wild Cattle Park** *(chillinghamwildcattle.com)*, which was originally part of the castle grounds and is still home to 130 Chillingham wild cattle, thought to be the last descendants of the aurochs that once roamed Britain until becoming all but extinct during the Bronze Age, making them one of the world's rarest breeds of any species. Tours lasting one hour are led by a park warden; wear sturdy shoes.

From Alnwick, it's a 14-mile journey: take the B6346 northwest through forest and farmland to Chillingham.

08 Craster

Sandy, salty Craster is a small, sheltered fishing village that's famous for its kippers. In the early 20th century 2500 herring were smoked here daily. The kippers still produced today by **L Robson & Sons** *(kipper.co.uk)* are said to have graced the late Queen's breakfast table. Four generations have operated this traditional fish smokers. It's best known for its kippers, but also smokes salmon and other fish.

The dramatic 1.5-mile walk along the coast from Craster (it is not accessible by car) is the most scenic path to moody, weather-beaten **Dunstanburgh Castle** *(english-heritage.org.uk)*. Its construction began in 1314 and it was strengthened during the Wars of the Roses, but then left to crumble, before falling into ruin by 1550. Parts of the original wall and gatehouse keep are still standing and it's a tribute to its builders that so much remains.

THE DRIVE: This section of the drive skirts the edge of

beautiful Embleton Bay, a pale wide arc of sand that stretches from Dunstanburgh past the endearing, sloping village of Embleton and curves in a broad vanilla-coloured strand around to end at Low Newton-by-the-Sea. En route, several side roads lead down to the water. From Craster, it's a 5.9-mile journey.

09 Low Newton-by-the-Sea

This tiny whitewashed, National Trust–preserved village centres on its village green, adjoining brewery-pub the **Ship Inn** *(shipinnnewton.co.uk)*.

Behind the bay is a path leading to the Newton Pool Nature Reserve, an important spot for breeding and migrating birds such as black-headed gulls and grasshopper warblers. There are a couple of hides where you can peer out at them. You can continue walking along the headland beyond Low Newton, where you'll find Football Hole, a delightful hidden beach between headlands.

THE DRIVE: Bamburgh is just 11 miles north of Low Newton-by-the-Sea via the small villages of Beadnell and Seahouses (the departure point for the Farne Islands). Between Beadnell and Seahouses you'll have a sweeping view of the white-sand beach on your right; after Seahouses, the dunes rise up between the road and the shore.

10 Bamburgh

High up on a dolerite crag, Northumberland's most dramatic castle looms over the quaint village's clutch of houses centred around a pleasant green.

Bamburgh Castle *(bamburghcastle.com)* was built around a powerful 11th-century Norman keep by Henry II. The castle played a key role in the border wars of the 13th and 14th centuries, and in 1464 was the first English castle to fall during the Wars of the Roses.

It was restored in the 19th century by the great industrialist Lord Armstrong, and is still home to the Armstrong family. Its name is a derivative of Bebbanburg, after the wife of Anglo-Saxon ruler Æthelfrith, whose fortified home occupied this basalt outcrop 500 years earlier. Antique furniture, suits of armour, priceless ceramics and artworks cram the castle's rooms and chambers, but top billing goes to the neogothic King's Hall with wood panelling, leaded windows and hefty beams supporting the roof.

THE DRIVE: It's 16 miles to Holy Island (Lindisfarne). Check tide times at lindisfarne.org.uk – the island is only accessible at low tide. You must park in the signposted fee-paying car park. A shuttle bus runs from the car park to the castle every 20 minutes from Easter to September; alternatively, it's a level 300m walk to the village.

11 Holy Island (Lindisfarne)

There's something otherworldly about this tiny, 2-sq-mile island. Connected to the mainland by a narrow causeway that only appears at low tide, cut off from the mainland for about five hours each day, it's fiercely desolate and isolated, little changed from when St Aidan arrived to found a monastery in 635. As you cross the empty flats, it's easy to imagine the marauding Vikings who repeatedly sacked the settlement between 793 and 875, when the monks finally took the hint and left. They carried with them the illuminated Lindisfarne Gospels (now in the British Library in London) and the miraculously preserved body of St Cuthbert, who lived here for a couple of years.

The skeletal, red and grey ruins of **Lindisfarne Priory** *(english-heritage.org.uk)* are an eerie sight and give a glimpse into the isolated life of the Lindisfarne monks. The later 13th-century **St Mary the Virgin Church** *(stmarysholyisland.org)* is built on the site of the first church between the Tees and the Firth of Forth. The adjacent museum displays the remains of the first monastery and tells the story of the monastic community before and after the Dissolution.

Built atop a rocky bluff in 1550, tiny **Lindisfarne Castle** *(nationaltrust.org.uk)* was extended and converted by Sir Edwin Lutyens from 1902 to 1910 for Edward Hudson, the founder of *Country Life* magazine – you can imagine some of the decadent Gatsby-style parties that graced its alluring rooms.

THE DRIVE: Again, check tide times before leaving the island. Every year drivers are caught midway by the incoming tide and have to abandon their cars. From the island, it's 14 miles north to beautiful Berwick-upon-Tweed.

12 Berwick-upon-Tweed

England's northernmost city is a picturesque fortress town, cut in two by the River Tweed and spanned by historic bridges. Between 1174 and 1482 this fought-over settlement changed hands 14 times between the Scots and the English.

Only a fragment remains of the once-mighty border castle but you can walk the whole length of Berwick's hefty **Elizabethan walls** *(english-heritage.org.uk)*, begun in 1558 to reinforce an earlier set built during Edward II's reign. The mile-long walk has wonderful, wide-open views.

Lindisfarne Castle
MICHAEL CONRAD/SHUTTERSTOCK

PHOTO OPPORTUNITY

An imposing 16th-century castle on Holy Island (Lindisfarne).

0 50 km
0 25 miles
Irish Sea
St George's Channel
Cardigan Bay
ATLANTIC OCEAN
Bristol Channel
Liverpool Bay
ENGLAND
Amlwch
Holyhead
Beaumaris
Bangor
Llandudno
Colwyn Bay
Rhyl
Holywell
Liverpool
Wigan
Warrington
Chester
Denbigh
Caernarfon
Llanberis
Capel Curig
Llanrwst
Betws-y-Coed
Ruthin
Wrexham
Pen-y-Pass
Blaenau Ffestiniog
Corwen
Llangollen
Porthmadog
Harlech
Pwllheli
Abersoch
Llŷn Peninsula
Bala
Eryri (Snowdonia) National Park
Barmouth
Fairbourne
Dolgellau
Welshpool
Shrewsbury
Tywyn
Machynlleth
Newtown
Borth
Aberystwyth
Llanidloes
Devil's Bridge
Rhayader
Knighton
Ludlow
Presteigne
Aberaeron
New Quay
Tregaron
Llandrindod Wells
Cardigan
Lampeter
Cambrian Mountains
Llanwrtyd Wells
Builth Wells
Hay-on-Wye
Hereford
Fishguard
Newport
Newcastle Emlyn
Llandovery
Brecon
Libanus
St Davids
Carmarthen
Llandeilo
Bannau Brycheiniog (Brecon Beacons) National Park
Haverfordwest
Narberth
Abergavenny
Monmouth
Laugharne
Kidwelly
Merthyr Tydfil
Amroth
Pembroke
Tenby
Llanelli
Swansea
Chepstow
Pontypridd
Port Talbot
Newport
Rhossili
Mumbles
Porthcawl
Bridgend
CARDIFF
Bristol
A55
A499
A496
A487
A483
A5
A40
A477
M4
25
26
27
28
29

SERGII FIGURNYI/SHUTTERSTOCK

Caernarfon Castle (p243)

WALES

EXPLORE

WALES

Wales is simply sumptuous: even greener and gentler than rural England, it's blessed with a varied landscape and plenty of lightly trafficked rural routes. For such a small country, Wales has so much to offer the road tripper.

Coastal fans are blessed: the Pembrokeshire Coast National Park alone offers 186 miles of dramatic cliffs and secret beaches. Further north there's more to astonish: Ceredigion/Cardigan Bay and the Llŷn Peninsula. Inland lie wilderness and solitude aplenty – especially in Eryri (Snowdonia) and Bannau Brycheiniog (Brecon Beacons) National Parks. Plus, Wales' turbulent history has left a legacy of castles unmatched elsewhere in Britain.

Cardiff

The Welsh capital, the country's biggest urban centre, is easy to access and ideal for launching your tour, especially if you're exploring the south of the country. With frequent rail connections from London (direct trains take just under two hours), Cardiff is a thriving modern city with all your accommodation, car-rental, shopping and nightlife needs covered.

In terms of these itineraries, the city is best used as a base for the 'Lyrical Southeast Wales' (p232) and 'Southwest Coast' (p216) routes. It also has an airport, intermittently connecting with destinations across Europe and linked to the city by shuttle bus (around 10 minutes).

Swansea

Wales' second city is a little bit grittier than Cardiff and offers some less expensive accommodation options – most obviously in the form of old-school seafront B&Bs. There are quite a few car-rental options and supermarkets to stock up for your trip. Swansea is most convenient for the 'Southwest Coast' (p216) and 'Wilderness Wales' (p238) itineraries.

Aberystwyth

A mid-size university town on Ceredigion/Cardigan Bay, Aberystwyth has the advantage of proximity to these itineraries: 'Wilderness Wales' (p238), 'Southwest Coast' (p216) and even the southern reaches of 'Eryri (Snowdonia) National Park' (p226). A once-grand resort town, it has plenty of accommodation

WHEN TO GO

Winter can present problems in parts of Wales, such as the Cambrian Mountains, Bannau Brycheiniog (the Brecon Beacons) and especially Snowdonia. Low temperatures, higher altitudes and winding, skinny roads make for icy, hazardous winter driving. Conversely, hot spots such as Snowdon, St Davids and Llandudno can be overrun in summer. It's best to time your visit for the shoulder seasons.

options, most at the midrange-to-budget end of the spectrum. Arrive with your own wheels, as it's not well served for long-distance transport. There are enough shops to stock up for your trip.

Caernarfon

In many ways the capital of northwest Wales, Caernarfon is a Roman-founded port town dominated by one of Britain's most impressive castles. There's a reasonable range of accommodation, plus adequate supermarkets on the outskirts (and boutique suppliers in the old centre). The nearest car-rental place is in Bangor, 10 miles away. Caernarfon is best treated as a destination in its own right, with easy access to the 'Eryri (Snowdonia) National Park' (p226) and 'Northwest Wales' (p242) driving routes.

Abergavenny

If you're looking for a smaller town with decent choices for accommodation, supermarkets and easy access to Bannau Brycheiniog (the Brecon Beacons), Wye Valley and the 'Lyrical Southeast Wales' (p232) driving tour, Abergavenny is an excellent choice. Although it's only 45 minutes by train from Cardiff, it's best to arrive by car.

TRANSPORT

Connections to Wales lag behind those to more populated parts of Britain. Usually, your best bet is to head from London to Cardiff by train, hire a car and proceed from there under your own steam. Wales is refreshingly lacking in motorways, so while distances are not huge, the winding roads are slow to drive.

RESOURCES

Welsh Tourism
The first site you should consult when planning any trip here. *Visitwales.com*

Mid-Wales
Invaluable source of news, events and attractions in Mid-Wales. *Discover ceredigion.wales*

Welsh Culture & History
An unparalleled source of information on Welsh history and culture. In Cardiff. *Museum.wales/stfagans*

Welsh Language
Learn some Welsh online before you arrive. *Nantgwrtheyrn.org/languagecourses*

WHAT'S ON

Hay Festival
Britain's best-known literary festival brings this lovely riverside town alive for 11 days in late May.

National Eisteddfod of Wales
Held over eight days in August, this huge festival of Welsh music and culture moves to a new site each year.

World Bog Snorkelling Championships
The little Mid-Welsh town of Llanwrtyd Wells holds this bizarre event, along with several others, in August.

WHERE TO STAY

In the repurposed 1860 terraced cottages of an abandoned coastal granite quarry, Nant Gwrtheyrn Cottages, Llŷn Peninsula, offers 24 cosy rooms, plus classes in the Welsh language.

Plas Tan Y Craig, Beddgelert, Snowdonia, is a super-cosy, award-winning B&B in a charming town at the junction of the Glaslyn and Colwyn rivers.

Penrhiw Hotel, St Davids, was a late-Victorian priory, and is now an architect-designed boutique hotel set among landscaped gardens and meadows.

By the Wye, Hay-on-Wye, offers off-grid glamping in treetop safari tents and rewilding activities from nature trails to forest bathing.

Denmark Farm Eco Lodge & Conservation Centre, Ceredigion, has family-friendly self-catering cottages and camping sites with activities and courses.

25

★ BEST FOR

FAMILIES

Splashing about on the beach at Tenby.

WALES

SOUTHWEST COAST

Oystermouth Castle

DURATION: 4 DAYS

DISTANCE: 129 MILES / 207KM

GREAT FOR: HISTORY, FAMILIES

BEST TIME TO GO: JUNE, JULY AND AUGUST OFFER THE BEST BEACH WEATHER BUT BEACHES ARE LESS CROWDED IN APRIL, MAY AND SEPTEMBER.

This route links two distinctly Welsh cities – Wales' second largest and the UK's tiniest – by way of Wales' two most famously beautiful tracts of coast. The broad sandy arc of Swansea Bay is only a teaser for what is to come. Waves crash against sheer cliffs painted from a rapidly changing palate of grey, purple and inky black. This trip takes you to some of Britain's very best beaches: glorious sandy stretches and remote coves alike.

LINK YOUR TRIP

27 Lyrical Southeast Wales
It's an 80-minute (50-mile) drive from Abergavenny to Swansea via Merthyr Tydfil along the southern edge of the Brecon Beacons.

28 Wilderness Wales
From St Davids it's a simple matter of continuing up a scenic stretch of the Pembrokeshire coast to Cardigan, 35 miles away.

01 Swansea

Wales' second city has gritty charm and an enviable setting on 5-mile-long, sandy Swansea Bay. An active bar scene is enthusiastically supported by a large student population, while a new brace of affordable ethnic eateries and seafood restaurants have improved the city's once drab food scene no end.

Literature lovers will relish the handsome Uplands area, where the country's best-known writer, Dylan Thomas, was born, bred, inspired and inebriated.

Fuel up on everything from wondrous Welsh cakes to tantalising Thai food to delicious fresh produce at one of the nation's best markets, **Swansea Market** *(swanseaindoormarket.co.uk)*. Next, dive into the whizz-bang **National Waterfront Museum** *(museum.wales/swansea)* for a history lesson.

Dylan Thomas fans can do a tour of the district surrounding his

TONY MARTIN LONG/SHUTTERSTOCK

birthplace *(dylanthomasbirthplace.com)*, explore his legacy at the **Dylan Thomas Centre** *(dylanthomas.com)* before visiting some of the (many!) nearby pubs that he famously frequented.

THE DRIVE: Broad Oystermouth Rd traces the edge of Swansea Bay, changing its name to Mumbles Rd halfway along. It's only 4 miles from central Swansea to the heart of the Mumbles strip.

02 Mumbles

Swansea's swanky seaside suburb sprawls along the western curve of Swansea Bay and terminates in the pair of rounded hills which may have gifted the area its unusual name (from the French *Les Mamelles* – 'the breasts') The Norman fortress of **Oystermouth Castle** *(swansea.gov.uk/oystermouthcastle)* stands guard over fashionable Newton Rd and sea-fronting Mumbles Rd with their spread of tempting restaurants and bars.

Pick up an ice cream at **Joe's** *(joes-icecream.com)*, a Swansea institution founded by an Italian immigrant in 1922, and take a stroll along the waterside promenade to the Victorian **pier** *(mumbles-pier.co.uk)*. There's a pretty little sandy beach tucked just beneath it. If you're peckish, there are good cafes and restaurants spread along the waterfront, some serving the region's highly regarded seafood, and plenty of pubs and bars too.

THE DRIVE: From Mumbles it's 6 miles to Parkmill on the Gower Peninsula. Head uphill on Newton Rd, following the Gower signs. Eventually, houses give way to fields and, at the village of Murton, a sharp right-hand turn leads to the B4436 and on to the A4118, the main Gower road.

03 Parkmill

The spectacular coastal landscape of the Gower Peninsula was declared the UK's first Area of Outstanding Natural Beauty (now National Landscape) in 1956.

In the gateway village of Parkmill 12th-century mill buildings have been converted into the **Gower Heritage Centre** *(gowerheritagecentre.co.uk)*. Despite its worthy (sounding) name, it's a great place to take kids with craft workshops, a playground and farm animals to pet. Nearby **Parc-le-Breos** contains the remains of a 5500-year-old burial chamber.

However, the real reason to stop in Parkmill is to take a stroll to **Three Cliffs Bay**. Right up there among Britain's most beautiful sandy beaches, Three Cliffs has a memorable setting, with a ruined 13th-century **castle** above and a triple-pointed rock formation framing a natural arch at its eastern end.

THE DRIVE: From Parkmill, head west along the A4118, following the signs to Rhossili. Eventually, the road turns left towards the village of Scurlage and the Rhossili turn-off. In all, it's a distance of 10 miles along good roads, but it's quite likely you'll be sporadically stuck behind a slow-moving camper van or tractor.

04 Rhossili

The three miles of surf-battered golden sands of Rhossili Bay make it the Gower Peninsula's most spectacular strand. Rhossili village, at the southern end of the beach, makes the best casual stop. There's a **National Trust visitor centre** *(nationaltrust.org.uk/rhossili-and-south-gower-coast)* here, and the excellent cafe and bar **View Rhossili** *(theviewrhossili.com)* bigging up local produce. Beware of swimming here: tides can make it dangerous.

This end of the beach is abutted by **Worms Head**, a dragon-shaped promontory which turns into an island at high tide and is home to seals and many seabirds. It's safe to explore on foot for 2½ hours either side of low tide. Don't get cut off by incoming tides!

Surfers tend to prefer Llangennith, near the north end of the beach, as a base.

THE DRIVE: It's only 31 miles from Rhossili to Kidwelly, but allow an hour as the first part of the journey zigzags along tiny byways on the Gower Peninsula's northern edge. Before and after navigating the scraggly outskirts of Llanelli, it's a pleasantly rural drive.

05 Kidwelly

Castles are a dime a dozen in this part of Wales – a legacy of a time when Norman 'Marcher' lords were given authority and a large degree of autonomy to subjugate the Welsh in the south and along the English border. The cute little Carmarthenshire town of Kidwelly has a particularly well-preserved example.

Originally erected in 1106, only 40 years after the Norman invasion of England, **Kidwelly Castle** *(cadw.gov.wales)* got its current configuration of imposing stone walls in the 13th century. Wander around and explore its remaining towers and battlements, or just stop by to take a photo of the grey walls looming above the peaceful river far below.

STAY IN DYLAN THOMAS' HOUSE

Dylan Thomas fans can stay in the house where the poet was born and spent his first 23 years. The house has been diligently maintained in period style, and you'll have the choice of staying in the bedrooms once occupied by Nancy (his sister), DJ and Florrie (his parents), and of course Dylan himself.

Booking at the **Dylan Thomas Birthplace** *(dylanthomasbirthplace.com)* entails exclusive use of the house; a tour is included in the deal.

Extensive **Pembrey Country Park** *(pembreycountrypark.wales)* is 5 miles south of Kidwelly. With 202 hectares of trail-crossed woods abutting one of Wales' longest sandy beaches, you could spend a few hours mooching about here.

THE DRIVE: From Kidwelly, motor north along the A484 through the green fields of Carmarthenshire. At Carmarthen, a pleasant but unremarkable county town, switch to the A40 dual carriageway to St Clears, and then follow the A4066 south to the becalmed estuary town of Laugharne: 21 miles in total.

06 Laugharne

While shooting down the highway between Carmarthen and Tenby, it's worth considering taking a left at St Clears to visit the town of Laugharne (pronounced 'larn') on the Taf estuary. Perched picturesquely above the reed-lined shore, **Laugharne Castle** *(cadw.gov.wales)* is a hefty 13th-century fortress, converted into a mansion in the 16th century.

Swansea may have been Dylan Thomas' birthplace, but Laugharne is where he lived out his final years. It's been suggested he got inspiration for voices in his classic play *Under Milk Wood* here. Many fans make the pilgrimage to visit the **boathouse** *(cofgar.wales/venues/dylan-thomas-boathouse)* where Thomas lived, the shed

Dylan Thomas' boathouse, Laugharne
TONY MARTIN LONG/SHUTTERSTOCK

PHOTO OPPORTUNITY

The boathouse where Dylan Thomas spent his final years, overlooking the Taf estuary.

where he wrote and his final resting place, found in the graveyard of St Martin's Church.

Also worth a visit is **Brown's Hotel** *(browns.wales)*, one of his favourite watering holes. Then there is the **Dylan Thomas Birthday Walk** *(dylanthomasbirthdaywalk.co.uk)*, taking you on a trail around the town and nearby estuary to spots associated with the poet.

Laugharne is situated 4 miles off the highway: allocate a few hours to explore it properly. Although you can continue southwest from here on narrow roads, you're better off backtracking to the A477 to get to Tenby.

THE DRIVE: Twenty miles of verdant farmland separate Laugharne from Tenby via the A477 and then, once you hit Kilgetty, the A478.

07 Tenby

Sandy, family-friendly beaches spread out in either direction from this pretty pastel-hued resort town tumbling over the headland above. Pembrokeshire's (if not Wales') premier seaside resort it is, but Tenby's eclectic blend of architecture and steep twisty streets, still part-wrapped by Norman walls, almost evoking Greek island towns at times, impress most.

The beaches are the major attraction here, plus the variety of eateries stashed away amid the sinuous cobbled streets. The other big draws – the sea-bashed crag of **St Catherine's Island** *(saintcatherinesisland.co.uk)* topped by its bombastic fort, along with the **Tenby Boat Trips** *(tenbyboattrips.co.uk)* out to Caldey Island, home to seals, seabirds, beaches and a community of Cistercian monks – are lovely additional strings to Tenby's bow.

THE DRIVE: From Tenby, it's a short, sweet 10-mile hop to Pembroke. From the town centre, head west on Greenhill

Laugharne Castle (p218)

PHOTOFIRES/SHUTTERSTOCK

Rd, go under the railway bridge and turn right at the roundabout. Follow Heywood Lane (the B4318) through a patchwork of fields until you reach the Sageston roundabout. Turn left onto the A477, and then veer left on the A4075; or plump for the equally distanced but quieter A4139 via Jameston, where enticing lanes shoot off to the likes of Manorbier and Freshwater East Beaches.

St David's Day

St David's Day is to the Welsh what St Patrick's Day is to the Irish – a day to celebrate one's essential Welshness, albeit somewhat more soberly than Ireland does. If you're in Wales on 1 March, there's no better place to be than the saint's own city, St Davids. Around the cathedral, a host of golden daffodils flower seemingly right on cue; people pin leek, daffodil or red dragon badges to their lapels; streets are strung with flags bearing the black-and-gold St David's cross; and *cawl* (a traditional soupy stew) is consumed in industrial quantities. You should also visit the cathedral, where the saint's remains lie year-round in a recently restored shrine.

08 Pembroke

Pembroke is dominated by hulking **Pembroke Castle** *(pembroke-castle.co.uk)*, which looms over the end of the town's main street. The fortress is best viewed from the Mill Pond, a pretty lake that forms a moat on three sides of the headland from which the castle rises.

Pembroke played a leading role in British history as the birthplace of the first Tudor king, Henry VII. The castle is in extremely good condition, with lots of well-preserved towers, dungeons and wall walks to explore.

A strip of mainly Georgian and Victorian buildings leads down from the castle, featuring good pubs and some excellent food at **Williams** cafe.

THE DRIVE: The 24-mile journey to Solva heads through the port town of Pembroke Dock, crosses the Daugleddau estuary and then traverses Pembrokeshire's nondescript county town, Haverfordwest. Exit Haverfordwest on the A487, trundling through farmland before reaching the coast at Newgale, a vast sandy surf beach backed by a high bank of pebbles. From here the road more or less shadows the coast.

DETOUR

West of Pembroke

Start: 08 Pembroke

The remote peninsula that forms the bottom lip of the long, deep-sea harbour of Milford Haven has some of the Pembrokeshire coast's most dramatic geological features and blissful little beaches. An especially lovely area includes the golden sands of **Barafundle Bay** and **Broad Haven South**, and a network of walking tracks around **Bosherston Lily Ponds**.

The B4319 winds south from Pembroke to Bosherston. Continue past Bosherston to the coast and a short, steep path leads to the photogenic shell of **St Govan's Chapel**, wedged into a slot in the cliffs just above the pounding waves. Sadly, the coast here and just west is part of a military firing range: when red flags are flying there's no public access to some of the Pembrokeshire coast's most arresting natural sights – neither the chapel, nor **Elegug Stacks** nor the gigantic arch known as the Green Bridge of Wales.

After sidestepping the firing range, the road continues on to **Freshwater West** – a moody, wave-battered stretch of coast that has provided a brooding backdrop for movies such as *Harry Potter and the Deathly Hallows* and Ridley Scott's *Robin Hood*. It's widely held to be Wales' best surf beach, but also one of the most dangerous for swimmers.

From Pembroke, it's just over 6 miles to Barafundle Bay (heading southeast) or 8 miles to Freshwater West (heading west). For all these sights, you could easily make a day of it. Best is to take the B4319 heading south from Pembroke; Bosherston and the Elegug Stack Rocks are reached from narrow country lanes branching off it. The B4319 continues past Freshwater West and terminates at the B4320, where you can turn right to return to Pembroke.

09 Solva

Clustered around a long, hook-shaped harbour, Solva is the classic Welsh fishing village straight out of central casting. Pastel-hued cottages line the gurgling stream running through its lower reaches, while Georgian townhouses cling to the cliffs above. When the tide's out, the water disappears completely from the harbour, leaving the sailing fleet striking angular poses on the sand.

Lower Solva is the part of most interest to travellers. Amble about antique shops and galleries, settle in somewhere cosy for a meal or walk a section of the Pembrokeshire Coast Path, which approaches its most exquisite stretch around Solva.

If you need to shed some calories afterwards, a 1-mile walk will take you upstream to the **Solva Woollen Mill** *(solvawoollenmill.co.uk)*, the oldest working mill of its kind in Pembrokeshire.

THE DRIVE: You really can't go wrong on the 3-mile drive to St Davids. Just continue west.

10 St Davids

A city only by dint of its prestigious cathedral, pretty St Davids (p224) feels more like an oversized village. Yet this little settlement looms large in the Welsh consciousness as the hometown of Wales' patron saint and has a very special vibe as a result.

Mesmeric **St David's Cathedral** *(stdavidscathedral.org.uk)* stands on the site of the saint's own 6th-century religious settlement. Wonderful stone and wooden carvings decorate the interior, and there's a treasury and historic library hidden within.

St David was born at **St Non's Bay**, a ruggedly attractive section of coast with a holy well and a cute little chapel, a short walk from the centre of town. If it's a swim or surf you covet, head to broad, beautiful Whitesands Bay (Porth Mawr), although there are other quieter beaches dotted between the headlands hereabouts.

Also not to be missed are the city's distinguished bunch of cafes and restaurants, which are ever-ready to sate weary travellers' bellies. One of our favourite spots for its sheer novelty is **MamGu Welshcakes**, a lively cafe specialising in wacky takes on the typical Welsh sweet snack of Welsh cakes.

Do not just dally in St Davids now that you have come this far west. Get out and roam the emerald-green, undulating landscape around as it bows to sandy and stony bays where you will truly feel the significance of the Welsh word 'Penfro', which explains how Pembrokeshire gets its name. The meaning? 'Land's End'.

WHERE TO SAMPLE TEMPTING WELSH CAKES

You'll see the humble Welsh cake in a whole new light after a visit to **MamGu** *(mamguwelshcakes.com)*. Friends Becky and Thea travelled the world before landing in St Davids.

At their cafe in the atmospheric 14th-century ruins of St Davids Cathedral Rectory, Welsh cakes traverse the entire taste spectrum, with flavours from leek and cheese to ginger and chili-chocolate.

Altar, St Davids Cathedral

MAKASANA PHOTO/SHUTTERSTOCK

STAY AWHILE

ST DAVIDS

BY KERRY WALKER

Gazing out over a heart-thumpingly beautiful stretch of coast, Britain's cutest city, St Davids, is a laid-back place to break from the wheel.

For me, the Pembrokeshire coast feels wildest when you chuck on boots for a seashore walk with **Really Wild Foraging** *(reallywild emporium.co.uk)*, with seabirds soaring, waves booming and the cold Atlantic slapping your ankles. I love tuning into nature while combing the rock pools for seaweeds, from sea spaghetti to laverbread and truffle-like pepper dulse. Afterwards, I might stop by the rustic-chic **Really Wild Emporium** for a seaweed brownie or full-on tasting menu playing up foraged ingredients in dishes like laver hash with wild garlic and brill with celeriac, brown butter and kelp – all delicious.

If I had to pick just one coastal hike it would be the 3.7-mile, two-hour loop of **St Davids Head** *(nationaltrust.org.uk)*, starting at the surf-bashed sweep of Whitesands Bay. The hike clambers over gorse-clad cliffs to **Porthmelgan**, a boulder-flanked crescent of sand, an Iron Age hillfort and the neolithic burial chamber of **Coetan Arthur**.

On blue-sky days, hook up with **TYF Adventure** *(tyf.com)* to explore the ragged, cave-riddled shore with the very Welsh sport of coasteering, which involves scrambling, cave swimming, wildlife encounters and jumping off cliffs just for the sheer hell of it.

As day fades into dusk, I would slide over to **Blas** *(blasrestaurant.com)*, a subtly lit, street-art-splashed restaurant with tide-to-table dishes like Solva crab with pickled kohlrabi. For something less formal, head to **Grain** *(grain.wales)* for wood-fired pizza and Welsh craft beer in the courtyard.

LINK YOUR TRIP

The beautiful coastal 25 **Southwest Coast drive** ends in St Davids, or head northeast for the cliffs and mountains of 28 **Wilderness Wales**.

DAVID LYONS/ALAMY

IAN BOTTLE/ALAMY

Left: Coetan Arthur;
Right: Caerfai Bay campsite

PLACES TO STAY

St Davids has hands-down the pick of Pembrokeshire's most original places to stay.

Caerfai Camping
Awarded the Green Key for its eco credentials, this camping site sits on a 73-hectare organic dairy farm above the deep imprint of Caerfai Bay and the wave-smashed Atlantic. *caerfaibay.co.uk*

Twr y Felin
This striking architect-designed windmill conversion entices with minimalist-chic rooms, specially commissioned art, an intimate spa and a gourmet restaurant, Blas. *twryfelinhotel.com*

Crug Glâs
For total peace, book this 12th-century farm and romantic country house, with rooms decked out in ornate beds and period grandeur. Home-cooked meals make Pembrokeshire produce sing. *crug-glas.co.uk*

26

WALES

ERYRI (SNOWDONIA) NATIONAL PARK

DURATION: 4 DAYS

DISTANCE: 165 MILES / 266KM

GREAT FOR: HISTORY, OUTDOORS

BEST TIME TO GO: SUMMER IS BEST, ALTHOUGH TRAILS CAN GET CROWDED DURING THE SCHOOL HOLIDAYS (JULY AND AUGUST).

Great fortresses of rock rising steeply from glittering lakes and ancient forests: this drive takes you deep into the Wales you've always dreamt of. The treasures of the national park the Welsh call Eryri (The Highland) are laid before you, as you follow this wild, winding route. You'll want to stop often to scramble up scree-scattered slopes, wander slate-built towns, venture down slate mines and explore some of the mightiest castles in the British Isles.

LINK YOUR TRIP

28 Wilderness Wales
Hop off the route at Dolgellau, heading 11 miles south on the A470 and A487 to Corris, to see another side of Wales' wild heart.

29 Northwest Wales
Jump ship at Conwy or Caernarfon to see more of what the northwest corner of Wales has to offer.

01 Llanberis

Ground zero for rock climbers and mountain lovers, Llanberis is an offbeat little town that also offers a fantastic introduction to Snowdonia's industrial heritage.

Climbers can sign up for a day stint with **Boulder Adventures** *(boulderadventures.co.uk)*, while history buffs are drawn by the atmospheric ruins of **Dolbadarn Castle** *(cadw.gov.wales)* and the **National Slate Museum** *(museum.wales/slate)*, a fascinating recreation of the area's industrial past. To get a similar sense of its present, **Engie** *(engie.co.uk)* uncovers the science (and 10 miles of tunnels) of nearby Dinorwig, Europe's largest pumped-storage hydroelectric scheme.

If you're looking to summit Mt Snowdon, Llanberis is the starting point for the Victorian-built **Snowdon Mountain Railway** *(snowdonrailway.co.uk)*, a rack-and-pinion train that scales Wales' highest peak; alternatively, just take the Llanberis Path to the top.

THE DRIVE: The 11-mile drive to Capel Curig offers an immediate introduction to Snowdonia's heady heights: the views from

★ BEST FOR

OUTDOORS

The mountain ranges surrounding Capel Curig.

EDDIE/500PX

Y Pincin, above Capel Curig

the Pen-y-Pass are impressive. Take the winding A4086 east out of Llanberis, then all the way to Capel Curig.

02 Capel Curig

Little more than an intersection, Capel Curig is a hugely popular walkers' base. From the hamlet, you can do a demanding half-day 5-mile ridge hike up Moel Siabod, or head for the nearby Ogwen Valley. Those seeking to polish their Bear Grylls skills should check out the excellent **Plas y Brenin National Mountain Sports Centre** *(pyb.co.uk)*.

THE DRIVE: The 26-mile drive to historic Conwy is worth it simply for the trip through the starkly beautiful Ogwen Valley, straddled by the Carneddau and Glyderau ranges. Take the A5 northwest from Capel Curig, then the North Wales Expressway northeast to Conwy.

DETOUR

Ogwen Valley Treks

Start: 02 Capel Curig

If the wild calls when heading from Capel Curig to Conwy, give in to temptation to tackle some of Snowdonia's most scenic and challenging hikes. These are found in the Glyderau and Carneddau ranges, above the Ogwen Valley's glacial lakes, Llyn Ogwen and Llyn Idwal.

At the west end of Llyn Ogwen, **YHA Idwal Cottage** *(yha.org.uk)* is the starting point for trails up the sharply angled Tryfan (918m) that take you high above Llyn Idwal (A5). Both Tryfan via Heather Terrace (4 miles) and Tryfan's North Ridge (4 miles) are demanding half-day treks; allow a full day to do the Glyder Traverse (6 miles) that takes in the other-worldly rock formations of the Castle of the Winds and Devil's Kitchen. On the other side of the A5, the spectacular 9-mile Carnedd Loop (A5, Tal-y-Llyn Ogwen Farm) awaits: a full-day adventure that comprises four mighty Carneddau peaks, including Carnedd Llewelyn (1064m), two highland lakes and some scrambling.

From Capel Curig, head 5 miles northwest on the A5 to the bridge at Pont Pen-y-Benglog, where both lakes and walking trails begin. The YHA Idwal Cottage is your only overnighting option, but a good one. To rejoin the route, just continue up the A5 to Conwy.

03 Conwy

Ringed by medieval stone walls, Conwy is a banquet for medieval-history buffs. Its impressive **castle** *(cadw.gov.wales)*, commanding a narrow point in the mouth of the River Conwy, is complemented by the most complete set of **town walls** *(cadw.gov.wales)* in Britain. Both were built in the late 13th century when this was an English garrison town lording it over the recently subdued Welsh.

Within the town, there are plenty more historical sights to be unearthed. **Plas Mawr** *(cadw.gov.wales)* is one of the finest Elizabethan houses in Britain, while Aberconwy House is a merchant's house of the same vintage as the castle and town walls. And let's not skip over the excellent dining scene, either.

> **PHOTO OPPORTUNITY**
>
> The perfect medieval symmetry of Conwy's castle and walls.

THE DRIVE: The 7-mile hop from Conwy to Bodnant Estate takes you down the bucolic Conwy Valley. Take the Llanrwst Rd (B5106) south from near the castle, turning east onto the B5279 to cross the Conwy River, then north onto the A470, from which Bodnant Estate is signposted.

04 Bodnant Estate

Bodnant Estate is a beautiful place that no fan of British landscaping should miss. Its horticultural collections are internationally renowned, while the **Bodnant Farm Shop** *(bodnant-welshfood.co.uk)* is stocked with local and organic produce. There's also the excellent **Hayloft Bar & Grill** *(bodnant-welshfood.co.uk)*, a revamped barn spotlighting season-led cooking, and plenty of courses (gardening, cooking, farming) throughout the year.

THE DRIVE: Rejoin the A470, heading south to Llanrwst, then take the B5106 back over the Conwy and into Betws-y-Coed: about 13 miles all told.

05 Betws-y-Coed

The outdoor-adventure capital of Snowdonia, Betws is a slate-coloured village commanding the junction of the Conwy and Llugwy rivers. In summer its many B&Bs are booked solid by walkers, climbers and other fresh-air seekers.

Nearby, check out the **Conwy Falls** *(conwyfalls.com)*, and head below ground for adrenaline-packed via ferrata scrambles, subterranean zip-lining and freefalls into darkness in a disused slate mine with **Go Below Underground Adventures** *(go-below.co.uk)*. If you're looking for something more sedate,

Bala Lake Railway

PHILIP ENTICKNAP/ALAMY

Fairy Glen is worth a walk and a swim, while **Gwydyr Forest** and **Swallow Falls** also attract their share of outdoorsy types. Finish off with some Spanish-Welsh tapas and an overnight stay at Olif.

THE DRIVE: The 27-mile drive to Bala is best appreciated taking narrow, winding B roads through ancient forest and past lakes: leave the A5 a few miles south of town, take the B4406 south through Penmachno, the B4391 east to the Tryweryn River, and the A4212 into Bala.

06 Bala

Quiet Bala is a jumping-off point for white-water rafting and kayaking with the **National White Water Centre** *(nationalwhitewatercentre.co.uk)* on the River Tryweryn, and other forms of aquatic entertainment on **Llyn Tegid**, Wales' largest natural lake, with **Bala Adventure & Watersports Centre** *(balawatersports.com)*.

Those preferring to keep dry might be tempted by a scenic ride on the narrow-gauge **Bala Lake railway** *(bala-lake-railway.co.uk)*, or a blowout meal at **Tyddyn Llan** *(tyddynllan.co.uk)*, a short drive from town.

THE DRIVE: From Bala, it's a straightforward 18-mile drive southwest on the A494 (Bala Rd) to Dolgellau, skirting the northern shore of Llyn Tegid.

07 Dolgellau

Built of handsome dark stone, Dolgellau contains more than 200 heritage-listed buildings (the highest density of any town in Wales). With natural attractions such as the hikers' favourite **Cader Idris** on its doorstep, plus the bird-filled **Mawddach Estuary** *(visitmidwales.co.uk)* and the mountain bikers' playground of **Coed y Brenin Forest Park** *(naturalresources.wales/coedybrenin)*, it's well served with B&Bs, outlying farmstays and country houses, as well as a range of imaginative restaurants, such as the **Fork, Cork and Feathers**.

SOSN-A/SHUTTERSTOCK

View from Cader Idris

WHAT TO PACK?

Pack your hiking boots, your camera and your sense of wonder: they'll all get a thorough workout.

THE DRIVE: The 20-mile drive to Harlech flanks the north side of the Mawddach Estuary, passing through the resort town of Barmouth and skirting the Cardigan Bay coast. Take the Cader Rd west out of town to the A493, head over the Mawddach to the A496 and follow it west through Barmouth, then north to Harlech.

08 Harlech

One of Wales' splendid 13th-century **castles** *(cadw.gov.wales)* – and perhaps the most dramatically situated – commands the hill-town of Harlech.

With views across Cardigan Bay to the Llŷn Peninsula in one direction, and towards Snowdonia's peaks in another, it's worth diverting up the steep road. Once there, you'll find top-notch B&Bs, cosy teashops, and some of the best bistros and Welsh comfort food for miles around.

THE DRIVE: From Harlech, follow the Stryd Fawr (High St)/B4573 northeast, merging with the A496 as it follows the River Dwyryd further inland through woodlands. In all, this leg is 14 miles.

09 Blaenau Ffestiniog

Surrounded by striking mountains of shattered slate, Blaenau has made the most of its slate-mining heritage. It's the northern terminus of the former slate-carrying **Ffestiniog Railway** *(festrail.co.uk)*, which winds its way through the dramatic hills from coastal Porthmadog.

Visitors may also explore the fascinating **Llechwedd Slate Caverns** *(zipworld.co.uk)*, zip wire over vast open quarries, and tackle the challenging mountain-bike trails of **Antur Stiniog** *(anturstiniog.com)*.

THE DRIVE: Backtrack southwest along the A496 to where the B4410 branches off to the west. Join the A498 at Prenteg, and follow its narrow curves north through dense forest and along the River Glaslyn to Beddgelert: all up a journey of 16 miles.

10 Beddgelert

Beautifully preserved Beddgelert, built of dark local stone at the junction of the Colwyn and Glaslyn rivers, is surrounded by photogenic hills and rolling farmland.

This is prime walking country: consider dropping into the National Trust–owned **Craflwyn Hall** *(nationaltrust.org.uk)* and taking on the 60-minute round-trip ramble to the hilltop of **Dinas Emrys**, legendary site of a castle built by King Vortigern. Alternatively, challenge yourself with a half-day ascent of **Moel Hebog Ridge** (off the A4085), or take a gentle wander along the river to the legendary **Gelert's Grave**.

THE DRIVE: Skirting the southern slopes of Snowdon and the northern shore of Llyn Cwellyn, the narrow valley road, A4085, winds its way 13 miles northwest to your last stop, Caernarfon.

11 Caernarfon

Any visit to Caernarfon inevitably focuses on its mighty **castle** *(cadw.gov.wales)*; its banded, hexagonal towers were designed in the 13th century to pay aesthetic tribute to the sturdy walls of Byzantium.

Ironically, for a town that figures strongly in both the Roman and English domination of Wales, Caernarfon is now a vibrant centre of Welsh language and culture.

Well-stocked with characterful B&Bs, it also has some excellent pubs and restaurants – the Tuscan flavours of **Osteria** are standouts – and is the perfect base for forays across the Menai Strait to Anglesey, or along the less-trodden Llŷn Peninsula.

WONDERFUL PLACES TO EAT AND SLEEP

Kicking Dolgellau's dining scene up a notch, the elegantly rustic **Fork, Cork and Feathers** *(theforkcorkandfeathers.co.uk)* takes pride in local sourcing. Ingredients take centre stage at this deli cafe, wine bar and bistro, whether you go for a tasting platter of cured meats, a gourmet sandwich or Welsh tapas. Dishes like Snowdonia Wagyu beef oxtail slow-cooked in red wine are simple but sensational.

Victoria House *(victoriahouse.wales)* is pretty much the perfect guesthouse – a delightful, solid Victorian building in Caernarfon's old town with four spacious, Victorian-style rooms.

On a hilltop perch overlooking the slate landscapes of Blaenau and framed by the Moelwynion mountains, **Llechwedd Glamping at Plas Weunydd** *(plasweunydd.co.uk)* is a terrific base for outdoor activities from downhill mountain biking to peak bagging. Here stylish glamping tents come with snug beds, wood-burning stoves and private decks where you can watch zipliners whizz past.

Bridge, Beddgelert, made of local dark stone

STEVE ROSENBACH/SHUTTERSTOCK

CAERNARFON

27

WALES

LYRICAL SOUTHEAST WALES

DURATION: 3 DAYS

DISTANCE: 75 MILES / 121KM

GREAT FOR: HISTORY

BEST TIME TO GO: THIS ROUTE IS ENJOYABLE YEAR-ROUND BUT CONSIDER MAY AND JUNE FOR SPRING FLOWERS AND THE HAY FESTIVAL.

★ BEST FOR

HISTORY

Exploring the hidden nooks of Chepstow and Raglan Castles.

Raglan Castle

The Wye Valley was the birthplace of British tourism. From 1760, English high society flocked here to view Tintern Abbey and the many castles along the way. The romantic vistas that fired the likes of Turner, Coleridge and Wordsworth remain substantially intact today. The trip continues through rural Monmouthshire and the beautiful Bannau Brycheiniog (Brecon Beacons) National Park.

LINK YOUR TRIP

11 Winchester, Glastonbury & Bath
It's a 45-minute (30-mile) drive from Bath to Chepstow via the M4 and Severn Bridge.

16 Industrial Heritage
From Great Malvern, it's 45 miles to Chepstow (allow 1¼ hours); head south to Gloucester and take the A48.

01 Chepstow

If you were in any doubt this was a border town, check out **Chepstow Castle** *(cadw.gov.wales)*, standing guard over the River Wye, which still marks the divide between the two nations of Wales and England. This colossal fortress was founded by the Normans immediately after their conquest of England, making it among Britain's oldest castles. It's a fascinating place to poke about in, but try not to wake King Arthur, who's believed to be snoozing in a cavern underneath the castle, until he's needed to save the day.

The town itself was once held in the castle's stony embrace by a surrounding wall, sections of which still remain.

The old part of Chepstow is a likeable place to potter about in, with good eateries, pubs and shops, and a little **local history museum** *(visitmonmouthshire.com)*.

THE DRIVE: From Chepstow, take the A466 north past

MAYUMI.K.PHOTOGRAPHY/SHUTTERSTOCK

Chepstow Racecourse and along the wooded Wye Valley to Tintern. It's an enchanting 5-mile drive, rendered rather mysterious when the morning mist, as it often does, lingers thickly.

02 Tintern

Immortalised by painters and poets down the ages, the enigmatic ruins of **Tintern Abbey** (*cadw.gov.wales*) are ridiculously picturesque. Part of it is the setting, with the River Wye on one side and forested hills fanning all around. The rest is down to the soaring grandeur of the Gothic architecture, made no less stirring by the lack of a roof or windows. Founded in 1131 by the Cistercian order, it was left to fall into elegant ruin after Henry VIII dissolved all of Britain's monasteries in the 16th century.

Tintern village spreads along the river for about a mile. There are some cracking local walks, including easy riverside tracks in the vicinity of the **Old Station** (*visitmonmouthshire.com*) visitor centre-cum-cafe and the classic Devil's Pulpit hike up into those thickly wooded hills.

THE DRIVE: Beautiful landscapes keep unfurling as you progress up this tree-lined river valley. The road crosses the river into England and back before reaching Monmouth, a journey of 12 miles.

03 Monmouth

The county town of Monmouthshire is as English a town as you'll find in Wales. In fact, the border has shifted backwards and forwards over the centuries, shunting it between the two countries.

The rivers Monnow and Wye curl around the historic town centre, creating a natural moat to what was once a walled town attached to **Monmouth Castle** (*monmouthcastlemuseum.org.uk*). All that remains of this august fortress – the birthplace of Henry V – is a small section of wall and part of a tower. In a much better state of repair is **Monnow Bridge**, the UK's only remaining medieval fortified bridge, which abuts the main street.

Monmouth's other famous son was Charles Stewart Rolls, co-founder of Rolls-Royce. Discover more about his life in the **Nelson Museum & Local History Centre** (*visitmonmouthshire.com*). The museum also has extensive displays dedicated to Admiral Horatio Nelson.

THE DRIVE: From Monmouth, take the busy A40 dual carriageway southwest for 9 miles. Raglan Castle rears into view to the right of the highway. Continue on to the roundabout near Raglan village before doubling back to enter the site.

04 Raglan Castle

Standing in majestic ruin beside a busy highway, **Raglan Castle** (*cadw.gov.wales*) is much more ornate than any castle needs to be. That's because defence was only part of its purpose – showing off the wealth, power and good taste of its owners was equally important. Much of the sandstone used in its construction has a pinkish hue, and elegant courtyards were backed by halls decorated with elaborate windows and fireplaces.

Raglan fell into disrepair after the English Civil War of the 1640s. Still, much of the structure is intact and you should allow at least an hour to explore the site.

THE DRIVE: From the castle, backtrack down the highway to the nearest roundabout before swinging back past the castle on the A40 to Abergavenny. On the 11-mile trip, the mountains of Brecon Beacons National Park loom distractingly ever-nearer.

05 Abergavenny

Sitting on the doorstep of Brecon Beacons National Park, ringed by oddly shaped mountains, the Monmouthshire market town of Abergavenny makes a great base for walkers and other active types. It has also become a gastronomic hot spot, with a selection of top-quality farm produce, an outstanding September food festival and a handful of high-profile restaurants scattered about the surrounding countryside.

In the town, the main attraction is **St Mary's Priory Church** *(abergavenny.church)*, filled with so many grand tombs that it's been dubbed the 'Westminster Abbey of Wales'. Once attached to a monastery, it survived Henry VIII's reforms by being converted into a parish church. The neighbouring 12th-century **Tithe Barn** *(abergavenny.church/the-tithe-barn)* now holds a heritage centre and food hall showcasincg a range of Welsh products.

Abergavenny's castle is humble by Welsh standards, with only a few stretches of curtain wall and a **local history museum** *(abergavennymuseum.co.uk)* where the keep once stood.

On a literary note, modern writer Owen Sheers went to school here.

THE DRIVE: Leaving Abergavenny via the A40, you'll quickly enter Brecon Beacons National Park and cross into Powys. The highway shadows the River Usk, albeit from a distance, with the Sugar Loaf mountain to the right. You'll reach Crickhowell after 6 miles.

DETOUR

Blaenavon

Start: 05 Abergavenny

You have done pastoral, but industrial is just as much a defining landscape of this part of Wales. The coal mines of the South Wales Valleys once fuelled Britain's industrial revolution and powered the might of the British Navy. That all came to a standstill during the mine closures of the 1980s. The close-knit communities of the valleys took a major hit, unemployment soared and whole towns faced extinction.

One such place was Blaenavon, a town that came into being in the 18th century after the world's biggest ironworks were constructed. In the year 2000, 20 years after its Big Pit coal mine was closed, Blaenavon's unique conglomeration of industrial sites was awarded World Heritage status by UNESCO, igniting a rebirth of sorts.

Start your visit at the excellent **Blaenavon World Heritage Centre** *(visitblaenavon.co.uk)* to put everything into perspective. The town's main attraction is the **Big Pit National Coal Museum** *(museum.wales/bigpit)*, where you can get a feel for what life was like working the coal seam. The biggest attraction involves heading 90m down into the pit depths under the guidance of former miners, and the above-ground museum is fascinating in its own right.

The historic **Blaenavon Ironworks** *(cadw.gov.wales)* are another must-see, the hulking ruins brought to life through audio-visual displays. A group of local enthusiasts has also resurrected a section of the **Pontypool & Blaenavon Railway** *(bhrailway.co.uk)*, which once hauled coal down from the mines. Check online to see if/when steam trains are running to **Whistle Stop**, the highest train station in both Wales and England.

Another byproduct of the town's reinvention is the **Blaenafon Cheddar Company** *(chunkofcheese.co.uk)*, which produces award-winning cheeses, some of which are matured in historic cellars. Try adventurous flavours such as chiili-spiced Dragon's Breath or even cider-laced Taffy Apple.

HISTORIC PUB TO VISIT

If only every village in Wales had a pub like this...Looking back on 600 years of history, the **Bear Hotel** *(bearhotel.co.uk)* in Crickhowell was once an overnight stop on the horse-drawn coach journey from London to west Wales. Now a delightfully old-school gastropub and hotel, it's full of creaky character, with oak beams, log fires and cosy nooks.

CHRIS HOWES/WILD PLACES PHOTOGRAPHY/ALAMY

Blaenafon Cheddar Company

Blaenavon is 7 miles southwest of Abergavenny via the B4246. From here you can continue back to the Head of the Valleys Rd and on through Llangattock to Crickhowell; 10 miles all told.

06 Crickhowell

The picturesque, flower-festooned village of **Crickhowell** is encircled by contorted Black Mountains peaks, which form the eastern section of Brecon Beacons National Park.

Aside from a crumbling castle, its main feature of interest is an elegant bridge over the River Usk, which has more arches on one side than the other. That is in addition to the proudly, prettily independent shops, restaurants and pubs that contributed towards this little honeypot winning 'Best Place to Live in Wales' in 2025, according to the *Sunday Times*.

Crickhowell takes its name from **Crug Hywel** (Table Mountain), a flat-topped mountain with the remains of an Iron Age fort at its summit. It makes an excellent target for a steep 3-mile-return walk. The **Crickhowell Walking Festival** *(crickhowellfestival.com)* in March throws further light on the region's delightful hikes.

THE DRIVE: It's under 3 miles from Crickhowell to Tretower, your next stop. Take the A40 out of town and then veer right onto the A479. Look for the sign to Tretower Court on your left.

07 Tretower

By the 15th century, the Vaughan family, like many toffs of the time, had tired of living in their drafty old castle and decided to build a more comfortable pad nearby. The result was **Tretower Court** *(cadw.gov.wales)*, a large fortified house, still standing today in the unassuming hamlet of Tretower.

Most rooms have been left bare, but the kitchens and banqueting hall have been enlivened with period-style furnishings and implements. The house has also been used for period dramas, including the movies *Restoration* and *The Libertine*.

Don't forget to check out the medieval garden beside the house and to cross the fields to the Vaughans' old digs – the sturdy Norman motte-and-bailey castle, reminiscent of a giant's abandoned chess piece.

THE DRIVE: Continue along the lane past Tretower Court to rejoin the A40, which leads to Brecon. It's a good, scenic road through the pastures that comprise the Brecon Beacons foothills. The journey is less than 12 miles; allow 20 minutes.

08 Brecon

At the confluence of the rivers Usk and Honddu, Brecon is a ruggedly handsome market town and major trailhead/activity hub for hiking and other outdoor pursuits in Brecon Beacons National Park.

When the Normans did their conquering hereabouts, inevitably they built a castle and a monastery. **Brecknock Castle** (Castle Sq) has largely been consumed by a hotel, but the monk's church has fared better, being subsequently converted into impressive **Brecon Cathedral** *(breconcathedral.org.uk)*. If you're interested in military history, don't miss the **Regimental Museum of the Royal Welsh** *(royalwelshmuseum.wales)*.

Brecon is the northern terminus of the **Monmouthshire & Brecon Canal**. Regular cruises depart from the Canal Basin, or you can hire your own boat for a self-guided trip. The canal towpath is a popular walking and cycling route.

Walkers are drawn to the craggy summits of the Brecon Beacons, protruding like immense upturned antique irons near town. The key target is the summit of **Pen-y-Fan**.

THE DRIVE: For the 17-mile jaunt to Hay-on-Wye, bear east out of town along the Watton and then turn left onto the A470, which eventually becomes the A438. The road to Hay (the B4350) branches off at Glasbury.

09 Hay-on-Wye

If there's anywhere more bookish than Hay-on-Wye we'd be seriously surprised. Once a pretty but nondescript agricultural centre, Hay reinvented itself in the 1970s under the instigation of local maverick Richard Booth, who opened the world's largest bookshop in a defunct cinema, bought crumbling **Hay Castle** *(haycastletrust.org)*, declared himself king, attracted national attention and saved the town from the decline facing many rural communities at the time.

Others took note and now there are literally dozens of new, second hand, specialist and antiquarian bookshops in this small Powys town. On top of that, Hay-on-Wye is now the setting for the **Hay Festival** *(hayfestival.com)* in late May, arguably the most famous literature event in the world and famously dubbed 'Woodstock of the mind' by former US president Bill Clinton. Spend your Hay time alternating between bookshops, antique stores and pubs, and be sure to check out some of the excellent local eateries.

TREETOP GLAMPING IN HAY-ON-WYE

Reclining in ancient native woodland on the River Wye's banks, eco-minded **By the Wye** *(bythewye.uk)* takes glamping to a luxury level.

Perched on stilts high in the tree canopy, the safari tents are sublime, with fantasy-like beds handmade from gnarly driftwood and lots of above-and-beyond details, including welcome baskets with local goodies, firepits, decks overlooking the river, plus binoculars for an afternoon of bird-spotting.

Tintern Abbey

CLAUDIO DIVIZIA/SHUTTERSTOCK

PHOTO OPPORTUNITY

The spectral ruins of Tintern Abbey.

28

WALES

WILDERNESS WALES

★ BEST FOR

WILDLIFE

Red kites wheeling over Rhayader and other locales in the Cambrian Mountains.

Devil's Bridge

DURATION: 4 DAYS

DISTANCE: 125 MILES / 201KM

GREAT FOR: FAMILIES

BEST TIME TO GO: SUMMER FOR HIKING, EVENTS AND DOLPHIN-SPOTTING. DECEMBER TO FEBRUARY BRINGS SNOW TO THE CAMBRIAN MOUNTAINS.

From the diving dolphins of Cardigan Bay to the red kites soaring above the Cambrian Mountains, Wales' wild heart will take your breath away. This drive takes you from the historic port of Cardigan, through bright beach towns, Victorian spa country, pretty market towns, the great 'Desert of Wales' (as the empty Cambrian Mountains often get called), and the forests and estuaries of the green northwest. We guarantee you won't forget this tour.

LINK YOUR TRIP

26 Eryri (Snowdonia) National Park
Extend your stay to see more of what the northwest corner of Wales has to offer.

29 Northwest Wales
This is easily accessed from Aberystwyth by heading northeast on the A487, 24 miles to Corris.

01 Cardigan

An important medieval and Elizabethan port, Cardigan has emerged from long obscurity to stake a claim as a major centre of culture in Mid-Wales. Its riverside **castle** *(cardigancastle.com)*, Castell Aberteifi in Welsh – where, in the 12th century, the first Eisteddfod was held – has been carefully restored, and serves once again as a bastion of Welsh culture, offering self-guided tours, performances, a sophisticated restaurant and more. Beyond, the vast sweep of Cardigan Bay promises stunning **encounters** *(baytoremember.co.uk)* with dolphins, seals and birdlife (book boat trips online beforehand), while quiet sandy beaches like **Mwnt** *(nationaltrust.org.uk)* speckle the coastline heading north.

THE DRIVE: Take the A487 out of town as it heads northeast and inland for 22 miles, before rejoining the coast just outside pretty harbour town Aberaeron.

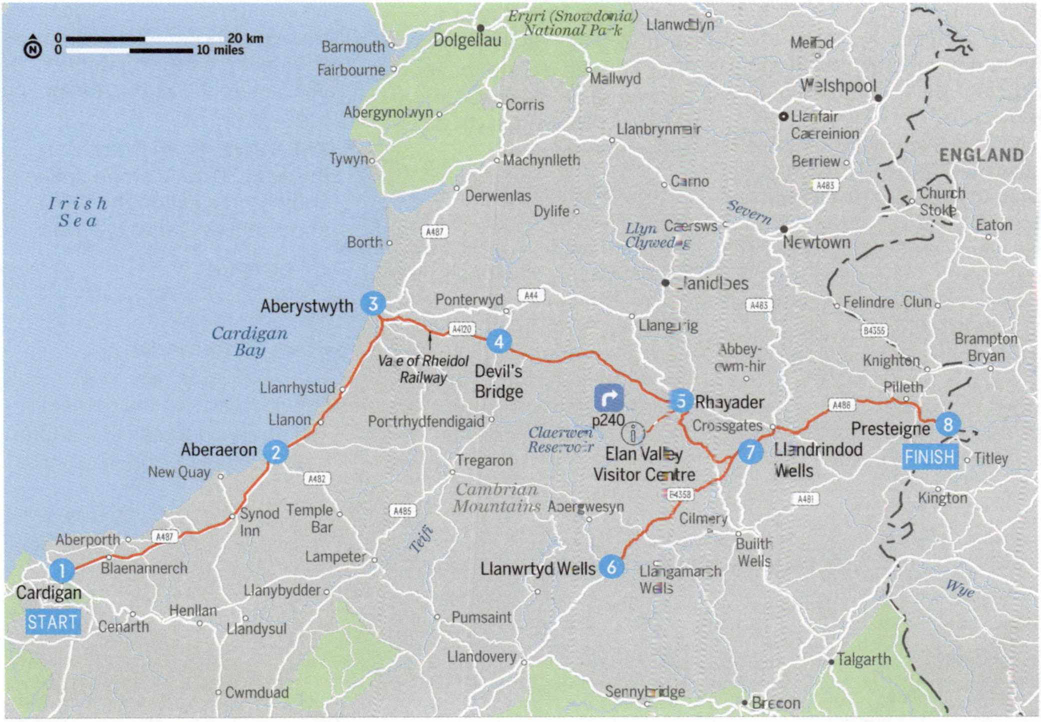

JAX10289/SHUTTERSTOCK

02 Aberaeron

With its colourful quayside rows of Georgian houses and shipping offices, many now occupied by top-notch B&Bs and hotels, Aberaeron makes a great stop alongside a tempestuous stretch of coast. Most of the appeal – such as the beautiful boutique hotel and restaurant **Harbourmaster** *(harbourmaster.com)* – is to be found along Pen Cei on the waterfront, but it's well worth the 2.5-mile trek out of town to visit **Llanerchaeron** *(nationaltrust.org.uk)*, a lovely Georgian country estate.

THE DRIVE: Continue cruising north up the coast until you hit the Mid-Wales metropolis of Aberystwyth (population under 20,000); in all, the journey is 16 miles.

03 Aberystwyth

Not exactly the wilderness, but a very diverting place to spend an afternoon (or evening, or night) between your wild adventures, Aberystwyth is a lively student town lining a long, sandy beach with a big mix of attractions. Culturally, it's hard to go past the **National Library** *(library.wales)*, which surmounts a hill befitting its eminence behind the town, or the brilliant **Aberystwyth Arts Centre** *(aberystwythartscentre.co.uk)*.

There's also a picturesque ruined **castle** (King St) and pubs aplenty to keep students and seaside drinkers happy. Dining-wise, there are many gems among Aber's twisting streets. Importantly, gorgeous countryside is also close: the northern Cambrian Mountains and Southern Snowdonia are extremely easy to access from town.

THE DRIVE: From Aberystwyth, it's a 12-mile climb on the A4120 to the wooded ravine of Devil's Bridge.

04 Devil's Bridge

The eponymous **bridge** *(devilsbridgewaterfalls.co.uk)* is the main attraction at this otherwise out-of-the way corner of Mid-Wales. Spanning a cataract where the River Rheidol plunges into the homonymous gorge, it's actually a palimpsest of three overlapping bridges: the top built of iron in the early 20th century, the middle of stone in the mid-18th, and the first (also of stone) in the 11th.

It's worth paying the few pounds to descend into the gorge and the **Coed Rheidol National Nature Reserve**, with its dripping oaks and photogenic glimpses of the bridge. Devil's Bridge is also the inland terminus of the **Vale of Rheidol Railway** *(vor.wales)*, a narrow-gauge industrial train preserved as a tourist attraction that clings to the slopes as it wends its picturesque way to coast-hugging Aberystwyth.

THE DRIVE: From Devil's Bridge, you'll be venturing further into the back of beyond, skittering on narrow, remote lanes via Cwmystwyth, 18 miles to Rhayader.

05 Rhayader

An important agricultural centre, Rhayader is most appealing for its access to surrounding wild places. It's the closest centre to the delightfully dramatic Elan Valley, with its monumental Victorian and Edwardian dams, and is also handy for the beginning of the **Wye Valley Walk** *(wyevalleywalk.org)*. Watch out for red kites wheeling overhead throughout these Cambrian uplands. For refreshment, try the diminutive but characterful **Triangle Inn** *(triangleinn.co.uk)*.

THE DRIVE: From Rhayader, the next 20-mile stage snakes south and west on the A470 and A483 to Llanwrtyd Wells.

DETOUR

The Elan Valley

Start: 05 Rhayader

From Rhayader, you really should head into the human-sculpted wilderness of the **Elan Valley**. It feels immediately wild

Craig Goch Dam, Elan Valley

PHOTO OPPORTUNITY

The mighty Victorian dams of the Elan Valley.

STEPHEN REES/SHUTTERSTOCK

once you leave civilisation behind, yet its defining features are the four mighty **Victorian and Edwardian dams** that were created to ensure water supplies to, ahem, Birmingham.

Inevitably controversial, the dams nonetheless created a 70-sq-mile chain of lake, forest and bog environments in Mid-Wales in which many rare plants and animals, and the totemic red kites, thrive. Nant-y-Gro, an early dam built here, was used in 1942 as target practice by Sir Barnes Neville Wallis, inventor of the 'dam-busting' bouncing bomb.

Elan Valley Visitor Centre *(elanvalley.org.uk)* has all the information a visitor could need, including the specifics of many local hikes. In season, Penbont House makes for a delightful lunch or tea stop, and can provide accommodation too. From Rhayader, the visitor centre is less than 4 miles southwest on the B4518; backtrack to rejoin the main route.

06 Llanwrtyd Wells

Mid-Wales' capital of kooky, little Llanwrtyd and its surrounding hills are home to a variety of weird and wonderful annual events, including **bog snorkelling** *(green-events.co.uk)* and a **fell-running competition** *(green-events.co.uk)* in mid-June that pits human against horse. Dining, drinking and sleeping options are also in rich supply for such a tiny town, and include **Drovers Rest** *(food-food-food.co.uk)* and the **Neuadd Arms** *(neuadd armshotel.co.uk)* – a hub of the local community.

The town is also a great base for forging out into the Cambrian Mountains to the north.

THE DRIVE: Jaunt along the A483 northeast from Llanwrtyd, switching to the B4358 at Beulah. Continue past Newbridge-on-Wye, joining the A4081 for a while to arrive at Llandrindod Wells; 17 miles all told.

07 Llandrindod Wells

The Victorian-Edwardian heyday of this spa town is still evident in the grand architecture of its hotels and terraces, however quiet they may be today. Hotel-spas still fly the flag of formal luxury, the mineral fountains and rambling gardens of Rock Park hint at bygone glory days, when visitors from around Britain would arrive to take the waters, and there is a 5-hectare lake with a Welsh water-spouting dragon at its centre for further ambles. For freewheeling fans there is also the **National Cycle Museum** *(cyclemuseum.org.uk)*.

THE DRIVE: A 20-mile drive from here ushers you to Presteigne on the A483, A44, A488 and B4356 through the hills of historical Radnorshire. You journey via Crossgates and then Pilleth, site of an important battle victory for Owain Glyndŵr against the English under Sir Edward Mortimer, during the ultimately unsuccessful Welsh War of Independence.

> ❤ DON'T MISS
>
> ### HISTORIC B&B
>
> A classic B&B in a rambling, Arts and Crafts–style Edwardian house in Llandrindod Wells, the **Cottage** *(thecottagebandb.co.uk)* exhibits comfortable period-style rooms with heavy wooden furniture and myriad original features, set within a winsome garden.

08 Presteigne

The beauty of the former county of Radnorshire can be seen at something like its best in pretty little Presteigne, with its winsome timber-framed buildings, independent shops and sophisticated air. In town, the **Judge's Lodging** *(judgeslodging.org.uk)* reanimates a Victorian rural magistrate's household in exacting detail.

Outside of town, you land in a gentle chunk of unsung undulating Welsh countryside, with the 16th-century **Offa's Dyke** *(nationaltrail.co.uk)* national trail on the doorstep. Bang on the border with England, it is also a fitting place to end your wild wanderings through Wales. Toast your trip in one of the nation's best real country pubs, the **Harp Inn** at Old Radnor, 6.5 miles south-west of Presteigne.

29

★ BEST FOR

HISTORY

The mock-Byzantine splendour of Caernarfon Castle.

WALES

NORTHWEST WALES

DURATION: 4 DAYS

DISTANCE: 141 MILES / 227KM

GREAT FOR: HISTORY, FAMILIES

BEST TIME TO GO: FLOWERS IN BLOOM AND WARM WEATHER MAKE MAY A LOVELY TIME TO VISIT.

Victorian pier, Llandudno

Shaped by pilgrims, conquerors and the restless sea, northwest Wales is an extraordinary corner of the British Isles that begs to be explored from behind the wheel. Starting from the bustling seaside resort of Llandudno, whose Victorian spirit lingers, this trip takes in some of the mightiest castles, the medieval towns of Conwy, Beaumaris and Caernarfon, plus the most dramatic coastline in the country and bird-rich wetlands.

LINK YOUR TRIP

26 Eryri (Snowdonia) National Park
Join this circuit of Wales' most famous uplands at Dolgellau.

28 Wilderness Wales
Follow the A487 for 34 miles southwest of Dolgellau to start this tour of Wales' wild heart in reverse, at Aberystwyth.

01 Llandudno

Strikingly situated below the towering limestone plateau of Great Orme (Y Gogarth), where you can explore the most extensive **Bronze Age mine** *(greatormemines.info)* yet discovered, Llandudno retains many of the attractions of its Victorian heyday: a grand promenade, a **Victorian pier** *(llandudnopier.com)*, a **rack-and-pinion tramway** *(greatormetramway.co.uk)* and even a Punch and Judy show.

Add a huge range of B&Bs and restaurants, **Mostyn Gallery** *(mostyn.org)*, and this amounts to one of the highlights of the entire North Wales seaboard.

THE DRIVE: This first leg is just 4 miles, south down the A546 to Llandudno Junction, then take the third exit to cross the river to Conwy.

02 Conwy

Conwy is a near-perfect medieval walled town with a superlative

CKTRAVELS.COM/SHUTTERSTOCK

castle. Built in the 13th century as a key part of Edward I's 'Iron Ring', **Conwy Castle** *(cadw.gov.wales)* has survived centuries of mixed fortunes; you can stroll along sections of its mighty town wall for great views.

The Old Town is studded with other historical and cultural attractions, such as **Plas Mawr** (Great House). Excellent accommodation, real ale pubs, such as the **Albion Ale House** *(albionalehouse.weebly.com)*, and fantastic eating options encourage you to linger longer.

THE DRIVE: The Bangor Rd/A547 heads west out of Conwy to the A55. Cross the Menai Strait on the Pont Britannia, then take the A5 east into the town of Menai Bridge, following Dale St, then High St/Cadnant Rd until it joins Beaumaris Rd. It's 23 miles to your next stop.

03 Beaumaris

Beaumaris' broad streets, lined with handsome Georgian buildings, lead the visitor inevitably to the waterfront, and the town's unsurpassed **castle** *(cadw.gov.wales)*, a 13th-century masterpiece considered to be the most perfectly designed fortress in all the British Isles.

There's also the 17th-century **courthouse** *(visitanglesey.co.uk)* and Georgian **Gaol** *(visitanglesey.co.uk)* to explore, as well as **Penmon Priory** *(cadw.gov.wales)*, a short drive north.

It's also worth a **Seacoast Safaris** *(seacoastsafaris.co.uk)* cruise to Puffin Island to view its clamouring bird population.

Finish with a showstopper meal at the Michelin-starred **Sosban & the Old Butchers** *(sosbanandtheoldbutchers.com)* in nearby Menai Bridge.

THE DRIVE: Backtrack along the roads from Beaumaris to Menai Bridge, turn south over the eponymous bridge itself to join the A487, and head southwest for 13 miles to reach Caenarfon.

04 Caernarfon

Built during the same 13th-century push for English military consolidation as Conwy and Beaumaris, Caernarfon's **castle** *(cadw.gov.wales)* is just as impressive. Its hexagonal Byzantine-style walls tower over the Menai Strait and medieval town. Just outside the town walls are the remains of **Segontium** *(cadw.gov.wales)*, a Roman fort from an earlier conquest, while inside there are excellent pubs, B&Bs and restaurants.

THE DRIVE: The 18-mile leg to Nant Gwrtheyrn on the Llŷn Peninsula starts on the A487, south of Caernarfon. Take the A499 to the southwest, then the B4417 at Llanaelhaearn. The minor road over the hill to Nant Gwrtheyrn is signposted from Lithfaen.

05 Nant Gwrtheyrn

Reachable via the hairpin bends of a steep and narrow road, the 19th-century buildings of Nant Gwrtheyrn have been revived as the **Welsh Language & Heritage Centre** *(nantgwrtheyrn.org)*, a bastion of Welsh culture. From the car park above the village, you can also do a wonderful hill walk to the **Tre'r Ceiri Hillfort**, one of the best-preserved Iron Age forts in Europe, for tremendous views of the Llŷn Peninsula from the top.

THE DRIVE: Backtrack over the hill and then back down to Lithfaen, taking the B4417 west through Pistyll and Nefyn, and further west once you join the B4413. It's 19 miles to Aberdaron.

06 Aberdaron

It's worth going to the end of the Llŷn Peninsula. The rocky tip of this barren outpost of Celtic Britain is starkly beautiful and Aberdaron fishing hamlet is the natural base from which to explore this landscape.

You can detour to **Porthor** *(nationaltrust.org.uk)*, aka Whistling Sands, to ride the waves there. And the view of the Pilgrims' Island of **Bardsey**, across the gun-metal sea from the headland of **Mynydd Mawr** *(nationaltrust.org.uk)*, is one of north Wales' most arresting sights. In summer cross the waters with **Bardsey Boat Trips** *(bardseyboattrips.com)* to go birding or walking on the 'Isle of 20,000 Saints'.

> **PHOTO OPPORTUNITY**
>
> Bardsey, the Holy Island of Pilgrims, from Braich-y-Pwll at the tip of the Llŷn Peninsula.

THE DRIVE: The narrow, scenic 13-mile drive to Abersoch follows the B4413 uphill and inland, then south along a signposted minor road into town.

07 Abersoch

Laid-back and lovely even in the colder months, with its Blue Flag beach and views across Cardigan Bay to Snowdonia, Abersoch gets particularly lively in summer.

If you have the time to work on your sailing, wakeboarding, kite-surfing or surfing skills, then try **Abersoch Hydro** *(abersochhydro.com)* or **Offaxis** *(offaxis.co.uk)*.

THE DRIVE: Take the A499 northeast, through Llanbedrog to Pwllheli. From there the A497 follows the coastal railway, through Criccieth to Porthmadog: all up, it's 20 miles.

08 Porthmadog

The former slate port of Porthmadog is a natural stopping point when driving from the Llŷn Peninsula to the northwest Welsh coast. It's also the start of two classic Welsh heritage railways – the **Welsh Highland** *(festrail.co.uk)*

Mawddach Estuary, Barmouth

JANUSZKUREK.COM/SHUTTERSTOCK

and **Ffestiniog** (p229) lines – and a central point on the Cambrian Coast line to Pwllheli.

Real ale fans will appreciate the **Australia** *(facebook.com/australia porthmadog)*, a pub run by Purple Moose Brewery, which is a leading craft brewer in northern Wales.

THE DRIVE: The 21 miles to Barmouth take in the sweep of Cardigan Bay. Take Porthmadog High St north, and join the A487 heading east. Leave the A487 at Penrhyndeudraeth, take Briwet Bridge south, join the A496 and pass through Harlech on the way to Barmouth.

DETOUR

Portmeirion

Start: 08 Porthmadog

This fantasy village, created by visionary architect Sir Clough Williams-Ellis over five decades from 1925, is in a category of its own. Occupying a peninsula with a microclimate mild enough to grow many exotic plants, it's a homage to what Williams-Ellis saw as the ideal human-made environments of the Mediterranean. Spend an hour or two wandering its fanciful Italianate piazzas, set-piece landscapes and visually delightful follies. The cult 1960s TV show *The Prisoner* was filmed here: every year the PortmeiriCon (Prisoner Convention; *portmeiricon.com*) convention draws together devoted fans.

Portmeirion is a 3-mile dash along High St/Britannia Tce from central Porthmadog, heading southeast over the broad Glaslyn River Estuary. When you reach Minffordd, take the signposted road to Portmeirion. Just retrace your steps to restart the itinerary.

IAN SHAW/ALAMY

Portmeirion

09 Barmouth

Barmouth may be a typical seaside resort, but its Victorian architecture and proximity to the walks and birdlife of the **Mawddach Estuary** (p229) make it special. Its impressive railway bridge, built in the town's heyday, spanning 699m of the mouth of the Mawddach, is its most distinctive feature. It's well worth scrambling up Dinas Oleu hill for the panoramic views of the estuary and checking out **Tŷ Crwn Roundhouse** *(barsailinst.org.uk/crwn.html)*, the former prison for drunk sailors and slatterns.

THE DRIVE: The last, winding 10-mile stretch skirts the northern edge of the wide, sandy Mawddach Estuary. The A496 takes you to the junction with the A470, just north of the Mawddach River; from here, head south into Dolgellau.

10 Dolgellau

The charming market town of Dolgellau is one of the highlights of northwest Wales. This former wool and gold town has many listed buildings and an enviable natural setting. Dolgellau's proximity to **Cader Idris**, the walking and cycling trails passing through the Mawddach Estuary and the mountain-biking playground of **Coed y Brenin Forest Park** (p229), make it a natural base for fresh-air fans.

Superb B&Bs, coupled with creative tapas and wine bars such as **Gwin Dylanwad Wine** *(dylanwad.co.uk)* and the **Fork, Cork and Feathers** (p230), add to the town's appeal.

0 100 km
0 50 miles
Orkney
Stromness
Kirkwall
Dunnet Head
John O'Groats
Strathy Point
Thurso
ATLANTIC OCEAN
Butt of Lewis
Cape Wrath
Durness
Melvich
Tongue
North Sea
Kinlochbervie
Wick
A894
Lybster
Stornoway
Outer Hebrides
Lochinver
The Minch
Helmsdale
A9
Lairg
Brora
Tarbert
Ullapool
Dornoch
A832
Moray Firth
Fraserburgh
Gairloch
Invergordon
Elgin
Banff
Lochmaddy
Uig
Trotternish
Strathpeffer
Black Isle
Nairn
Craigellachie
Peterhead
33
A890
Inverness
36
Huntly
Dunvegan
Portree
Dufftown
Loch Ness
A9
Grantown-on-Spey
Skye
Kyle of Lochalsh
A82
Aviemore
Five Sisters of Kintail
Fort Augustus
A939
Aberdeen
A93
Kingussie
Mallaig
Cairngorms National Park
Braemar
Stonehaven
Sea of the Hebrides
35
34
A90
Fort William
Ben Nevis
A9
Kinlochleven
Pitlochry
Brechin
Montrose
Tobermory
Glencoe
Glencoe
Aberfeldy
Forfar
Salen
A82
Arbroath
Mull
Dunkeld
Taynuilt
Dundee
Iona
Oban
A85
Crieff
Perth
Fionnphort
St Andrews
Loch Lomond & The Trossachs National Park
37
Inveraray
ATLANTIC OCEAN
Kinross
Arrochar
Kilmartin
Aberfoyle
Kirkcaldy
A83
Stirling
31
Lochgilphead
Berwick-upon-Tweed
32
Greenock
Dumbarton
Jura
EDINBURGH
Haddington
M8
Kennacraig
Glasgow
Motherwell
A68
30
Portnahaven
Islay
Ardrossan
Peebles
Kelso
Coldstream
Kintyre
Arran
Brodick
Kilmarnock
Melrose
A841
Jedburgh
Ayr
Campbeltown
Firth of Clyde
Mull of Kintyre
Moffat
Girvan
St John's Town of Dalry
Northumberland National Park
Coleraine
North Channel
Galloway Forest Park
NORTHERN IRELAND
Dumfries
Newcastle-upon-Tyne
Larne
Stranraer
Newton Stewart
Castle Douglas
Carlisle
Portpatrick
Kirkcudbright
ENGLAND
Mull of Galloway
Burrow Head
BELFAST

TTSTUDIO/SHUTTERSTOCK

Inveraray Castle (p262)

SCOTLAND

EXPLORE

SCOTLAND

Want to get lost in Britain? Nowhere is as wild, dramatic and empty as Scotland. It's more a question of how lost you want to get – and amid what kind of landscape. The Lowlands' rolling farmland hides centuries of bitter border warfare, evident in 'peles' (defensive towers) and ruined abbeys. The Central Belt encompasses Scotland's great cities, Glasgow and Edinburgh, with imposing medieval monuments such as Stirling Castle. The Highlands are an endless procession of jaw-dropping glens and shimmering lochs, and the isles are truly a world apart: all wave-wracked coastlines and prehistoric monuments.

Edinburgh

Scotland's capital and handsomest city can be the natural start for most of these drives. It's under five hours by train from London, and there are excellent train, tram and other links to Edinburgh Airport – Scotland's busiest, connecting with over 150 destinations. Car hire is easily arranged at the airport or in town. Edinburgh is blessed with historical and cultural riches, and has plenty of places to stay, from old-school British B&Bs in Georgian houses to swanky hotels. You're sure to find something to match your budget and tastes, and will have plenty of supermarkets and delis to garner supplies.

Glasgow

Scotland's second city is the gateway to the southern Highlands and islands. The train journey from London is only slightly longer than the one to Edinburgh (closer to six hours), and Glasgow has its own airport (smaller and serving mainly European and UK destinations). Naturally, the city has plenty of car-hire outfits, and sleeping and shopping options. You're more likely to find cheaper accommodation here than in Edinburgh, but only if you book well ahead.

Stirling

Well placed for the 'Stirling & Fife Coast' (p254), 'Lower West Coast' (p258), 'Royal Highlands & Cairngorms' (p276) and 'Great Glen' (p284) tours, Stirling is a historic destination in its own right. Only 50 minutes by train from Edinburgh, it has plenty of accommodation and

WHEN TO GO

Scottish winters can be bleak, even brutal. While you may enjoy cold, sunlit, short days, the reality is November to March can be harsh – expect rain, snow, rough seas and icy roads. Summer can be divine (despite the late-afternoon clouds of midges), but the shoulder seasons – April to June and September and October – are usually mild and crowd-free.

supermarkets, plus half a dozen car rental outlets. It's best to drive here if you are using it as your main base.

Inverness

At the head of the Great Glen and the River Ness, Inverness is well stocked with accommodation, car-rental offices and supermarkets. It's a good choice for the 'Great Glen' (p258) and 'Upper West Coast' (p244) drives. Edinburgh is a three-hour drive or 3¾-hour train ride away.

Fort William

A regional hub, especially for hikers, Fort William sits at the southern end of the Great Glen, making it ideal for launching trips into the Highlands, Western Isles and central Scotland. It has two independent car-hire businesses and a multitude of restaurants, but decent places to stay book out quickly.

Oban

A serene jumping-off point for the 'Lower West Coast' (p258), 'Great Glen' (p284) and 'Ferry-Hopping' (p296) itineraries, seaside Oban is well stocked with accommodation, pubs and restaurants. It has two independent car-rental outlets but you'd be best prepared by arriving here with your own wheels.

TRANSPORT

The high-speed train that links London and Edinburgh, terminating at Waverley station in the heart of the Scottish capital, is a popular means of access. Alternatively, there are trains to Glasgow from London. Edinburgh and Glasgow Airports are linked with more than 150 destinations, predominantly in Europe. It's a long drive (7½ hours) from London to Edinburgh.

RESOURCES

Scottish Tourism
Scotland's official tourism website, listing events, activities, sights and other highlights. *Visitscotland.com*

Historic Environment Scotland
Offers a comprehensive list of historic sites and opportunities to get involved in their protection. *historicenvironment.scot*

Caledonian MacBrayne
Accurate, seasonal information on Caledonian MacBrayne's extensive ferry network. *calmac.co.uk*

WHAT'S ON

Edinburgh International Festival
For four weeks in August this immense, city-wide festival makes Edinburgh the centre of the performing-arts world. Accommodation becomes scarce and very expensive.

Braemar Gathering
Better known as 'The Highland Games', with traditional Scottish sports testing strength. Takes place on the first Saturday of September.

Ullapool Guitar Festival
If you're in Ullapool in October, stay for this three-day festival of guitar performances and workshops.

WHERE TO STAY

Cameron House, St Andrews, has beautifully decorated rooms and warm, cheerful hosts – a real home away from home.

Friars Wynd, Stirling, is a thoughtfully renovated 19th-century townhouse in which period features mix with modern luxuries.

A stately Georgian townhouse, 14 Hart St, Edinburgh, offers three lovingly appointed, family-friendly suites.

Opposite Kelvingrove Park, the Alamo Guesthouse, Glasgow, comprises 10 peaceful rooms close to some of the city's best museums and restaurants.

The Old Mill Inn, Pitlochry, is a welcoming and family-friendly retreat at the gateway to the Highlands.

30

★ BEST FOR

FAMILIES

Mountain biking and forest zip lines at Glentress.

SCOTLAND

THE BORDERS

DURATION: 2–3 DAYS

DISTANCE: 90 MILES / 144KM

GREAT FOR: HISTORY, NATURE

BEST TIME TO GO: LATE SPRING OFFERS BLOOMING FLOWERS, GREEN FIELDS AND LOCAL FESTIVALS.

Rosslyn Chapel, Roslin

Romance and strife coincide in the Borders region, whose rough history of war and plunder is encapsulated by the magnificent ruins of four abbeys. Templar mysteries add an extra layer at atmosphere-packed Rosslyn Chapel, while a number of welcoming villages with ancient traditions pepper the countryside and grandiose mansions await exploration. Over it all is poised the benevolent ghost of Sir Walter Scott, quill in hand.

LINK YOUR TRIP

24 Northumbria
It's a pleasantly leisurely drive alongside the Tweed from Kelso to reach the coast at Berwick, where you can take on the Northumbria route in reverse.

31 Stirling & Fife Coast
It's 80 miles northwest from Kelso via Edinburgh's southern bypass to Stirling and this coastal route.

01 Roslin

It's only a 7-mile journey through city suburbs from central Edinburgh to Roslin, where the success of Dan Brown's novel *The Da Vinci Code* shot Scotland's most beautiful and enigmatic church, **Rosslyn Chapel** *(rosslynchapel.com)*, to prominence. The chapel was built in the mid-15th century for William Sinclair, 3rd Earl of Orkney, and the ornately carved interior – at odds with the architectural fashion of its time – is a monument to the mason's art, rich in symbolic imagery.

As well as flowers, vines, angels and biblical figures, the carved stones include many examples of the pagan 'Green Man'; other figures are associated with Freemasonry and the Knights Templar.

Intriguingly, there are also carvings of plants from the Americas that predate Columbus' voyage of discovery. The symbolism has led some to conclude that Rosslyn is a secret Templar repository with

NEVERSTOPLOOKINGUP/SHUTTERSTOCK

hidden vaults concealing anything from the Holy Grail or the head of John the Baptist to the body of Christ himself.

THE DRIVE: The A701 is easily accessed just outside Roslin, and it's an easy drive south along it and the A703 to Peebles, 15 miles away.

02 Peebles

With a picturesque main street set on a ridge between the lovely River Tweed and Eddleston Water, Peebles is one of the most handsome of the Border towns. Though it lacks a major sight, the agreeable atmosphere, fine eating and snacking choices, and good walking options in the rolling, wooded hills thereabouts will entice you to linger.

Two miles east of Peebles off the A72, **Glentress forest** *(7stanes mountainbiking.com)* has one of the best of the network of mountain-biking hubs known as the 7Stanes. The shop here hires rigs and will put you on the right trail for your ability. Classes are available also. These are some of Britain's best biking routes.

There are also marked walking trails, **forest zip lines** *(goapezoo.uk)* and osprey-viewing available.

THE DRIVE: Cross the Tweed in Peebles and continue along the quiet country road B7062, or take the main A72 east and turn right in Innerleithen to reach Traquair House, which is well signposted. It's about a 7-mile drive whichever way you choose.

> PHOTO OPPORTUNITY
>
> Snapping Sir Walter's favourite vista from lovely Scott's View.

03 Traquair House

One of Scotland's great country houses, **Traquair House** *(traquair.co.uk)* has a powerful, ethereal beauty. Odd, sloping floors and a musty odour bestow a genuine feel, and parts of the building are believed to have been constructed long before the first official record of its existence in 1107. The massive tower house was gradually expanded but has remained virtually unchanged since the 17th century.

Since the 15th century, Traquair has belonged to the Stuart family, and the family's unwavering Catholicism and loyalty to the Stuart cause led to famous visitors, including Mary, Queen of Scots and Bonnie Prince Charlie, but also to numerous problems as life as a Jacobite became a furtive, clandestine affair.

One of Traquair's most interesting places is the concealed room where priests secretly lived and performed Mass. Other beautiful time-worn rooms hold fascinating relics and letters.

In addition to the house, there's a garden maze, a small brewery producing the tasty Bear Ale and a series of craft workshops.

THE DRIVE: Head back to the A72 and head east towards Galashiels and Melrose. A couple of miles before Melrose, you'll reach Abbotsford, after a total drive of 17 miles.

04 Abbotsford

Just outside Melrose, **Abbotsford** *(scottsabbotsford.com)* is the place to discover the life and works of Sir Walter Scott, to whom

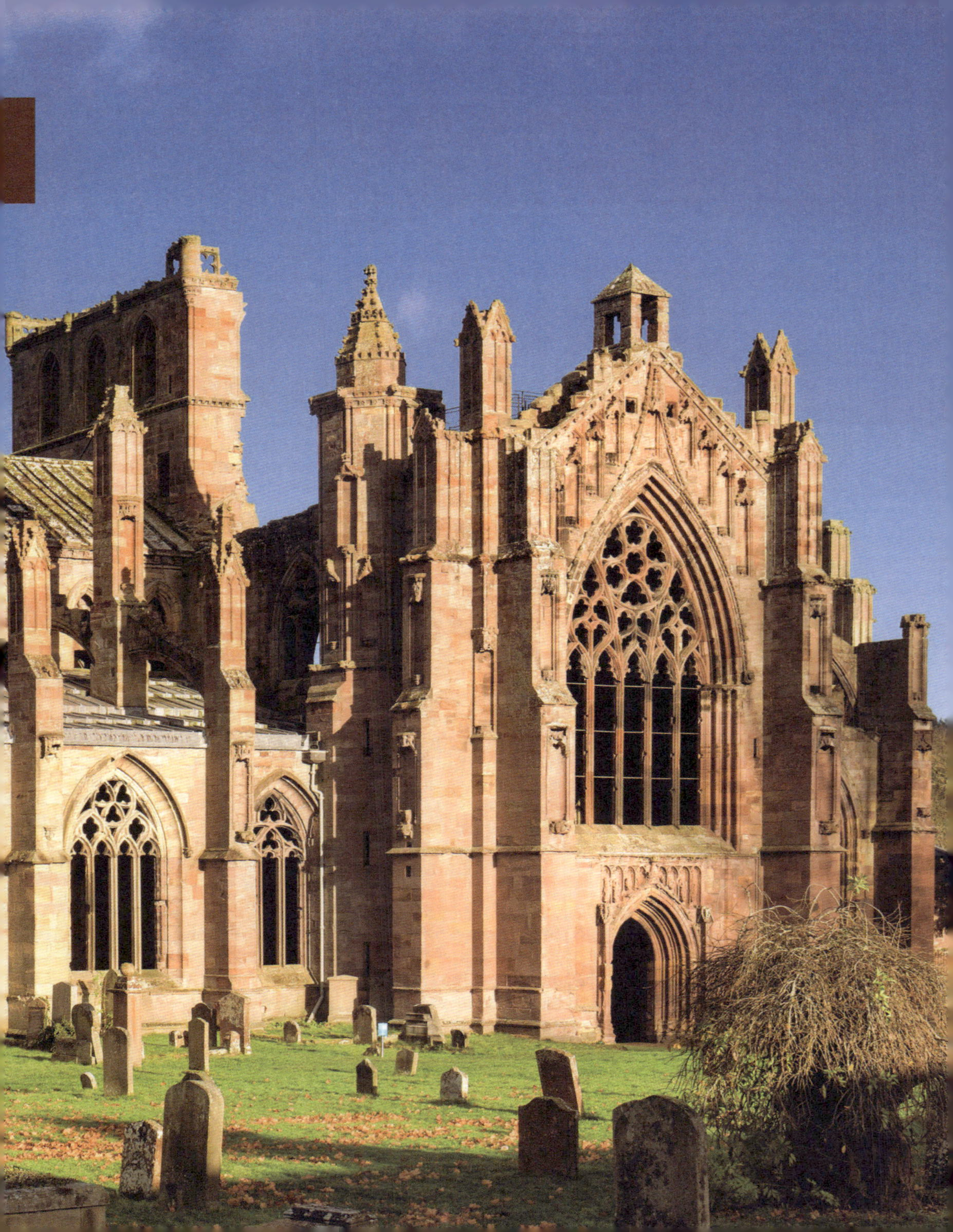

we arguably owe both the modern novel and our mind's-eye view of Scotland. This whimsical, fabulous house where he lived – and which ruined him when his publishers went bust – really brings this 19th-century writer to life. The grounds on the banks of the Tweed are lovely, and Scott drew much inspiration from rambles in the surrounding countryside.

A modern visitor centre displays memorabilia and gives an overview of the man, before a swish audio-guide system – with one designed for kids – shows you around the house. Within are some gloriously over-the-top features, with elaborate carvings, enough swords and dirks to equip a small army, a Chinese drawing room, and a lovely study and library. There's a cafe-restaurant atop the visitor centre.

THE DRIVE: Abbotsford to Melrose is just a couple of miles.

05 Melrose

Tiny, charming Melrose is a polished village running on the well-greased wheels of tourism. Sitting at the feet of the three heather-covered Eildon Hills, Melrose has a classic market square and one of the great abbey ruins.

Red-sandstone **Melrose Abbey** *(historicenvironment.scot)* was repeatedly destroyed by the English in the 14th century. The remaining broken shell is pure Gothic and the ruins are famous for their decorative stonework – look out for the pig gargoyle playing the bagpipes. Though Melrose had a monastery way back in the 7th century, this abbey was founded by David I in 1136 for Cistercian monks, and later rebuilt by Robert the Bruce, whose heart is buried here. Ask for details of local walks.

Melrose Abbey
PHOTO-LOCI/ALAMY

In the immediate vicinity of the abbey, and all free to enter, it's worth exploring a couple of elegant gardens as well as an exhibition on local Roman heritage.

THE DRIVE: Head east on Main St from Melrose before taking the A68 towards Edinburgh at the roundabout. Take a right onto B6360 towards Dryburgh and keep following signs for the abbey. Altogether, the journey is just over 9 miles.

06 Dryburgh Abbey

Dryburgh Abbey *(historicenvironment.scot)* is the most beautiful and complete of the Border abbeys, partly because the neighbouring town of Dryburgh no longer exists (another victim of the wars) and partly for its lovely site by the Tweed in a sheltered birdsong-filled valley.

Dating from about 1150, the abbey belonged to the Premonstratensians, a religious order founded in France, and conjures 12th-century monastic life more successfully than its nearby counterparts. The pink-hued stone ruins are the burial place of Sir Walter Scott.

THE DRIVE: From Dryburgh Abbey, retrace your steps to the A68 and turn south on it. After 15 miles you'll reach Jedburgh.

HISTORIC ENVIRONMENT SCOTLAND

Several of the attractions along this route are run by **Historic Environment Scotland** (HES; *historic environment.scot*), a national heritage organisation. If you'll be visiting these and other highlights, such as Stirling or Edinburgh Castles, consider joining up, as entry is free for members.

07 Jedburgh

Attractive Jedburgh, where many old buildings and wynds (narrow alleys) have been intelligently restored, invites exploration on foot. It's centred on the noble skeleton of its **ruined abbey** *(historicenvironment.scot)*. Dominating the town, this was the first of the great Border abbeys to be passed into state care, and it shows – audio and visual presentations telling the abbey's story are scattered throughout the carefully preserved ruins (good for the kids). The red-sandstone ruins are roofless but relatively intact, and the ingenuity of the master mason can be seen in some of the rich (if faded) stone carvings in the nave.

THE DRIVE: It's 11 miles from Jedburgh to Kelso. Head north up the A68, then right on to the A698.

08 Kelso

Kelso, a market town with a broad, cobbled square flanked by Georgian buildings, has a cheery feel and historic appeal. During the day it's busy, but after 8pm you'll have the streets to yourself. The town has a lovely site at the junction of the Tweed and Teviot, and is one of the most enjoyable places in the Borders.

Once one of the richest abbeys in southern Scotland, **Kelso Abbey** *(historicenvironment.scot)* was reduced to ruins by English raids in the 16th century. What remains today is some of the finest surviving Romanesque architecture in Scotland.

Grandiose **Floors Castle** *(floorscastle.com)* is Scotland's largest inhabited mansion, home to the Duke of Roxburghe, and overlooks the Tweed about a mile west of Kelso. Built by William Adam in the 1720s, the original Georgian simplicity was 'improved' in the 1840s.

31

SCOTLAND

★ BEST FOR

HISTORY

Exploring the beautifully preserved medieval village of Culross.

STIRLING & FIFE COAST

DURATION: 2–3 DAYS

DISTANCE: 82 MILES / 131KM

GREAT FOR: HISTORY

BEST TIME TO GO: JULY AND AUGUST FOR SUMMER FUN ON THE BEACH AT ELIE.

National Wallace Monument

Stirling and St Andrews, two of Scotland's top tourist magnets, bookend this trip along the less well known southwest coast of Fife, taking in the red pantiled roofs and crow-stepped gables of 17th-century Culross' cobbled lanes (regularly used as a film set), the golden-sand beaches and seaside walks of Elie and Earlsferry, and the pretty-as-a-picture fishing harbours of the East Neuk, one of central Scotland's most picturesque corners.

LINK YOUR TRIP

32 Lower West Coast
A short 20-mile hop to Callander links up with our trip around the scenic and historic highlights of Loch Lomond, the Trossachs and Argyll.

30 The Borders
From St Andrews you can head south across the Forth to Rosslyn Chapel to begin our trip around the Borders' market towns, castles and stately homes.

01 Stirling

With an impregnable position atop a mighty wooded crag, Stirling's beautifully preserved Old Town is a treasure trove of historic buildings and cobbled streets winding up to the ramparts of its impressive castle, which offers views for miles around. Nearby is Bannockburn, scene of Robert the Bruce's pivotal triumph over the English in 1314.

Many visitors find **Stirling Castle** *(stirlingcastle.scot)* even more atmospheric than Edinburgh Castle – the location, architecture, historical significance and commanding views combine to make for a truly memorable experience. The undisputed highlight of a visit is the fabulous Royal Palace, its exterior studded with beautiful sculptures.

Sloping steeply down from Stirling Castle, the **Old Town** has a remarkably different feel to modern Stirling. Its cobblestone streets are jam-packed with 15th- to 17th-century architectural gems, and

FOTO-JAGLA.DE/SHUTTERSTOCK

surrounded by Scotland's best-surviving city wall.

THE DRIVE: Head north from Stirling city centre along Causewayhead Rd towards Bridge of Allan; at the junction with the A907 to Alloa, keep straight on and follow signs to the National Wallace Monument (total 2.5 miles). From the visitor centre car park, walk or shuttle-bus up the hill to the monument itself.

02 National Wallace Monument

Perched high on a crag above the floodplain of the River Forth, the Victorian **Wallace Monument** *(nationalwallacemonument.com)* is so Gothic it deserves circling bats and croaking ravens. Built in the shape of a medieval tower, it commemorates William Wallace, the hero of the bid for Scottish independence depicted in the film *Braveheart*. The view from the top over the flat, green gorgeousness of the Forth Valley, including the site of Wallace's 1297 victory over the English at Stirling Bridge, almost justifies the steep entry fee.

The climb up the narrow staircase inside leads through a series of galleries including the Hall of Heroes, a marble pantheon of lugubrious Scottish luminaries. Admire Wallace's 1.68m of broadsword and see the man himself recreated in a 3D audiovisual display.

THE DRIVE: Return to the junction and head east on the A907 through Alloa and Clackmannan, then south on the A977 to Kincardine; at the junction with the A985, keep straight, following signs for Fife Coastal Tourist Route until you reach Culross (16 miles).

03 Culross

Familiar to fans of the TV series *Outlander*, in which it appears as the fictional village of Cranesmuir, Culross (koo-ross) is Scotland's best-preserved example of a 17th-century town. Limewashed white and yellow-ochre houses with red-tiled roofs stand amid a maze of cobbled streets. The winding Back Causeway to the abbey is lined with several whimsical cottages.

Culross Palace *(nts.org.uk)* – more large house than palace – was the 17th-century residence of local laird Sir George Bruce and features an interior largely unchanged since his time. The decorative wood panelling and painted timber ceilings are of national importance, particularly the allegorical scenes in the Painted Chamber, which survive from the early 1600s.

Don't miss the recreation of a 17th-century garden at the back, with gorgeous views from the top terrace.

THE DRIVE: Continue east via the B9037 and A994 to Dunfermline (8 miles).

04 Dunfermline

Dunfermline is a large town rich in history. The focus is evocative **Dunfermline Abbey** *(historic environment.scot)*, founded by King David I in the 12th century as a Benedictine monastery.

The abbey and its neighbouring palace was already favoured by religious royals; Malcolm III married the exiled Saxon princess Margaret here in the 11th century, and both chose to be interred here. There were many more royal burials, none more notable than Robert the Bruce, whose remains were interred here in 1329.

THE DRIVE: Take the M90 towards the Queensferry Crossing, but leave at Junction 1C (signposted A921 Inverkeithing) and continue east to the attractive seaside village of Aberdour. Stay on the A921 as far as Kirkcaldy, then take the faster A915 (signposted St Andrews) as far as Upper Largo, where you follow the A917 to Elie (35 miles).

05 Elie & Earlsferry

These two attractive villages have great sandy beaches, golf courses and good walks along the coast – seek out the **Chain Walk**, an adventurous scramble along the rocky shoreline at Kincraig Point, west of Earlsferry (allow two hours and ask local advice about tides before setting off). On a more relaxing note, there's nothing better than a lazy summer Sunday in Elie, watching the local team play cricket on the beach. **Elie Watersports** *(eliewatersports.com)* hires out windsurfers, sailing dinghies, canoes and mountain bikes, and offers instruction.

THE DRIVE: Continue east along the Fife coast on the A917 through the pretty fishing villages of St Monans and Pittenweem to Anstruther (6 miles).

06 Anstruther

Once one of Scotland's busiest fishing ports, cheery Anstruther (pronounced en-ster by locals) offers a pleasant mixture of bobbing boats,

Puffins, Isle of May

GRAFXART/SHUTTERSTOCK

PHOTO OPPORTUNITY

Puffin-spotting on the Isle of May, the largest puffin colony on the east coast of Britain.

historic streets and visitors ambling around the harbour grazing on fish and chips or contemplating a boat trip to the **Isle of May** *(nature.scot)*.

The super **Scottish Fisheries Museum** *(scotfishmuseum.org)* covers the history of the Scottish fishing industry in fascinating detail, including plenty of hands-on exhibits for kids.

Displays include the Zulu Gallery, which houses the huge, partly restored hull of a traditional Zulu-class fishing boat, redolent with the scents of tar and timber. Afloat in the harbour outside the museum lies the *Reaper*, a fully restored Fifie-class fishing boat built in 1902.

THE DRIVE: It's just a short 4-mile drive east to Crail.

07 Crail

Little Crail has a much-photographed stone-built **harbour** surrounded by quaint cottages with red-tiled roofs. The village's history is outlined in the **Crail Museum** *(crailmuseum.uk)*, but the main attraction is just wandering the winding streets and hanging out by the harbour.

THE DRIVE: The A917 continues north for 10 miles to St Andrews, passing Kingsbarns Distillery and Cambo Walled Garden.

08 St Andrews

For a small town, St Andrews has made a big name for itself, firstly as a religious centre and place of pilgrimage, then as Scotland's oldest (and Britain's third-oldest) university town. But it is its status as the home of golf that has propelled it to even greater fame, and today's pilgrims mostly arrive with a set of clubs in hand.

The **Old Course** *(standrews.com)*, the world's most famous golf links, has a striking seaside location at the western end of town – it's a thrilling experience to stroll the hallowed turf. You are free to walk over the course on Sunday, or follow the footpaths around the edge at any time.

The ruins of **St Andrews Cathedral** *(historicenvironment.scot)* are testimony to what was once one of Britain's most magnificent medieval buildings. There's also a museum that contains the late-8th-century St Andrews Sarcophagus, Europe's finest example of early medieval stone carving.

St Andrews Castle *(historicenvironment.scot)*, too, is mainly in ruins, but the site itself is evocative and offers some dramatic coastline views.

NADEZHDA KLIMENKOVA/SHUTTERSTOCK

The Old Course Hotel, overlooking the Old Course

PLAYING GOLF AT A WORLD-FAMOUS COURSE

The **Old Course** *(standrews.com)* is the oldest and most famous golf course in the world. Golf has been played here since the 15th century – by 1457 it was apparently so popular that James II had to ban it because it was interfering with his troops' archery practice. Although it lies beside the Royal & Ancient Golf Club, the Old Course is a public course.

To play the Old Course, you'll need to book in advance via the website, or by phoning the Reservations Department (or Reception, if just one day in advance or on the day). Reservations open on the last Wednesday in August the year before you wish to play.

Unless you've booked months in advance, getting a tee-off time is literally a lottery; enter the ballot at the caddie office (or online or by phoning Reception) before 2pm two days before you hope to play (there's no Sunday play). Be warned that applications by ballot are normally heavily oversubscribed.

If you play on a windy day, expect those scores to balloon: Nick Faldo famously stated, 'When it blows here, even the seagulls walk'. Teeing off here also makes for a great photo opportunity.

32

★ BEST FOR

FOODIES

Dining on seafood in Oban.

SCOTLAND

LOWER WEST COAST

DURATION: 4–6 DAYS

DISTANCE: 222 MILES / 355KM

GREAT FOR: HISTORY

BEST TIME TO GO: MAY AND JUNE HAVE THE BEST WEATHER AND THE BRIGHTEST ROADSIDE FLOWERS.

Sir Walter Scott steamship

The scenery is the star of this trip, which winds its way from the shining waters, shady forests and foaming cascades of the Trossachs to the intricately fretted seaboard of Argyll, with its craggy hills and narrow, probing sea lochs. But history, too, is always close; you'll explore castles both medieval and Victorian, and touch the very heart of the nation at Kilmartin's ancient glen.

LINK YOUR TRIP

31 Stirling & Fife Coast
From Callander, the start of this castles and coastline tour in Stirling is just 20 miles to the southeast.

37 Ferry-Hopping
This trip intersects with the Ferry-Hopping one at Oban, from where you can take off on a tour of the islands.

01 Aberfoyle

Aberfoyle is one of the gateways to **Loch Lomond & the Trossachs National Park**. Picturesque waymarked trails start from the nearby **Lodge Forest Visitor Centre** *(forestryandland.gov.scot)*, ranging from a light 20-minute stroll to a nearby waterfall – with great interactive play options for kids – to a hilly 4-mile circuit. The centre has a popular cafe as well as magnificent views and live wildlife cameras offering a peek at some of the local red squirrels.

Also here, **Go Ape!** *(goape.co.uk)* will bring out the monkey in you on its exhilarating adventure course of long zip lines, swings and rope bridges among the trees. Look out, too, for the spooky mirror sculptures by local artist Rob Mulholland.

THE DRIVE: Head north on the A821, which leads high over Duke's Pass, pausing for a photo opportunity at the crest of the hill before descending to

RICHARD P LONG/SHUTTERSTOCK

Loch Achray, where a left turn leads along a narrow glen to a car park at Trossachs Pier on Loch Katrine (7 miles).

02 Loch Katrine

Lovely Loch Katrine lies at the heart of the Trossachs, a National Landscape with thickly forested hills, romantic lochs, and excellent walking and cycling routes.

Cruises *(lochkatrine.com)* depart from Trossachs Pier at the loch's eastern end, including on the fabulous centenarian steamship **Sir Walter Scott**, or you can walk or cycle along the northern shore of the loch; **Katrine Wheelz** *(katrine wheelz.co.uk)* hires out good bikes.

THE DRIVE: Return to the A821 and drive east along the northern shores of Lochs Achray and Venachar, then turn right to arrive in the town of Callander (10 miles).

03 Callander

Callander, the principal Trossachs town, has been pulling in tourists for over 150 years, and has a laid-back ambience that quickly lulls visitors into lazy pottering. It's home to the **Hamilton Toy Collection** *(thehamiltontoy collection.co.uk)*, a powerhouse of 20th-century children's memorabilia, chock-full of dolls' houses, puppets and toy soldiers.

Impressive **Bracklinn Falls** are reached by track and footpath from Bracklinn Rd (30 minutes each way from the car park). Also off Bracklinn Rd, a woodland trail leads up to **Callander Crags**, with great views over the surroundings; a return trip from the car park is about 4 miles.

THE DRIVE: The A84 leads north from Callander along Loch Lubnaig and Strathyre. Stop briefly at Balquhidder to pay respects at Rob Roy's grave; you might continue down the single-track road to Monachyle Mhor for a coffee or a posh lunch – the drive is worth it in any event. Back on the main road, continue north to Killin (22 miles).

04 Killin

This lovely village sits at the western end of Loch Tay and has a spread-out, relaxed feel, particularly around the scenic **Falls of Dochart**, which tumble through the centre. On a sunny day, people sprawl over the rocks by the bridge, pint or picnic in hand. There is fine walking around the town, and mighty mountains and glens close by.

Five miles northeast of Killin, Ben Lawers (1214m) rises above Loch Tay. Walking routes abound; one rewarding circular walk heads up into the Acharn Woods southwest of town, emerging above the treeline to great views of Loch Tay and Ben Lawers. **Killin Outdoor Centre** *(facebook.com/killinoutdoor)* provides walking advice as well as hiring bikes, canoes and kayaks.

Glen Lochay runs westwards from Killin into the hills of Mamlorn. You can take a mountain bike up the glen; the scenery is impressive and the hills aren't too difficult.

Loch Tay is famous for its fishing – salmon, trout and pike are all caught here. **Fish on Scotland** *(fishonscotland.com)* can kit you out for a day's fishing with a boat, tackle and guide.

THE DRIVE: Head southwest from Killin, following the A85 along Glen Dochart to Crianlarich, then turning south on the A82. Stop and stretch your legs at the Falls of Falloch, then continue to Tarbet (total 30 miles).

05 Tarbet

Tarbet is a tiny village at a road junction on the western shore of **Loch Lomond**. **Cruise Loch Lomond** *(cruiselochlomond.co.uk)* offers boat trips from Tarbet and nearby Luss, including options that explorw loch islands, Rob Roy's cave, Arklet Falls, or walking a section of the West Highland Way from Inversnaid. The Tarbet Circular cruise offers a one-hour exploration of the northern end of the loch, taking in waterfalls and mountain views.

THE DRIVE: Strike west from Tarbet on the A83, which soon enters mountainous territory, climbing through Glen Croe and over the high pass known as the Rest and Be Thankful (a memorial stone in the car park at the top explains the name) to reach the sea at Loch Fyne. Continue around the head of this stunning loch and you'll reach Inveraray (23 miles).

DETOUR

Isle of Bute

Start: 05 Tarbet

Bute lies pinched between the thumb and forefinger of the Cowal Peninsula, separated from the mainland by a narrow, scenic strait. The Highland Boundary Fault cuts through the middle of the island so that, geologically speaking, the northern half is in the Highlands and the southern half is in the central Lowlands.

Rothesay, the island's main town, was once one of Scotland's most popular holiday resorts, bustling with day-trippers disembarking from numerous steamers crowded around the pier. Cheap foreign holidays saw Rothesay's fortunes decline, but a nostalgia-fuelled resurgence of interest has seen many Victorian buildings restored. The grassy, flowery waterfront and row of noble villas make it a lovely place to be once again.

Splendid ruined 13th-century **Rothesay Castle** *(historicenvironment.scot)*, with seagulls and jackdaws nesting in the walls,

Falls of Dochart (p259)

PHOTO OPPORTUNITY

The Falls of Dochart seen from the bridge in Killin.

CORNFIELD/SHUTTERSTOCK

was once a favourite residence of the Stuart kings. It is unique in Scotland in having a circular plan, with four stocky round towers. The landscaped moat, with manicured turf, flower gardens and lazily cruising ducks, makes a picturesque setting.

The true jewel in Bute's crown is **Mount Stuart** *(mountstuart.com)*, 5 miles south of Rothesay. The 19th-century family seat of the Stuart Earls of Bute is one of Britain's more magnificent stately homes, the first to have a telephone, underfloor heating and a heated pool. Its eclectic interior, with a magnificent central hall and chapel in Italian marble, is heavily influenced by the third Marquess' interests in Greek mythology and astrology. The drawing room has paintings by Titian and Tintoretto among other masters.

From Tarbet, follow the A83 towards Inveraray. As you descend Glen Kinglas towards Loch Fyne, the A815 forks to the left just before Cairndow; follow it 10 miles south to Strachur, then take the A886 for another 24 miles to Colintraive; a five-minute ferry crossing (departing every 30 minutes) takes you to Bute.

06 Inveraray

This historic planned village is all black and white – even the familiar logos of high-street chain shops conform. Spectacularly set on the shores of Loch Fyne, Inveraray was built by the Duke of Argyll in Georgian style in the 18th century.

Inveraray Jail *(inverarayjail.co.uk)* has been turned into an interactive tourist attraction where you can sit in on a trial, try out a

JAROSLAV MORAVCIK/SHUTTERSTOCK

View of Loch Lomond

LOCH LOMOND

The 'bonnie banks' and 'bonnie braes' of Loch Lomond have long been Glasgow's rural retreat – a scenic region of hills, water and healthy fresh air within easy reach of Scotland's largest city. Today the loch's popularity shows no sign of decreasing.

Loch Lomond is mainland Britain's largest lake and, after Loch Ness, the most famous of Scotland's lochs. Its proximity to Glasgow (20 miles away) means that the tourist honeypots of Balloch, Loch Lomond Shores and Luss get pretty crowded in summer. The eastern shore, which is followed by the West Highland Way long-distance footpath, is quieter and offers a better chance to appreciate the loch away from the busy main road.

Loch Lomond straddles the Highland border. The southern part is broad and island-studded, fringed by woods and Lowland meadows. However, north of Luss the loch narrows, occupying a deep trench gouged out by glaciers during the Ice Age, with 900m mountains crowding either side.

There are around 60 islands, large and small, in the loch. Most are privately owned, and only two (Inchcailloch and Inchmurrin) can be reached without your own boat or canoe. Inchcailloch is a nature reserve reached by boats from Balmaha or Luss, while privately owned Inchconnachan is only accessible by boat or canoe. Unusually, it is home to a herd of wallabies, introduced by a previous owner in the 1940s

Inchmurrin has walking trails, beaches, self-catering cottages and a restaurant that is open from Easter to October. There's a passenger ferry from Arden, but only for guests of the restaurant or accommodation; see *inchmurrinlochlomond.com*.

cell and discover some of the harsh tortures that were meted out to unfortunate prisoners.

The stunning **Inveraray Castle** *(inveraray-castle.com)* has been the seat of the Dukes of Argyll – chiefs of Clan Campbell – since the 15th century. The 18th-century building, with its fairy-tale turrets and fake battlements, houses an impressive armoury hall, its walls patterned with more than 1000 pole-arms, dirks, muskets and Lochaber axes.

Loch Fyne Oyster Bar *(lochfyne.com)*, 9 miles north of Inveraray, is a great place to try the local molluscs or other Scottish seafood, eat in or take away. Nearby **Fyne Ales** *(fyneales.com)* is an excellent craft brewery with tours and a lovely bar-cafe where you can taste the beers; our favourite is the light, citrussy Jarl.

THE DRIVE: A ceremonial arch at the east end of town marks the beginning of the A819, which snakes north through low hills and dense forest to reach the shores of Loch Awe. When you reach the A85 junction, turn left and continue around the head of the loch to Lochawe village (16 miles).

07 Lochawe

Loch Awe is one of Scotland's most beautiful lochs, with rolling forested hills around its southern end and spectacular mountains in the north. It is the longest freshwater loch in Scotland – about 25 miles – but is less than 1 mile wide for most of its length. At its northern end, it escapes to the sea through the narrow Pass of Brander, where Robert the Bruce defeated the MacDougalls in 1309.

Just east of Lochawe village are the scenic ruins of the much-photographed **Kilchurn Castle** *(historicenvironment.scot)*. Built in 1440, it enjoys one of Scotland's finest settings. There's a scenic stroll to it from the car park on the A85, just west of the Inveraray turn-off between Dalmally and Lochawe. At the time of research the castle was closed for conservation works, but you can still walk around the outside.

Three miles west of the village you can visit the free exhibition at **Cruachan hydroelectric scheme's visitor centre** *(visitcruachan.co.uk)*. The power station is housed in a vast subterranean chamber half a mile inside Ben Cruachan; guided tours into 'the hollow mountain' are on hold until maintenance works are completed in 2028.

A further 6 miles will bring you to Taynuilt, where you can visit the fascinating **Bonawe Furnace** *(historicenvironment.scot)*, a picturesque historical iron smelting complex. It's now a tranquil, beautiful place, with the old buildings picturesquely arranged around a green hillside, and there's great background information on the iron industry. Take a picnic.

THE DRIVE: Continue west on the A85 to Oban (21 miles from

Mount Stuart (p261)

CAROLE MACDONALD/SHUTTERSTOCK

Lochawe), stopping at Connel Bridge to see the Falls of Lora, white-water rapids under the bridge caused by the tide flowing in and out through the narrow rocky mouth of Loch Etive (depends on tide times).

08 Oban

Oban, the main ferry terminal for crossings to the Scottish islands, enjoys a fine setting on a broad bay with glorious views west to the hills of Mull. Some of Britain's standout places to enjoy fish and shellfish are to be found here, whether you go for no-frills crab shacks like the **Oban Seafood Hut**, or more upmarket restaurants such as **Ee-usk** *(eeusk.com)* or **Waterfront Fishouse** *(waterfrontfishouse.co.uk)*. Sustainable sourcing of fish is an important element that's widely practised.

In the centre of town, handsome **Oban Distillery** *(obanwhisky.com)* has been producing whisky since 1794. The standard guided tour leaves regularly (worth booking) and includes a dram, a take-home glass and a taste straight from the cask.

Crowning the hill above town is a Colosseum-like Victorian folly, **McCaig's Tower**, commissioned in 1890 by a local landowner with the philanthropic intention of providing work for unemployed stonemasons. To reach it on foot, make the steep climb up Jacob's Ladder (a flight of stairs) from Argyll St; the bay views are worth the effort.

A pleasant 1-mile stroll north along the coast road leads to **Dunollie Castle** *(dunollie.org)*, built by the MacDougalls of Lorn in the 13th century and unsuccessfully besieged for a year during the 1715 Jacobite rebellion. It's ruined, but ongoing conservation work is offering increasing access. The nearby **1745 House** – seat of Clan MacDougall – is an intriguing museum of local and clan history, and there are pleasant wooded grounds and a cafe. Free tours run twice daily.

THE DRIVE: Head south from Oban for 29 miles on the A816 to Kilmartin Glen.

DETOUR

Isle of Seil

Start: 08 Oban

The small Isle of Seil is best known for its connection to the mainland – the graceful bridge over the Atlantic, designed by Thomas Telford and opened in 1793.

On the west coast of the island is the pretty conservation village of **Ellenabeich**, with whitewashed cottages and rainwater barrels backed by a wee harbour and rocky cliffs. It was built to house local slate workers, but the industry collapsed in 1881 when the sea broke into the main quarry – the flooded pit can still be seen.

Just offshore is small, charming **Easdale Island**, which has more old slate-workers' cottages and an interesting **folk museum** *(easdalemuseum.org)* with displays about the slate industry and social history. Once housing 450 people, the island's population fell to just seven old-timers by 1950 but now has a healthier few dozen after a programme welcoming incomers. Climb to the top of the island (a 38m peak) for great views of the surrounding area. Easdale island is reached by a five-minute passenger ferry from the harbour at Ellenabeich.

Seafari Adventures *(seafari.co.uk)* runs a series of exciting boat trips in high-speed boats to Corryvreckan whirlpool (call for dates of 'Whirlpool Specials', when the tide is strongest), as well

ESCAPADES OF ROB ROY

Nicknamed Red ('ruadh' in Gaelic, anglicised to 'roy') for his ginger locks, Robert MacGregor (1671–1734) was the wild leader of the wildest of Scotland's clans, outlawed by powerful neighbours, hence their sobriquet, Children of the Mist. Incognito, Rob became a prosperous livestock trader, before a dodgy deal led to a warrant for his arrest.

A legendary swordsman, the fugitive from justice then became notorious for daring raids into the Lowlands to carry off cattle and sheep. Forever hiding from potential captors he was twice imprisoned, but escaped dramatically on both occasions. He finally turned himself in and received his liberty and a pardon from the king. He lies buried – perhaps – in the churchyard at Balquhidder; his uncompromising later epitaph reads 'MacGregor despite them'.

His life has been glorified over the years due to Sir Walter Scott's novel and the 1995 film. Many Scots see his life as a symbol of the struggle of the common folk against the ownership of vast tracts of the country by landed aristocrats.

as summer whale-watching trips and several other excursions.

A car-ferry hop from Seil's southern end takes you to neighbouring **Isle of Luing**, a quiet backwater that has no real sights but is appealing for wildlife walks and easy-going bike rides.

To reach Seil, 10 miles south of Oban, follow the A816 to Kilninver and turn right on the B844. To rejoin the main trip, retrace your route to the A816.

09 Kilmartin Glen

This magical glen is the focus of one of the biggest concentrations of **prehistoric sites** in Scotland. Burial cairns, standing stones, stone circles, hill forts and cup-and-ring-marked rocks litter the countryside. Within a 6-mile radius of Kilmartin village there are 25 sites with standing stones and more than 100 rock carvings.

In the 6th century, Irish settlers arrived in this part of Argyll and founded the kingdom of Dál Riata (Dalriada), which eventually united with the Picts in 843 to create the first Scottish kingdom.

Their seat of power was the hill fort of **Dunadd**, on the plain 3.5 miles to the south of Kilmartin. Rising out of the boggy plain of Moine Mhor Nature Reserve, it's an atmospheric spot. A slippery path leads to the summit, where you can gaze out on much the same view that the ancient kings of Dál Riata enjoyed 1300 years ago. Atop the hill, you can find a footprint, faint rock carvings of a boar and an ogham inscription may have been used in inauguration ceremonies.

At **Kilmartin Museum** (*kilmartin.org*; Kilmartin) you can see ancient artefacts close to where they were found and join guided walks around these amazing ancient sites.

THE DRIVE: Continue south on the A816 and A83 through Lochgilphead and Ardrishaig to Tarbert (21 miles). If you fancy a longer, more scenic route, turn right on the B8024 south of Ardrishaig, which follows the west coast of Knapdale with views to the hills of Jura (42 miles).

10 Tarbert

The attractive fishing village and yachting centre of Tarbert is the gateway to Kintyre, and most scenic, with buildings strung around its excellent natural harbour. A crossroads for nearby ferry routes, it's a handy stepping stone to Arran or Islay, but is well worth a stopover on any itinerary. The picturesque harbour is overlooked by the ivy-covered ruins of **Tarbert Castle**, rebuilt by Robert the Bruce in the 14th century. You can hike up via a signposted footpath 50m beyond **Loch Fyne Gallery**, a shop which showcases the work of local artists.

Try to time your trip to fit in a takeaway from the **Silver Darlings seafood truck** (*facebook.com/silverdarlingstarbert*), parked on the north side of the harbour. The menu varies according to what's fresh off the local fishing boats that day; check Facebook for opening hours.

THE DRIVE: Continue south from Tarbert on the A83 and, just past the ferry terminal at Kennacraig, turn left on the B8001 to Claonaig and another left to the road end at Skipness (13 miles).

11 Skipness

Tiny Skipness is pleasant and quiet with great views of Arran. Beyond the village rise the substantial remains of 13th-century **Skipness Castle** (*historicenvironment.scot*), a former possession of the Lords of the Isles. It's a striking building, composed of dark-green local stone trimmed with contrasting red-brown sandstone from Arran. The 16th-century tower house was occupied until the 19th century. From the top you can see the roofless, 13th-century St Brendan's Chapel down by the shore. The kirkyard contains some excellent carved grave slabs.

Attached to Skipness House, near the castle, is the **Seafood Cabin** (*skipnessseafoodcabin.co.uk*), a great place for lunch on a fine summer day, serving no-frills but delicious local fish and shellfish at outdoor picnic tables with grand views over the grassy coast. It's famous for crab rolls, which are on the small side: add on a pot of mussels or plate of gravadlax.

Continuing the theme, nearby **Skipness Smokehouse** (*skipnesssmokehouse.com*) produces sensational hot smoked salmon among other goodies.

THE DRIVE: Return to Claonaig and turn left to follow the B842 down the eastern shore of the

♥ DON'T MISS

FOR A ROMANTIC GETAWAY

Soothingly situated on a lake (yes, it's the only non-loch in Scotland) 3 miles east of Aberfoyle, the **Karma Lake of Menteith Hotel** (*karmagroup.com/finddestination/karma-resorts/karma-lake-of-menteith*) makes a great romantic getaway. Though all rooms are excellent, with a contemporary feel, it's worth an upgrade if possible to the enormous superior ones with a view of the water: it really is a sensational outlook.

NIKIFOROV ALEXANDER/SHUTTERSTOCK

Tarbert Castle

Kintyre Peninsula to Campbeltown (30 miles), a twisting roller coaster of a road that climbs high above the sea then swoops down to remote bays, with breathtaking views across the water to Arran's rocky peaks.

12 Campbeltown

Blue-collar Campbeltown, set around a beautiful harbour, still suffers from the decline of its fishing and whisky industries but is rebounding on the back of golf tourism. The spruced-up seafront backed by green hills lends the town a distinctly optimistic air.

There were once no fewer than 32 **distilleries** around Campbeltown, but most closed in the 1920s. Today **Springbank** *(springbank.scot)* is one of only three that are operational. It is also one of the few around that distils, matures and bottles all its whisky on the one site, making for an interesting tour. It's a quality malt, one of Scotland's finest. Various premium tours take you deeper into the process.

Campbeltown's most unusual sight awaits in a cave on the southern side of Davaar Island, at the mouth of Campbeltown Loch. On the wall of the cave is an eerie painting of the **Crucifixion** by local artist Archibald MacKinnon, dating from 1887. You can walk to the island at low tide: check tide times with the community information centre. Near Campbeltown, the **Machrihanish Golf Club** *(machgolf.com)* is a classic links course, designed by Old Tom Morris. It's remarkably good value compared to courses of a similar standard elsewhere in Scotland. The famous first hole requires a very decent drive across the bay, or you will literally end up on the beach.

Close by is the much newer **Machrihanish Dunes** *(machrihanishdunes.com)*, an impressive seaside experience and very welcoming: the clubhouse is a convivial little hut, it's child-friendly and there are often website offers.

DETOUR

Mull of Kintyre

Start: 12 Campbeltown

A narrow winding road, 15 miles long, leads south from Campbeltown to the Mull of Kintyre, passing good sandy beaches near Southend. This remote headland was immortalised in Paul McCartney's famous song – the former Beatle owns a farmhouse in the area. From where the road ends, a 30-minute steep downhill walk leads to a clifftop lighthouse, with Northern Ireland, only 12 miles away, visible across the channel. Don't leave the road when the frequent mists roll in as it's easy to become disoriented.

33

SCOTLAND

UPPER WEST COAST

DURATION: 3–5 DAYS

DISTANCE: 360 MILES / 575KM

GREAT FOR: FOOD & DRINK

BEST TIME TO GO: JUNE IS BUSY BUT OFFERS LONG EVENINGS AND DREAMY LIGHT. SEPTEMBER IS QUIETER, WITH FEWER MIDGES.

Quintessential highland country such as this, marked by single-track roads, breathtaking emptiness and a wild, fragile beauty, leaves an indelible imprint on the soul. Scotland's far northwest coastline is a feast of deep inlets, forgotten beaches and surging peninsulas; looming inland are some of Scotland's most imposing and emblematic peaks. Whether in blazing sunshine or murky greyness, the character of the land is amazingly unique.

LINK YOUR TRIP

35 Great Glen
This trip can be tackled before or after this drive, either by heading from Fort William to the ferry at Mallaig and thence to Skye, or by dropping down from Durness to Inverness.

37 Ferry-Hopping
Link these trips via Oban and the Mallaig ferry to Skye.

01 Portree

Portree is Skye's largest and liveliest town. It has a pretty harbour lined with brightly painted houses, and there are great views of the surrounding hills. Its name (from the Gaelic for King's Harbour) commemorates James V, who came here in 1540 to pacify the local clans.

MV Stardust *(skyeboat-trips.co.uk)* offers 1½-hour boat trips into the Sound of Raasay, with the chance to see seals, porpoises and – if you're lucky – white-tailed sea eagles. There are also four-hour cruises to Kilt Rock and the Isle of Rona.

THE DRIVE: Follow the road north through the centre of Portree to leave town on the A855, which after about 6 miles brings you to the first sights on the Trotternish Peninsula.

02 Trotternish Peninsula

The Trotternish Peninsula to the north of Portree has some of Skye's most spectacular scenery.

PAJOR PAWEL/SHUTTERSTOCK

★ BEST FOR

FOODIES

The local seafood is sublime.

Old Man of Storr

Whatever the weather, it is difficult not to be blown away by the savage beauty of this place.

The 50m-high, pot-bellied pinnacle of crumbling basalt known as the **Old Man of Storr** is prominent above the road 6 miles north of Portree. Walk up to its foot from the car park at the northern end of Loch Leathan (round trip 2 miles). Eight miles north of the Old Man of Storr car park is a popular clifftop lookout over spectacular Kilt Rock, whose columnar cliffs resemble kilt pleats.

At the northern end of the peninsula at Kilmuir, the peat-reek of crofting life in the 18th and 19th centuries is preserved in the thatched cottages, croft houses, barns and farm implements of the evocative **Skye Museum of Island Life** *(skyemuseum.co.uk)*. Behind the museum is Kilmuir Cemetery, where a Celtic cross marks Flora MacDonald's grave.

THE DRIVE: Keep following the road around the peninsula, through Uig's ferry port and on to Borve, where you take a right on to the A850 to Dunvegan. From the Old Man of Storr it's about 54 miles via this route.

03 Dunvegan Castle

Skye's most famous historic building, and one of its most popular tourist attractions, **Dunvegan Castle** *(dunvegancastle.com)* is the seat of the chief of Clan MacLeod. In addition to the usual castle stuff – swords, silver and family portraits – there are interesting artefacts, including the Fairy Flag, a diaphanous silk banner that dates from some time between the 4th and 7th centuries, and Bonnie Prince Charlie's waistcoat and a lock of his hair.

The oldest parts are the 14th-century keep and dungeon but most of it dates from the 17th to 19th centuries, when it played host to Samuel Johnson, Sir Walter Scott and, most famously, Flora MacDonald. Look out for Rory Mor's Drinking Horn, a beautiful 16th-century vessel of Celtic design that could hold half a gallon of claret. Upholding the family tradition in 1956, John MacLeod – the 29th chief, who died in 2007 – downed the contents in one minute and 57 seconds 'without setting down or falling down'.

THE DRIVE: It's 24 scenic miles across the heart of the island along the A863 to Sligachan, a crossroads and walkers' haven watched over by the brooding Cuillin Hills.

☑ TAKE A BREAK

The pretty harbour village of **Plockton** is a good place to stop for lunch, or even an overnight, with a good range of places to stay and a couple of good eateries. Top spots for lunch include the refurbished 19th-century **Plockton Inn** *(highlandcoasthotels.com/plockton-inn)*, with a menu of high-quality local seafood and a regular Sunday roast. At Duirinish, 2 miles south of Plockton, the **Croft Cafe** *(facebook.com/thecroftcafe)* serves up hearty breakfasts, burgers and toasties.

04 Cuillin Hills

The Cuillin Hills are Britain's most spectacular mountain range (the name comes from the Old Norse *kjöllen*, meaning 'keel-shaped'). Though small in stature (Sgùrr Alasdair, the highest summit, is only 993m), the peaks are near-alpine in character, with knife-edge ridges, jagged pinnacles, scree-filled gullies and hectares of naked rock. While they are a paradise for experienced mountaineers, the higher reaches of the Cuillin are off-limits to the majority of walkers.

The good news is that there are also plenty of good low-level hikes within the ability of most walkers, several leaving from Sligachan.

THE DRIVE: It's a 30-mile drive from Sligachan on the A87 along the Skye coast, past the Raasay ferry at Sconser, through Broadford and over the bridge onto the mainland at Kyle of Lochalsh. In town, take a left up the hill and follow this road to Plockton.

DETOUR

Elgol

Start: 04 Cuillin Hills

On a clear day, the 15-mile journey along the road from Broadford to Elgol is one of the most scenic on Skye. It takes in two classic postcard panoramas – the view of Blà Bheinn across Loch Slapin (near Torrin), and the superb view of the entire Cuillin range from Elgol pier. Elgol itself is a tiny settlement with a cafe and seafood truck at the end of this long, single-track road.

05 Plockton

Idyllic little **Plockton**, with its perfect cottages lining a perfect bay, looks like it was designed as a film set. And it has served as just that – scenes from *The Wicker Man* (1973) were filmed here, and the village eventually became famous as the location for the 1990s TV series *Hamish Macbeth*.

There's no denying its appeal, with 'palm trees' (actually hardy New Zealand cabbage palms) lining the waterfront, a thriving small-boat sailing scene and several good places to stay, eat and drink. The local langoustines (Plockton prawns) are famous.

It's fun to get out on the water here. **Calum's Seal Trips** *(calums-sealtrips.com)* runs friendly seal-watching cruises – there's a seal colony just outside the harbour, and the trip comes with an excellent commentary. **Sea Kayak Plockton** *(seakayakplockton.co.uk)*, offers everything from beginners' lessons to multiday trips around Skye to highly challenging odysseys.

THE DRIVE: Head to the A890, running northeast beside Loch Carron. Turn left along the A896 along the loch's opposite side and through likeable Lochcarron village before taking a left turn to Applecross. The magnificent Bealach na Bà (Pass of the Cattle; 626m) climbs steeply and hair-raisingly via hairpin bends (not suitable for caravans or large motorhomes), then drops dramatically to the village with views of Skye (36 miles total).

Plockton
LONEROC/SHUTTERSTOCK

THE QUIRAING

Staffin Bay, on the east side of the Trotternish Peninsula, is dominated by the dramatic basalt escarpment of the Quiraing, whose impressive land-slipped cliffs and pinnacles constitute one of Skye's most remarkable landscapes. Instead of driving around the north end of Trotternish, you can cut across from Staffin to Uig via a steep and twisty minor road. From a parking area at the highest point of the road, a well-worn, occasionally rocky path leads in half an hour into the heart of the dramatic and photogenic jumble of basalt towers, blocks and pinnacles.

06 Applecross

The delightfully remote seaside village of Applecross feels like an island retreat due to its isolation and magnificent views of Raasay and the hills of Skye that set the pulse racing, particularly at sunset. Book ahead for a bed or meal at the **Applecross Inn** *(applecrossinn.co.uk)*.

THE DRIVE: It's 25 winding miles of single-track road from Applecross around the north coast of the peninsula to the pretty waterside village of Shieldaig where you rejoin the A896 and head east for the majestic 7 miles to Torridon, along the shore of the sea loch of the same name.

07 Torridon

The road running through Glen Torridon is dwarfed by some of Britain's most dramatic mountain scenery. Carved by ice from massive layers of ancient sandstone that takes its name from the region, the mountains here are steep, shapely and imposing.

The road from lovely Shieldaig, which features an attractive main street of whitewashed houses right on the waterfront, reaches the head of the sea loch at spectacularly sited Torridon village. It's a base for excursions to the Torridon peaks: **Liathach** (1054m; pronounced 'lee-agakh', Gaelic for 'the Grey One'), **Beinn Eighe** (1010m; 'ben ay', 'the File') and **Beinn Alligin** (986m; 'the Jewelled Mountain'). These are big, serious mountains for experienced hill walkers only.

THE DRIVE: Follow the A896 northeast to Kinlochewe, then turn left along the A832, which continues to Gairloch (27 miles total). The road follows the shore of beautiful Loch Maree. From a car park 1.5 miles past Beinn Eighe visitor centre, there's a great waymarked 4-mile return walk to a plateau and cairn on the side of Beinn Eighe, offering magnificent views.

08 Gairloch

Gairloch is a knot of villages around the inner end of the loch of the same name. It's a good base for whale- and dolphin-watching excursions, and the surrounding area has beautiful sandy beaches, good trout fishing and birdwatching.

Gairloch Marine Life Centre & Cruises *(porpoise-gairloch.co.uk)* has audiovisual and interactive displays, lots of charts, photos and knowledgeable staff. From here, cruises run three times daily (weather permitting); during the two-hour trips you may see basking sharks, porpoises and minke whales. The crew collects data on water temperature and conditions, and monitors cetacean populations, so you are subsidising important research.

Six miles north of Gairloch, splendid **Inverewe Garden** *(nts.org.uk)* is a welcome splash of colour on this otherwise bleak coast. The climate here is warmed by the Gulf Stream, which allowed Osgood Mackenzie to create this exotic woodland garden in 1862.

THE DRIVE: It's a slow, winding 42 miles along the A832 from Gairloch north and east to the junction with the A835. Relax and enjoy the scenic solitude.

09 Falls of Measach

Just west of the junction of the A835 and A832, a car park and visitor centre give access to the Falls of Measach, which spill 45m into spectacularly deep and narrow Corrieshalloch Gorge. You can cross the gorge on a swaying suspension bridge, and walk west for 250m to a viewing platform that juts out dizzyingly above a sheer drop. The thundering falls and misty vapours rising from the gorge are very impressive.

THE DRIVE: From the road junction, it's 12 miles northwest on the A835 to Ullapool.

10 Ullapool

This pretty port on the shores of Loch Broom is the largest settlement in Wester Ross and one of the most alluring spots in the Highlands, a wonderful destination in itself as well as a gateway to the Western Isles.

Offering a row of whitewashed cottages arrayed along the harbour and special views of the loch and its

Liathach and Loch Clair, Glen Torridon

DANIEL LANGE/SHUTTERSTOCK

flanking hills, the town has a very distinctive appeal. The harbour served as an emigration point during the Clearances, with thousands of Scots watching Ullapool recede behind them as the diaspora cast them across the world.

Housed in a converted church, **Ullapool Museum** *(ullapoolmuseum.co.uk)* relates the prehistoric, natural and social history of the town and Lochbroom area, with a focus on the emigration to Nova Scotia and other places. Leaving from Ullapool's harbour, **Seascape** *(sea-scape.co.uk)* runs enjoyable two-hour tours out to the Summer Isles in an orange rigid inflatable boat. It also runs shorter trips, plus excursions to nearby Isle Martin.

THE DRIVE: It's 26 miles north along the A835 then A837 to the Skiag Bridge road junction at the heart of the Assynt region. Stop along the way to appreciate the mountainscapes and keep an eye out in the rear-view mirror, as many of the best perspectives unfold behind you.

DETOUR

Coigach

Start: 10 Ullapool

The region west of the main A835 road from Ullapool to Ledmore Junction is known as **Coigach** *(visitcoigach.com)*. A single-track road off the A835 9 miles north of Ullapool pierces this wilderness, leading through gloriously wild scenery to remote settlements.

Coigach is a wonderland for walkers and wildlife enthusiasts, with a patchwork of sinuous silver lochs dominated by the isolated peaks of **Cul Mor** (849m), **Cul Beag** (769m), **Ben More Coigach** (743m) and **Stac Pollaidh** (613m). The main settlement is the straggling township of Achiltibuie, 15 miles from the main road, with the gorgeous Summer Isles moored just off the coast, and silhouettes of mountains skirting the bay.

You could head back to the main road to continue your journey, or, at the western end of Loch Bad a' Ghaill, a branch road leads north to Lochinver, a scenic backroad so narrow and twisting that it's nicknamed the Wee Mad Road (not suitable for caravans or large motorhomes).

HANDY PLACES TO STAY AND EAT

Gairloch, about halfway between Applecross and Ullapool, is a handy place to break your journey. Overnight options include rustic **Gairloch Sands Youth Hostel** *(hostellingscotland.org.uk)* or **Muldoanich B&B** (muldoanichbandb.co.uk) for a more luxurious alternative. For coffee and cake, head for the **Mountain Coffee Company** *(facebook.com/MountainCoffee.Gairloch)* – this offbeat spot is a shrine to all things mountaineering, with a lazy, chilled-out vibe and a hearty menu, best enjoyed in the conservatory.

11 Assynt

With its other-worldly scenery of isolated peaks rising above a sea of crumpled, lochan-spattered gneiss, Assynt epitomises the wild magnificence of the northwest. Glaciers have sculpted the Torridonian sandstone into spectacular peaks, including Suilven's distinctive sugarloaf and ziggurat-like Quinag. The area is the centrepiece of what has been designated the **Northwest Highlands Geopark** *(nwhgeopark.com)*.

Half a mile south of the Skiag Bridge road junction, perched on an island at the edge of Loch Assynt, are the romantic ruins of **Ardvreck Castle**, a 15th-century stronghold of the MacLeods of Assynt. There are rumoured to be several ghosts at Ardvreck, including the daughter of a MacLeod chieftain who was sold in marriage to the devil by her father. Nearby are the ruins of a barrack house built by the Mackenzies in the 1720s. There are wonderful summer sunsets over the castle and loch.

THE DRIVE: Head west 10 miles from Skiag Bridge along the A837 to reach Lochinver. The road runs along the northern shore of wild and moody Loch Assynt.

12 Lochinver

Lochinver (p274) is Assynt's main settlement, a busy little fishing port that's a popular pit stop thanks to its laid-back atmosphere, good facilities and striking scenery.

Using local landscapes as inspiration, **Highland Stoneware** *(highlandstoneware.com)* ensures you can relive the northwest's majesty every time you have a cuppa.

North Coast Sea Tours *(northcoastseatours.co.uk)* give a good taste of this spectacular coastline.

Just north of Lochinver (or if coming from the north, not far south of Kylesku), a 23-mile detour on the narrow B869 rewards with spectacular views and fine beaches. From the Point of Stoer lighthouse, a one-hour cliff walk leads to the spectacular sea stack **Old Man of Stoer**.

THE DRIVE: Head north from Lochinver up the narrow B869 coastal route. This takes you past Clashnessie beach and Drumbeg. After 23 miles, you join the A894 just south of Kylesku.

13 Kylesku & Around

Hidden away on the shores of Loch Glencoul, tiny Kylesku served as a ferry crossing until it was made redundant by beautiful **Kylesku Bridge** in 1984. It has an excellent inn and is a good base for walks; you can hire bikes here.

Five miles southeast, in wild, remote country, lies 213m-high **Eas a'Chuil Aluinn**, Britain's highest waterfall. You can hike to the top from a parking area at a sharp bend in the main road 3 miles south of Kylesku, a 6-mile round trip; very rough and boggy. It can also be seen on **boat trips** from Kylesku.

THE DRIVE: It's 10 spectacular miles up the A894 from Kylesku to Scourie. Look behind you for the best views.

14 Scourie & Handa Island

Scourie is a pretty crofting community with decent services, halfway between Durness and Ullapool. A few miles north lies **Handa Island** *(scottishwildlifetrust.org.uk)*, a nature reserve run by the Scottish Wildlife Trust. The island's western sea cliffs provide nesting sites for important breeding populations of great skuas, arctic skuas, puffins, kittiwakes, razorbills and guillemots. Reach the island from Tarbet, 6 miles north of Scourie, via a **ferry** *(handa-ferry.com)*.

THE DRIVE: Continue 7 miles northeast from Scourie on the A894, then north 19 miles on the A838 to reach Scotland's north coast at Durness.

15 Durness

Scattered Durness is wonderfully located, strung out along cliffs rising from pristine beaches. When the sun shines, the effect of the blinding white sand, seabirds' cries and jade-green seas is magical.

Walking around the sensational sandy coastline is a highlight, as is a visit to Cape Wrath. Durness' beautiful beaches include **Rispond** (also known as Ceannabeinne) to the east, **Sango Sands** below town and **Balnakeil** to the west. At Balnakeil, a craft village occupies a former early-warning radar station. A walk along the beach to the north leads to **Faraid Head**, where you can see puffin colonies in early summer.

A mile east of the village is a path down to **Smoo Cave**. From the vast main chamber, you can head through to a smaller flooded cavern where a waterfall sometimes cascades from the roof. There's evidence the cave was inhabited about 6000 years ago. You can take a **boat trip** *(smoocavetours.com)* to explore a little further into the interior.

DETOUR

Cape Wrath

Start: 15 Durness

Though its name comes from the Norse word *hvarf* (turning point), there is something daunting and primal about **Cape Wrath**, the remote northwesternmost point of the British mainland. The danger of the hazardous, stormy seas led to the building of the lighthouse at the cape by Robert and Alan Stevenson in 1828. The last keepers had left by 1998, when people were replaced by automation. Three miles east are the seabird colonies of **Clo Mor**, the British mainland's highest vertical sea cliffs (195m).

Part of the moorland has served for decades as a bombing range. The island of **An Garbh-Eilean**, 5 miles from the cape, has the misfortune to be around the same size as an aircraft carrier and is regularly ripped up by RAF bombs and missiles. There is no public access when the range is in use; restrictions are announced at *gov.uk/government/publications/scotland-firing-times*.

Getting to Cape Wrath involves a **boat ride** *(capewrathferry.wordpress.com)* – passengers and bikes only – across the Kyle of Durness (10 minutes), and then a **minibus** *(visitcapewrath.com)* running 11 miles to the cape (50 minutes). This service has limited capacity, so plan on waiting in high season, and call ahead to make sure the ferry is running. The ferry leaves from 2 miles southwest of Durness, and runs twice daily from May to September. If you decide against the minibus, it's a spectacular 11-mile ride or hike from the boat to the cape over bleak scenery.

SINGLE-TRACK

Along much of this drive you will find single-track roads wide enough for one vehicle only. Passing places (usually marked with a white diamond sign, or a black-and-white striped pole) are used to allow oncoming traffic to get by. Passing places are also for overtaking – you must pull over to let faster vehicles pass. Be wary, too, of sheep straying onto the road.

Faraid Head
TOM RICHARDSON SCOTLAND/ALAMY

PHOTO OPPORTUNITY

Views of the dramatic Cape Wrath, the most north-westerly point in Great Britain, from Faraid Head's summit.

STAY AWHILE

LOCHINVER

BY NEIL WILSON

There are many places in the northwest Highlands where I'd be happy to stop and relax for a day or two, but Lochinver is the pick of the crop. This picturesque harbour village lies on the western coast of Assynt, amid an array of Scotland's finest scenery.

A necklace of golden sand beaches adorns the coast to the northwest of town – Achmelvich, Clachtoll and Clashnessie – but Lochinver is also within easy reach of many fine hikes and hill walks, from the easy trails at **Leitir Easaidh** and **Culag Woods** to more challenging hikes to **Inverkirkaig Waterfall** and on to the summit of **Suilven**.

With a day to spend, I'd head north along the B869 and make the short walk to the less well-known **Alltan na Bradhan beach** (between Achmelvich and Clachtoll), a secret sandy cove below the ruins of a 17th-century watermill. After a quick morning swim, I'd continue north to **Stoer Lighthouse** *(stoerlighthouse.co.uk)*, the starting point for a fine coastal walk to the **Old Man of Stoer**, a spectacular sea-stack rock climb that's still on my wish list.

In 1993, the North Assynt Estate was purchased by the **Assynt Crofters Trust** *(theassyntcrofters.co.uk)*; Scotland's first community land buyout set a precedent for local people taking control of the land they work and live on. The trust's **information office**, a wee timber building near Stoer village, has displays about Assynt's history. They could sell me a fishing permit for the estate's numerous trout lochs if I wanted to head off into the hills to chase the evening rise.

LINK YOUR TRIP

Lochinver is a popular stopover on the epic 01 **North Coast 500** and the scenic 33 **Upper West Coast** drive.

DANIEL KARFIK/SHUTTERSTOCK

ANDREW PETER BRIGGS/SHUTTERSTOCK

Left: Stoer Lighthouse; Right: Lochinver, with Suilven (background)

PLACES TO STAY

You're spoilt for choice of places to stay in and around Lochinver. Campervans and motorhomes have the added option of a superb 'wild camping' spot at Strone Viewpoint, 3 miles north of town.

Shore Caravan Site
Informal grassy campsite in an attractive setting just north of Lochinver, next to Achmelvich's gorgeous sandy beach. *shorecaravansite.co.uk*

An Cala Bunkhouse
A comfortable, community-run hostel housed in the former fishermen's mission down by the harbour. *ancalacafeandbunkhouse.co.uk*

Davar Guest House
A more luxurious option is this excellent B&B with a fabulous view across the bay to Suilven. *davar-lochinver.co.uk*

34

SCOTLAND

ROYAL HIGHLANDS & CAIRNGORMS

DURATION: 4–5 DAYS

DISTANCE: 149 MILES / 238KM

GREAT FOR: HISTORY, WILDLIFE

BEST TIME TO GO: JULY AND AUGUST MEAN GOOD WEATHER AND ALL ATTRACTIONS ARE OPEN.

★ BEST FOR

WILDLIFE

Watching the nesting ospreys at Loch Garten.

Braemar Castle

The heart of the Scottish Highlands features castles and mountains, wild roller-coaster roads and the chance to see Highland wildlife up close. You'll tick off the highlights of Royal Deeside and the central Highlands as you make this circuit around Cairngorms National Park. Queen Victoria kick-started the Scottish tourism industry when she purchased the original Balmoral Castle in the 19th century, and her descendants still holiday here.

LINK YOUR TRIP

31 Stirling & Fife Coast
A scenic 46 miles lead south from Aberfeldy to Stirling, the start of our tour of the historic and cultural jewels of Fife.

32 Lower West Coast
From Aberfeldy it's a lovely 23-mile drive along Loch Tay to Killin, where you can pick up our tour of the Argyllshire coast.

01 Braemar

Braemar is a pretty little village with a grand location on a broad plain ringed by mountains where the Dee valley and Glen Clunie meet. In winter this is one of the coldest places in the country – temperatures as low as -29°C have been recorded.

Just north of the village, turreted **Braemar Castle** *(braemarcastle.co.uk)* dates from 1628 and served as a government garrison after the 1745 Jacobite rebellion. It was taken over by the local community in 2007, and now offers self-guided tours of the historic castle apartments.

There are Highland games in many towns and villages throughout the summer, but the best known is the **Braemar Gathering** *(braemargathering.org)*, which takes place on the first Saturday in September and has been running since 1832.

THE DRIVE: The upper valley of the River Dee stretches east from Braemar to Aboyne. Made famous by its long

ARCH WHITE/ALAMY

association with the monarchy, the region is often called Royal Deeside. Head east from Braemar on the A93 for 9 miles to the car park at the entrance to Balmoral Castle.

02 Balmoral Castle

Built for Queen Victoria in 1855 as a private residence for the royal family – the old building was demolished – **Balmoral Castle** *(balmoral castle.com)* kicked off the revival of the Scottish Baronial style of architecture that characterises many of Scotland's 19th-century country houses.

General admission tickets include an audioguide tour of the castle gardens and grounds; as for the castle itself, only the ballroom, which displays a collection of Landseer paintings and royal silver, is included.

A limited number of much more expensive tickets are available for guided tours of the castle interior, where you will be shown rooms used by King Charles and the royal family when they visit.

You can buy a booklet with several waymarked walks within Balmoral Estate; the best is the climb to Prince Albert's Cairn.

THE DRIVE: Continue east on the A93 for 8 more miles to Ballater.

03 Ballater

The attractive village of Ballater owes its 18th-century origins to the curative waters of nearby Pannanich Springs (now bottled commercially as Deeside Natural Mineral Water), and its prosperity to nearby Balmoral Castle.

After the original station was destroyed by fire in 2015, the **Old Royal Station** building – restored to exactly replicate the one built in 1866 to receive Queen Victoria when she visited Balmoral by train – reopened in 2018. It houses a tourist office, a tearoom and a cafe-bistro. Behind the tourist office is a replica of Queen Victoria's carriage.

There are many pleasant walks in the area. The steep woodland walk up Craigendarroch (400m) takes just over one hour; ask at the tourist office for more info. You can hire bikes from **CycleHighlands** *(cyclehighlands.com)* and **Bike Station** *(bikestationballater.co.uk)*, which also offer guided bike rides and advice on local trails.

THE DRIVE: The A939 strikes north through the mountains from Ballater to Tomintoul (25 miles). The section beyond Cock Bridge is a magnificent roller-coaster of a road, much loved by motorcyclists, summiting at the Lecht pass (637m), where there's a small skiing area (it's usually the first road in Scotland to be blocked by snow when winter closes in).

04 Tomintoul

Tomintoul (tom-in-towel) is a pretty, stone-built village with a tree-lined main square. It was built by the Duke of Gordon in 1775 on the old military road that leads over the Lecht pass from Corgarff, a route now followed by the A939. The **Tomintoul & Glenlivet Discovery Centre** celebrates local history, with reconstructions of a crofter's kitchen and a blacksmith's forge.

There's excellent mountain biking at the **Bike Glenlivet** *(bikeglenlivet.co.uk)* trail centre, 4.5 miles north of Tomintoul, off the B9136 road.

♥ WHY I LOVE THIS TRIP

NEIL WILSON, WRITER

I live just south of Blairgowrie, so this tour around the fringes of Cairngorms National Park is home territory. For me, the Cairngorms mean famous salmon rivers lined with gnarled Scots pines; celebrated castles and pretty villages hewn from pink and grey granite; hulking, wind-blasted hills and iconic wildlife. Red deer and mountain hares roam the hillsides, red squirrels and Scottish wildcats haunt the forests, while golden eagles and ospreys soar above. This trip has it all.

THE DRIVE: Continue northwest from Tomintoul on the A939 for 8.5 miles before turning left on a minor road to the village of Nethy Bridge. In the village, turn left towards Aviemore on the B970 then, after 600m, turn left again on a minor road to Loch Garten (total 17 miles).

05 Loch Garten

A car park on the shores of Loch Garten, amid beautiful open forest of Scots pine, gives access to the **RSPB Loch Garten Osprey Centre** *(rspb.org.uk/lochgarten)*. Ospreys nest in a tall pine tree on the reserve – you can watch from a hide as the birds feed their young, and see live CCTV feeds from the nest.

These rare and beautiful birds – the only bird of prey in the world that eats only fish – migrate here each spring from Africa, arriving in April and leaving in August (check the website to see if they're in residence).

THE DRIVE: The minor road leads back to the B970, where you turn left along the banks of the River Spey to Coylumbridge; turn right here to reach Aviemore (11 miles).

06 Aviemore

The gateway to the Cairngorms, Aviemore may not be the prettiest town in Scotland – the main attractions are in the surrounding area – but when bad weather puts the hills off limits, Aviemore fills up with hikers, cyclists and climbers (plus skiers and snowboarders in winter) cruising the outdoor-equipment shops or recounting their latest adventures in the cafes and bars.

Strathspey Steam Railway *(strathspeyrailway.co.uk)* runs steam trains on a section of restored line between Aviemore and Broomhill, 10 miles to the northeast, via Boat of Garten. There are four or five trains daily from June to August, and a more limited service in April, May, September, October and December, with the option of enjoying afternoon tea in a first-class carriage compartment.

THE DRIVE: From Aviemore, drive south on the B9152, which follows the valley of the River Spey; after 8.5 miles, soon after passing through the village of Kincraig, you'll see a sign on the right for the Highland Wildlife Park.

DETOUR

Cairn Gorm Mountain

Start: 06 Aviemore

Cairn Gorm Mountain (1245m), 10 miles southeast of Aviemore, is the sixth-highest summit in the UK and home to Scotland's biggest ski area. From Aviemore, it's a 10-mile drive to Coire Cas car park at the end of Ski Rd; from here a funicular railway will whisk you to the edge of the Cairngorm plateau (altitude 1085m) in just eight minutes. Unfortunately, for environmental and safety reasons, you're not allowed out of the top station in summer.

From Aviemore, the road to Cairn Gorm Mountain passes through the Rothiemurchus Estate, famous for having one of Scotland's largest remnants of Caledonian forest, the ancient forest of Scots pine that once covered most of the country. The **Rothiemurchus Centre** *(rothiemurchus.net)* has maps detailing more than 50 miles of footpaths and cycling trails, including the 4-mile trail around Loch an Eilein, with its ruined castle and peaceful pine woods.

Six miles east of Aviemore, the road passes Loch Morlich, surrounded by some 8 sq miles of pine and spruce forest that make up the Glenmore Forest Park. Its attractions include a sandy beach (at the east end) and a water-sports centre.

Nearby, the **Cairngorm Reindeer Centre** *(cairngormreindeer.co.uk)* runs guided walks to see and feed Britain's only herd of reindeer, which are free-ranging but very tame. Walks take place at 11am daily (weather permitting), plus another at 2.30pm from May to September. Book tickets in advance.

REFUEL IN AVIEMORE

The busy town of Aviemore is the obvious place to stretch your legs and refuel. Many eating places are clustered along the main drag, but it's worth seeking out **Route 7 Cafe** *(route7.co.uk)*. This place, named after the cycle route that passes the door, takes a bit of finding (at the end of the side road that passes Cairngorm Brewery), but is well worth seeking out for its hearty menu of burgers, grilled sandwiches and vegan dishes.

07 Highland Wildlife Park

The **Highland Wildlife Park** *(highlandwildlifepark.org)* features a drive-through safari park and animal enclosures that offer the chance to view rarely seen native wildlife, such as Scottish wildcats, red deer,

Deer, Highland Wildlife Park
MARTEN_HOUSE/SHUTTERSTOCK

pine martens and red squirrels. It is also home to species that once roamed the Scottish hills but have long since disappeared, including wolves and lynx, plus endangered species from around the world. Last entry is two hours before closing.

THE DRIVE: Continue southwest on the B9152 through Kingussie to the Highland Folk Museum (6.5 miles).

08 Highland Folk Museum

The old Speyside towns of Kingussie (kin-yew-see) and Newtonmore sit at the foot of the great heather-clad humps known as the Monadhliath Mountains.

Newtonmore is best known as the home of the excellent **Highland Folk Museum** *(highlifehighland.com/highlandfolkmuseum)*, an open-air collection of historical buildings and artefacts revealing many aspects of Highland culture and lifestyle. Laid out like a farming township, it has a community of traditional thatch-roofed cottages, a sawmill, a schoolhouse, a shepherd's bothy (hut) and a rural post office.

> PHOTO OPPORTUNITY
>
> The gorgeous view of Schiehallion mountain from Queen's View on Loch Tummel.

THE DRIVE: Join the main A9 Inverness to Perth road and follow it south for 35 miles to Blair Atholl, passing through bleak mountain scenery and climbing to a high point of 460m at the Pass of Drumochter.

09 Blair Atholl

The picturesque village of Blair Atholl dates only from the early 19th century, built by the Duke of Atholl, head of the Murray Clan, whose seat – magnificent **Blair Castle** *(atholl-estates.co.uk/blair-castle)* – is one of the most popular tourist attractions in Scotland.

Thirty rooms are open to the public and they present a wonderful picture of upper-class Highland life from the 16th century on. The original tower was built in 1269, but the castle underwent significant remodelling in the 18th and 19th centuries. Highlights include the 2nd-floor Drawing Room with its ornate Georgian plasterwork and Zoffany portrait of the 4th duke's family, complete with a pet lemur called Tommy; and the Tapestry Room draped with 17th-century wall hangings created for Charles I. The dining room is sumptuous – check out the 9-pint wine glasses.

There are more than 50 miles of cycling trails through the estate; hire a bike from **Blair Atholl Bike Hire** *(segway-ecosse.com/bike-hire)*.

THE DRIVE: Follow the B8079 southeast out of Blair Atholl for a few miles, past the historic battle site of Killiecrankie, and turn right on the B8019 Strathtummel road. This gloriously scenic road leads along **Loch Tummel** (stop for photographs at Queen's View) to Tummel Bridge; turn left

Highland Folk Museum

ERIC MURPHY/ALAMY

here on the B846 over the hills to Aberfeldy (29 miles in total).

10 Aberfeldy

Aberfeldy (p282) is the gateway to Breadalbane (the historic region surrounding Loch Tay), and a good base: adventure sports, angling, art and castles all feature here.

It's a peaceful, pretty place on the banks of the Tay, but if it's moody lochs and glens that steal your heart, you may want to push further west into Glen Lyon. You arrive in the town by crossing the River Tay via the elegant Wade's Bridge, built in 1733 as part of the network of military roads designed to tame the Highlands.

At the eastern end of town is **Aberfeldy Distillery** *(dewarsaberfeldydistillery.com)*, home of the famous Dewar's whisky; entertaining tours of the whisky-making process are followed by a tasting of venerable Aberfeldy single malts and others.

DETOUR

Glen Lyon

Start: 10 Aberfeldy

The 'longest, loneliest and loveliest glen in Scotland', according to Sir Walter Scott, stretches for 32 miles of rickety stone bridges, native woodland and heather-clad hills, becoming wilder and more uninhabited as it snakes its way west. The ancients believed it to be a gateway to Faerieland, and even the most sceptical of visitors will be entranced by the valley's magic.

There are no villages in the glen – the majestic scenery is the main reason to be here – just a cluster of houses at Bridge of Balgie, where the **Glenlyon Tearoom**, with a suntrap of a terrace overlooking the river, serves as a hub for walkers, cyclists and motorists. The owners are a fount of knowledge about the glen – their cakes and scones are legendary.

There are several waymarked woodland walks beginning from a car park a short distance beyond Bridge of Balgie, and more challenging hill walks into the surrounding mountains *(walkhighlands.co.uk/perthshire)*.

From Aberfeldy, the B846 leads to the pretty village of Fortingall, famous for its ancient yew tree, where a narrow minor road strikes west up the glen; another steep and spectacular route from Loch Tay crosses the hills to meet it at Bridge of Balgie. The road continues west as far as the dam on Loch Lyon, passing a memorial to Robert Campbell (1808–94), a Canadian explorer born in the glen.

ROBERT HARDING VIDEO/SHUTTERSTOCK

Red squirrel, Cairngorms

BEST CAIRNGORMS WILDLIFE TOURS

- **Her Alvie & Dalraddy Estates** *(alvie-estate.co.uk)*: See the Cairngorms from the saddle at this estate near Kincraig, which offers pony trekking, quad-bike tours and red squirrel photography trips.
- **Speyside Wildlife** *(speysidewildlife.co.uk)*: Grantown-on-Spey operator offering bespoke trips and evening badger and pine marten watching.
- **Instinct Guides** *(instinctguides.com)*: Birdwatching specialists with exclusive access to black grouse 'lekking', when blackcock males battle for territory.
- **Cairngorm Mountain** *(cairngormmountain.co.uk)*: Ride the funicular railway and take a guided walk to the top of Cairngorm mountain with a national park ranger to learn about the flora and fauna on the subarctic summit plateau.

STAY AWHILE

ABERFELDY

BY NEIL WILSON

This lovely little town in the heart of Highland Perthshire is a great place to slow down and relax. I like to stretch my legs at the **Birks of Aberfeldy,** a woodland path that climbs beside an impressive waterfall immortalised in verse by Robert Burns, before relaxing with a cappuccino at **Fika Coffee Shop**.

My favourite excursion from Aberfeldy is along the shores of Loch Tay to the fascinating **Scottish Crannog Centre** *(crannog.co.uk)* then over the mountain road to **Bridge of Balgie**. The National Trust for Scotland car park on this road is the starting point for a superb hill walk to the summit of **Ben Lawers**. The road then descends into gorgeous Glen Lyon where I always stop at the **Glenlyon Tearoom** for coffee and scones before heading back. An easy 48 miles in the car, or a challenging full day on the bike.

A shorter bike ride heads down the minor road on the far bank of the River Tay, past JK Rowling's country house at Killiechassie, to the bridge at Grandtully for lunch at the **Inn on the Tay** *(theinnonthetay.co.uk)*, returning to Aberfeldy via the old railway cycle path.

Wet-weather options include a tour of the **Aberfeldy Distillery** *(dewarsaberfeldydistillery.com)* or **whitewater rafting** *(rafting.co.uk)* on the River Tay, but I usually just retreat to the **Watermill** *(aberfeldywatermill.com)*, a great little cafe and one of the best bookshops in the country; I can never leave without buying yet another book.

LINK YOUR TRIP

Aberfeldy is the end point of the 34 **Royal Highlands & Cairngorms** trip and a short drive from Killin on the 32 **Lower West Coast** drive.

STEPHEN FINN/ALAMY

IZZET CAKALLI/SHUTTERSTOCK

Left: Aberfeldy Caravan Park; Right: Glenlyon Tearoom

PLACES TO STAY

Aberfeldy's accommodation caters to all tastes.

Aberfeldy Caravan Park
Tents, campervans and motorhomes are all welcome at this riverside site, just five minutes' walk from the town centre. *aberfeldycaravanpark.co.uk*

Pitilie Pods
Two miles south of town on the A826, these luxurious glamping cabins have underfloor heating and fantastic views; some have hot tubs. *pitiliepods.com*

Townhouse Aberfeldy
Set in a grand old Victorian building that was once the railway station hotel, this great-value B&B is right in the middle of town. *townhouseaberfeldy.co.uk*

Ailean Chraggan
Superb food and a warm welcome are the trademarks of this small, family-run hotel just across the river from town. *chraggs.co.uk*

35

★ BEST FOR

FAMILIES

Taking a Nessie-hunting cruise from Fort Augustus.

SCOTLAND

GREAT GLEN

DURATION: 2–3 DAYS

DISTANCE: 147 MILES / 235KM

GREAT FOR: FAMILY TRAVEL

BEST TIME TO GO: APRIL TO SEE SNOW ON THE MOUNTAINS, OCTOBER FOR AUTUMN COLOURS IN THE FORESTS.

Aonach Eagach ridge

The Great Glen is a geological fault running in an arrow-straight line across Scotland, filled by a series of lochs including world-famous Loch Ness – here be monsters! This trip through some of the Highlands' scenic hot spots follows the A82 road along the glen (completed in 1933 – a date that coincides with the first sightings of the Loch Ness monster) and links two National Landscapes – Glen Coe to the south, and Glen Affric to the north.

LINK YOUR TRIP

33 Upper West Coast
The stirring wilderness of the northwest Highlands awaits – Skye lies 60 miles northwest of Fort Augustus along the A87.

36 Whisky Trails
A short drive east from Inverness to Elgin (39 miles) links to our trip around the heartland of Scotland's whisky distilleries.

01 Glen Coe

Scotland's most famous glen is also one of its grandest. The A82 leads over the **Pass of Glencoe** and into the narrow upper glen. The southern side is dominated by three massive, brooding spurs, known as the Three Sisters, while the northern side is enclosed by the continuous steep wall of the knife-edged **Aonach Eagach** ridge, a classic mountaineering challenge.

Glencoe Visitor Centre *(nts.org.uk)* provides comprehensive information on the geological, environmental and cultural history of Glencoe, charts the development of mountaineering in the glen, and tells the story of the Glencoe Massacre in all its gory detail.

THE DRIVE: From Glencoe village at the foot of the glen, head east on the B863 for 7 miles along the southern shore of Loch Leven to Kinlochleven.

02 Kinlochleven

Kinlochleven is hemmed in by high mountains at the head

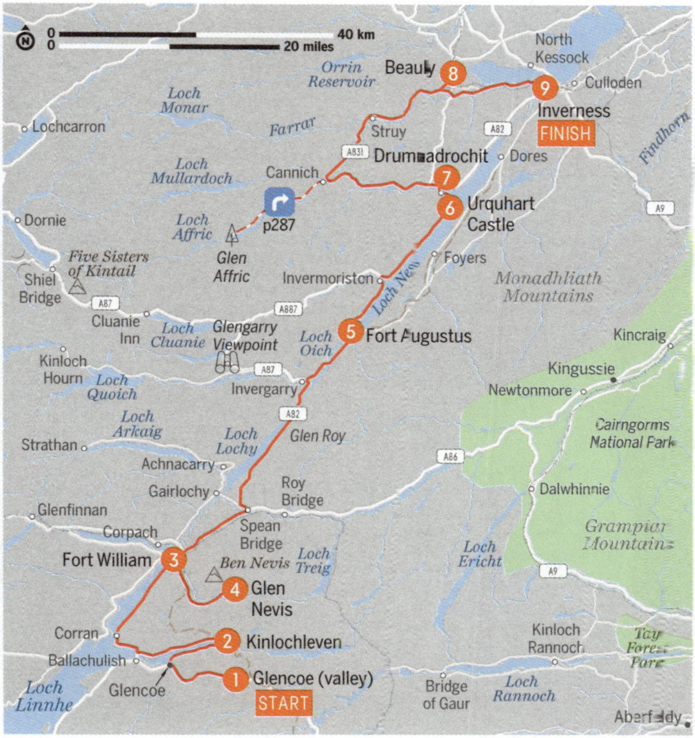

SCOTLAND'S SCENERY/SHUTTERSTOCK

of beautiful Loch Leven, where the West Highland Way brings a steady stream of hikers through the village.

It is also the starting point for walks up the glen of the Allt a'Chumhainn, through pleasant woods to the Grey Mare's Tail waterfall, and harder mountain hikes into the Mamores.

Scotland's first **Via Ferrata** *(verticaldescents-scotland.com)* – a 500m climbing route equipped with steel ladders, cables and bridges – snakes through the crags around the Grey Mare's Tail, allowing non-climbers to experience the thrill of climbing (you'll need a head for heights, though).

THE DRIVE: Return west along the north side of Loch Leven, perhaps stopping for lunch at the excellent Lochleven Seafood Cafe, then head north on the A82 to Fort William (22 miles).

03 Fort William

Basking on the shores of Loch Linnhe amid magnificent mountain scenery, Fort William has one of the most enviable settings in the whole of Scotland. If it wasn't for the busy dual carriageway crammed between the less-than-attractive town centre and the loch, and one of the highest rainfall records in the country, it would be almost idyllic. Even so, the Fort has carved out a reputation as Outdoor Capital of the UK *(visitwesthighlands.co.uk)*.

The small but fascinating **West Highland Museum** *(westhighlandmuseum.org.uk)* is packed with all manner of Highland memorabilia. Look out for the secret portrait of Bonnie Prince Charlie – after the Jacobite rebellions, all things Highland were banned, including pictures of the exiled leader, and this tiny painting looks like nothing more than a smear of paint until viewed in a cylindrical mirror.

THE DRIVE: At the roundabout on the northern edge of Fort William, take the minor road that runs into Glen Nevis; it leads to a car park at the far end of the glen, 6.5 miles away.

> **PHOTO OPPORTUNITY**
>
> Failing a shot of the Loch Ness monster, crossing the wire bridge at Steall Falls.

04 Glen Nevis

Scenic Glen Nevis – used as a filming location for *Braveheart* and the *Harry Potter* movies – wraps around the base of **Ben Nevis** (1345m), Britain's highest mountain. The **Ben Nevis Visitor Centre** is situated 1.5 miles up the glen, and provides information on hiking, weather forecasts and on climbing Ben Nevis.

From the car park at the end of the road, 5 miles beyond the visitor centre, there is an excellent 1.5-mile walk through the spectacular, verdant **Nevis Gorge** valley to **Steall Falls**, a 100m-high bridal-veil waterfall. You can reach the foot of the falls by crossing the river on a wobbly, three-cable wire bridge – one cable for your feet and one for each hand – a real test of balance.

CLIMBING BEN NEVIS

Here are some hard facts to mull over before you think about climbing Ben Nevis. The summit plateau has a subarctic climate – it can snow on any day of the year. The summit is wrapped in cloud nine days out of 10. In thick clouds, visibility at the summit can be 10m or less, and in such conditions, the only safe way off the mountain requires careful use of a map and compass. On average there are 80 to 100 rescues and six deaths each year. Seek advice at the **Ben Nevis Visitor Centre** *(highlifehighland.com/bennevis/visitor-centre).*

THE DRIVE: Return down Glen Nevis and head north on the A82. At Invergarry, turn left onto the A87, which climbs high above Loch Garry; stop at the famous Glengarry Viewpoint (lay-by on left). By a quirk of perspective, the lochs to the west appear to form the map outline of Scotland. Return to the A82 and continue to Fort Augustus (44 miles).

05 Fort Augustus

Fort Augustus, at the junction of four old military roads, was originally a government garrison and the headquarters of General George Wade's road-building operations in the early 18th century. Today, it's a neat and picturesque little place bisected by the Caledonian Canal. Boats using the canal are raised and lowered 13m by a 'ladder' of five consecutive locks. It's fun to watch, and the neatly landscaped canal banks are a great place to soak up the sun. The **Caledonian Canal Centre**, beside the lowest lock, has information on the history of the canal.

Cruise Loch Ness *(cruiselochness.com)*, at the jetty beside the canal bridge, operates one-hour cruises on Loch Ness accompanied by the latest high-tech sonar equipment so you can keep an underwater eye open for the Loch Ness monster.

THE DRIVE: It's a straightforward but scenic 17-mile drive along the shores of Loch Ness to Urquhart Castle.

06 Urquhart Castle

Commanding a superb location with outstanding views over Loch Ness, **Urquhart Castle** *(historicenvironment.scot)* is a popular Nessie-hunting hot spot. The castle was repeatedly sacked and rebuilt (and sacked and rebuilt) over the centuries; in 1692 it was blown up to prevent the Jacobites from using it. The five-storey tower house at the northern point is the most impressive remaining fragment and offers wonderful views across the water.

The visitor centre includes displays of medieval items discovered in the castle and a video theatre; the film, with a dramatic 'reveal' of the castle at the end, can be downloaded onto your phone using a QR code if the visitor centre is closed.

THE DRIVE: A short hop of 2 miles leads to Drumnadrochit.

07 Drumnadrochit

Deep, dark and narrow, **Loch Ness** stretches for 23 miles between Inverness and Fort Augustus. Its bitterly cold waters have been extensively explored in search of Nessie, the elusive Loch Ness monster, but most visitors see her only in the form of a cardboard cut-out at Drumnadrochit's monster exhibitions.

The **Loch Ness Centre** *(lochness.com)* adopts a scientific approach that allows you to weigh the evidence for yourself on the Nessie question. Exhibits include the original equipment – sonar survey vessels, miniature submarines, cameras and sediment coring tools – used in various monster hunts, as well as original photographs and film footage of sightings. You'll find out about hoaxes and optical illusions, as well as learning a lot about the ecology of Loch Ness – is there enough food in the loch to support even one 'monster', let alone a breeding population?

THE DRIVE: Head west on the A831, which leads to the village of Cannich – jumping-off point for the Glen Affric detour – before turning north along lovely Strathglass to reach Beauly (30 miles).

> ♥ DON'T MISS
>
> ### LOCHSIDE SEAFOOD
>
> The **Lochleven Seafood Cafe** *(lochlevenseafoodcafe.co.uk)* lies 5 miles west of Kinlochleven, with a splendid setting on the north shore of the loch – for warm days there's an outdoor terrace with a view across the loch to the Pap of Glencoe. The menu offers superb fresh shellfish from seawater tanks, including Loch Leven mussels, Loch Creran oysters, Loch Linnhe langoustines, crabs and lobsters, plus a daily fish special and some non-seafood dishes.

DETOUR

Glen Affric

Start: 07 Drumnadrochit

Glen Affric, one of Scotland's most beautiful glens, extends deep into the hills beyond Cannich, halfway between Drumnadrochit and Beauly. The upper reaches of the glen, now designated as Glen Affric Nature Reserve, is a wonderland of shimmering lochs, rugged mountains and native Scots pine forest, home to pine martens, wildcats, otters, red squirrels and golden eagles.

Ben Nevis
CAMROSPHOTOGRAPHY/SHUTTERSTOCK

A narrow, dead-end road leads southwest from Cannich for 11 miles to the River Affric car park and picnic site at the eastern end of Loch Affric, where there are several short walks along the river and the loch shore; this is also the starting point for a longer circuit of Loch Affric, and ascents of the surrounding Munros.

08 Beauly

Mary, Queen of Scots is said to have given this village its name in 1564 when she visited, exclaiming in French: *'Quel beau lieu!'* ('What a beautiful place!'). Founded in 1230, the red-sandstone **Beauly Priory** is now an impressive ruin, haunted by the cries of rooks nesting in a magnificent centuries-old sycamore tree.

Corner on the Square eatery makes a good place to break your journey; it's well worth the stop.

THE DRIVE: Drive east on the A862 for 12 miles to Inverness.

09 Inverness

Inverness has a great location astride the River Ness at the northern end of the Great Glen. In summer it overflows with visitors intent on monster hunting at nearby Loch Ness, but it's worth a visit in its own right for **Inverness Castle** *(invernesscastle.scot)*, a pink-sandstone confection dating from the 1840s that replaced a medieval castle blown up by the Jacobites in 1746. The castle served as courthouse and prison until 2020, and reopened in 2025 after a regeneration project to create the city's top attraction.

A leisurely stroll along the river to the **Ness Islands**. Planted with mature Scots pine, fir, beech and sycamore, and linked to the riverbanks and each other by elegant Victorian footbridges, the islands make an appealing picnic spot. They're a 20-minute walk south of the castle - head upstream on either side of the river (the start of the Great Glen Way), and return on the opposite bank.

GLEN AFFRIC WALKS

- **Plodda Falls:**
  A short trail (20 minutes) southwest of Tomich leads to a restored Victorian viewing platform above the top of the falls, with a dizzying view down the 40m-high cascade.
- **Dog Falls:**
  A scenic spot where the River Affric squeezes through a narrow, rocky gorge. Waymarked walking trail (two hours) from Dog Falls car park, 4 miles from Cannich.
- **River Affric Trail:**
  Short (allow 45 minutes) and easy but beautiful riverside walk signposted from the River Affric car park.
- **Loch Affric Circuit:**
  A five-hour trek (or two-hour mountain bike ride) around Loch Affric, starting at the River Affric car park.

Ness Islands

JONATHAN FUSSELL/ALAMY

36

SCOTLAND

WHISKY TRAILS

DURATION: 2–3 DAYS

DISTANCE: 39 MILES / 62KM

GREAT FOR: DRINKING, HISTORY

BEST TIME TO GO: EARLY MAY, WHEN THE SPIRIT OF SPEYSIDE FESTIVALS TAKE PLACE.

★ BEST FOR

SHOPPING

Stocking up on gourmet goodies at Elgin's Gordon & Macphail.

Whisky barrels, Macallan Distillery

As well as visiting half a dozen famous whisky distilleries, you'll discover ancient crafts and traditions such as barrel-making, wool-spinning and hand-loom weaving on this tour of historic Speyside. The old county of Moray, centred on the town of Elgin, lies at the heart of an ancient Celtic earldom and is famed for its mild climate and rich farmland – the barley fields here traditionally provided the raw material for Speyside's whisky distilleries.

LINK YOUR TRIP

35 Great Glen
Inverness, the final stop on our tour of Highland highlights, is 39 miles west of Elgin along the A96.

34 Royal Highlands & Cairngorms
You can extend your trip in the Cairngorms National Park by following the second half of this tour: join it at Tomintoul, 19 miles southwest of Dufftown.

01 Elgin

Elgin, dominated by a hilltop monument to the 5th Duke of Gordon, has been the provincial capital of Moray for more than eight centuries.

Many people think that the ruins of **Elgin Cathedral** *(historicenvironment.scot)*, known as the 'lantern of the north', are the most beautiful and evocative in Scotland; its octagonal chapter house is the finest in the country.

The town is also home to Scotland's oldest independent **museum** *(elginmuseum.org.uk)*, a captivating collection beautifully displayed in a purpose-built Victorian building. Exhibits range from Ecuadorian shrunken heads to Peruvian mummies, and include internationally important fish and reptile fossils discovered in local rocks; call ahead to check opening times.

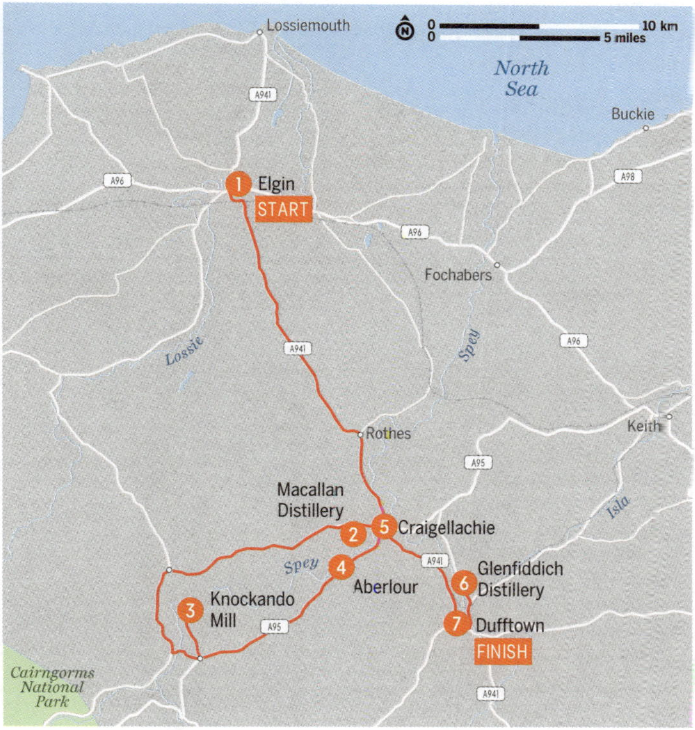

HORST FRIEDRICHS/ALAMY

Look out for **Gordon & Mac Phail** *(gordonandmacphail.com)*, the world's largest specialist malt-whisky dealer. More than a century old and offering around 450 different varieties, this Elgin shop is a place of pilgrimage for whisky connoisseurs.

Founded in 1797, **Johnstons of Elgin** *(discover.johnstonsofelgin.com/our-story/mill-experiences)* on Newmill Rd is famous for its cashmere woollen clothing, and is the only UK woollen mill that still sees the manufacturing process through from raw fibre to finished garment. There's a retail outlet with a restaurant on the edge of town, and guided tours of the works.

THE DRIVE: Follow the A941 south from Elgin to reach the River Spey at Rothes, where a welter of distillery signs announce that you have arrived in Speyside, the heart of Scotland's whisky industry. South of Rothes, turn right on the B9102, which soon leads to the Macallan Distillery (14 miles).

02 Macallan Distillery

The Macallan – known as the king of Speyside malts – is produced in a range of sherry and bourbon finishes.

The **Macallan Distillery** *(themacallan.com)* enjoys a lovely location 1 mile west of Craigellachie and is housed in a spectacular turf-roofed visitor centre made from engineered timber that also contains an exhibition, restaurant, whisky bar and gift boutique. Tours must be pre-booked.

THE DRIVE: Continue west on the B9102 for 7 miles to the Knockando Woolmill. It's down a short side road on the left – look out for the signpost.

03 Knockando Woolmill

Hidden in a fold of the hills beneath Cardhu distillery, **Knockando Woolmill** *(kwc.co.uk)* is a rare survival of an 18th-century woollen mill that has been lovingly restored to full working order.

The ancient looms clank away Monday to Friday, turning out plaid and tweed textiles that can be purchased in the neighbouring shop. You can take a guided tour to find out more.

Beyond the mill, on the banks of the Spey, lie two more distilleries, Tamdhu and Knockando.

THE DRIVE: Return to the B9102 and turn left. After 4 miles, turn left again to cross the River Spey, and once more on the A95. You will soon pass the small, friendly and independent Glenfarclas Distillery before arriving in Aberlour (total 11 miles).

04 Aberlour

Aberlour *(morayspeyside.com/visit/aberlour)* – or Charlestown of Aberlour, to give it its full name – is a pretty village straggling along the banks of the River Spey. **Aberlour Distillery** *(aberlour.com)* is right on the main street, and offers an excellent, detailed tour with a proper tasting session.

Other attractions include spots for salmon fishing on the Spey, and some lovely walks along the Speyside Way.

As the home of Walkers, shortbread and Aberlour single malt, the village is rightly proud of its local produce, and you can browse a huge selection of Scottish food and drink in the village's own **Spey Larder** *(speylarder.com)* or sit down to a meal and a few nips of whisky at the **Mash Tun** beside the River Spey.

THE DRIVE: From Aberlour, it's a short hop of just under 2 miles to Craigellachie.

05 Craigellachie

Craigellachie Hotel is famous for its wonderfully old-fashioned, hunting-lodge atmosphere, from the wood-panelled lobby to the opulent drawing room, where you can sink into a sofa in front of the log fire.

HOW TO BE A MALT WHISKY BUFF

'Love makes the world go round? Not at all! Whisky makes it go round twice as fast.' *Whisky Galore*, Compton Mackenzie (1883–1972).

How should a single malt be drunk? Either neat, or with a little water added. To appreciate the aroma and flavour to the utmost, a measure of malt whisky can be cut (diluted) with one-third to two-thirds as much spring water. Ice, tap water and (God forbid) mixers are for philistines. Would you add lemonade to a glass of Chablis?

Whisky tasting today is big news: being able to tell your Ardbeg from your Edradour is de rigueur among the whisky nosing set, so here are some pointers to help you impress your friends.

What's the difference between malt and grain whiskies? Malts are distilled from malted barley – that is, barley that has been soaked in water, then allowed to germinate for around 10 days until the starch has turned into sugar – while grain whiskies are distilled from other cereals, usually wheat, corn or unmalted barley.

So what is a single malt? A single malt is a whisky that has been distilled only from malted barley and is the product of a single distillery. A blended malt is a mixture of single malts from several distilleries, whereas a blended whisky comprises a mixture of various grain whiskies (about 60%) and malt whiskies (about 40%) from different distilleries.

Single malts vs blends? A single malt, like a fine wine, somehow captures the terroir or essence of the place where it was made and matured – a combination of the water, the barley, the peat smoke, the oak barrels in which it was aged and (in the case of certain coastal distilleries) the sea air and salt spray. Each distillation varies from the one before, not unlike different vintages that hail from the same vineyard.

Mash Tun, Aberlour
JOHN MACPHERSON/ALAMY

ATMOSPHERIC SPOT FOR A WEE DRAM

Housed in a curious stone building made for a sea captain in the outline of a ship, the luxurious **Mash Tun** *(mashtun-aberlour.com)* B&B in Aberlour has a famous whisky bar – a place of pilgrimage for whisky enthusiasts – which has a collection of old and rare single malts, and a walk-in humidor for cigar connoisseurs. The bar also includes a fine-dining restaurant serving lunch and dinner – it's best to book ahead to avoid disappointment.

PHOTO OPPORTUNITY

A whisky-barrel maker at work in the Speyside Cooperage.

The hotel's Quaich Bar, lined with more than 900 varieties of single malt whisky, is a particularly compelling drawcard.

On the southern edge of the village is the **Speyside Cooperage** *(speysidecooperage.co.uk)*, where you can watch the fascinating art of barrel-making during a 45-minute guided tour.

THE DRIVE: Drive south along the A941 for 4 miles to Glenfiddich Distillery.

06 Glenfiddich Distillery

Along with Glenmorangie, Glenfiddich is among the most famous of single malt whisky brands, and kept the flame of whisky appreciation alive during the dark years of the 1970s and '80s, before the welcome revival of interest in all things distilled.

Glenfiddich Distillery *(glenfiddich.com)* is big and bustling. You can tour the distillery to find out more about the history and sample some of its fine whiskies. It is best to pre-book.

THE DRIVE: Continue into the centre of Dufftown, just 0.75 miles south.

07 Dufftown

Rome may be built on seven hills, but Dufftown's built on seven stills, say the locals. Founded in 1817 by James Duff, 4th Earl of Fife, Dufftown lies at the heart of the Speyside whisky-distilling region.

With seven working distilleries nearby, Dufftown has been dubbed Scotland's malt-whisky capital and is host to the annual **Spirit of Speyside** *(spiritofspeyside.com)* whisky festival.

Speyside Cooperage

SUE BURTON PHOTOGRAPHY/SHUTTERSTOCK

TRAVELLING TOURIST/SHUTTERSTOCK

Glenfiddich Distillery

WHILE ON THE SUBJECT OF DISTILLERIES...

Scotland is famous throughout the world for its whisky, and rightly so, but it is also making a mighty fine name for itself in the world of craft gin. See p42.

As well as housing a superb selection of single malt whiskies and Scottish gins, the town's **Whisky Brother shop** *(whiskybrother.co.uk)* holds monthly barrel-top tasting sessions (usually noon to 3pm on a Saturday) where you can learn what to look for in a fine single malt. Check the Facebook page *(facebook.com/whiskybrotheruk)* for dates.

The **Keith & Dufftown Railway** *(keith-dufftown-railway.co.uk)* sees trains hauled by 1950s diesel motor units running at weekends from April to September, plus Fridays from July to September.

37

★ BEST FOR

WILDLIFE

Mull's white-tailed eagles and whale watching.

SCOTLAND

FERRY-HOPPING

DURATION: 6–8 DAYS

DISTANCE: 255 MILES / 410KM (PLUS FERRIES)

GREAT FOR: DRINKING, OUTDOORS

BEST TIME TO GO: MAY IS OFTEN GREAT, WITH A WHISKY FESTIVAL ON ISLAY AND SURPRISINGLY GOOD WEATHER.

Brodick Castle

Taking in four of Scotland's most enticing islands plus the vibrant city of Glasgow, this is an in-depth exploration of southwestern Scotland. The route covers stunningly scenic Arran, Islay's welcoming distilleries, Oban's seafood scene, Mull's heart-lifting landscapes and the enchanting holy isle of Iona. The ferry trips themselves – offering sensational coastal perspectives and wildlife-spotting opportunities – are part of the adventure.

LINK YOUR TRIP

32 Lower West Coast
Once you've visited Mull, head back to Oban and explore the Kintyre Peninsula on this trip.

35 Great Glen
From Tobermory, you can get a ferry across to Kilchoan and approach Fort William by a lonely, scenic route.

01 Glasgow

Full of excellent art, design, food and pubs, Glasgow is an intoxicatingly vibrant place with a legendary live-music scene and loads to see.

The city's cathedral is one of Scotland's most interesting and atmospheric; don't miss a stroll in the adjacent Necropolis.

To the west of the centre, **Kelvingrove Art Gallery & Museum** has a fabulous display of paintings and much more, while the **Burrell Collection** *(burrellcollection.com)* has a soothing parkland settingand a great collection of art. Keep an eye out for the work of architecture and design genius Charles Rennie Mackintosh at places such as **Mackintosh House** *(gla.ac.uk/hunterian/visit/our-venues/mackintosh-house)*.

Glasgow is a shopping paradise, with the boutiques of the central pedestrianised area counterbalanced by the vintage shops and delis of the bohemian West End.

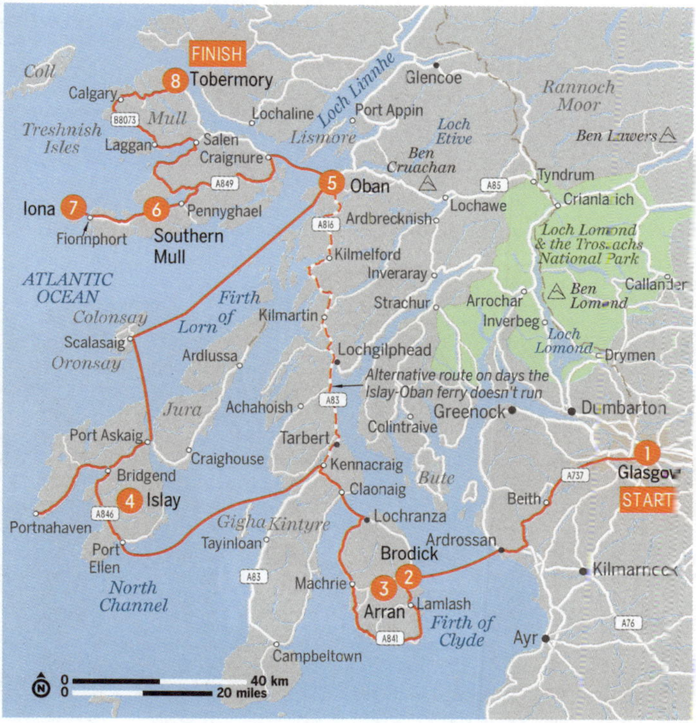

DAVID WOODS/SHUTTERSTOCK

THE DRIVE: Take the M8 out of Glasgow to the west, then exit for the A737, which runs down to the Ayrshire coast, where you pick up the A78 west for the last few miles to Ardrossan and the Arran ferry. The total drive is 33 miles.

02 Brodick

The Ardrossan ferry arrives at Brodick, beating heart of the Isle of Arran, rising from a coastal road that follows the long curving bay. On a clear day it's a spectacular vista, with Goatfell looming over the forested shore.

Two miles north, elegant **Brodick Castle** *(nts.org.uk)* evolved from 13th-century origins into a stately home and hunting lodge for the dukes of Hamilton. The extensive grounds, now a country park with various trails among the rhododendrons, justify the entry fee.

Nearby, the walk up and down **Goatfell**, the island's highest point, is 8 miles return (allow six hours).

THE DRIVE: Take the A841 southbound to do a leisurely clockwise near-circuit of the island. It's 42 miles this way right around to Lochranza, otherwise only 14 miles away heading north.

03 Arran

Lamlash, just 3 miles south of Brodick, is in a dazzling setting, strung along the beachfront. Just offshore is Buddhist-run **Holy Island** *(holyisle.org)*, which you can visit.

The landscape in the south of Arran is gentler than in the north; the road drops into little wooded valleys, and Kildonan has pleasant sandy beaches, basking seals and a gorgeous water outlook.

Another spectacular coastal setting is at the **Lagg Distillery** *(laggwhisky.com)*, a modern setup producing a robust, peaty style.

On the western side of the island is **Machrie Moor Stone Circle**, a pleasant 1.25-mile stroll from the parking area on the coastal road.

The village and ferry port of Lochranza is characterised by numerous red deer and a picturesque ruined 13th-century **castle** *(historicenvironment.scot)*.

THE DRIVE: A car ferry runs at least five times daily from Lochranza to Claonaig on Kintyre. From Claonaig, the B8001 crosses the peninsula to Kennacraig (5 miles) and the ferry to Islay, which docks at either Port Askaig in the island's east or Port Ellen in the south. From Tarbert, it's 5 miles south on the A83 to Kennacraig.

04 Islay

The home of some of the world's greatest and peatiest whiskies, whose names reverberate on the tongue like a pantheon of Celtic deities, Islay (eye-lah) is a wonderfully friendly place and the birdlife, fine seafood, turquoise bays and basking seals are ample non-whisky reasons to visit.

Islay has 10 working distilleries, with three more on the way. All welcome visitors and run tours. It's worth booking ahead; you'll certainly need to for the more involved premium tours. Pick up the invaluable pamphlet listing tour times from the tourist office.

The island's 'capital', Bowmore, has a round church to leave the devil no corners to hide in, and the **Bowmore distillery** *(bowmore.com)*.

which malts its own barley. Three of the biggest, peatiest names in single malt are close together near Port Ellen in the south: **Laphroaig** *(laphroaig.com)*, **Lagavulin** *(malts.com/en-gb/distilleries/lagavulin)* and **Ardbeg** *(ardbeg.com)*.

On the western side of the island, two excellent distilleries are **Bruichladdich** *(bruichladdich.com)*, near Port Charlotte, and boutique-sized **Kilchoman** *(kilchomandistillery.com)*.

Head past Port Charlotte to Portnahaven to watch seals on the harbour rocks.

Three miles from Port Askaig, tumbledown ruins of houses and a chapel on an islet in a shallow loch mark **Finlaggan** *(finlaggan.org)*, all that remains of the stronghold of the Lords of the Isles. Start your exploration at the visitor centre. The islet itself is open at all times.

THE DRIVE: Try and time your exit from Islay for a Wednesday or Saturday when there's a ferry from Port Askaig to Oban via Colonsay. Otherwise, head back to Kennacraig then north up the A83, turning left on to the A816 at Lochgilphead. It's 56 miles from Kennacraig to Oban. If going this way, stop at Kilmartin's interesting museum and prehistoric sights.

05 Oban

Oban, main gateway to many of the Hebridean islands, is a waterfront town on a delightful bay, with sweeping views to Kerrera and Mull.

In summer the town centre is crowded with holidaymakers and travellers headed for the archipelago. But the setting is still lovely, and Oban's brilliant seafood restaurants are marvellous places to be as the sun sets over the bay.

Oban

TOTAJLA/SHUTTERSTOCK

13THREEPHOTOGRAPHY/SHUTTERSTOCK

Caledonian MacBrayne ferry

FERRY IMPORTANT

Scotland's west-coast ferries are operated by **Caledonian MacBrayne** *(calmac.co.uk)*. A comprehensive timetable booklet is available from tourist offices and on the website. There's a summer timetable and one for winter, when services are somewhat reduced. It's important to book car spaces ahead online or by phone; several days ahead for Islay, Mull and Arran is best. If there are no spaces left you can still turn up and wait in the standby queue; you'll often, but not always, squeeze on. Downloading the Calmac app is also a good idea, as it has the latest information on cancelled services and so on.

Basking Shark Scotland *(baskingsharkscotland.co.uk)* runs entertaining boat trips with optional snorkelling, focused on finding and observing basking sharks – the world's second-largest fish – and other notable marine species. Book these trips weeks or even months ahead.

Sea Kayak Oban *(seakayakoban.com)* has a well-stocked shop, rental, great route advice and sea-kayaking courses, including an all-inclusive two-day intro for beginners.

THE DRIVE: From the centre of Oban, get the ferry across to Craignure on the island of Mull. It takes about an hour.

06 Southern Mull

Mull can lay claim to some of the finest and most varied scenery in the Inner Hebrides. Noble birds of prey soar over mountain and coast, while the western waters provide good whale-watching.

Near the Craignure ferry slip, **Duart Castle** *(duartcastle.com)*, the ancestral seat of the Maclean Clan, enjoys a spectacular position on a rocky outcrop overlooking the Sound of Mull.

Contact **Mull Wildlife Tours** *(mullwildlifetours.co.uk)* to observe the white-tailed eagle, Britain's largest bird of prey. Tours also offer the chance to spot golden eagles, hen harriers, grey seals and otters. **Mull & Iona Ranger Service** *(mulliona rangerservice.com)* provides weekly guided walks at the widlife hides on the island.

Great walks in the southern part of the island include the popular climb of Ben More and the spectacular trek to Carsaig Arches.

THE DRIVE: From the ferry at Craignure, it's 37 miles of imposing scenery along the A849 to Mull's southwestern tip at Fionnphort. From here, a passenger ferry zips to Iona, just across the strait.

07 Iona

Like an emerald teardrop off Mull's western shore, enchanting, idyllic Iona, holy island and burial ground of kings, is a magical place that lives up to its lofty reputation.

Iona's ancient but heavily reconstructed **abbey** *(historicenviron ment.scot)* is the spiritual heart of the island. The spectacular nave, dominated by Romanesque and early Gothic vaults and columns, is a powerful space; a door on the left leads to the beautiful cloister, where medieval grave slabs sit alongside modern religious sculptures. Out the back, the museum displays some fabulous carved high crosses.

Next to the abbey is an ancient graveyard where there's an evocative Romanesque chapel as well as a mound that marks the burial place of 48 of Scotland's early kings, possibly including Macbeth.

Trips from Iona run to the spectacular accordion-like island of Staffa and its awe-inspiring basalt-columned **Fingal's Cave**.

THE DRIVE: Get the ferry back to Fionnphort and drive back up the A849 for 18 miles before taking a left onto the B8035. Follow this, then the B8073, a spectacular drive along the Mull coastline for a slow, single-track 50 miles to the capital, Tobermory.

08 Northern Mull & Tobermory

The highlights of northern Mull, apart from the spectacular drive, are the glorious beach and gallery-cafe complex at Calgary; and the pretty capital, Tobermory, with colourful houses arrayed along a pretty picture-book harbour. It makes a great base, with a good selection of accommodation and fine seafood.

Book your place on a boat with **Sea Life Mull** *(sealifemull.co.uk)*, which runs whale-watching trips that head out from Tobermory harbour to the waters north and west of Mull. Shorter seal-spotting jaunts are also available.

WHERE TO EAT THE FRESHEST FISH

Seafood doesn't come much fresher than the stuff served at **Cafe Fish** *(thecafefish.com)*, a warm and welcoming little restaurant overlooking Tobermory harbour. Crustaceans go straight from boat to kitchen to join rich seafood stew, fat scallops, fish pie and catch-of-the-day on the daily-changing menu, where occasional use of Asian ingredients adds an extra dimension. Book ahead.

Fingal's Cave

LASSE JOHANSSON/SHUTTERSTOCK

PHOTO OPPORTUNITY

The impressive basalt columns of Fingal's Cave.

TOOLKIT

ARRIVING, p304

GETTING AROUND, p305

ACCOMMODATION, p306

ARRIVING

If you're coming into London, contactless payment for public transport is easiest and cheapest (check overseas transaction fees with your bank). From Heathrow, the Elizabeth Line runs to East London via Paddington and Liverpool St stations. Coaches serve London and cities such as Windsor and Oxford. From Gatwick, trains and 24-hour buses run to central London. Ride-shares/taxis start at £70/£100. You'll pay a premium for Heathrow Express and Gatwick Express trains.

AIRPORT CAR RENTALS

There are multiple car-rental options at Heathrow and Gatwick. However, if you are going to London first, catch public transport in and hire a car later: parking in London is expensive.

Aggregator websites such as *rentalcars.com* share deals from major companies, but check terms and conditions before booking as these vary. Cheap prices may mean limited mileage or a very small boot/trunk.

You will need your passport, driving licence and a credit card (not just a debit card) to rent a car. Holding deposits range from £200 to £700, which is locked away until you return the car. Budget accordingly.

You can rent a car on the spot but it's best to pre-book. You'll be asked to thoroughly check the vehicle before departing. Mark up any scratch, no matter how minor.

AIRPORT TO CITY CENTRE *

	LONDON (HEATHROW)	EDINBURGH	MANCHESTER
TRAIN	30mins £13.90	30mins £7.50	20mins £4-£7.40
BUS	60-90 mins £10+	30mins £6	60mins £2
TAXI	90mins £50+	20mins £35	30mins £35+

* London is served by several airports, with Heathrow and Gatwick being the largest. Distances from the centre vary considerably, with Luton and Stansted further from London.

UK ETA

Visitors who don't need a visa (including Australian, Canadian, Japanese, US, NZ and EU nationals – except Ireland) – need an electronic travel authorisation (ETA). A two-year, multi-entry ETA costs £16; allow three working days. See *gov.uk/eta*.

BORDER CONTROL

Since 2026, all British dual nationals need to present either a British or Irish passport, or a foreign passport with a Certificate of Entitlement, to enter the UK.

MOBILE PHONES

Local SIM cards can be bought at airports, but if you stick to free wi-fi until you're in town, you can visit a branded mobile store for more choice and service. Alternatively, you can buy an eSIM.

WI-FI

Free wi-fi at Heathrow and Gatwick airports requires email registration. Various temporary email-address services can create a 'burner' email account for your trip for protection from spamming or phishing.

GETTING AROUND

MOTORWAY SERVICES

You don't just pull into a service station for petrol and a comfort stop when you're driving on the UK's motorways. As well as multiple chain restaurants, coffee, toilets, fuel and EV-charging points, you'll also find many have mini-supermarkets, gaming rooms for a spot of gambling on your break and sometimes a motel if you need to stay the night. Services are signposted at regular intervals along major motorways.

DRIVING INFO

↑↓

In Britain, cars drive on the left. On motorways, stick to the left lanes unless overtaking.

999

Emergencies: call 999; AA roadside assistance: call 0333 004 6046.

.08

Blood-alcohol limit England and Wales: 80mg/ml (0.08%); Scotland: 50mg/ml (0.05%).

RAILCARDS

Trains zip you from city to city more quickly than driving, but the cost rapidly adds up. If you're planning to do a fair bit of train travel, purchase a Network Railcard (Digital) for discounted fares, including for family and friends in the London and South East area.

SPEED LIMITS

The speed limit is 30mph (48km/h) in built-up areas, 60mph (96km/h) on single carriageways and 70mph (112km/h) on motorways. More boroughs are reducing their speed limit to 20mph (32km/h).

CLEAN AIR ZONES

Many cities in the UK now have Clean Air Zones, such as London's ULEZ (Ultra Low Emission Zone; see p39), in which drivers are charged a fee for driving older pollution-emitting vehicles. New-model rental cars should all be compliant.

PARKING

Expect to pay for parking almost everywhere. In towns, and cities such as Oxford and Windsor, street parking is limited. Designated car parks are at the edge of town; you'll have to walk or ride a shuttle the rest of the way. Popular parking apps include RingGo and JustPark.

TRAVEL COSTS

Car rental From **£50–£120/day**

Petrol **Approx £1.32-£1.44/ litre**

EV charging **£0.54-£0.77/ kWh**

Train ticket from London to Bath **Pre-booked, off-peak fare from £30.50**

ACCOMMODATION

HOW MUCH FOR A NIGHT IN A...

Tent pitch (Unpowered)
£0–£30/day

Hostel dorm bed
£20–£45/day

Coaching inn double room
£100–£300/day

PUBS

Coaching houses, pubs, staging inns... Whatever you call them, you're experiencing peak Britain. Imagine an old stone pub with a low-beamed dining room, a crackling fire in winter and a sprawling beer garden in summer. Once annexed with horse stables for passing coaches, rural inns now usually have an adjoining car park. Some pubs are simple and inexpensive; others are beautifully decorated with luxury flourishes.

BOTHIES

A bothy is a basic shelter found in the remote mountains of Scotland, Northern England and Wales. Usually built from stone or wood, bothies are maintained by volunteers and are free to use as long as you respect the 'bothy code'. They may be full; so take overnight camping equipment just in case.

UNIVERSITY ROOMS

Fancy overnighting at the University of Cambridge or Oxford? During the holidays, many campuses offer student accommodation to visitors. Expect a simple, functional single or double room, sometimes in beautiful historic colleges. Self-catering flats are also available. See *universityrooms.com* for details.

HISTORIC BUILDINGS

With some truly memorable accommodation, the **Landmark Trust** *(landmarktrust.org.uk)* rents historic buildings from medieval castles and Napoleonic forts to remote lighthouses and ancient cottages. The **National Trust** *(nationaltrust.org.uk/holidays)* and **English Heritage** *(english-heritage.org.uk/visit/holiday-cottages)* also do stays in epic locations as well as campsites in summer.

GOING CAMPING

Camping is a summertime experience you shouldn't miss, especially if you're travelling with children. Beyond year-round tent and camper-van sites, temporary campgrounds spring up by rivers, lakes and beaches. Farmers deck grassy fields with bell tents, many with bonfires, hay-bale stacks, farm animals, and street-food markets at night. See *hipcamp.com* for ideas.

SECOND HOMES

Many local families have been priced out of the rental market in popular destinations such as Dorset and Cornwall as demand for houses skyrocketed (a trend exacerbated by the COVID-19 pandemic). Fuelled by websites such as Airbnb, investors bought and furnished places to let to holidaymakers, effectively turning small towns into multiple-accommodation businesses. Others have purchased seaside cottages as second homes to work from remotely. Doubling council tax is one way local councils hope to address the problem, while higher stamp duty land tax (SDLT) for additional properties aims to alleviate the broader affordable-housing crisis.

CARS

CERI BREEZE/SHUTTERSTOCK

HOW MUCH TO HIRE A CAR?

Small car
From £50/ day

EV/hybrid car
From £90/ day

Camper van
£450-£1400/week

CAR & CAMPER-VAN RENTAL

Major car-rental companies such as **Avis** *(avis.co.uk)*, **Budget** *(budget.co.uk)*, **Europcar** *(europcar.co.uk)*, **Hertz** *(hertz.co.uk)*, **Sixt** *(sixt.co.uk)* and **Thrifty** *(thrifty.co.uk)* have offices at airports and major train stations plus various city locations across Britain.

Lower-cost outfits such as **Keddy** (through Europcar) and **Green Motion** *(greenmotion.com)* are an option, but check online reviewer tips on potential hidden costs, or hassles when hiring (and returning) cars.

Note: most car rentals are manual drive, so if you need a car with automatic transmission make sure you tick that box.

Camper vans and motorhomes can be rented through **Bunk Campers** *(bunkcampers.com)*, **Indie Campers** *(indiecampers.com)* and **Swift Go** *(swiftgo.co.uk)*.

ELECTRIC VEHICLES

Electric and hybrid vehicles are not as common for short-term rentals as petrol- and diesel-fuelled vehicles just yet. They're classed as 'prestige model' cars, with prices (and commensurate customer service) to match.

Hyundai is a popular option for rental EVs, but you'll also see the Porsche Taycan and hybrid models from Audi to Volvo. Hybrids are recommended if you're planning to do a lot of long-distance driving – especially in the more remote parts of Scotland.

Public EV recharge stations are being added across the country and some fleets have their own networks.

You can reportedly drive between 150 miles (241km) and 300 miles (482km) on average before having to recharge your vehicle.

OTHER GEAR

Extras such as satnav and a baby, child or backless booster seat cost £10 to £15 per day (which can add considerably to your hire cost). Children up to the age of 12 (or 135cm, whichever they reach first) must use a correctly fitted child seat by law in the UK.

RESPONSIBLE TRAVEL

CLIMATE CHANGE & TRAVEL

Lonely Planet urges all travellers to engage with their travel carbon footprint, which will mainly come from air travel. While there often isn't an alternative, travellers can look to minimise the number of flights they take and use cleaner ground transport, such as trains.

One proposed solution – purchasing carbon offsets – unfortunately does not cancel out the impact of individual flights. While most destinations will depend on air travel for the foreseeable future, for now, pursuing ground-based travel where possible is the best course of action.

The **UN Carbon Offset Calculator** shows how flying impacts a household's emissions

The **ICAO's carbon emissions calculator** allows visitors to analyse the CO_2 generated by point-to-point journeys

Justice & Care
justiceandcare.org/spot-the-signs
Look out for signs of modern-day slavery

Wildlife Trust
wildlifetrusts.org
Grassroots organisations restoring nature

Extinction Rebellion
extinctionrebellion.uk
Activist group campaigning for change

SIGHTSEEING

For every Stonehenge, Isle of Skye and Mt Snowdon, there's an equally stunning, less popular alternative to visit. Don't skip the best of Britain, but also share your love (and sterling) around. Get spontaneous and stop somewhere unexpected.

SHOPPING

For a list of traders selling organic produce plus plastic-free stores, go to Better Food Traders *(betterfoodtraders.org)*. Many towns and cities also have farmers markets where you can shop directly from local producers.

AVIAN FLU

Highly pathogenic avian influenza, or bird flu, remains a serious concern in Britain. Follow biosecurity advice to avoid spreading disease: stay on footpaths and don't touch dead or sick wild birds or dropped feathers. Disinfect your hands after any contact with birds or feathers.

SAFE TRAVEL

CHECK YOUR INSURANCE POLICY

It's illegal to drive a car or motorbike in Britain without (at least) third-party insurance. This will be included with all rental cars. If you're bringing your own vehicle, check whether your insurance will cover you in Britain.

BREAKDOWNS AND ACCIDENTS

Roadside assistance is available from the AA *(theaa.com)* and RAC *(rac.co.uk)*, but car-hire companies have their own procedures in the event of a breakdown (or accident). Note the number to call before you go. Call emergency services (999) immediately if anyone is hurt, if the road is blocked or if the other party in a collision has left the scene.

THEFT

It goes without saying that leaving valuables in sight in your car is an invitation to theft (that includes any bags). Keep your eyes and ears open in most cities. In London, pickpockets typically operate in tourist centres: Westminster, Southwark and Camden. Thieves also snatch bags and mobile phones from unsuspecting pedestrians, and from tables at cafes (both inside and outside).

WINTER DRIVING

Heavy rainfall, flooding and freezing winter temperatures create dangerous driving conditions. Be prepared to change plans if an amber or red weather warning is issued (check the Met Office website: *metoffice.gov.uk*). Do not drive into flooded roads. Urban drains manage sewage with waste water in Britain: exposure to dangerous bacteria is a risk. Main roads are gritted and cleared of ice and snow, but back streets rarely are.

SCAMS

Online scams continue to innovate. Be suspicious of incoming calls, text messages and links sent to you. If someone contacts you purporting to be from an organisation, from the Home Office to your car-hire company, hang up and contact the organisation directly yourself. Beware of 'quishing' involving fake QR codes (eg stuck on parking meters).

ILLEGAL DRUGS

With the amount of marijuana smoking in the UK, you'd be forgiven for thinking it's been decriminalised. It hasn't, but CBD oil can be bought legally as a food supplement from health stores. Almost all other illegal drugs from cocaine to ketamine are classed 'A' or 'B', with proportionate consequences if found in your possession.

IN CASE OF EMERGENCY

999

Police, fire, ambulance
This is the main number for police, ambulance, fire brigade, coastguard and mountain rescue services.

111

Medical advice
For medical advice; not for emergencies.

112

Emergency number
This number works the same as 999 and is the standard European emergency line.

101

Police non-emergency number
To report a crime.

NUTS & BOLTS

GOOD TO KNOW

Time zone
GMT/UTC (BST April to October)

Country code
44

Emergency number
999

Population
69.5 million

CURRENCY: BRITISH POUND (£)

CASHLESS PAYMENTS

Establishments in Britain are increasingly cashless. Even a small market stall will have an electronic card reader. Some businesses have a minimum spend of around £2 for electronic transactions. You'll also come across businesses, usually restaurants, that only accept cash.

TAXES

Value-added tax (VAT) is a 20% sales tax levied on most goods and services. VAT is always included in sale prices. You can no longer claim a refund for VAT paid on goods you bought in Britain when you are leaving.

OPENING HOURS

Hours are typically 9am to 5.30pm or 6pm Monday to Saturday, 11am to 4pm or 5pm on Sunday. Late-night shopping (until 9pm) is common at big shopping centres.

INTERNET ACCESS

There are still spots when data is slow or unavailable. Don't rely on the internet for maps and tickets. Download essentials when you've got good service or wi-fi access.

TOILETS

Find free public toilets at train stations, museums and shopping centres. Park or street-side loos vary in cleanliness. Cafes, pubs and shops allow only customers in. See *toiletmap.org.uk*.

SERVICE CHARGES

A 'voluntary' service charge of around 12.5% is added to restaurant bills. If it's not added to the bill it's expected that diners will tip waitstaff directly. Keep this in mind when budgeting. You can refuse to pay the service charge, but that doesn't happen often.

ELECTRICITY 230V/50HZ

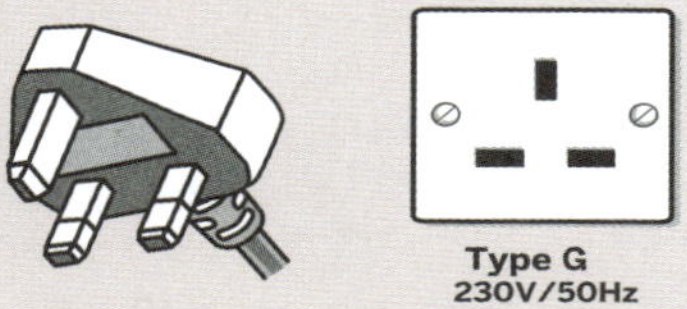

Type G
230V/50Hz

HOW MUCH FOR A...

Coffee
£2.60–£3.75

Tesco meal deal
£3.90

Sunday pub roast
£12–£30

Art-exhibition ticket
£5–£30

Drives 000
Map pages **p000**

INDEX

D

E

F

G

H

I

T

U

V

W

Y

Z

NOTES

NOTES

NOTES

NOTES

NOTES

THE WRITERS

This is the 4th edition of Lonely Planet's Best Road Trips Great Britain guidebook, updated with new material by Catherine Le Nevez, Kerry Walker and Neil Wilson. Writers on previous editions whose work also appears in this book are included below.

Catherine Le Nevez

A Lonely Planet author since 2004, contributing to well over 100 guides in some two dozen countries, Catherine has a Doctorate of Creative Arts in writing and insatiable wanderlust. *lonelyplanet.com/authors/catherine-le-nevez*

Kerry Walker

Kerry has been writing about Wales for Lonely Planet for the past decade. She loves returning to the country she once called home to hike in the Brecon Beacons and strike out along the Pembrokeshire coast in search of cliff-clasped bays, one-pub fishing villages and puffin islands. *@kerryawalker*

Neil Wilson

Neil is a travel writer who lives in Perthshire, Scotland, and has covered Scotland for Lonely Planet for more than 20 years. *@neil3965*

Contributing writers

Isabel Albiston, Oliver Berry, Joe Bindloss, Fionn Davenport, Belinda Dixon, Anthony Ham, Damian Harper, Anna Kaminski, Andy Symington, Tasmin Waby and Luke Waterson.

Send us your feedback

We love to hear from travellers – your comments keep us on our toes and help make our books better. Our well-travelled team reads every word on what you loved or loathed about this book. Although we cannot reply individually to your submissions, we always guarantee that your feedback goes straight to the appropriate writers, in time for the next edition.

BEHIND THE SCENES

This book was produced by the following:

Destination Editor
James Smart

Coordinating Editor
Bridget Blair

Production Editor
Ursula O'Sullivan-Dale

Image Researcher
Dorota Michalec

Cartographer
Jennifer Johnston

Assisting Editor
Peterjon Cresswell

Cover Researcher
Daisy Korpics

Thanks to
Marc Blackwell, Melanie Dankel, Jennifer McCann, Saralinda Turner, Clifton Wilkinson

Product Development
Sofie Andersen, Melinda Anderson, Marc Backwell, Alison Killilea, Darren O'Connell, James Smart, Robin Yule

Acknowledgments

Digital Model Elevation Data
Contains public sector information licensed under the Open Government Licence v3.0 website nationalarchives.gov.uk/doc/open-government-licence/version/3/

Cover photographs
Front: Thatched cottage at Westington, Chipping Campden, Cotswolds, England; Andrew Roland/Shutterstock
Back: Brighton pier; Pajor Pawel/Shutterstock

Visit **lonelyplanet.com/contact** to submit your updates and suggestions or to ask for help. Our award-winning website also features inspirational travel stories and news.

Note: We may edit, reproduce and incorporate your comments in Lonely Planet products such as guidebooks, websites and digital products, so let us know if you are happy to have your name acknowledged. For a copy of our privacy policy visit **lonelyplanet.com/legal**

lonely planet

Published by Lonely Planet Global Limited
CRN 554153
Digital Depot, Roe Lane off Thomas Street, Dublin
D08 TCV4, Ireland (EU authorised representative)
4th edition – Sep 2026
ISBN 9781837584536
© Lonely Planet 2026 Photographs © as indicated 2026
10 9 8 7 6 5 4 3 2 1
Printed in China